The Buddha's Tooth

BUDDHISM AND MODERNITY
A series edited by Donald S. Lopez Jr.

Recent Books in the Series
Seeking Śākyamuni (2019), by Richard M. Jaffe
The Passion Book (2018), by Gendun Chopel
A Storied Sage (2016), by Micah L. Auerback
Strange Tales of an Oriental Idol (2016), by Donald S. Lopez Jr.
Rescued from the Nation (2015), by Steven Kemper

The Buddha's Tooth

Western Tales of a Sri Lankan Relic

JOHN S. STRONG

University of Chicago Press
Chicago and London

The University of Chicago Press, Chicago 60637

The University of Chicago Press, Ltd., London

© 2021 by The University of Chicago

All rights reserved. No part of this book may be used or reproduced in any manner whatsoever without written permission, except in the case of brief quotations in critical articles and reviews. For more information, contact the University of Chicago Press, 1427 E. 60th St., Chicago, IL 60637.

Published 2021

Printed in the United States of America

30 29 28 27 26 25 24 23 22 21   1 2 3 4 5

ISBN-13: 978-0-226-78911-8 (cloth)
ISBN-13: 978-0-226-80173-5 (paper)
ISBN-13: 978-0-226-80187-2 (e-book)
DOI: https://doi.org/10.7208/chicago/9780226801872.001.0001

Library of Congress Cataloging-in-Publication Data

Names: Strong, John, 1948– author.
Title: The Buddha's tooth : western tales of a Sri Lankan relic / John Strong.
Other titles: Buddhism and modernity.
Description: Chicago : University of Chicago Press, 2021. | Series: Buddhism and modernity | Includes bibliographical references and index.
Identifiers: LCCN 2021001502 | ISBN 9780226789118 (cloth) | ISBN 9780226801735 (paperback) | ISBN 9780226801872 (ebook)
Subjects: LCSH: Gautama Buddha—Relics—Sri Lanka. | Buddhism and state—Sri Lanka.
Classification: LCC BQ924 .S767 2021 | DDC 294.3/3/77095493—dc23
LC record available at https://lccn.loc.gov/2021001502

♾ This paper meets the requirements of ANSI/NISO Z39.48-1992 (Permanence of Paper).

For Sarah
and for our children
Anna and Aaron
and our grandchildren
Isaac
Cyrus
Caleb
Esther
Madeline
Zoe

CONTENTS

Preface and Acknowledgments / *ix*
Note on Usage / *xiii*

Introduction / 1

PART I : THE PORTUGUESE AND THE TOOTH RELIC

ONE / The Tale of the Portuguese Tooth and Its Sources / 19

TWO / Where the Tooth Was Found: Traditions about the
Location of the Relic in Sri Lanka / 43

THREE / Whose Tooth Was It? Traditions about
the Identity of the Relic / 73

FOUR / The Trial of the Tooth / 109

FIVE / The Destruction of the Tooth / 125

CONSPECTUS OF PART ONE / The Storical Evolution of
the Tales of the Portuguese Tooth / 145

PART II : THE BRITISH AND THE TOOTH RELIC

SIX / The Cosmopolitan Tooth: The Relic in Kandy before
the British Became Aware of It / 153

SEVEN / The British Takeover of 1815 and the Kandyan Convention / 177

EIGHT / The Relic Returns: The Tooth and Its Properties
Restored to the Temple / 203

NINE / The Relic Lost and Recaptured: The Tooth and
the Rebellion of 1817–1818 / 223

TEN / The Relic Disestablished: Missionary Oppositions to the Tooth / 245

ELEVEN / Showings of the Tooth: The Story of the King
of Siam's Visit (1897) / 267

TWELVE / Showings of the Tooth: The Story of
Queen Elizabeth's Shoes (1954) / 285

Summary and Conclusion / 307

References / 317
Index / 339

PREFACE AND ACKNOWLEDGMENTS

This book has been simmering on a project back burner for many years. I first became interested in the topic of part 1 when I gave a lecture on the Portuguese destruction of the Buddha's tooth relic at the Center for the Study of World Religions at Harvard University in 1994. I thank the then director of the Center, Lawrence Sullivan, for inviting me to deliver it, and for his perceptive comments on that occasion. Three years later, I repeated more or less the same presentation as the Stewart Lecture at Princeton University, where Alexander Nehamas suggested I expand the talk into a book. My response, I fear, was to let the thing sit for over a decade while I pursued other projects. I revived the topic, however, in a paper I gave at a conference organized by Alexandra Walsham in 2008, at the University of Exeter, on the comparative study of relics (see Strong 2010). But it was not until 2015–2016, when a sabbatical from Bates College and a Guggenheim Fellowship gave me the leisure time needed for research, that I realized that my early forays into the subject matter had been severely limited in scope and perspective. I am grateful to both Bates and the Guggenheim Foundation for their backing. I would also like to thank Bates for its help in defraying some of the costs of publication of this book with a subvention; such support in the midst of the COVID-19 pandemic—especially after one's retirement—is remarkable.

The second part of this book has an even more distant origin, dating back to 1969 when, thanks to a "Wanderjahr fellowship" from the Watson Foundation, my wife and I lived for three months in an apartment on the top floor of the Queen's Hotel in Kandy, directly across the esplanade from the Palace of the Tooth (Dalada Maligawa). My first visits to the temple date from that time. They were continued in 1986–1987 when I lived in Kandy again, this time for over a year—first as director of the ISLE Study Abroad Program, and then as a Fulbright fellow teaching at the University of Peradeniya.

In those days, we lived in a house owned by Derrick Nugawela, whose relatives had, for generations from 1901 to 1961, succeeded one another as lay custodians (Diyawadana Nilames) of the tooth. At the same time, I gained new insights into the cult and history of the relic and its temple from the late Anuradha Seneviratne.

In the actual researching and writing of the book, the help of several colleagues and friends needs also to be recognized. First, at Bates College, thanks are due to Steven Kemper, who, unasked, constantly fed me a stream of offprints of microfilms or photocopies of original documents he had made of hard-to-obtain sources that I would never have found (or even realized existed) on my own. It is wonderful that, after forty years as colleagues at Bates, our research interests have finally come together. Also at Bates, I would like to thank Alison Melnick for her help and insights and for making my retirement possible by replacing me.

In London, I benefited from the assistance of Daniel Gilfoyle and Robert Harding at the National Archives in Kew, and of Edward Weech at the Library of the Royal Asiatic Society. I would also like to thank Beth and Paul Willatts in Southfields, for putting me up and putting up with me on repeated research trips.

A special word of gratitude is also due to Donald Stadtner who, in the midst of his writing his book on sacred sites in Sri Lanka, was always willing to take time out to send me photos and tidbits of information, and who facilitated my getting still more pictures from Igor Grunin, whom I wish to thank as well, though I have never met him.

In addition, I am grateful to a number of other individuals for answering specific oral or email questions—big and small—as they arose during the course of my research: Stephen Berkwitz, Zoltán Biedermann, Anne Blackburn, Loring Danforth, Wendy Doniger, Robert Goldman, John Holt, Margaret Imber, David Kolb, Philip Lutgendorf, Dennis McGilvray, John Rogers, Arshia Sattar, Alan Strathern, Sarah Strong, and Jonathan Walters. I would also like to thank Charles Hallisey and Kristin Scheible, who reviewed the draft of this work while it was in manuscript and whose comments much improved it. Needless to say, any mistakes remaining are due to my own shortcomings.

I am also grateful to Donald Lopez, the editor of this series, who initially encouraged me to submit this work, and to Alan Thomas, Kyle Wagner, Dylan Montanari, and Mark Reschke at the University of Chicago Press, for their interest in this book and their help in seeing it through to publication, as well as to Marianne Tatom, who expertly copyedited the manuscript.

Finally, let me say that the manuscript of this work was already complete by the time I belatedly became aware of Gananath Obeyesekere's *The Doomed King* (2017), a book that proved to be very difficult to obtain in an era of COVID-19, with library services shut down and the publisher in Colombo not exporting any copies. As a consequence, I was not able to fully incorporate his views into the body of my text but have only referred to them in appropriate places in footnotes, mainly in part 2. I would like to thank Anne Blackburn for generously sending me her copy of his work.

NOTE ON USAGE

For place names in Sri Lanka, I have generally used modern English appella-
tions without diacritical marks (e.g., Kandy for Senkadagala or Mahānuwara;
Kotte for Kōṭṭe). Exceptions occasionally occur when the context seems to
call for older names (e.g., Ceylon for Sri Lanka, Burma for Myanmar, Pegu
for Bago, etc.). For Sinhala names and words, I have also, on the whole, dis-
pensed with diacriticals, and opted for forms that are more commonly used
in English (e.g., Esala Perahera for Äsaḷa Perahära, Ehelepola for Ähälēpola).
This usually includes the use of "w" instead of "v" (e.g., Malwatta for Mal-
vatta or Malvatu; and Dalada Maligawa for Daḷadā Māligāva). Exceptions are
the titles of Sinhala works, where I have retained diacriticals. For specifically
Buddhist terms, I have given preference to standard Pali and sometimes
Sanskrit forms with diacriticals, except for words listed as English terms in
the Merriam-Webster dictionary (e.g., nirvana, sangha), which I transcribe
un-italicized. The same is true for Anglo-Indian terms (e.g., durbar) listed in
Yule and Burnell 1903.

Introduction

Beginning in the sixteenth century, the process of representing what India was in Europe became linked in a variety of ways to collecting objects and written materials on that part of the world. . . . The objects that were collected were sometimes of sufficient cultural density and complexity that they had to be interpreted and translated in the sense that a sheaf of cinnamon or a sack of pepper might not.

—Sanjay Subrahmanyam (2017, 18–19)

This is a book about two small but significant Sri Lankan objects—two pieces of bone. It is not a book about how *Sri Lankans* have viewed these objects—that was a topic I treated in an earlier work;[1] it is, rather, a book about some of the ways in which *Westerners* encountered and treated them, from the sixteenth to the nineteenth centuries.

The first of these bones (to be considered in part 1) is a tooth that was said to have been captured by the Portuguese c. 1560 during one of their incursions into Sri Lanka. It was eventually identified by them as being a tooth relic of the Buddha, although, as we shall see, they gave it several other identities as well. Reportedly enshrined in a jeweled case when they first found it in a temple, it was in their minds viewed by the local population as having some kind of religious significance, and the Portuguese took it back to Goa as a prize. For a while, they considered holding it for ransom, but after some deliberation, they decided they needed to make a stance against idolatry and publicly crushed it in a mortar, burned the fragments in a brazier, and threw them all into the river.

---

1. See Strong 2004b, 150–210. For a discussion of the Buddhist philosophy of objects including relics (mainly dealing with Japanese materials), see Rambelli 2007, 11–87.

The second bone I will look at (in part 2) is also a tooth, but a more famous one.[2] It has a long history in Sri Lankan tradition as a relic of the Buddha. In the period that interests me here—roughly 1800 to 1850, during early British colonial rule on the island—it was enshrined in the Dalada Maligawa (literally, the Palace of the Tooth Relic, aka the Temple of the Tooth) in Kandy, where it remains today. Accordingly, if only for practical reasons, I will call it the "Kandyan tooth" in order to distinguish it from the "Portuguese tooth."[3]

When the British first invaded Kandy in 1803, they were more or less oblivious to the importance of this Kandyan tooth which, in any case, had been removed from its temple by the king when he fled before their arrival. By the time they reconquered Kandy in 1815, however, recovery of the tooth became one of their prime preoccupations. They were successful in convincing the Kandyans to bring it back to the temple, and there they re-enshrined it with great ceremony. It was, however, soon stolen from its shrine during the Sri Lankan rebellion of 1817–1818, at the end of which the British recovered it, this time by force. Thereafter, for a few decades at least, back in Kandy, they became the facilitators and guarantors of its cult until Christian missionary pressures forced them to withdraw (pretty much, but not entirely) from that role.

The Western Discoveries of Buddhism

It is one of my hopes that a back-to-back consideration of the actions and attitudes of the Portuguese and the British toward these two pieces of bone can help us concretize and trace nascent and developing European understandings of the Buddha and more generally of Buddhism.

In the wake of Edward Said's *Orientalism* (1978), scholars interested in Indian and Buddhist studies soon began to think about the application of some of his insights to religions other than Islam and cultures beyond the Middle East. One of them, Philip Almond, started writing about the British "discovery" (or "invention," or "construction") of Buddhism during the course of the nineteenth century. It was, he claimed, only then that Buddhism really came to be seen as an independent religious tradition, "es-

---

2. It makes sense to treat the two tooth relics in this book as distinct objects, although, as we shall see, some Sri Lankans were to claim that they were one and the same—that the Portuguese failed to destroy the tooth they had captured because, as it was about to be crushed in the mortar, it miraculously vanished and flew to its shrine in Sri Lanka.

3. By "Portuguese tooth," I do not mean to imply that the tooth *qua* relic somehow belonged to the Portuguese, only that it was an object that much preoccupied them.

sentially constituted by its textuality," and that the Buddha "emerged from the wings of myth" as a human being, a historical figure (Almond 1988, 139–140).

Almond, however, may have short-sheeted his argument by not going back far enough. There was an earlier—though somewhat different—Western "discovery" of Buddhism, prior to that of the Victorians. This may be found in the writings of Europeans of various nationalities from the sixteenth to the early nineteenth centuries. These include first- and secondhand accounts by Christian missionaries, soldiers-of-fortune, colonial officials, profit-seeking traders, Church envoys, travelers, adventurers, traders, and expatriate aristocrats, to name but a few. In recent times, scholars such as Urs App (2010, 2012), Donald Lopez (2016), Sanjay Subrahmanyam (2017), and others have pointed to the importance of these materials in amplifying and correcting our picture of how "Buddhism" entered the Western imaginaire. These sources, for the most part, deal with observed things, not abstract doctrines, with concrete objects, not texts.

Objects and Stories

Arjun Appadurai has enlightened us to the significance of objects as a focal point for understanding the interaction of communities and cultures. As he put it, "we have to follow the things themselves, for their meanings are inscribed in their forms, their uses, their trajectories" (Appadurai 1986, 5). I think there is no doubt that the "trajectories" of the Sri Lankan tooth relics can help us see the interaction of Western and South Asian cultures and religions. I would only add that their meanings are also invested in the stories told about them, sometimes long after the object in question has disappeared.

In part 1 of this book, as mentioned, I will primarily be looking at stories about the Portuguese tooth and its ceremonial destruction. That destruction did not mean the end of the stories told about it; in fact, it may have marked their beginning. Over the next couple of centuries, the tale of the Portuguese tooth continued to be told and retold not only by Portuguese authors, but by other European writers as well. It was variously portrayed by them as having been captured in Jaffna, or on Adam's Peak, or near Galle in the South; and as being a tooth of the Devil, or a tooth of a monkey, or of the divinity Hanumān, and then, eventually, as a relic of the Buddha.

Since the first of these accounts dates from 1596, some thirty-five years after the "event" of the tooth's destruction, and since the subsequent narratives differ considerably from one another and extend over a period of

150 years, there is little hope of recapturing any historicity in this matter. But that is not my intent. I am less interested in the factuality of the events (though I am willing to minimally speculate about that) than I am in their "fictionality"—in how and why stories about those "events" arose and developed, and how those various stories may reflect the attitudes of the times. In this way, I will seek to trace what I call a "*storical* evolution" of this tradition.[4] As we shall see, this will involve not only paying attention to the chronological sequence in which our sources were written, but also reconstructing the development of the narrative elements of the stories they tell.

The tales of the Kandyan tooth, on the other hand, are rather different in nature. For one thing, they are *apparently* more historical, since our sources are often nearly contemporaneous (sometimes to the very day) to the events they describe and include things such as letters, newspaper reports, personal diaries, and even secret government telegrams. In spite of this, Gananath Obeyesekere (2017) warns us that even such sources often reflect a colonial agenda and should not too readily be accepted as "factual"—a good reminder that we are dealing here with stories. Obeyesekere, however, goes on to present an alternative view of the history of these times. Unlike him, I am less interested in correcting the historical record than in narrating it as a story—factual and/or fictional—and in focusing specifically on how the tale helps us understand British apprehensions of the Kandyan tooth during this period, and more generally their developing attitudes toward Buddhism and Sri Lanka.[5]

Relics are a special kind of object, however, in that they are ornamented not only by stories, but by other objects as well. In particular, they are surrounded by the precious gems and jewels that have been offered to them over the years or that form and adorn their reliquaries. Patrick Geary (1990, 5) has pointed out that a "bare relic," such as a bone, "carries no fixed code or sign of its meaning." It needs to be framed—to be "adorned"—in order to have significance, in order to become the relic that it is. The Portuguese would never have realized the importance of their tooth if they had not found it in a temple, in a bejeweled box. The Kandyans, as we shall see, in 1815 insisted that they could not bring the Buddha's tooth back to its temple unless and until all of its adornments were returned. In this sense, the

4. For an application of this approach to the life of the Buddha, see Strong 2001 and 2017.
5. I often regret that in English, at least at the lexical level, the word "history" has gotten divorced from the word "story." It would be nice to have a single word that would enable us to equivocate more readily between "fact" and "fiction"—something like the French "*histoire*," German "*Geschichte*," or Portuguese "*história*"—all of which can ambiguously overlap the two.

jewels are more than just markers of a relic's identity. Wannaporn Rienjang (2017, 146, 331), who has conducted extensive studies of gems in Buddhist archaeological sites in Gandhāra, has suggested that they may themselves be viewed as relics—either as "extended bodies" of the donors who offered them, or as alternate bodies of the Buddha himself, symbolizing his purity and permanence.[6] For purposes of this book, however, I will consider the jewels to be embodiments of the this-worldly royal dimensions of the tooth, and the "bare bone" they envelop as a somatic representation of the Buddha in his otherworldly ascetic aspect.

Details

Mircea Eliade (1969, 37) once quoted a French proverb that asserts that "details are the *only things* that count" ("Il n'y a que les détails qui comptent"). I am not sure this is always true, but I do think that many things can be learned from details, and the reader will find that I have included many in this book. I have done so for several reasons. First, as Eliade illustrates, details can occasionally be "unexpectedly illuminating." In narratives, they can serve to guard against too-easy generalizations by reminding us that events recalled may be more complex than they seem. For example, at the end of the 1817–1818 Sri Lankan rebellion, the British recaptured the tooth relic (which had been "stolen" by a monk from the temple) and brought it triumphantly back to Kandy. Unlike their invasion of 1815, which the British portrayed as a bloodless "liberation" of Kandy, their suppression of the 1817–1818 insurrection had all the marks of a ruthless and violent subjugation. And yet, at this very juncture, they agreed to ask a Sinhalese astrologer to determine the proper *nekata*—the astrologically auspicious moment—in order for them (the British) to bring the tooth back to its temple. This "detail" is not what one would expect of a regime that had just fiercely put down an uprising and lost all patience with "native" ways and superstitions. Its recall is thus a signal against simplistic understandings, a hint that, in the midst of colonial oppression, there was still some respect (for whatever reasons) for local traditions. Indeed, as we shall see in part 2, the primary British actors in Kandy at that time had rather complex motives and attitudes.

More broadly, an accumulation of "details" can also serve to give a down-to-earth and concrete feeling for the ambience of the times being recounted. I do not plan to comment on all the details that I present in this book; in

6. See also Strong forthcoming b; Skilling 2018, 3; and Schopen 1997, 114–147.

many cases they are simply of inherent interest (in my opinion), and add their own flavor to a larger story, making it come alive, and humanizing it in ways that abstractions often do not. Many of them come from often-forgotten books and articles published long ago; others, from unpublished documents in colonial archives.

Contexts

The stories and their details, however, also reflect the cultural, religious, and historical contexts in which they are set, and many of these I do plan to look at and analyze. The destruction of the tooth by the Portuguese, for instance, is informed by the fervent Catholicism of their time as well as the corrupt practices of their empire. It is surely no coincidence that the tooth was burned in Goa just as the Portuguese Inquisition was being introduced there, and but a few years after the full-body relic of Saint Francis Xavier was enshrined there. The stories about its destruction and its identification, however, also reflect the political concerns of a growing Portuguese Empire. Similarly, the British dealings with the tooth in Kandy, as we shall see, are marked by their own ongoing worldwide quest for empire, but also by an ideological tension between missionary-inspired Protestantism and an Enlightenment-informed pragmatism.

The Two Social Loops of Charismatic Objects

In the concluding chapter to his study of Thai Buddhist amulets, Stanley Tambiah (1984, 335) makes an important comment about the nature of the objects he has been studying. Max Weber, he points out, was "alive to the routinization . . . of charisma in institutional structures" but failed to study the "fetishism of objects," that is, "the *objectification* of charisma" in such items of ritual import as amulets, regalia, palladia, and relics. Tambiah then goes on to discuss two contexts in which this kind of charisma of objects operates—what he calls two social loops or cycles. The first of these is the ideological and devotional dimension that connects the worshippers of such objects to the divinity or saint they embody. Venerators of a relic such as the Kandyan tooth could relate through it to the Buddha, and in turn make merit and advance on the path to enlightenment through their veneration. The second is what Tambiah (1984, 336) calls the "cycle of transactions," in which charismatic objects are used for political or commercial or other "secular" purposes, in which a relic such as the tooth may be used "to influence, control, seduce, and exploit fellow [persons] for worldly purposes—in the corridors of politics, the stratagems of commerce, the intrigues of love, and the sycophancy of clientage." Things such as relics are important, therefore, because, as objectifications of charisma, they bridge two aspects of experienced reality—what might (too simplistically for sure) be called the "sacred" and the "secular," or, in Buddhist terms, the "supramundane" (*lokottara*) and the "worldly" (*laukika*).[7] We shall see that the Portuguese tooth as well as the Kandyan tooth operate in both of these dimensions. The Portuguese, for instance, destroy the tooth for religious reasons—to score points against heathenism, to combat idolatry and demonolatry. But they also do it for mytho-symbolic geopolitical reasons—to make it clear that they are the new foreign conquerors of Sri Lanka, who are now replacing other "foreign" conquerors of the past. At the same time, before destroying it, they toy with the idea of holding their tooth for ransom by the highest bidder, clearly seeing it as a valuable commodity. Similarly, as we shall see, the British are first interested in the jewels of the Temple of the Tooth as possible "booty," before deciding to give up that claim in order to use the tooth to bolster their own political sovereignty over the island, before, again, giving up their custody of the tooth under Christian missionary pressure.

We can begin to see, here, how the two tales of the Portuguese and the Kandyan relics, though they end up with very different treatments of the tooth as an object, nonetheless have certain attitudinal points in common. Though this book is divided into two distinct parts, there is a sense that together they present one continuous saga of stories reflective of changing European mindsets, as I shall spell out in due time, in my concluding discussion. This does not mean, however, that we should expect a single conclusion about any one Western viewpoint. Because this is a book that pays attention to details and that takes seriously the variants of stories, it is almost inevitable that we shall end up with a diversity of positions and a multitude of smaller conclusions. As Subrahmanyam puts it in the preface to his *Europe's India* (2017, xv), "different forms of knowledge and modes of knowledge-production existed [among Europeans in early colonial South Asia], and sometimes they and their adherents struggled bitterly with one another. This is the reason a close attention to context is always essential, and this is also the reason it is no simple matter to provide a stark outline of this work and its main thrust."

7. See also Rambelli's comments (2007, 172–210) about how certain objects can act as mediators between the Sacred and the Profane.

The Chapters of Part 1

Subrahmanyam's warning notwithstanding, in what follows, I will try to present the contents and major findings of each of my chapters in summary fashion, to give readers a preliminary outline of the book as a whole—a sort of guide-map to the arguments that follow. I will start with the chapters of part 1.

Most scholars who deal with the story of the Portuguese tooth base themselves (either directly or indirectly) on a single source: the account of the historian Diogo do Couto (1542–1616). There are many other versions of the tale, however. In chapter 1, I will introduce fourteen of them (including Do Couto's), written over the course of about 150 years.[8] Some of these are only snippets of narrative, but others are veritable sagas. By compiling all of these and seeing their redundancies and repetitions, as well as their additions and novelties, one can form a better idea of the supposed whole. My assumption is that many (if not all) versions of a story need to be looked at, for they all can "count" in our understanding of its overall significance.[9] One can see in such an approach how variant "details" might become important.

I have chosen to present my fourteen sources in chronological order, beginning with the account of the Dutch Jan Huyghen van Linschoten in 1596, and ending with that of the German Johann Wolffgang Heydt in 1744. In between, I will consider twelve other narratives by authors variously writing in Portuguese, French, Dutch, and Spanish. These sources will form the basis for the rest of the chapters in part 1. By looking at all of them together, we can get a picture of which details are ongoing and which are new, as well as an idea of how the stories themselves may have "circulated." As we shall see, it is possible more or less to isolate two "families" or lineages of tales: a Franco-Portuguese one and a Dutch-German one. One of the things that distinguishes these two families of sources is their differing accounts of (a) *where* in Sri Lanka the tooth was first captured by the Portuguese, and (b) *whose tooth* they thought it was that they had captured.

8. These are the ones that I have chosen, for a variety of reasons, to use in my analysis of the overall tale. In addition, I am aware of a few other colonial-era sources that touch on the story of the Portuguese tooth, but that add little to it. See, for example, the brief mentions in Herbert [1634] 1638, 306–307; De la Boullaye-le-Gouz 1653, 179; Ribeiro [1685] 1701, 118–119; Picart et al. 1723–1743, 4: 135; and Hurd 1780, 94.

9. This assumption is doubtless due to distant influences on me of Claude Lévi-Strauss's (1963) insights on the study of myth and Vladimir Propp's (1968) methods for analyzing folktales.

I will look at variant answers to the first of these questions in chapter 2. As we shall see, there are two basic Western traditions about the location of the tooth when the Portuguese captured it. On the one hand, the Dutch-German lineage asserts that the tooth was found by them on or near Adam's Peak (aka Śrī Pada), a sacred mountain and pilgrimage place in Central Sri Lanka that is famous for having a rock on its top marked by a large imprint of a foot, variously venerated by Muslims, Hindus, Buddhists, and even Christians.[10] On the other hand, the Franco-Portuguese tradition maintains that the tooth was found in the temple of Nallur in Jaffna, in the far north of the island. As we shall see, both of these claims are historically problematic but "storically" interesting. In my analysis, I will be particularly concerned with why the storytellers might wish to locate the tooth at these sites, and the implication of those choices.

Drawing on a number of recent theoretical discussions on the "place of place" in cultural and religious studies, James Robson (2009) has shown the value of looking at religious practices not in terms of various historically defined "-isms" (e.g., Buddhism, Hinduism, Daoism), but in terms of traditions associated with a particular place (in his case, the Chinese mountain Nanyue). In his view, such a site is a locale where we can see both the syncretistic sharings of different traditions, and the emergence of definitional boundaries between them. As Robson (2009, 4) puts it, looking at Nanyue as a place makes us alive to both "complementarities and tensions."

In my understanding, Adam's Peak and, less obviously perhaps, the temple of Nallur in Jaffna are also such places—where a multiplicity of traditions come together, but where their very contiguity encourages distinctions. The storical placing of the tooth relic at such sites, then, is imaginatively conducive to questions about the interaction of religious traditions, as well as the identity of the tooth itself—about whose tooth it was that the Portuguese captured.

This question of identity I will treat in chapter 3. Here again our two families of sources differ from one another, although the situation is a bit messier. The Dutch and German authors are now joined by the French in generally asserting that the tooth was that of some sort of monkey. Most

10. Adam's Peak is located in Central Sri Lanka, not far from Ratnapura. It was visible from far out to sea and so was a landmark for navigators and marked as such on maritime charts. See Paranavitana and de Silva 2002, 43, 52, 55, 118. As we shall see, however, in the time of our sources, it was also sometimes thought to be in far southern Sri Lanka and identified with the site of Mulgirigala, which the Dutch called "Adams Berg." The two places shared some of the same stories.

of the Portuguese, on the other hand, while mentioning the monkey tooth theory, proffer the alternative view that the tooth was the Buddha's, and eventually assert this as being true.

Among all those who identify the tooth as a simian's fang, however, there are further variants. Some say the tooth was that of an ordinary ape and mock the Sri Lankans for idolizing an animal's bone. Others claim it belonged to a special white monkey, a designation that is replete with ambiguous overtones. Finally, a goodly number say the simian tooth was that of Hanumān, the divine monkey in the *Rāmāyaṇa* epic who was instrumental in the Indian god-king Rāma's invasion of the island.

I shall explore the implications of all of these identifications but pay particular attention to the cases of Hanumān and the Buddha. As we shall see, in Portuguese sources, there is a gradual but definite transition between these two identities. Simply put, the tooth, over time, goes from being recognized as a tooth of Hanumān to being identified as a tooth of the Buddha. The reasons for this, I claim, are contextual and essentially political, and reflect Tambiah's aforementioned "cycle of [worldly] transactions" that characterizes one dimension of charismatic objects.

In addition to being an object of devotion to a particular divinity (e.g., Hanumān or the Buddha), in the Sri Lankan context, the tooth relic was also a palladium of rule—a legitimator of royal sovereignty. It was at once symbolic of the supremacy of the divinity and of the king associated with that divinity. Thus, whose sovereignty was being legitimated depended on the identity of whose tooth it was thought to be. I will argue that Hanumān, besides being an Indian divinity, was also a symbol of the hegemonic authority of the empire of Vijayanagara, the largest and most important political and economic power in South India at the time of the Portuguese arrival there. By destroying "Hanumān's tooth," the Portuguese were symbolically putting an end to (or marking the end of) Vijayanagara's claims to hegemony, at least in Sri Lanka, and more broadly in the region as a whole. They were announcing, in effect, that "there was a new sheriff in town."

The Vijayanagara Empire, it should be said, was already in decline by the time the Portuguese captured the tooth (1560). In due time, but even before its final demise (it lasted until 1646), the Portuguese realized there was another important player in their part of the world: the Burmese and very Buddhist kingdom of Pegu [today, Bago]. This behooved a new identity for the tooth: Hanumān's tooth gradually became the Buddha's tooth, and by destroying the latter, the Portuguese were symbolically challenging the dominance of Pegu in the region. At the same time, the destruction of the Buddha's tooth also enabled the Portuguese to undermine native claims to sovereignty in Sri Lanka itself, especially by the newly emergent king of Kandy, whose recently acquired Buddha's tooth relic they could now claim was a fake since they had destroyed the real one.

Chapters 4 and 5 will deal with the "trial" of the tooth and accounts of its destruction. Frankly, in composing this book, I went back and forth about where to place these two chapters. In some ways, they could have been put at the very start of part 1, for, in my view, they recount events that must have marked the tooth as an important object and engendered subsequent stories about it. For practical and narrative reasons, however, it eventually made sense to place them here at the end.

Chapter 4 concerns the "trial" of the tooth, by which I mean the debate that was held by the Portuguese in Goa to decide what to do with the captured relic. The argument was essentially between those who wanted to sell it to the highest bidder (mostly, the *fidalgos* and the military men), and those who wanted to destroy it (the archbishop and other clerics). Caught in between was the viceroy, Dom Constantino da Bragança. Once again, here, Tambiah's distinction between the worldly and otherworldly dimensions of charismatic objects can be helpful, for both sides surface in the course of the debate: arguments about practical concerns (the Portuguese Empire's need for money) are opposed by biblical citations invoking the divine obligation to destroy idols. In the end, the "other-worldlies" win the day, and the verdict is reached: the tooth must be destroyed.

It is noteworthy, however, that during the whole course of this "trial," no mention is made of the different identities (monkey, Hanumān, the Buddha) variously proposed for the tooth. It is as though those traditions were irrelevant to the debaters or had not yet been developed. Instead, the relic is demonized by the Portuguese and presented solely as a "tooth of the Devil." This is an example of what I think of as Portuguese "other-worldly myopia."[11] Because of the nature of their Christianity, the Portuguese in seventeenth-century Goa, while easily able to grasp the potential economic value of the tooth in this-worldly terms, were, with few exceptions, incapable of seeing its divine referent—Hanumān or the Buddha—in legitimate otherworldly terms. The few exceptions will be dealt with briefly in an addendum to chapter 4 entitled "Paths Not Taken."

In chapter 5, I will finally come to the story of the destruction of the tooth. Following its trial, we are told, in many of our sources, that the tooth was publicly rendered to fragments in a mortar, burned on a brazier, and

11. On the somewhat analogous notions of "cultural incommensurability" and "epistemological deficit," see Subrahmanyam 2012, 5–24; and 2017, 103.

then disposed of in water. I will discuss these details in terms of several different contexts: Hindu funerary practices, Portuguese iconoclasm, the Inquisition and the use of *autos-da-fé* in Goa, and Christian and Buddhist understandings of relics focusing in particular on the contrast between the tooth and the immaculate full-body relic of the soon-to-be-sainted Francis Xavier, whom the Jesuits had just enshrined in Goa.

The Chapters of Part 2

In 1874, T. W. Rhys Davids, a British Buddhist scholar and former civil servant in Ceylon, wrote a review of Muthu Coomaraswamy's translation of the Pali *Dāṭhavaṃsa* [Chronicle of the tooth]. In it, he sums up the story of the destruction of the tooth by the Portuguese, and then vehemently denies its historicity. For him, the tooth could never have been in Jaffna, for it "was always an outlying and unimportant part of the Ceylon kingdom." The Portuguese, he declares, were duped, they were "imposed upon," and he has "every reason to believe that the very tooth referred to in the work edited by Sir Coomāra Swāmy [which was brought to the island in the fourth century CE] is preserved to this day in Kandy" (Davids 1874, 340).

What Rhys Davids does not say, of course, is that the British, having conquered the Kandyan kingdom (the last remaining independent polity on the island), had a vested interest in the genuineness and uniqueness of the Buddha's tooth relic now in their possession, and so a motive to belittle or disregard altogether the Portuguese claims presented above.

Not all British writers agreed with Rhys Davids, however. Many, in fact, argued just the opposite—that the Kandyan relic could not be the "genuine" tooth of the Buddha because that was what the Portuguese had destroyed two and a half centuries earlier (e.g., Farrer 1908, 80; Woolf 1961, 144)! Either way, both views are assuming that we are dealing here with two distinct material objects, but then arguing for elevating the historicity of one of them *qua* relic over the other. I am willing to follow them in their assumption but not in their argument: for me, storically speaking, both relics have an equal authenticity.

Part 2 of this book will examine the story of the gradual investment of the British in the Kandyan tooth and then their gradual divestment of it. In other words, chapter by chapter, I will trace how they came to see the tooth as an object of value whose cult should be maintained, and then how they eventually reversed course on that realization. This progressive episodic approach will mean that this part of the book will differ somewhat from that in part 1, where the discussion was more topical.

By way of background, in chapter 6, I will first look at the place of the tooth in Kandy just prior to its takeover by the British in 1815, during the reigns of the Nāyakkar kings of Kandy whose dynasty traced their origins to South India. Generally speaking, the tooth relic has been viewed as an emblem of Sinhalese Buddhist sovereignty. It is sometimes claimed, therefore, that the Nāyakkar kings did so much to bolster the cult of the Kandyan tooth because they were trying to compensate for their own foreignness—to show what good supporters of Sinhalese Buddhism they were, despite their family's connection to Śaivism. In fact, this is only one side of the coin. Basing my reasoning on an insight of Victor Goloubew (1932), I will argue that the Buddha's Kandyan tooth was an ideal palladium for the Nāyakkars, for it was, like them, of "foreign" origination (storically, it came from India), and its cult, like their own beliefs, was a syncretic mix of Buddhist and Hindu elements. The tooth, in other words, was a cosmopolitan object that could easily bridge the gaps between Sri Lanka and India, Sri Lanka and the rest of the Buddhist world, Buddhists and Hindus, and so on. In my view, this same cosmopolitanism eventually was a factor that facilitated the British usurpation of the tooth as a symbol of their own legitimacy as new foreign rulers.[12]

The British were slow, however, to realize its importance. Toward the end of chapter 6, I will deal with the fiasco of their first invasion of Kandy in 1803, during which they pretty much ignored the potential of the tooth for their own purposes, thinking instead that they had to replace Śrī Vikrama, the last of the Nāyakkar kings, with a new (also Nāyakkar) puppet-ruler of their own choosing, Muttusāmi.

Chapter 7 will then be given over to the British reinvasion of Kandy in 1815, by which time, I will argue, they had realized their mistake. This will involve a consideration of two things: their decision not to replace King Śrī Vikrama, after they captured him, with a Kandyan monarch of their choosing; and their decision to start using the tooth relic as an indigenous symbol of their own sovereignty. The tooth, however, was still at large; prior to the British invasion, it had been ferreted away to the countryside for safekeeping, and it had not been seized along with Śrī Vikrama. A significant part of the chapter, therefore, will be devoted to the story of how the British got the Kandyans to agree to bring the tooth back to the temple. This will involve evaluating the role of John D'Oyly, the British Resident in Kandy at the time, who played a key role in this, as well as analyzing the text of the Kandyan

---

12. For general discussion of "the problem of cosmopolitanism," but in a Sri Lankan context, see Strathern and Biedermann 2017, 3–7.

Convention (the treaty between the British and the Sinhalese) in which the colonial government agreed to support the practice of Buddhism on the island. In this crucial document, the British commit to maintaining and protecting the tooth relic as part of their more general pledge to consider the Buddhist religion "inviolable."

In chapter 8, I will examine in detail the story of the actual return of the tooth to Kandy in 1815—something that took time and diplomacy. One of the problems, as we shall see, is that the Kandyan monastic leaders insisted that the considerable number of jewels, ornaments, gems, gold, ritual vessels, precious artifacts, and the like—temple properties that had also been sent to various places in the countryside for safety—must all be returned to the temple before the relic could be brought back and its cult restored. It would be inappropriate, they claimed, for the tooth to be venerated again in Kandy without its proper "ornamentation."[13] The British, however, argued (at least initially) that much of this wealth belonged to the former king and so it properly should be given over to the British Army as a war prize. We have here almost a classic case of one group (the Kandyans) merging the notions of "Church and State," and another (the British) distinguishing between them.

A second issue in this chapter concerns the matter of D'Oyly's participation in the grand *perahera* (procession) that returned the tooth to the temple, and his subsequent involvement in the ritual re-enshrining of the tooth. In D'Oyly's eyes (but not in the eyes of various Christian commentators on the island), this ceremony was a great success for, by it, as he wrote later to Governor Brownrigg, "we obtained the surest proof of the confidence of the Kandyan Nation and their acquiescence in the dominion of the British government" (CO 54/56, 129B).[14]

This "acquiescence" was not to last very long, however. Just two years later, in 1817, a major millenarian uprising broke out on the island. In chapter 9, I present the story of this "Kandyan Rebellion," focusing primarily on three things: the theft of the tooth from within the precincts of the temple and its use by the rebels to bolster their legitimacy; the serendipitous recapture of the tooth by the British toward the end of the rebellion; and the British decision to allow the cult of the tooth to resume in Kandy but to now openly use

13. The tooth in Kandy is enclosed in the smallest of seven nesting golden reliquaries, which are covered with gems, strings of precious stones, gold ornaments, and the like. All of these must be taken off one by one whenever the tooth itself (on rare occasions) is shown to important visitors.

14. For abbreviations of references to archival materials, see the bibliography at the end of the book.

it to legitimate their own rule. As Doctor John Davy, Governor Brownrigg's personal physician, who was in Kandy at the time, put it: "Now the English are indeed masters of the country; for [as the people say] they who possess the relic have a right to govern" (Davy 1821, 169).

British sponsorship of the tooth relic (if even for their own purposes) continued for some decades, but, as mentioned, objections to it soon arose from missionary societies in England, and from Christian ministers in Sri Lanka. Chapter 10 traces the story of these objections. I shall begin with an examination of the arguments in an influential pamphlet entitled *The British Government and the Idolatry of Ceylon*, written by the Wesleyan missionary R. Spence Hardy in 1839, and I shall stop around 1853, when the issue was more or less settled in favor of putting an end to any official relationship of the colonial government to the Kandyan tooth (and to Buddhism more generally). In between, as we shall see, British policy wavered back and forth between the poles of continued engagement with the tooth (and Buddhism) and total disengagement from it. One of the things that is particularly interesting in all this are the parallels between this British debate and the "trial" of the Portuguese tooth in Goa in 1561. Both events featured oppositions between those who wanted to use the tooth for practical this-worldly purposes and those who wanted to disassociate themselves from it for religious reasons. In both cases, the latter parties win out, with the difference that disassociation for the Portuguese meant destruction, while for the English it meant divorce.

The saga of the British government's relationship to the tooth, however, did not completely end with this divorce. In chapter 11, as an example of the British continued involvement with the tooth at the end of the nineteenth century, I will present the story of the visit made to the tooth in Kandy by King Chulalongkorn of Siam (now Thailand) in 1897. He famously asked to be allowed to touch the tooth, and when he was told he could not, he felt insulted and stomped out of the temple, ordering all the offerings he had brought with him to be withdrawn. This is usually interpreted as a sign of royal petulance by an absolute monarch, or officious haughtiness by the Sri Lankans officiating at the temple, or both. Without disagreeing with either of these views, I will instead seek to further an argument recently made by Steven Kemper (2017, 2019) that the insult to Chulalongkorn was staged by the British. The colonial authorities may well have disassociated themselves (and their own ruler, Queen Victoria) from the tooth, but they were not about to let the monarch of another country hook up to it.

Finally, in chapter 12, I will present another story of a monarch's visit to the Kandyan tooth, this one illustrative of British attitudes toward the relic in the period when Sri Lanka was newly independent but still a part of the Commonwealth. This is the curious case of Queen Elizabeth II's viewing the tooth in 1954.[15] For months ahead of time, a debate raged between Whitehall, Downing Street, Buckingham Palace, Kandy, and Colombo about whether or not Her Majesty would have to remove her shoes inside the temple. On the one hand, there were those who felt that the Queen, as head of the Anglican Church and Defender of the Faith, should in no way be involved in showing respect to an "idol." On the other hand, there were those who argued that removing one's shoes was simply a local custom that had nothing to do with religion, and that the future of Ceylon's relationship to England depended on Her Majesty's treatment of the tooth. Once again, we have here another instance of the opposition between those who see the tooth in a religious context and those who view it in practical this-worldly terms. This time, however, the this-worldlies win; the Queen takes off her shoes.

In a final concluding discussion, at the end of the book, I will sum up by presenting some points of commonality and contrast between the findings of the chapters in part 1 and those in part 2.

15. An oral version of this chapter was presented by me remotely via Zoom to Whitman College as the 2020 David Deal Lecture on October 27, 2020. See https://www.whitman.edu /academics/majors-and-minors/asian-and-middle-eastern-studies/david-deal-lecture-series.

PART ONE

The Portuguese and the Tooth Relic

ONE

The Tale of the Portuguese
Tooth and Its Sources

Stories reveal things that are not easily gleaned from the harder disciplines.

—Wendy Doniger (1988, 2)

Many Buddhologists and historians of Sri Lanka are familiar with the story of the Portuguese capture and destruction of the Buddha's tooth relic in 1560–1561, however they might evaluate its historicity. By and large they know it from a single source—the account of the official chronicler of the Portuguese Empire in Asia, Diogo Do Couto (1542–1616).[1] Both prior to and after Do Couto, however, other renderings of this tale of the tooth were told by a number of authors—adventurers, churchmen, merchants, scholars—whose various versions differ significantly from his, as they do from one another's. These were written in a variety of languages (Dutch, Portuguese, French, Spanish, German, and English), and date anywhere from the end of the sixteenth to the early eighteenth centuries.

When we look at all of these sources together, it becomes clear that there are significant discrepancies and divergences between them. For instance, while some, like Do Couto, claim that the tooth was captured in Jaffna, at the northern end of the island, in 1560, other (especially Dutch) sources affirm that it was taken in 1554 on or near Adam's Peak (aka Śrī Pada), in south-central Sri Lanka. Still others maintain it was found somewhere near Galle, in the far south (see fig. 1.1). Perhaps more significantly, while Do Couto and others following him indicate that the tooth itself was considered to be the tooth relic of the Buddha, all the sources before him, and quite a few

---

1. See Do Couto 1783, 316–18, 428–31 (English translations: Tennent 1859, 2: 213–216; Da Cunha 1875, 41–52; and Ferguson [1908] 1993, 191–192, 211–214).

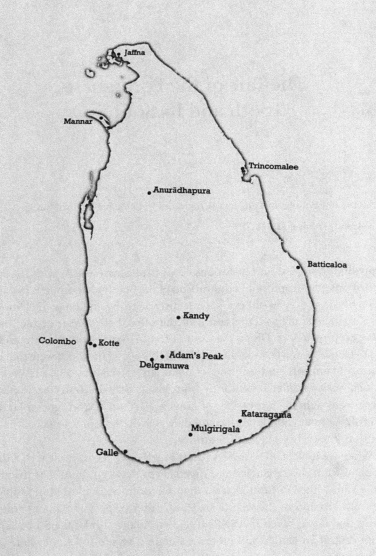

Figure 1.1. Map of Sri Lankan sites relevant to the Portuguese tooth.

afterward, declare it to be the tooth of a monkey, whom they sometimes further identify as the Hindu divine being Hanumān.

I shall discuss these and other discrepancies episodically in chapters two through five below. First, however, by way of introduction, I want to present, in chronological order, the sources and accounts that I will be considering. In doing this, I will also say something about the storytellers themselves, as this can help us contextualize their particular narratives and understand some of the divergences between them. The purpose of this chapter, then, is to begin to familiarize readers with the developing saga of the Portuguese tooth, with the authors who recounted and embellished it, and a bit with the tonality of the times. This will, of necessity, involve some repetition, but I will try to keep this at a minimum.

(1) JAN HUYGHEN VAN LINSCHOTEN (1596). The first known account of the Portuguese capture and destruction of the tooth dates from 1596 and was written not in Portuguese but in Dutch. Jan Huyghen Van Linschoten was born in Holland in 1562 and brought up in a Catholic family in the generally Protestant town of Enkhuizen, an important port on the Zuydersee, and the center of the booming sixteenth-century Dutch herring industry (Méndez-Oliver 2016, 341).[2] Even as a young lad, he was obviously bright, ambitious, capable, and observant. He also suffered from wanderlust, and at the age of fourteen he apprenticed himself to his brother, who was a merchant in Seville. He then moved to Lisbon, and after a few years there managed to get appointed as secretary to the newly named Portuguese archbishop of Goa, João Vicente da Fonseca. Together with the archbishop, he departed for the colony in 1583, where he continued to be employed in the monsignor's household until 1589. He kept a meticulous record of his observations of life in Goa—what he saw, what he learned, the political situation, the people, their customs, and the stories they told. He also spent time sketching many scenes of daily life.[3] All this he edited and published upon his return to Holland, as the first part of his magnum opus, *Itinerario*. What he is most famous for, however, is having surreptitiously copied many of the secret Portuguese nautical maps providing key data on currents, islands, reefs, and so on, throughout the Indies, along with eighty years of navigational

2. It is doubtful that Van Linschoten could have ever held the position he did later in the household of the archbishop of Goa as a Protestant. After his return from India, however, he did convert to the Dutch Reformed Church, and Wojciehowski (2011, 193–198) looks at his version of the tooth narrative as a "Protestant account."

3. On these sketches, see the comments of Subrahmanyam 2017, 132–133.

observations and sailing directions recorded by Portuguese pilots and captains, starting with Vasco da Gama. Apparently, Van Linschoten gained access to many of these documents during his long layover in the Azores on his return trip home from India (Parr 1964, 165; Méndez-Oliver 2016, 342). These he published as the second part of his work, entitled *Reysgeschrift* [Travel writings], to which he added personal observations about the dilapidated state of the Portuguese fleet. *Reysgeschrift* was almost immediately translated into English, Latin, and French, and it had a tremendous impact. Suffice it to say that it was this book, perhaps as much as anything else, that enabled the Dutch (and, to some extent, the British) to break the Portuguese monopoly on trade in Asia, and eventually confine them to enclaves of influence.[4]

The passage that interests us, however, occurs in chapter 44 of the *Itinerario*, where Van Linschoten deals with Indian "temples, idols, indulgences, pilgrimages, ceremonies, and other superstitions." After a brief description of the Indian Buddhist caves at Kāṇherī (being used in his day as a cloister by a group of Franciscan brothers [Van Linschoten 1885, 1: 289–291]),[5] he then abruptly switches to Adam's Peak in south-central Sri Lanka.[6] On top of that mountain, he says, there is a great building, wherein there stands a famous "pagode"—a Portuguese term then meaning either a heathen temple or an idol of some sort (see Yule and Burnell 1903, 652–656). In 1554 (*sic*), a group of Portuguese soldiers, looking for booty, climbed the mountain and ransacked the temple, where they found nothing except a little bejeweled coffer, in which was a "tooth of an ape [*aap*] or monkey [*simme*], shrined in gold and precious stones." It was, he states, "the holiest thing in India," and attracted more pilgrims than the shrines of Santiago de Compostella in Galicia or Mont Saint Michel in France. Van Linschoten then goes on to describe how it was taken to Goa, where the kings of Pegu [today, Bago], Sion [present-day Mumbai], Bisnagar [Vijayanagar], and others offered great sums of money for it (700,000 ducats in gold), but were rejected by Archbishop Gaspar, his employer's predecessor, who had the tooth destroyed by

4. In particular, Van Linschoten made clear to his countrymen the potential of Java, and the direct southern route to that island. On his influence, see Parr 1964; Kamps 2001, 160; and, for a different perspective, Méndez-Oliver 2016.

5. On the repossession of the caves at Kāṇherī, see also Xavier and Županov 2015, 124–125.

6. Adam's Peak (aka Śrī Pada, or Pico de Adam, as Van Linschoten calls it) was, at least from the twelfth century on, most famous for the "footprint" located on its peak, variously attributed by followers of different religions to visits of the Buddha, Śiva, Adam, or Saint Thomas (see Strong 2004b, 92–94). Van Linschoten makes no mention of the footprint here, but he does in a different passage on the mountain elsewhere (1885, 1: 79). For general discussions of the mountain and pilgrimages there, see Aksland 2001; Skeen [1870] 1997.

fire. Not long thereafter, however, a clever merchant got another ape's tooth and made the "heathens" believe that it was the very same relic that the archbishop thought he had destroyed, declaring its location had been revealed to him in a vision that also assured him that the tooth had slipped through the bottom of the mortar when it was supposedly being smashed and had reappeared in his temple in Lanka. That merchant later sold that fake tooth to the (Hindu) king of Vijayanagar in India (Van Linschoten 1885, 1: 292–94; see also Wojciehowski 2011, 196–198).

Van Linschoten makes no mention of the Buddha but identifies the tooth as that of a monkey. He does, however, clearly know about offers having been made to ransom it, its destruction by fire in Goa, and a version of the tale of its post-mortem reappearance—all themes that we shall encounter again in subsequent narratives.

Van Linschoten's dating of the Portuguese raid on Adam's Peak to 1554 is noteworthy as it differs from the later, and more usual, affirmation that it was taken in Jaffna in 1560. Burnell and Tiele (Van Linschoten 1885, 1: 292n5), on the basis of Do Couto, deem 1554 to be "clearly mistaken." For the time being, however, it is best to take both the date (1554) and the location (Adam's Peak) at face value. By the early 1550s, the Portuguese viceroy Afonso de Noronha (in office 1550–1554) had invaded the kingdom of Kotte just east of Colombo, and his men had engaged in destruction and plunder in the area, including the looting of the royal treasure in the Temple of the Tooth in Kotte itself.[7] It may be that they ransacked Adam's Peak around the same time. In any case, subsequent Dutch writers (e.g., Philipus Baldaeus and François Valentijn) uncritically followed Van Linschoten in both his dating (1554) and location (on Adam's Peak) of the tooth's capture, although by their time, as we shall see, the locale of Adam's Peak had become confused.

(2) NICOLAUS PIMENTA (1605).[8] Our next reference to the tooth's destruction probably dates to 1605. It comes from a letter by Nicolaus Pimenta (1546–1613) and is much shorter than Van Linschoten's. Father Pimenta went out to Goa in 1597, where he acted as Visitor to the Jesuits, responsible

---

7. See below. See also Biedermann (2018, 171) on the importance of this event. As we shall see, there is no mention that the tooth was then located in its temple in Kotte. By that time, according to Sri Lankan sources, the relic had been taken from Kotte to Delgamuwa. If Van Linschoten, in Goa, had heard that this had happened, his location of the relic is a bit more understandable, since Delgamuwa is but twenty-five kilometers from Adam's Peak and is right next to Kuruwita, one of the traditional take-off points for pilgrims intending to ascend the mountain.

8. His name is also spelled Pementa.

for keeping in touch with, and tabs on, all the order's missionaries in the Orient.[9] In this function, he traveled extensively throughout South and Southeast Asia, sending letters back to Rome on what he was finding, and what his fellow Jesuit priests were doing. In one of these letters, he has a section entitled "Superstitious madness of Jogues [Yogis, i.e., non-Christian ascetics and priests of all kinds]." In this he claims that the ape's tooth found in Sri Lanka (he does not say where) was actually a relic of the Hindu "Monkey God" Hanumān (Purchas [1625] 1905, 10: 208).

In the Hindu *Rāmāyaṇa* epic, Hanumān, a simian figure with divine powers, is famous for being an ardent devotee of Rāma. When Rāma's wife Sītā is abducted by Rāvaṇa, the ten-headed demon-king of Lanka, Hanumān is dispatched to the island to locate her. He then later helps Rāma defeat the demon and rescue her.[10] Hanumān's fame in the epic guaranteed him a place in the Hindu pantheon, and he is today (and was in the sixteenth century) venerated pretty much throughout India.[11]

Pimenta's account of his story is rather truncated. He writes only that in a certain Hindu temple of Perimal [= Perumal, a Tamil form of Viṣṇu] in South India, there was "worshipped an Ape called Hanimant [= Hanumān], whom they report to have beene a God, but who, for some offence or another, along with many other thousands of gods (similarly metamorphosed), [was] transformed into an Ape" (Purchas [1625] 1905, 10: 208, slightly altered). He goes on to recount how one day this monkey, lacking a ship, jumped over the waters between Rameśvaram in South India and Sri Lanka, at every bound causing a small island or sandbar to appear (the present so-called Adam's Bridge in the Palk Straits between India and Sri Lanka). He then adds, as though the story were well known, that "they say it was his Tooth which the Viceroy Constantine cast into the fire, notwithstanding the Ethnikes' [natives'] offer of three hundred thousand ducats for [its] redemption" (Purchas [1625] 1905, 10: 208–209, slightly altered). Again, Pimenta makes no mention of the Buddha and no mention of Jaffna or the capture, but the story of the rejected ransom and Dom Constantino destroying the relic has obviously reached him.

9. I would like to thank David Kolb for his email of April 24, 2020, clarifying the evolving role of the Visitor in the Jesuit Order.
10. In Hinduism, Rāma is an avatar of Viṣṇu and Rāvaṇa is a devotee of Śiva; in some Buddhist traditions (e.g., the "Dasaratha jātaka"), Rāma is a previous incarnation of the Buddha and Rāvaṇa (e.g., in the *Lankāvatāra sūtra*) is a devotee of the Buddha. For a comparative study, see Reynolds 1991.
11. On the cult of Hanumān, see Lutgendorf 2007.

(3) PIERRE DU JARRIC (1610). The first of our authors to place the capture of the tooth in Jaffna is Pierre Du Jarric (1566–1617). He was born in Toulouse and entered the Jesuit Order at the age of sixteen. His desire to become a missionary was never realized; instead, he became a professor of philosophy at Bordeaux, where he spent much of the rest of his life chronicling the mission work of his Portuguese brethren who did go to the Indies (Huonder 1913). In his magnum opus of 1610 on "The history of the more memorable things that happened in the East Indies as well as in other countries discovered by the Portuguese, concerning the establishment and progress of the Christian Faith; and of the role played in this by the Religieux of the Company of Jesus, and what they endured for the same cause,"[12] he recalls that, following Dom Constantino's invasion of Jaffna in 1560, "what the King and several other Princes of India deplored most of all was the loss of a white monkey's tooth which had been held sacred and worshipped by practically all the Pagans of the East" (Du Jarric 1610, 397; see also Gaspard 1918, 15).

He then tells the story of Hanumān who, he says, was demoted from divine status to that of monkey, and who passed over from the city of Perimal in the land of the "Badagas" (i.e., Vijayanagara) to Sri Lanka, a small island appearing at each jump so he would not wet his paws. Hanumān, he claims, died in Sri Lanka, where "the people kept this one relic of him, namely the tooth which . . . was held as something sacrosanct and divine by the Pagans of these parts" (Du Jarric 1610, 397–398; Gaspard 1918, 15–16).

Even though he asserts that the tooth is that of Hanumān, who originally came from Vijayanagara in South India, Du Jarric goes on to recount the king of Pegu's offer of 300,000 crowns (écus) to ransom the relic, and explains that this resulted in much debate over what to do. Some wanted to accept the Peguan proposal, but Don Constantino held a council and it was decided that since that would only promote idolatry, the tooth should be destroyed instead. There then follows a rather elaborate description of its being crushed in a mortar and burned in a brazier, to which we shall return (Du Jarric 1610, 398–399). Unfortunately, Du Jarric does not cite any of his sources, but it is obvious that, sitting in Bordeaux, he had read much and perhaps heard much, probably from fellow Jesuits, with whom he corresponded extensively.

---

12. *Histoire des choses plus mémorables advenues tant ez Indes Orientales, que autre païs de la descouverte des Portugais, en l'establissement et progrez de la foy Chrestienne et Catholique: et principalement de ce que les Religieux de la Compagnie de Iesus y ont faict, et enduré pour la mesme fin.*

(4) PEDRO TEXEIRA (1610). Our next source, also written in 1610, comes from the pen of Pedro Texeira. Texeira was a Portuguese Crypto-Jewish merchant and adventurer who embarked for Goa in 1586 and slowly circumnavigated the world, living for some years in different parts of the Near East and Asia, including Goa and Malacca. He then returned to Portugal in 1601 via Manila, Acapulco, Mexico City, Veracruz, Havana, Florida, and Seville. In 1603, however, he was obliged to go back to Goa to settle some financial matters (debts are mentioned). Having quickly taken care of that business, he decided this time to return to Europe via the Middle East (by ship to Hormuz, and then, following various caravan trails, to Basra, Baghdad, Karbala, Aleppo, and finally Iskenderun ["Little Alexandria"], whence he sailed to Venice, arriving there in April 1605).[13] By 1608 he settled in Antwerp, where he wrote, in Spanish, a tripartite work comprising histories of the kings of Persia, and of Hormuz, and an account of his travels in the Middle East.[14] The following is a story he presumably came across in Goa, but was reminded of when writing about the ransoming of the Kaaba (which he calls "a superstitious stone") in Mecca in 932 by an Abbasid Caliph:

[By way of contrast,] Don Constantine de Braganza, being Viceroy of India for the crown of Portugal, among the other noble actions becoming his high birth . . . was the subduing of the kingdom of Jafanapatan [Jaffna], whence, besides many other things of value, [he] brought away a monkey's tooth, held in mighty veneration, and adored by those heathens, as having belonged to a monkey, into which they said one of their gods had transformed himself, and done mighty wonders in rescuing the wife of one of those gods, which had been stolen away from him. . . . This monkey's tooth being carried to Goa, the neighboring infidels . . . resolve[d] to send a solemn embassy to Goa, to propose the ransoming of it. (Texeira 1715, 251; original text in Texeira 1610, 271)

Texeira then goes on to describe the rejection of that offer and the destruction of the tooth in some detail. A council was called to debate the question, and its resolution was that, "notwithstanding the considerable sum offered for the tooth, they ought rather to prefer their zeal for God's Honour, and to deprive the Gentiles of so considerable an object of idolatry." Accordingly, they summoned those ransom offerers to a square by the

13. On Texeira's life, see Fuente del Pilar 2015, 631–634; Ferguson 1897; and Kayserling 1907. He should not be confused with his near contemporary and namesake, the Pedro Texeira who was the first to travel the length of the Amazon River.
14. See Texeira 1610, 1902, and 1715.

viceroy's palace, and, in their presence, pulverized the tooth in a mortar and cast it into the river (Texeira 1715, 251).

(5) FRANÇOIS PYRARD DE LAVAL (1611). Like Du Jarric, Texeira situates the capture of the tooth in Jaffna, and identifies it as Hanumān's, though he does not use that god's name. However, our next, very brief account, written a year later in 1611 by François Pyrard de Laval (c. 1578–1623), takes us back to southern Sri Lanka. Pyrard was a French adventurer who embarked from Saint Malo on the *Corbin* in 1601, probably as the ship's purser. The boat was part of the first French expedition to India, aimed at challenging the Portuguese monopoly over the sea routes. The voyage ends badly, however, when in 1602, the *Corbin* is shipwrecked in the Maldive Islands.[15] Pyrard and a few other survivors are marooned there, where they are kept in captivity (actually under "island arrest") by the local sultan for five years.[16] His confinement comes to an end when a hostile fleet from Chittagong, in Bengal, bent on getting the cannons from the wrecked *Corbin* and other booty from the islands, attacks the Maldives and kills the sultan. The Bengalis take Pyrard de Laval and his three fellow French survivors with them back to Bengal. From there, he eventually makes his way to the west coast of India, where he is cordially received by the Zamorin of Calicut. Unfortunately, while on an excursion outside the city, he is betrayed and arrested (as an enemy Frenchman) by a band of Portuguese, who take him prisoner to Cochin, and then on to Goa in June 1608. There, he manages to gain his freedom through the intervention of a French Jesuit, but with the understanding that he will now have to serve as a soldier on a Portuguese vessel. He does so on two expeditions, one of which takes him for a short while to Sri Lanka, where he is "able to gather a quantity of hearsay information about the island" (Gray 1887, 2: xiii). Upon his return, he resides in Goa for half a year longer. Eventually, he makes it back to France, via Brazil and Spain (where he goes to Compostella to fulfill a pilgrimage vow), and in 1611, in Paris,

---

15. There were two ships on the 1601 French expedition to the East Indies. The other, the *Croissant*, managed to go on to Sumatra, but its voyage, like the *Corbin*'s, ended badly; on its return journey to Europe, it was intercepted off the coast of Spain by three Dutch privateers who appropriated all of its cargo. The surgeon on board the *Croissant* later wrote an account of its voyage, which was published when he finally got back to Saint Malo (see Martin De Vitré 1604). For a summary of Martin de Vitré's adventures and an account of his career as an apothecary both before and after this expedition, see Irissou 1946.

16. He occupies his time, in part, in learning the local language, and eventually writes the first lexicon of the Maldivian language, which he appends to his book.

he publishes the first edition of his account of his adventures (Gray 1887, 1: xliv–xlviii).[17]

In the chapter of his book devoted to Ceylon, Pyrard first gives a somewhat confused narrative about a king (whom he calls Don Iouan) who spent a long time in Goa, then returned to Sri Lanka where, however, he renounced his Christianity and betrayed the Portuguese. This can only be Konappu Bandara, who spent some time in Goa, where he was baptized as Don João [= Don Iouan] da Austria. At first allying himself with the Portuguese, Konappu Bandara helped them invade and capture (for a while) the town of Kandy. As soon as the bulk of the Portuguese forces had left, however, he rallied the Sinhalese population in a rebellion against his former overlords and took over the throne for himself, reigning from 1592 to 1604 as Vimaladharmasuriya. According to Sri Lankan tradition, Vimaladharmasuriya built the first Temple of the Tooth in Kandy, where he enshrined the relic that he purported to have gotten from Delgamuwa near Adam's Peak. It was, for him, an important legitimizer of his somewhat dubious claim to the Kandyan throne.

These events would have just recently happened when Pyrard was in Sri Lanka (1609) and hence be fresh in his interlocutors' minds. Pyrard says nothing about "Don Iouan" being the one who first brought the tooth relic to his kingdom, but he goes on to state that "they [i.e., the people of his kingdom] worshipped a monkey's tooth, and, since it was taken by the Portuguese, they wanted to buy it back for great riches, but there was no desire to give it back and so it was publicly burned in Goa" (Pyrard de Laval 1619, 2: 152).

That is all Pyrard states, but this snippet of information is nonetheless important, for it would appear that this may be an early indication of Western awareness that there was a tooth in Kandy. Even though Pyrard makes no mention of Kandy by name and seems to think that Don Iouan's (i.e., Vimaladharma Suriya's) residence is "near Galle" (1619, 2: 152) in southern Sri Lanka,[18] the story he tells makes it clear that it is about Kandy. And the

---

17. A number of seventeenth-century writers doubted the authenticity of Pyrard de Laval's authorship of this work (some even questioning his existence), and attributed its writing instead to Jerome Bignon or Pierre Bergeron, who made use of either notes by Pyrard and/or conversations with him (see Gray 1888, 1, xxxiii–xxxviii). Gray, however, does not doubt that Pyrard was the ultimate source of information for the book. Bergeron, as we shall see, was also responsible in part for the publication of Vincent Le Blanc's account of his journeys.

18. Actually, Pyrard's account is even more confusing than this because he says that Don Iouan and his whole kingdom were conquered (along with the monkey's tooth) by André Fur-

immediate segueing into the story of the tooth (still that of a monkey) suggests that some of his interlocutors were aware of the relic's presence there, even though this information then got trumped by the story of the Portuguese destruction of the tooth in Goa.

(6) DIOGO DO COUTO (1616). As mentioned, scholars narrating the Portuguese capture and destruction of the tooth for the most part confine themselves to the account found in Diogo Do Couto's *Da Asia*—understandably, perhaps, given that it presents a more extended version of the story than any of those we have touched on so far.

Diogo Do Couto (1542–1616) was a man of humble birth. Raised in Lisbon, at the age of seventeen he set out for Portuguese India, where he remained for the better part of fifty years, the first ten of which he spent as an ordinary soldier.[19] Eventually, by dint of his native skills, self-promotion, and a few key sponsors, he became the keeper of the Portuguese archives in Goa, and was commissioned to continue writing *Da Asia*, the great official history that had been begun by his predecessor, the historian João De Barros (1496–1570), subtitled "On the feats of the Portuguese in the conquest and discovery of the lands and seas of the East."[20] Do Couto labored on this magnum opus for the rest of his life, often against great odds (manuscripts were repeatedly lost, or censored by church or by state).[21] The portion that describes Dom Constantino's expedition and the capture of the tooth relic falls in what is known as Decada VII [The 7th Decade], dealing with events between 1554 and 1565. Its manuscript was first finished in 1602, but then lost while on its way to Lisbon for official approval and printing when the carrack it was on, the *Santiago*, was captured and almost sunk by two Dutch corsairs off the island of Saint Helena in the South Atlantic Ocean.[22] When

---

tado de Mendosa. André Furtado was the Portuguese captain who was famed for finally conquering the Jaffna peninsula, but not until 1591. See Queiros 1930, 446–456.

19. Based on his life as a soldier, Do Couto wrote a scathing critique of the corruption rampant in Portuguese Asia in the guise of a conversation between a veteran soldier, a nobleman, and a crown official. See Do Couto [1612] 1937, translated in Do Couto 2016.

20. "Dos feitos, que os Portuguezes fizeram na conquista, e descubrimento das terras, e mares do Oriente."

21. The multiple volumes of the 1778–1788 Portuguese edition of this work may be found online at http://purl.pt/7030/3/.

22. Some claim that the *Santiago* was sunk; however, according to an Italian merchant, Francesco Carletti (1573–1636), who was on board on his way home after an eight-year circumnavigation of the world, the Dutch managed to patch it up and sail it away as a prize to Amsterdam, where the carrack and what was left of its cargo were auctioned (Carletti 1964, 238–245). On

he heard the news (the equivalent of a hard-disk crash with no backups), Do Couto resignedly rewrote the whole *decada* the following year (1603), apparently, this time, making a couple of copies. This version, however, was not given the go-ahead for printing for ten years and did not actually get published until 1616 (Boxer 1948, 13–15).[23] I therefore am considering it at this point in this chronological survey of sources, but it should be remembered that it reflects what Do Couto thought at the turn of the seventeenth century, even though it had no influence on what others thought until after 1616. This may or may not be important in considering the development of the tooth story over time.[24]

Do Couto prefaces his account of the capture of the tooth with a lengthy description of the events leading up to the Portuguese invasion of Jaffna in 1560—a story we shall look at in chapter 2. Suffice it to say here that after taking the city, the troops start looking for booty, and that is when they find the relic. As Do Couto puts it:

From their principal temple,[25] they brought to the Viceroy an enchased tooth, which was commonly said to be that of a monkey, [but] which was held by those heathens to be their most sacred object of worship. They immediately advised the Viceroy of this, and they assured him that it was the greatest treasure that he could have gotten, because he could receive a large sum of gold for it. Those heathens maintained that this tooth was that of their Budão [Buddha]. . . . In his legend, they relate that this Budão, after leaving Ceylon, traveled to parts of Pegu, and, in all those realms, converted heathens and performed miracles. And when he came to die, he wrenched this tooth from his mouth, and sent it to Ceylon as a very great relic of his. And thus it was considered so great among them, and among all the heathens of the

---

board the *Santiago* were thousands of pieces of Chinese porcelain, whose sale marked the start of a large-scale Dutch commerce in such dishware, which came to be known as "kraak [from *carrack*] porcelain." No mention is made of De Couto's manuscript being saved. (See Nilsson n.d.a and n.d.b.)

23. For a lively account of the many vicissitudes encountered by Do Couto in publishing his overall work, see Winius 1985, 6–7.

24. This may actually be a moot point, since it is not clear that any of Do Couto's near contemporaries were familiar with his book. Do Couto himself complains that no one was reading his work and that very few copies had been distributed, and that, although he had made presents of his books to the viceroy, the archbishop, and all the captains, "none of them gave me in return so much as a jar of marmalade" (Boxer 1948, 22).

25. Most probably the Hindu temple of Nallur Kandaswamy, which was and still is an important Śaivite center of worship dedicated to the god Murugan (aka Kataragama), but which served also as a kind of ceremonial center close by the royal palace.

principalities of Pegu, that there was nothing that they valued more highly. (Ferguson [1908] 1993, 191, slightly altered)[26]

Do Couto then goes on to describe how the tooth is taken to Goa and how the viceroy is originally inclined to accept the king of Pegu's offer (the sum of three to four hundred thousand *cruzados* is mentioned). Just as he is about to conclude the agreement, however, the archbishop of Goa, Dom Gaspar, hears of the affair. Accompanied by some members of the Inquisition (that was then just beginning to establish itself in Goa), Dom Gaspar approaches the viceroy and tells him that the tooth cannot be ransomed, for such a sale would be an insult to God that would only encourage idolatry. This gives pause to Dom Constantino, and, after some back-and-forth, he agrees to a resolution that the relic be destroyed. Accordingly, the viceroy formally hands the tooth over to the archbishop, who "there, in the presence of all throws it into a mortar, and with his own hand pounds it and reduces it to fragments, and casts them into a brasier . . . and commands the ashes and cinders to be thrown into the midst of the river in the sight of all, who witnessed it from the verandas and windows that looked on to the sea" (Ferguson [1908] 1993, 212–213, slightly altered; original text in Do Couto 1783, 430–431).

Do Couto, however, does not end his account here. He goes on to state that the reactions to this, both in Goa and in Portugal, were mixed. On the one hand, some praised Dom Constantino as a pious and religious man who had chosen to stand against idolatry and the temptations of avarice. On the other hand, some protested against the archbishop's act, and declared Dom Constantino to be a fool, saying the gold he turned down could have been used to replenish the nearly empty coffers of the empire in Asia (not to mention his own pockets). Besides, the "pagans" would probably just make another tooth to worship, out of a piece of bone or something (Do Couto 1783, 431–432; Eng. trans., Ferguson [1908] 1993, 213–214). Indeed, we are told that not long after the events described above, João Dharmapala, the king of Kotte, let it be known that the "real" tooth had never gone to Jaffna, that he, Dharmapala, had hidden it away, and had it all along. This then he promptly sold to the same king of Pegu who had been rebuffed by the Portuguese. But some decades later, in the 1590s, the emergent king of Kandy, Vimaladharmasuriya, contradicted this claim, asserting that, contrary to this, he had the "real" tooth relic of the Buddha in his possession. This he too

---

26. Original text in Do Couto 1783, 316–318. For alternative translations, see Tennent 1859, 2: 213; and Wojciehowski 2011, 188.

tried to sell to the king of Pegu, informing the latter that he had been duped by Kotte. The king of Pegu rebuffed him, however; apparently, he was not interested in admitting the tooth he had gotten was fake (Do Couto 1786, 74–87; Eng. trans., Ferguson [1908] 1993, 242–253).[27] I shall return to all these stories in due time. For now, suffice it to say that Do Couto not only locates the capture of the tooth in Jaffna, but he is the first to affirm that the natives (although not necessarily he himself) thought of it not as the tooth of a monkey but as that of the Buddha.

(7) PAULO DA TRINDADE (1636). Our next account of the tooth comes from the pen of Paulo da Trindade, who was born in Macao in 1570 but spent most of his life in Goa. Between 1630 and 1636, he wrote *The Spiritual Conquest of the Orient*[28] in three volumes. Trindade is heavily dependent on the works of earlier Portuguese historians, especially De Barros and Do Couto, whom he often paraphrases or plagiarizes (see Biedermann 2016). His work is interesting, however, because he was a Franciscan friar and, as such, presents a somewhat different attitude toward "heathens" than did the Jesuits. As is commonly recognized, the two Catholic orders were long in competition with each other in Asia. In Sri Lanka, the Franciscans held a fiercely guarded monopoly of sorts over missionary activity on the island until 1602, when the Jesuits were finally allowed to establish themselves there. The Dominicans followed in 1605, and the Augustinians in 1606. Thenceforth, Ceylon became "a battlefield for Catholic missionary work—strongly influenced by the rivalry between the various orders, and particularly by the dispute between the Franciscans and the Jesuits" (Carita 2007, 268).

As Zoltán Biedermann (2016, quoting Trindade [1630–1636] 1962–1967, 3: 3) has pointed out, Trindade was very much interested in Sri Lanka because "of the singular services that were performed there to God and to the Crown of Portugal by the friars of Saint Francis . . . irrigating with their blood the new plants they planted." He also appears to have been obsessed with idolatry, bemoaning "the vile doctrine of many different sects . . . the false theology of vain gods, accompanied by many rites, ceremonies, diabolic sacrifices and witchcraft" (Trindade [1630–1636] 1962–1967, 1: 83).

27. Strathern (2007, 1) suggests that there may be a distant reference to this story and to Vimaladharmasuriya in Don Quijote's hallucinated figure of the "mighty emperor Alifanfaron, lord of the great isle of Taprobana [i.e., Ceylon]." See Cervantes 1885, 287, and also 406–418 for his account of Doña Maguncia, the queen of "the famous kingdom of Kandy." Cervantes wrote *Don Quixote* in 1605.

28. *Conquista spiritual do Oriente.*

It makes sense, therefore, that he should dedicate a whole chapter to the destruction of the tooth relic, entitled "On the Tooth of the Monkey [*dente do bugio*] that was Captured in Jaffna, and what was done by the Council of Theologians." He begins by decrying the "worship by the infidels of the East of false gods, brute animals, non-sentient things, and, worse, the very devil himself represented by the most ugly and astounding figures that ever could be" (Trindade [1630–1636] 1962–1967, 3: 181). The tooth of the white monkey [*bugio branco*], in his view, was a prime example of "these different abominations." Trindade acknowledges that the natives thought of this as the tooth "of their Buddha [Budão] whom they held to be a great saint" and whose story he quickly summarizes in almost the same language as Do Couto. But, obsessed with demonolatry, he focuses most of all on Dom Constantino's "very wise and praiseworthy" decision to have the tooth destroyed (Trindade [1630–1636] 1962–1967, 3: 182–183).

(8) VINCENT LE BLANC (1648). The next account of the tooth is from a work by Vincent Le Blanc (1554–1640), redacted and published by Pierre Bergeron in 1648 as *Les voyages fameux du Sieur Vincent LeBlanc, Marseillois*.[29] Le Blanc is presented as an extraordinary adventurer who traveled for almost sixty years, visiting not only the Near East and Africa but "the East and West Indies, Persia and Pegu etc." As this was a time of the publication of many fictitious narratives pretending to be accounts of real voyages to real or poorly known places, some have suspected that LeBlanc's work is basically fictional and that he himself may never have existed. However, the French literary scholar Geoffroy Atkinson, who has studied this genre of "extraordinary voyages," disagrees. For him, the *Voyages* of Le Blanc are in all probability what they purport to be—"the diary and *mémoires* of a man who traveled extensively, published with additions and revisions by a lawyer, [i.e., Pierre Bergeron]" (Atkinson 1920, 26). Atkinson admits that the third part of the work dealing with America and the Antilles was evidently plagiarized from other sources, but, he declares, there is "a convincing realism of personal experience in the First and Second Parts of the book, dealing respectively with Asia and with Africa. Whether this personal and realistic element of the first part of the book is that which originally existed in the diary of one man, Vincent Le Blanc, or whether it is a composite of various such diaries,

29. An English translation was soon published under the title *The World Surveyed: Or, the Famous Voyages and Travailes of Vincent le Blanc, of Marseilles* (Le Blanc, 1660).

matters little after all" (Atkinson 1920, 27). That is also true from a "storical" perspective.

Though the work was not published until 1648, there is evidence that LeBlanc's notes were already known to Bergeron sometime before 1634 (Atkinson 1920, 26). Moreover, the experiences they were based on may be much older. At the start of part 1 of his work, LeBlanc (1648, 3–4) tells us that he was not yet fourteen when he embarked in 1567 for Alexandria without the permission of his father. He then narrates adventures in Syria (in 1569), in Arabia, and at Aden on the Red Sea. He goes to Hormuz, then visits Persia, then sails along the coast to Gujarat, Diu, and Goa (Le Blanc 1648, 7–79). Unfortunately, it is not clear how long all this takes, but by chapter 20, he is on the "Isle of Zeilan" [Ceylon]—perhaps in 1571. If this is the case, and if we believe the story he tells of the tooth is something he heard at that time, or before, in Goa, this would actually make LeBlanc one of our oldest sources. In any case, once again, there is no mention of the Buddha, but only of the monkey, who is once more identified as Hanumān. His account is as follows:

> This island [of Ceylon] . . . formerly had a single king, of a race that was said to be descendant from the Sun. His reign was extinguished by a king of Jaffna, and since then, the country [Kotte] has been divided into several kingdoms. The Portuguese went to war with the king of Jaffna, who, once conquered, was constrained to cede to them the Isle of Man[n]ar. . . . In this war against this king, the Portuguese captured, among other things, that renown idol of a monkey's tooth, adored by all those Indians, and enriched by precious stones. The king of Pegu esteemed it so much that he used to send every year some ambassadors, simply to attain an impression of it in amber, musk, and other perfumes, which he then held in great reverence. After its capture, he wanted to buy it from the Portuguese very dearly, but they preferred to lose the idol rather than profit from it, and burned it, something that caused a very stinking smoke. There are thousands of stories about this white monkey, named Hanimam—that he had been a god who was chased from heaven because of some misdeed and transformed into a monkey; then that he came to the land of the Badages in Bisnagar,[30] and from there passed over to Ceylon, where, after his death, he was worshipped, and his tooth kept as a relic. (Le Blanc 1648, 104)

30. "Badages" is a reference to the "Northerners" (Tamil, *Vaḍagar*), that is, the originally Telugu people who invaded Tamil lands and came to rule Vijayanagar (= Bisnagar). See Yule and Burnell 1903, 46.

(9) PHILIPPUS BALDAEUS (1672). Our next source dates from 1672 and comes from the pen of the Dutch missionary Philippus Baldaeus (1632–1671). He was raised in Delft by his grandfather, having lost his parents to the plague. He studied theology at Leiden and became a minister of the Reformed Church, and soon embarked for Asia in the employ of the Dutch East India Company. He joined the Dutch forces in their wars against the Portuguese in Ceylon and South India and eventually settled in Jaffna, where he studied various languages, including Tamil and Sanskrit, and became one of the first Western scholars to document Tamil culture and life in northern Sri Lanka. He spent his years on the island actively preaching to both Hindus and Catholics, seeking to convert them to Calvinism. After disputes with both the Dutch East India Company (VOC) and the Reformed Church, he returned to Holland, where he became a pastor in the small town of Geervliet, where he wrote *A Description of ye East India Coasts of Malabar and Coromandel with their Adjacent Kingdoms & Provinces & of the Empire of Ceylon* (Baldaeus [1703] 2000),[31] and where he passed away at a comparatively young age.[32]

In his book, which deals extensively with Tamil ethnology, mythology, history, and geography, he touches briefly on the story of the tooth, in the context of his discussion of Hanumān. Despite his familiarity with Portuguese sources, and his claim that his information is coming from them, what Baldaeus has to say here seems entirely dependent on the account of his Dutch compatriot Van Linschoten:

> This Ape [Hanumān] had divers celebrated *Pagodes* erected to him by the Indians. We read in the Portuguese Histories, that in 1554, when they plunder'd the famous Pagode upon the Adams Mount in Ceylon, they found an Ape's Tooth (the most sacred Relick of the Pagans of Pegu, Ceylon, Malabar, Bengale, Coromandel and Bisnagar [Vijayanagara]) encofed in a box set with precious stones, which they carried to Goa; some of the Indian Princes offered 700,000 Ducats to redeem it, but it was not accepted, by reason the Bishop of Goa opposed it. (Baldaeus [1703] 2000, 839; original Dutch text in Baldaeus 1672, part 3 [on Heathen Idols]: 26)

All that Baldaeus has added to Van Linschoten's account is the specification that the ape was Hanumān, and the addition of a few kingdoms

---

31. Original title: *Naauwkeurige Beschrijvinge van Malabar en Choromandel der Zelver aangrenzenden Ryken en het machtige Eyland Ceylon* (see Baldaeus 1672). Parts of his work have been shown to be plagiarisms of several earlier accounts (see Subrahmanyam 2017, 129).

32. For a short biography of Baldaeus, see Joosse 2015.

who were interested in acquiring his tooth. Nevertheless, his account is important because it shows the continuation of the Dutch claim that the tooth was captured in 1554 on Adam's Peak, or more precisely on what he calls Adam's Peak—we shall see that there was some Dutch confusion about this. This, however, is in spite of his good familiarity with Jaffna and its traditions. One would expect that had there been a Tamil tradition about the worship of Hanumān's (or the Buddha's) tooth in Jaffna, Baldaeus would have known about it and not had to resort to repeating the claims of Van Linschoten, whose version seems to have become the standard Dutch iteration of the tooth story.

(10) MANUEL FARIA E SOUZA (1674). Manuel Faria e Souza (1590–1649) was an independent Portuguese scholar and poet who often wrote in Spanish. Faria e Souza was born in Lisbon. He got in trouble with the Inquisition for portions of his commentary on Luis De Camões's great poetic epic *The Lusiads*, but survived that to start on his own huge history of the Portuguese everywhere—in Europe, in Africa, in America, in Asia. Of that, *Asia Portuguesa* was published in three volumes between 1666 and 1675, but was probably written in the 1640s, before his death in 1649 (Faria e Souza 1666–1675).[33] The story that interests us is contained in the second volume, which came out in 1674.

Like Le Blanc, Faria e Souza seems to be unaware of Do Couto's view that the tooth was a relic of the Buddha; instead, he picks up on the tradition already mentioned by Du Jarric that the simian in question was a "white monkey":

> In the treasure taken from the king of Jaffna, whom we recently vanquished by our arms, there was an idol celebrated in the whole of Asia. It was so coveted by all of the princes [in the region] that some of them had sought to get imprints of it in precious materials such as amber. In particular, the King of Pegu, every year, sent his ambassadors with rich gifts for that monarch, in the hopes that he would consent to an impression of the idol being taken, since he could not obtain the original. Those copies were re-presentations of that idol and were adored as much as it. It was a white monkey's tooth. (Faria e Souza 1666–1675, 2: 350)

33. For an often-problematic, somewhat abridged translation by John Stevens, see Faria e Souza 1695, 2: 208–209. In what follows, I will refer only to the original Spanish text.

Faria e Souza goes on to present several different accounts of this white monkey and its relic, then a lengthy account of the Portuguese debates over whether to sell or destroy the tooth, and then the story of the kings of Kotte and of Kandy "inventing" new false tooth relics. All of these will be examined in due time.

(11) FERNÃO QUEIROS (1687).[34] Our next author is one of the great Portuguese historians of Sri Lanka.[35] Fernão Queiros completed his *Temporal and Spiritual Conquest of Ceylon*[36] in 1687. The following year, it received an "Imprimatur" in Portugal, but then, three months later, Queiros died and, although his manuscript was ready to go to press, for some reason, it was never printed. Instead, it languished for a couple of centuries in the royal archives in Lisbon until they were moved to Brazil when King João VI and his court fled there in 1807 during the Napoleonic Wars. In time, the manuscript was presented to the National Library of Rio De Janeiro (where it remains to this day),[37] and in 1834, a single copy was made to be housed at the Historical and Geographical Institute of Brazil. That copy was eventually purchased by P. E. Pieris of Sri Lanka, who first used it in writing his *Ceylon: The Portuguese Era* (1914), and who then published (though not critically) the original in 1916 (Queiros 1916). So here we have the case of a book whose contents reflect seventeenth-century attitudes, but whose wider influence on scholarly knowledge was delayed until the twentieth.[38]

Queiros was born in Portugal in 1617 and entered the Jesuit novitiate at the age of fourteen. In 1635, he went to Goa, where he studied philosophy and theology, where he held various posts in the Jesuit establishment for the next fifty-three years, and where he served for sixteen of those years as one of the inquisitors. He died in Goa in 1688.[39] His three-volume history was written after the Portuguese lost their colony in Ceylon to the Dutch, and part of Queiros's intention was to explain that loss (which he blames

34. His name is also spelled Queiroz.
35. See, however, the reservations expressed in Strathern (2005, 86) concerning Queiros's agendas.
36. *Conquista temporal e espiritual de Ceylão* (see Queiros 1916 and 1930).
37. It has now been digitized; see http://objdigital.bn.br/acervo_digital/div_manuscritos/mss1233568/mss1233568.pdf.
38. See Perera's account of all this and more in his "Introduction" to Queiros 1930, 20*–22*. For a discussion, see Strathern 2005, 48. For a list of Queiros's writings, see Schurhammer 1929, 210. In what follows, I shall use S. G. Perera's English translation (Queiros 1930).
39. For a tabular chronology of his life, see Schurhammer 1929, 210–215.

on "the captains and merchants," thereby exonerating the religious orders), and to strongly argue for the reconquest of the island.[40] At the same time, he seeks to bring Do Couto's history up to date—to "elucidate, correct, criticize and even reprehend" it by the use of additional sources (Queiros 1930, 11). Queiros himself never visited Sri Lanka. Nonetheless, as an armchair scholar in Goa, he provides what is the most detailed account so far of Don Constantino's invasion of Jaffna, with new details on how the tooth got there in the first place (see chapter 2 below). He says very little about the destruction of the tooth in Goa, probably because his focus remains on events in Sri Lanka.

Queiros does distinguish, however, the tooth of the Buddha captured by the Portuguese from another tooth of the Buddha—the one enshrined in Kandy—which he describes in some detail:

Near the Palace [in Kandy] there is a Pagode, which . . . has two skylights which let into it the light by means of which, under an arch of the altar, can be seen [images of] Demons whom that heathendom venerates as gods, with snouts of pigs, monkeys, dogs and elephants. . . . They call it *Daladaz Guey* [Sinhala, Daḷadā-ge], which means "house of the tooth," because there is on the very altar under seven golden caskets, each inside the other, the tooth of a buffalo, holding it for certain that it is of Buddum, which the Devil makes them believe by means of miracles, imaginary and ridiculous. Another tooth of Buddum the Viceroy D. Constantino de Bragança brought from Jafanapa-taõ [= Jaffna] of which our historians make mention, and of the piety and nobility with which he acted, ordering it to be reduced to powder without accepting the great ransom which the King of Pegu offered for it; though they [i.e., our historians] call it an ape's tooth. (Queiros 1930, 1: 59–60)

(12) FRANCISCO DE SOUSA (1710). Our next source is by Francisco De Sousa, a Portuguese who was born in Brazil but then moved to Goa to further his studies at the Jesuit seminary there. In 1710, he wrote *The East Conquered for Jesus Christ by the Jesuit Fathers of the Province of Goa*.[41] De Sousa's work, though late, is of considerable significance, in part because the magnum opus of his predecessor, Queiros, was not published until the twenti-

40. Abeyasinghe 1980–1981, 36, 47. Queiros's views were strongly influenced by the prophetic and visionary writings of a Jesuit lay brother named Pedro de Basto. See Strathern 2005, 50–52; and Magone 2012, 254.

41. *Oriente conquistado a Jesu Christo pelos padres da Companhia de Jesu da Provincia de Goa* (see De Sousa 1710).

eth century. But it is also noteworthy for us because, by his time, knowledge of Buddhism had progressed somewhat in Portuguese and Jesuit circles. De Sousa, for example, knows, from his brethren in Japan that the Budu [Buddha] of Sri Lanka and Southeast Asia is the same as the Xaca [Śākyamuni] of Japan. He even recognizes that tooth relics of the Buddha (whom he calls a "famous philosopher, who lived a thousand years before Christ") are common, mentioning that in the court of the emperor in Meaco [Miyako, i.e., Kyoto], Japan, they have a tooth of the Buddha (De Sousa 1710, 199). He is aware that some "common Portuguese" call the relic in Sri Lanka the tooth of a monkey, but he disputes that. For him it was the tooth of the Buddha, and failure to destroy it would have been the equivalent of canonizing the Buddha as a saint (De Sousa 1710, 199). The importance of De Sousa's work for our purposes, then, lies in the fact that, finally, 150 years after the event, he unambiguously affirms that the tooth destroyed in Goa was the Buddha's. With regard to the saga of its actual destruction, his intent seems to be largely to defend and praise Dom Constantino for his action, concluding that he "was the best Portuguese who ever went to India, and this is the greatest feat which the Portuguese will ever accomplish" (De Sousa 1710, 197).

(13) FRANÇOIS VALENTIJN (1726). Our penultimate source was written in Dutch. François Valentijn (1666–1727) was, like his countryman Baldaeus, a minister of the Reformed Church. After his studies in Leiden and Utrecht, he joined the Dutch East India Company (VOC). He served two terms (1685–1695 and 1705–1713) as a missionary on the island of Ambon in the Moluccas, where he undertook a translation of the Bible into Malay, which he never managed to get published due to opposition on the part of powerful individuals in both the VOC and the Church. After returning to Dordrecht in his late forties, he completed a massive (5,144 pages, 1050 illustrations) history of the Dutch East India Company, *Old and New East-Indies*,[42] which was published in 1726. For years thereafter, this was looked to as an authoritative source on the subject (Arasaratnam 1978, 1–14).

Valentijn never lived in Ceylon, but this did not keep him from including a long account of it in his work, based on the books and materials he had accumulated over the years. In the context of his discussion of Adam's Peak, he repeats some of what Do Couto had to say about the mountain, and then reiterates more or less the same story that his fellow Netherlander, Van Linschoten, had told 130 years earlier: in a temple on the mountaintop,

42. *Oud en Nieuw Oost-Indien* (see Valentijn 1726).

there was a monkey's tooth (*aapen-tand*). The Portuguese captured it there in 1554 and took it back to Goa with them. It was the "greatest idol (*afgod*) [of the Ceylonese], and desired by the kings of Ceylon, Pegu, Siam, Bengal, Bisnagar [Vijayanagara], Malabar, Coromandel, Aracan, etc.," who offered "35 tons of gold" (*sic!*) for it.[43] But the money was refused by the viceroy, and the Portuguese archbishop Dom Gaspar crushed it, burned it, and threw the ashes into the air, and into the sea. Like Van Linschoten, he then adds the story of the clever merchant who manufactures another tooth out of a stag's horn and manages to sell it to the king of Bishnagar. He then cites Vincent Le Blanc to the effect that it was also thought that the tooth of the monkey in question was an idol of Hanumān (Valentijn 1726, 5: 382–383).

When, however, Valentijn goes on to give more precise descriptions of Adam's Peak (based, he says, on further documentary evidence [see Ferguson 1911, 202–205]), it becomes clear that, like many of his Dutch contemporaries, he has confused and conjoined the "real" Adam's Peak (Śrī Pada) near Ratnapura with the rocky outcropping known as Mulgirigala (but called "Adams Berg" by the Dutch) in far southern Sri Lanka. I shall return to this topic in a subsequent chapter. For now, suffice it to say that, for over a hundred years, from the mid-seventeenth to the mid-eighteenth centuries, some Dutch visited Mulgirigala thinking it was Adam's Peak, with the result that people like Valentijn (who had been to neither of the mountains) readily confused the two.[44] Thus, when Valentijn echoes Van Linschoten (and Baldaeus and Le Blanc) in proclaiming that the Portuguese captured a monkey's tooth on Adam's Peak, it is not clear where he is locating the mountain.

Unlike Van Linschoten, however, Valentijn also tells of another tooth. For, in the midst of his discussion of "Adam's Peak" (which one he means is again not clear, since he views them as one and the same), he states that "near this place, and not far from an imperial palace," there is a famous building with two towers that light up an altar decorated with carvings of idols with snouts of elephants, monkeys, and dogs. This pagoda is called the "House of the Tooth," and on its altar, enclosed in seven golden caskets, is "a tooth of a buffalo [*een tand van een buffel*], which the locals considered to be the tooth of their prophet Buddha" (Valentijn 1726, 5: 382).

It is not clear where Valentijn is getting this information; it is very reminiscent (it reads almost like a plagiarism) of Queiros, who, as we have seen

---

43. Valentijn 1726, 5: 382–383.
44. Valentijn 1726, 5: 376–378. See also Ferguson 1911, 202–204; and De Silva and Beumer 1988, 189–201.

above, gives a similar description of the temple of the tooth in Kandy and its buffalo-tooth relic of the Buddha. But Valentijn does not locate this tooth in Kandy and makes no mention of it or its temple in his later accounts of Dutch expeditions to that city. Moreover, in Valentijn's day, Queiros's work, though written a half century before him, had not yet been published and existed only in a single manuscript copy in the royal archives in Lisbon. It is thus doubtful that Valentijn had any access to it, and we are left supposing that perhaps there was some other, now lost, source that both Queiros and Valentijn drew upon.

(14) JOHANN WOLFFGANG HEYDT (1744). Finally, we come to our last source, written in German by Johann Wolffgang Heydt in 1744. We know little about Heydt. He was a cartographer and artist who, after working for the Palatinate court in the Rhineland, entered the service of the Dutch East India Company and embarked for Ceylon in 1733. He remained on the island for four years, where he befriended several persons of influence. One of these was Governor Diederik van Domburg (1685–1736), who sent him out to make drawings and maps of important places on the island. Another was Daniel Aggreen, whose embassy to Kandy in 1736 he joined as a quarter-master in charge of transport. In 1737, Heydt left Ceylon and moved on to Batavia, where he continued his work of drawing and illustrating landmarks. Soon, however, he became ill, and, in 1740, he was allowed to resign from the VOC and return to Germany, where he took a post as surveyor and archi-tect for a town not far from Nürnberg (Heydt 1952, v; see also De Silva and Beumer 1988, 457). It was there that he wrote *A completely new collection of geographical and topographical depictions of Africa and the East Indies*,[45] a book that consists of a presentation of and commentary on drawings or paintings of scenes made either by himself or (in the case of some instances in the Ceylon section of the book) by his friend, the Dutch artist Arent Jansen.[46]

Like Valentijn, Heydt confuses the two Adam's Peaks (Śrī Pāda and Mul-girigala). It is in regard to the second place, which he calls "Adams Berg,"

45. *Allerneuester Geographisch- und Topographischer Schau-Platz von Africa und Ost-Indien* (see Heydt 1744).

46. Jansen (or Jansz) was a resident of Colombo who was also commissioned by Governor-General van Domburg to travel and sketch various places of importance in Ceylon, including, as we shall see, "Adams Berg." See the account by De Vos, in Appendix B to Ferguson 1911, 239. For a brief account of his life and character, see De Silva and Beumer 1988, 456. Jansen's works may be found in Heydt 1744, 224–239; and Heydt 1952, plates 75–80. Some of these engravings are reproduced in De Silva and Beumer 1988, 192–199.

that he actually refers twice to the story that interests us. First, in commenting on his own distant drawing of "Adams Berg" seen from the outskirts of Galle, he tells us:

> Now on this peak Budu [= Buddha], the first man, as they call Adam, is said to have remained a long time, and, as Baldaeus states, the golden ape's-tooth (*goldene Affen-Zahn*) which the Portuguese took away with them was also preserved on it. Yet as it was told me both by natives and by Europeans who had themselves been on this mountain, it was stolen away from these [Portuguese] later. (Heydt 1744, 203; Eng. trans. in Heydt 1952, 44)

Second, a bit further on, in the midst of his commentary on one of Jansen's close-up depictions of "Adams Berg" (Mulgirigala—Heydt never actually visits the place), he declares:

> The Portuguese, who for long had this land in their possession before the Dutch, have said much in their annuals (*Jahr-Büchern*)[47] concerning an ape's tooth, which they captured on Adam's Hill [Adams-Berg] and for which the local kings offered 700,000 ducats if it should be returned to them; but, according to some authorities, they took it away to Goa, or, as others assert, they crushed it to powder and threw it into the sea. (Heydt 1952, 63, slightly altered; original text in Heydt 1744, 230)

Heydt makes no mention of a tooth of the Buddha. We will return to Heydt's account and his overlapping descriptions of both Śrī Pada and Mulgirigala in a subsequent chapter. For now, suffice it to say that it is remarkable to find him, a century and a half after Van Linschoten, still echoing the assertion that what the Portuguese destroyed was the tooth of an ape. This was a tradition that did not die easily.

---

47. Ferguson (1911, 233n94) posits that these are yearly letters sent back home by the Jesuits.

TWO

Where the Tooth Was Found:
Traditions about the Location
of the Relic in Sri Lanka

There is a high Hill called Pico d'Adam, or Adams Hill. . . . In this place in time past there was a Toothe of an Ape, shrined in Gold and precious stones . . . which for costlynes and worthynes was esteemed the holyest thing in all India.

—Jan Huyghen Van Linschoten [1598] 1885, 1: 292

And from their principal temple [in Jaffna] they brought to the Viceroy an enchased tooth, which was commonly said to be that of a monkey, [but] which was held by those heathens to be their most sacred object of worship.

—Diogo do Couto 1783, 316–317 (see Ferguson [1908] 1993, 191)

Given the nature of the sources described above, the fact that they were written over a period of 150 years in multiple languages, and the uncertainty (in some cases) of their specific dates of publication and (in all cases) of their distribution and readership, it is probably impossible to know, historically, the answer to the question "What 'really' happened with regard to the Portuguese and the tooth?" But it may be that we can trace some "storical" evolutions or lineages by treating all of our sources as valid reflectors of variant Western attitudes and opinions, and by looking at the elaboration (or lack thereof) of a number of themes, and the sometimes signal importance of certain details.

In table 2.1, I have noted the appearance or nonappearance of a number of narrative elements found in the sources considered. No doubt others could be added. In rows 5–8, it can be seen that, in virtually all of our sources, there is general agreement about a number of things: a tooth was captured by the Portuguese, then ransom offers were made for it and

Table 2.1 Synopsis of stories about the Portuguese tooth

	Source	Van Linschoten	Pimenta	Du Jarric	Texeira	Pyrard De Laval	Do Couto	Trindade	Le Blanc	Baldaeus	Faria e Souza	Queiros	De Sousa	Valentijn	Heydt
2	Date	1596	1605	1610	1610	1611	1616	1636	1648	1672	1674	1687	1710	1726	1744
3	Nationality of author	Du.	Por.	Fr.	Por.	Fr.	Por.	Por.	Fr.	Du.	Por.	Por.	Por.	Du.	Ger.
4															
5	Tooth captured	x	x	x	x	x	x	x	x	x	x	x	x	x	x
6	Ransom offer made and rejected	x	x	x	x	x	x	x	x	x	x	x	x	x	x
7	Tooth destroyed or destruction assumed	x	x	x	x	x	x	x	x	x	x	x	x	x	x
8	Destruction in Goa	x	[x]*	x	x	x	x	x	unclear	x	x	x	x	x	unclear
9															
10	Tooth captured:														
11	in Jaffna			x	x		x	x	x		x	x	x		
12	on Adam's Peak	x								x				x	x
13	uncertain/ unclear		x			x									

* The text does not actually mention Goa but appears to assume it, as it asserts the tooth was destroyed by the viceroy.

rejected, after which it was destroyed, probably in Goa. These common de-
nominators form the gist of our story. Beyond this, however, divergences
and discrepancies appear in the narrations of this bare-bones scenario. The
first of these, which I shall deal with in the rest of this chapter, concerns the
matter of where the tooth was found by the Portuguese. The second, variations in the identity of the tooth (i.e., answers to the question "Whose tooth
was this?"), will be examined in chapter 3.

With regard to the location of the tooth, rows 10–13 of table 2.1 make it
clear that we need to draw a distinction between two "lineages" of stories: a
Dutch-German tradition (Van Linschoten, Baldaeus, Valentijn, Heydt) that
portrays the capture of the tooth (said to be that of a monkey) as taking
place on or near Adam's Peak (wherever they locate that mountain); and a
Franco-Portuguese narrative line (Du Jarric, Texeira, Do Couto, Trindade,
Le Blanc, Faria e Souza, Queiros, De Sousa) that portrays the event as happening in Jaffna (where the tooth is variously said to be that of a monkey or
a white monkey or Hanumān or the Buddha). In addition, there are some
outlier sources (e.g., Pimenta and Pyrard) that do not specify where the capture took place or are unclear about the matter.

These various emplacements of the tooth are purely Western traditions;
the Sri Lankans at the time knew nothing about them. They did, however,
have their own notions about where their tooth was located during this period and where it had been in the past. By way of background and context,
therefore, before dealing with the question of where the Portuguese tooth
was captured, let me briefly survey Sinhalese traditions about their tooth's
movements in history to different locales in Sri Lanka. In a sense, the tooth
was a special kind of relic; as a movable object, it differed from a number
of other more stationary relics such as the Bodhi tree in Anurādhapura or
the Buddha's footprint on Adam's Peak. In recounting its movements in
Sri Lankan tradition, I will at the same time emphasize stories that curiously anticipate some of the Portuguese tales. As we shall see, the Portuguese were not the first to capture the tooth, to steal it away, or to attempt to
destroy it.

Movements of the Tooth Prior to Portuguese Times:
Stories of Theft and Attempted Destruction

According to the *Mahāparinibbāna sutta* [Discourse on the great extinction],
an ancient Pali text perhaps datable to the second century BCE, nothing was
left of the Buddha's body after his cremation except for a large number of

relics (*Dīgha Nikāya* 2: 164; Eng. trans., Walshe 1987, 275).[1] A later commentary on the text tells us that these came in three sizes; they were as big as mustard seeds, broken grains of rice, and split green peas and were said to resemble jasmine buds, washed pearls, and nuggets of gold (*Sumangalavilāsinī* 2, 603–604; Eng. trans., An 2003, 206). The sūtra goes on to talk of the initial distribution of these relics by a brahmin named Doṇa; as powerful and precious objects embodying the presence of the departed master, the relics were much sought after, and were quickly divided among eight North Indian kings, each of whom took away his share for enshrinement in his own country (*Dīgha Nikāya* 2: 164–167; Eng. trans., Walshe 1987, 275–277).

In an addendum to the Pali text, said to have been written at a later date by Sinhalese commentators (but already found in the Sanskrit version of the sūtra, though not in the Chinese translation of the text), mention is also made of four tooth relics—his four canines—that respectively go to Indra's heaven, to the city of Gandhāra, to the kingdom of Kalinga, and to the underwater world of the nāgas (*Dīgha Nikāya* 2: 167; Eng. trans., Walshe 1987, 277).[2] Of these, the one that interests us is the so-called Kalinga tooth, since that is the one that ends up in Sri Lanka.[3]

Storically speaking, in Sri Lanka, the movements of these four tooth relics were eventually explained by tales of theft. The thirteenth-century *Sinhala Thūpavaṃsa* [Chronicle of the Stūpa], for instance, recounts a story about how the brahmin Doṇa, when he was distributing the Buddha's bodily relics to the eight kings, pilfered one of the teeth and hid it in his turban, only to have the god Indra, observing this from above, swoop down invisibly and take the tooth from Doṇa's turban for himself (Berkwitz 2007, 126–127). A fourteenth-century Sri Lankan Pali text, the *Dhātuvaṃsa* [Chronicle of the relics], expands on this story and says Doṇa actually stole three of the original teeth, hiding one in his turban, one in his clothing, and one between his toes. The first one was then snatched by Indra, the second by a man from Gandhāra, and the third by a nāga coming up from beneath the earth (Trainor 1997, 132–133). The moral of this story would seem to be that the Kalinga tooth was the only one of the four eyeteeth that was *not* subject to theft, but, as we shall see, subsequent traditions were to belie that conclusion.

1. The word used for relics here is "*sarīra*," which literally means "body" but comes to mean "relics" in the plural. Walshe translates this as "bones."

2. For the Sanskrit version, see Waldschmidt 1950–1951, 450. For the Chinese version, see Ichimura 2015, 170–171.

3. On the fate of the other three teeth, see Strong 2004b, 185–190.

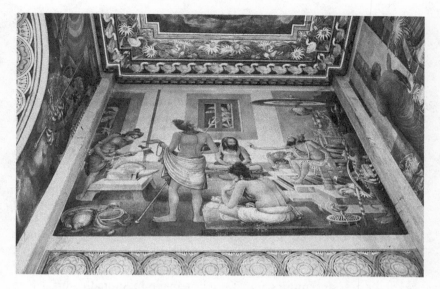

Figure 2.1. Attempted destruction of the tooth by King Paṇḍu (Solias Mendis mural in Kelaniya Temple). Photo courtesy Donald Stadtner.

Indeed, the legendary saga of the Kalinga tooth is much developed in several Sri Lankan sources.[4] According to the thirteenth-century Pali *Dāṭhāvaṃsa* [Tooth chronicle], the tooth is originally brought to Kalinga by a disciple of the Buddha named Khema and enshrined in the capital city of that country, which appropriately becomes known as Dantapura (Toothville).[5] There it is worshipped by the people and several generations of kings. After a while, however, it arouses the ire and jealousy of non-Buddhist "heretics" in the region, and the relic is taken away by a certain King Paṇḍu who tries, unsuccessfully, to destroy it: he has it thrown in a fire, but it does not burn; put on an anvil and smashed with a hammer, but it does not shatter; sunk in a tank of water, but it merely floats and swims around; buried in a pit and trampled by elephants, but it reemerges on a lotus blossom. Finally, Paṇḍu gives up trying to destroy it; he converts to Buddhism, and lets it return to Kalinga.[6] This story of its attempted destruction (which interestingly anticipates the tale of

4. I shall deal here only with the *Dāṭhāvaṃsa*. For references to other chronicle sources in Pali and Sinhala, see Strong 2004b, 194; and Herat 1994, 10–22. See also Holt 2017, 309–313.
5. On the possible location of Dantapura and Kalinga, see Strong 2004b, 191.
6. *Dāṭhāvaṃsa* 1884, 120–135; Eng. trans., Law 1925, 15–34.

what the Portuguese do to the relic) is still known today in Sri Lanka and is depicted in a mural by Solias Mendis[7] at the Kelaniya Temple (see fig. 2.1).

Later, however, another threat emerges: if relics cannot be destroyed, they can be captured. Thus, when Dantapura is again attacked by non-Buddhists, the king, desiring to keep the tooth from falling into the hands of these invaders, entrusts it to his daughter and son-in-law and tells them to flee with it to Sri Lanka, where the ruling monarch is known to be a Buddhist. After various adventures and mishaps, the couple eventually arrives on the island, where indeed the king receives them and has the relic enshrined in his palace compound in Anurādhapura in a building that is named the Dāṭhādhātu-ghara ("House of the Tooth Relic") (*Dāṭhāvaṃsa* 1884, 135–150; Eng. trans., Law 1925, 34–39). This is the first Sri Lankan tooth temple, usually dated to the fourth century CE (*Cūḷavaṃsa* 1980, 6–7; Eng. trans., Geiger 1929, 1: 7–8). Not long after its enshrinement there, the relic is visited by the Chinese pilgrim Faxian (journey, 399–414 CE), who gives an account of its annual ritual procession (Legge [1886] 1965, 38–39 [text], 105–107 [Eng. trans.]).[8]

For the next six centuries or so, the relic remains in Anurādhapura, where it is venerated together with the relic of the bowl of the Buddha with which it forms a pair.[9] At some point while there, the tooth is worshipped by the Chinese pilgrim Ming Yuan (aka Cintādeva), who is described only as a monk of the Tang Dynasty. He is so enamored of the tooth that, hiding himself in the shrine room after the king finishes his devotions to the relic, he tries to steal it and carry it off, but he is quickly apprehended. After this, it is said, new security measures for the tooth are adopted by the Sinhalese king; the relic is placed in a closely guarded high tower, behind several sets of locked doors, which can only be opened by a series of officials (Chavannes 1894, 54; Lahiri 1986, 33–34; Liu 1996, 32, 47).

We see, in this story, something of the growing international fame and importance of the tooth relic. However, it is really only from the eleventh or twelfth century on, when the capital is moved from Anurādhapura to Polonnaruwa and the movable tooth goes with it, that it becomes "the most prominent object of worship in Sri Lankan Buddhism" (Herath 1994, 194), replacing the Bodhi tree that remains rooted in the former capital. More specifically, the tooth is now seen as a palladium for the king's rule over

7. Solias Mendis (1897–1975) was a famed painter of Buddhist temple wall paintings in the modern era.
8. See also Deeg 2005, 165–166, 566–567.
9. The Buddha's begging bowl is said to have been brought to Sri Lanka by Aśoka's son Mahinda in the third century BCE (see Strong 2004b, 156). At some point, probably in the fourteenth century, the bowl relic drops out of the picture (see Strong 2004b, 195).

the island (or, more usually, a portion thereof, given the fact that few kings governed the whole island); a ruler's possession of it is thought not only to grant him legitimacy but to ensure adequate rainfall, abundant crops, victory in war, great merit, and so on. Thus, over the next five centuries, Sri Lankan kings desired closeness to the relic and, given this, the tooth follows the royal centers of power, as these move, and is enshrined in places such as Dambadeniya, Beligala, Yapahuwa, Kurunegala, and Gampola (*Cūḷavaṃsa* 1980, 512–513; Eng. trans., Geiger 1929, 2: 204–205).[10]

At the same time, it comes to be coveted by foreign rulers. For instance, sometime in the eleventh century when the tooth was in Polonnaruwa, the powerful Burmese king, Anawrahta, is said to have asked the Sinhalese king of Lanka to send the tooth relic to him in Pagan. He makes this request on the basis of a dream from the god Indra (Śakra), who tells him he is due to receive it. But the Sinhalese are loath to part with their relic, and in the end, according to Burmese sources, confrontation is averted by the action of the relic itself, which rises up into the air and miraculously produces a double of itself that is then given to Anawrahta (Tin and Luce 1960 [1923], 88–91). This event is passed over in silence in Sri Lankan sources, and modern scholars who recount it tend to interpret it as meaning simply that the Burmese are given a manufactured replica of the relic (Herath 1994, 58).

More successful, however (and this time acknowledged by Sri Lankan sources), were the efforts of a Pāṇḍyan general from South India named Āryacakravarti. At one point in the thirteenth century, when the relic is at the rock fortress capital of Yapahuwa, Āryacakravarti successfully invades the island and takes the tooth back with him to the Indian mainland, where he presents it to his king. There it remains from 1272 to 1284, until it is recovered by the military and diplomatic efforts of the next Sri Lankan monarch, Parākramabāhu III, who returns the relic to Polonnaruwa (Yapahuwa having been abandoned) (*Cūḷavaṃsa* 1980, 512–513; Eng. trans., Geiger 1929, 2: 205). Soon thereafter, it is moved to the new capital of Kurunegala. The story of this brief loss of the tooth is interesting not only because it confirms an occasion when the relic was taken by a "foreign" power coming from India, but also since the general who captured the tooth is commonly connected to the Āryacakravarti Dynasty that, with a few gaps, later ruled the Jaffna peninsula from the thirteenth to the early seventeenth centuries (thus overlapping the Portuguese incursion there of 1560) (Herath 1994, 70–73).

10. For a synoptic history of the tooth (and the bowl) relic in Sri Lanka, based on the *Mahāvaṃsa* and *Cūḷavaṃsa*, see Geiger 1960, 213–215. See also Strong 2004b, 191–195.

This, thus, may be a first indication of the interest of the Jaffna Dynasty in the tooth.

By the beginning of the fourteenth century, the capital has been moved to Gampola, and a hundred years later, the military strongman Alagakkonara, who has designs on the throne, establishes a fortress at Kotte (adjacent to present-day Colombo) in order to resist repeated military incursions from Jaffna. But Jaffna is not his only problem. He is also subject to attacks from the Chinese admiral Zheng He who, on his third naval expedition to the South Seas (1409–1411), conquers the Kotte fortress, takes Alagakkonara and several princes prisoner, and carries them back to China.[11] In some late Chinese sources, Zheng He is also said to acquire the (or a) tooth relic on this occasion and to take it back to China and present it to the emperor Yongle (together with his captives). For instance, a Ming Dynasty edition of accounts of Chinese voyages to the West credits the tooth with assuring Zheng He's fleet a safe passage home, and describes the measures the emperor Yongle took to welcome it when it arrived in the capital on July 9, 1411 (Levathes 1994, 116–117; see also Li 1996, 353–355). There is no mention of the tooth relic, however, in the more contemporary account of the "Veritable Record" of the emperor Yongle's reign (the *Taizong shilu*), and Edward Dreyer (2007, 69) suggests this may mean the story was fictional.[12]

Not surprisingly, perhaps, the story of Zheng He's capture of the tooth is also passed over in silence by Sri Lankan sources.[13] Indeed, they obviously assume the relic never left the island, since they portray the next king of Kotte, Parākramabāhu VI (r. 1412–1467), as building a large pavilion for the tooth right next to his new three-story palace in Kotte (to which he had officially moved the capital) (*Cūḷavaṃsa* 1980, 520; Eng. trans., Geiger 1929, 2: 215). Moreover, Dhammazedi, the king of Pegu in Myanmar, sends a great offering to the tooth relic in Kotte in 1476, obviously believing it to still be there.[14]

11. This is usually said to have happened on Zheng He's way back to China in 1411, but on this date, see Dreyer 2007, 73. The *Rājāvaliya* (Guṇaśekera 1900, 57) claims it was King Vijayabāhu VI who was captured and not Alagakkonara, who is said to stay in Kotte (keeping the tooth relic with him) and then to murder Vijayabāhu after he returns from China. This is also the view of Perera (1904, 292–293).

12. On this, see also Pelliot 1933, 281n.

13. Herath (1994, 81) suggests the Chinese may have carried off a replica of the tooth.

14. See Taw Sein Ko 1892, 78. In his "Kalyāṇī Inscription," Dhammazedi ranks the tooth relic above other Sri Lankan attractions such as the Bodhi tree and Śrī Pada (Adam's Peak). See also Herath 1994, 83.

Further Movements of the Relic:
The Tooth in Kotte and Delgamuwa

Located within the royal palace precincts, Parākramabāhu VI's Dalada Maligawa ("Tooth Palace") is one of the principal buildings of Kotte and serves as the realm's ritual center. The temple is described by the bird-messenger in the *Pärakumbā sirita* (a fifteenth-century Sinhalese panegyric poem) and in several other poetic sources of the period.[15] It is a stone building in the form of a crown, topped by a golden pinnacle, and containing within it not only the Buddha's Tooth, but, in adjunct structures, shrines to the four gods— Nātha, Saman, Viṣṇu, and Śiva—who safeguard the kingdom and help legitimate the rule of its king (Strathern 2007, 150–151; Perera 1910, 16).[16]

Parākramabāhu VI's sponsorship of the cult of the Buddha's tooth in Kotte does not mean that he himself was what we might today call a Buddhist (Rasanayagam [1926] 1984, 372). If such religious labels are necessary or even relevant for his time and context, one can say he was Hindu, and Hindu influence was certainly pronounced at the Kotte court (Perera 1910, 16). But it is probably best not to make such clear-cut distinctions. Religiously and culturally speaking, Sri Lanka was then generally characterized by a blend of what we would call Hindu and Buddhist beliefs, of Tamil and Sinhalese traditions. As Alan Strathern (2007, 151) has put it, religious beliefs at this time in Kotte were "highly syncretistic" and had an "incorporative tendency." In this regard, it should be noted that, while the tooth exalted in Kotte was certainly recognized as the Buddha's tooth, this does not necessarily mean that its cult was exclusively of concern to Buddhists or even Buddhistic in its formulation (Rasanayagam [1926] 1984, 372).[17]

Parākramabāhu VI's reign also represents somewhat of a golden age for late medieval Sinhalese civilization. It is marked by a flourishing literary culture and is also a time of territorial expansionism for the Kotte kingdom. In 1450, Parākramabāhu's adopted son, Sapumal Kumāraya, invades the kingdom of Jaffna, forcing the Āryacakravarti king there to flee to South India,

---

15. See Berkwitz 2016 on the *Pärakumbā sirita*. See also Ilangasinha 1992, 184–185; Perera 1910, 7; and Siriweera 1993/1995, 13).

16. At the foundation of the city of Kotte, the four shrines are to Viṣṇu, Saman, Vibhiṣana, and Skanda [Kataragama], but no mention is made of the tooth relic being there yet. See Perera 1904, 285; and Siriweera 1993/1995, 3. We will encounter the same basic pattern in Kandy, where the tooth relic is similarly associated with the four devas (although there Saman has been replaced by the goddess Pattini).

17. As we shall see in part 2 of this work, the same may be said of the Nāyakkar rulers of Kandy, who similarly promoted and emphasized the tooth relic.

and thus, for a while, placing the whole island of Sri Lanka under the single aegis of Kotte. For a couple of decades, Jaffna is directly ruled by Sapumal who, among other things, builds a new Kandaswamy Nallur temple next to his reconstructed palace there (Rasanayagam [1926] 1984, 372). In this, Sapumal seems, at least architecturally speaking, to be imitating his father by having, at the core of his city, his palace and its legitimating temple. This is interesting since, as we have seen, it was in this very same Nallur temple that the Portuguese were said to find the tooth relic about a century later. One wonders whether Sapumal might have enshrined in such a place his own replica of the Kotte tooth, and left it there when he returned to Kotte c. 1472 to succeed his father on the throne as Bhuvanekabāhu VI. It could thus have been there all along.

In 1505, the Portuguese arrive in Sri Lanka, and a few years later, they establish a fort and trading post in Colombo, on the coast not far from Kotte.[18] Their initial intention is to take over the island's commerce in cinnamon and to replace the Muslims who have hitherto controlled external trade. In time, however, they become thoroughly involved in the internal politics of the kingdom of Kotte. Seeking to exert control over it, they help defend it against the aggressions of other Sri Lankan kingdoms with whom they enter into an everchanging set of alliances and antagonisms: Sītāwaka (inland from Kotte), Raigama (farther down the coast)—which are soon in conflict with one another—Kandy (in the center and to the east of the island), and Jaffna (to the north). At the same time, they increasingly pressure the population and the king of Kotte to convert to Catholicism (Strathern 2007, 161–163; Holt 2007, 146–147).

In this regard, in 1556 or early 1557, they score what they consider to be a significant victory: at the age of seventeen, the young Kotte king Dharmapala, whom the Portuguese helped install on the throne as a child, agrees to be baptized (Strathern 2007, 66; Viterbo 1906, 60). In doing so, he adopts a new Christian name, Dom João (after the king of Portugal). Kotte now has a Christian king, and he quickly proceeds to take a number of steps that betoken his newly adopted faith (De Silva 1977, 26; Perniola 1989, 1: 352–353).[19] He confiscates all the lands belonging to the Buddhist and Hindu temples (vihāras and devales) of the kingdom, and directs that

18. On the Portuguese establishment in their empire of trading posts (feitorias) and forts (fortalezas), see Villiers 1986, 38. These were distinct from urban settlements (cidades) over which the Portuguese had full jurisdiction. By and large, however, the Portuguese had little interest in territorial conquest. The only cidades they established in the whole of their Asian realm were Goa, Cochin, Colombo, Malacca, and Macau (see Villiers 1986, 54).

19. For a Sri Lankan source, see Guṇasékara 1900, 68.

their revenues be made over to the colleges and seminaries established by the Franciscans (Trindade [1630–1636] 1962–1967, 3: 48; Queiros 1930, 330–331).[20] More specifically, around this time or somewhat before, the Temple of the Tooth in Kotte is opened up to being plundered, and then given over to the missionaries who transform it into the Church of the Holy Savior (Biedermann 2018, 141).[21]

Though the Portuguese were generally infamous for ransacking and destroying Sri Lankan places of worship, it is probably best, in this instance, not to think of marauding soldiers gone wild. The "looting" of the Temple of the Tooth in Kotte seems, rather, to have been an orderly affair—a methodical acquisition and transfer of wealth.[22] The Portuguese authorities were clearly aware that the temple was one of the richest and most important sanctuaries in the city, and that it, along with the royal treasury, contained valuables of interest to the king of Kotte, with whom they were trying to maintain an alliance of sorts. Thus, prior to its "looting," a contractual agreement was signed according to which half of the wealth in the temple was to remain in the king of Kotte's hands, and the other half was to devolve to the Portuguese viceroy (Viterbo 1906, 24). In order to effectuate this division fairly, a precise written list was kept of all the treasures that were found there.[23] Significantly, in this inventory of objects located in the temple or the palace, no mention is made of the tooth relic (although several golden "pagodes" of different sizes are alluded to). Nor is there any reference to the tooth being anywhere in Kotte in any other contemporary Portuguese sources. Indeed, it is not altogether clear how much the Portuguese were aware of the importance of what they were *not* finding.

According to Sinhalese tradition, this absence of the tooth in Kotte has a clear explanation. Sometime after the antagonism of the Portuguese to Buddhism first became evident, the relic was removed from the city and taken

20. For translations of the document of this donation, see De Silva 2009, 73–74; and Perniola 1989, 1: 352–353. At his death in 1597, Dharmapala wills the whole of his realm to the king of Portugal.

21. It is actually unclear when the Temple of the Tooth in Kotte was first looted by the Portuguese. They may have done so several times, starting as early as 1551. A Burmese tradition, however, speaks of the king of Pegu refurbishing the temple and sending gifts to the tooth in 1555. See Strathern 2007, 168–170; Queiros 1930, 330; and Pieris 1913, 140.

22. Dharmapala had, in theory, already transferred the wealth of the Temple of the Tooth to the Franciscan Order, but this did not recognize the state's interest in the treasure (see Biedermann 2018, 147).

23. The list was published as *O Thesouro do Rei de Ceylão* [The treasure of the king of Ceylon] and may be found in Viterbo 1906, 19–41.

to the neighboring kingdom of Sītāwaka for safekeeping.[24] An oft-repeated Sri Lankan story tells us that the man responsible for doing this was Keerawelle Hiripitiye, the chief lay custodian (the Diyawadana Nilame) of the Temple of the Tooth in Kotte, the very official responsible for the relic's safety. It is said that, in the midst of the turmoil of the times, as the Portuguese started destroying more and more Buddhist and Hindu temples in Kotte and all along the coast, Hiripitiye had a dream in which a venerable figure appeared to him and recited a verse in a mixture of Sinhala and Tamil, which he interpreted to mean that he should leave Kotte and take the tooth with him inland to Sītāwaka (Pieris 1913, 400–401).[25] Accordingly, he hid the tooth in his waistband and, sneaking out in the middle of the night, swam across the Diyawanna Oya Lake (today the site of the Sri Lankan parliament building), and fled with it to Sītāwaka, where he presented it to King Mayadunne. The latter promptly built a new shrine for it at Delgamuwa, not far from present-day Ratnapura in the center of the island (Pieris 1913, 401; see also Pieris 1920, 76). There the tooth was to remain for the next fifty years, and there, when it needed to be concealed from marauding Portuguese troops, it was hidden away under a great grinding stone, which remains famous to this day.[26]

It becomes understandable, then, why Sri Lankan sources seem little concerned about Portuguese claims to have captured and destroyed the tooth during this period; they knew those claims were false, because the tooth itself was safe and sound in Sinhalese territory. Indeed, the presence of the tooth in Delgamuwa seems to have been something of an open secret among Sri Lankans. There, after Mayadunne's death in 1581, it was honored by his son, Rājasinha I,[27] who established for it a regular annual tooth

24. It is unclear when this happened, exactly, but probably sometime before Dharmapala's conversion, and prior to the Portuguese transformation of the Temple of the Tooth there into a church. Ilangasinha (1992, 185) suggests a date of around 1543.
25. For a discussion of the wording of the verse, see Pieris 1920, 76.
26. For accounts of the Vihāra at Delgamuwa today, and of the great grinding stone in which the tooth relic was hidden, see *Sunday Observer* (Colombo), August 1, 2016; and De Silva 2017. For a contemporary Sinhalese poetic description of the shrine at Delgamuwa from Alagiyavanna's *Sävul Sandēśaya*, composed in the early 1580s, see Berkwitz 2013, 56–57. For pictures of the grinding stone and of murals from Delgamuwa, see Stadtner forthcoming. The *Cūḷavaṃsa* makes no mention of this story, but after describing the embellishments made to the relic in Kotte in 1409 (1980, 520–521; Eng. trans., Geiger 1929, 2: 215–216), its next reference to the tooth locates it in Delgamuwa. Geiger, in a footnote, says that it is not altogether clear why the tooth was taken there, but "probably the idea was to save it from the Portuguese" (Geiger 1929, 2, 228n).
27. Rājasinha I of Sītāwaka ruled from 1581 to 1592. At sixteen years of age, he was one of the warriors who defeated Vidiye Bandara (on whom, see below). During the 1570s, he fought several wars against the Kandyans, who were then supported by the Portuguese. At the end of the decade, he laid siege to the city of Colombo for two years (see De Silva 1981, 108–111).

procession (*perahera*) from Delgamuwa to the shrine of Mahā Saman (the god of Adam's Peak) in Ratnapura and back again.[28]

The tooth remained at Delgamuwa for almost fifty years, but it eventually got moved again. In 1590, Rājasinha, the king of Sītāwaka, faced a major revolt in the Kandyan highlands. He had previously managed to subdue the Kandyans, but this time, he was unable to prevail. He was defeated by Konappu Bandara (Vimaladharmasuriya I), who emerged as the new king of Kandy. Shortly thereafter, Vimaladharmasuriya made inquiries about the location of the tooth. Hearing it was in the Labujagāma-vihāra in Delgamuwa, he had it brought to Kandy, and there, sometime in the early 1590s, he built for it a brand-new "two-storeyed, superb relic temple [*dhātugeha*]," in the vicinity of his own palace (*Cūḷavaṃsa* 1980, 529; Eng. trans., Geiger 1929, 2, 228).[29] Since then, except for short periods that we shall examine in part 2 of this book, the tooth has stayed in Kandy, where it remains to this day, at least according to Sinhalese sources.

There are a number of things to be noted in this summary survey of Sri Lankan and other pre-Portuguese traditions about the tooth relic. First, the tooth was an import to Sri Lanka—a "foreign object" that was brought to the island from India and indigenized there. Second, once the tooth got established as a potent symbol of rule, it came to be an object coveted even by foreign rulers and sometimes said to be taken away by them. Third, in part for this reason, the tooth is a relic-on-the-move; it is subject to theft or attempted theft, and is commonly removed from the capital city for protection. Indeed, it was out of concern for the relic's safety that it was brought from India to Sri Lanka in the first place. Fourth, long before the Portuguese, attempts had already been made to destroy the tooth. Indeed, the various ways described above in which the "heretics" in India try to destroy the relic—by smashing, burning, submerging, and so on—are remarkably similar to the actions of the Portuguese, with the difference that the latter are said to succeed while the former do not. Finally, the tooth was a potent symbol of legitimacy not only for monarchs whose personal inclinations

28. Already at this time, the Delgamuwa *perahera* took on the form of the later Kandyan *perahera*, with the relic processing first, followed by the emblems of the protector gods. See Perera 1984, 296. By the time the Portuguese destroyed the Maha Saman Devale and Delgamuwa in 1618, the tooth had already been moved to Kandy.

29. The question of the arrival of the tooth in Kandy is complicated, however, by another indication in the *Cūḷavaṃsa* that an earlier ruler, Vīravikkama, built a shrine for a "resplendent relic" [*dhātum sobhanam*] of the Buddha in Kandy, as early as 1540. This passage does not specify, however, whether or not this meant the tooth relic (*Cūḷavaṃsa* 1980, 523; Eng. trans., Geiger 1929, 2: 220).

were Buddhistic, but also for those who might be labeled as Hindus. The cult of the tooth was as syncretistic as the culture of the times.

The Tooth at Adam's Peak

With all of these points in mind, we may now turn to a discussion of the claims of our Western sources that the tooth (whether of the Buddha or of a monkey or of Hanumān) was in Jaffna or on Adam's Peak when the Portuguese captured it. No mention is ever made of these locations in any of the Sri Lankan sources just surveyed, so the question must be posed: how did these European traditions arise, and how were they justified? I shall begin with the case of Adam's Peak.

Both our oldest and our latest sources—Van Linschoten and Heydt—and several others in between—Baldaeus and Valentijn (see table 2.1)—present the tooth (of a monkey or of Hanumān) as being captured on or near Adam's Peak and make no mention of Jaffna. Since three of these authors came from the Netherlands, and Heydt worked for the Dutch East India Company, one suspects that, for this story at least, they were reading one another and thus reinforcing a more or less parochial view.[30] Still, it is a story that persisted over the course of about 150 years, without apparently being influenced by the rival Franco-Portuguese tradition that placed the capture of the tooth in Jaffna.

Van Linschoten, it will be remembered, states that a looting party of Portuguese soldiers climbed Adam's Peak in 1554 and ransacked the "pagode" that they found on top. In the words of the old English translation of his work:

> When the Portingales made a road out of India and entred the Iland of Seylon, they went up upon the hill [Adam's Peak], where they thought to finde great treasure, because of the fame that was spread abroad of the great resort and offering in that place, where they sought the Cloyster and turned up everie stone thereof and found nothing but a little Coffer, made fast with many costly precious stones, wherein laye the Apes toothe. (Van Linschoten 1598, 81)

For the most part, modern scholars have found Van Linschoten's account to be "full of factual errors" (Wojciehowski 2011, 193n38), largely because

---

30. Baldaeus and Valentijn, in fact, cite Van Linschoten at various places.

it diverges as to place and date from Do Couto's. For instance, in their foot-notes, the editors of the English edition, Burnell and Tiele, readily point out all the places where Van Linschoten is "wrong," correcting him with information taken from Tennent's translation of Do Couto (Van Linschoten 1885, 1: 292–294nn). Thus, for them, the capture of the tooth did not take place in 1554 but in 1560, and not on Adam's Peak but in Jaffna. I am less interested in historical evaluations, however, than in stories, and where they may have come from, and, just as importantly, how long they lasted. Van Linschoten himself did not travel to Sri Lanka, so this must be something that he picked up elsewhere, probably in Goa.

In this regard, it is noteworthy that the tradition associating a tooth relic with Adam's Peak (itself a famed site in the eyes of not only Sri Lankans but other Asians, Muslims, and Westerners as well) is also mentioned by the Portuguese historian João De Barros, Do Couto's predecessor as author of *Da Asia*. In *Decada III* of that work, which appeared in 1563, De Barros describes Adam's Peak as follows:

> Twenty leagues from the seacoast is a mountain so high and steep that it rises to the height of seven leagues [*sic*!]; and on the summit of it is a flat surface . . . [about] thirty paces in diameter. In the middle of this is a stone two cubits higher than the flat surface in the manner of a table . . . on which is figured a man's footprint, two spans in length. This footprint is held in great reverence by the natives who assert it to be that of a holy man, a native of the kingdom of Delij [i.e., Delhi] in India, who came to this island where he stayed for many years, bringing men to the usage of believing and adoring only one God [*sic*]. (Ferguson 1909, 36, slightly altered; original text in De Barros [1563] 1777, 115)[31]

This holy man, De Barros goes on to say, is called "Budo" [Buddha] by the natives. After his stay on the island, Budo returned to India, "where he had a wife and children"; and when he passed away, many years later, "*he extracted one of his teeth and commanded that it should be sent to Sri Lanka*, and given to the king of the country, to be kept in memory of him be-side the footprint on the peak. And to this day, the [Lankan] kings view this tooth as a sacred relic to which they commit all their needs" (Ferguson

---

31. The "kingdom of Delhi," here, may simply be De Barros's way of referring to northern India as a whole, which in his time was under the control of the Mughal empire and ruled over by Emperor Akbar. We shall see below that, years later, De Sousa (1710, 199) and Queiros (1930, 118) still repeat this claim that the Buddha was a son of the king of Delhi.

1909, 36, slightly altered, emphasis added; original text in De Barros [1563] 1777, 116).[32]

It should be said that it is not altogether clear from this whether De Barros means the tooth was actually enshrined on the mountain. Ferguson, in his translation, seems to allow for the possibility of locating it there, in part since the story of the Buddha's sending the tooth is embedded in the middle of De Barros's account of Adam's Peak. The original text may be more ambiguous, however; the Portuguese *"além de"* (De Barros [1563] 1777, 116), which Ferguson translates as "beside," can also mean (like its English equivalent) "in addition to." It could be that this tooth, though connected in this story to Adam's Peak, was kept elsewhere by the king.

In fact, however, the tradition of there being a tooth relic on Adam's Peak predates De Barros and was already established by the time of Marco Polo (1254–1324). In his description of the mountain, the Venetian traveler relates the belief that the shrine at the top was the site of the Buddha's sepulcher,[33] and that, in it, there could be found a number of his relics: not only one but several of his teeth, in addition to his hair and bowl (Polo 1993, 2: 317–19). Polo then goes on to recount how Kublai Khan, hearing of these relics, sent ambassadors to Ceylon in 1284. Pressing their case, they convinced the king to allow them to carry off two of the Buddha's molars,[34] some of his hair, and his begging bowl, and return with them to Khanbaliq [the Mongol's Chinese capital, = Beijing]. There, he says, they were received with great joy, the whole population of the city coming out to welcome them (Polo 1993, 2: 320). Presumably Marco Polo himself was there in the Mongol capital when this happened and witnessed these events.

It is not clear whether De Barros or Van Linschoten ever read Marco Polo, but it is not impossible. We do know that the latter was interested in travel literature in his youth (Parr 1964, 12–16). More broadly, Polo's account was widely known around this time. It had, after all, inspired Christopher Columbus (who owned a copy of the book that he annotated), and other

32. It is noteworthy that De Barros makes no mention at all of the tooth being captured and destroyed by the Portuguese, probably because (as Ferguson [1909, 36n4] points out) he wrote this passage before 1561, when that event supposedly took place.

33. Polo (1993, 2: 319) also says it was thought (by Muslims) to be the site of Adam's tomb, but he disputes this since "according to the Holy Scripture of our [Christian] Church, the sepulcher of Adam is not in that part of the world [but in Jerusalem]."

34. Henry Yule (see Polo 1993, 2: 329–30), as a historicist, seeks to undermine the veracity of this claim by pointing out that "the" Sri Lankan tooth relic is traditionally said to be a canine, not a molar.

explorers in the sixteenth century were familiar with the work (Landström 1967, 27).[35]

Strangely, neither Van Linschoten nor Polo makes any mention of the stone footprint on Adam's Peak—which is described in such detail by De Barros, and which remains to this day the main attraction for pilgrims who climb the mountain. Baldaeus ([1703] 2000, 650), however, gives a lengthy description of it, saying that it is much visited by Sinhalese and Siamese pilgrims who gather up water that accumulates in the depression of the footprint and use it to purify themselves. Nearby on the mountaintop, he adds, there is a magnificent temple, and that was where the tooth (which for him was a relic of Hanumān) was found.

The pairing of Sri Lanka's two most famous relics—the footprint and the tooth—is also found in a report by an early fifteenth-century Chinese Muslim traveler and translator, Ma Huan (1380–1460), who went to Sri Lanka as part of Admiral Zheng He's sixth expedition in 1421. In his *Ying-yai shenglan* [The overall survey of the ocean's shores], he too mentions a stone footprint of the Buddha, in whose depression there was a constant supply of fresh water that never dried up and with which pilgrims could purify themselves. This, however, was not located at Adam's Peak but on the southwestern coast of the island, at a port the Chinese called Bieluoli, which has been identified with Beruwala, about forty-five kilometers south of Colombo.[36] Ma Huan tells us that this is not only where he himself went ashore, but where, long ago, the Buddha set down his foot when he came to Sri Lanka from the Nicobar and Andaman Islands (*sic!*) (Mills 1970, 125–126; Lévi 1900, 433–434).[37] He then goes on to tell us, like Marco Polo, that not too far away there was a temple, which was the place of the Buddha's sepulcher. It contained a large image of the Buddha lying on his right side in parinirvāṇa, and here, as well, was enshrined a tooth of the Buddha and several other relics.

It may be that Ma Huan is confusing this temple near Beruwala with the Galapatha Rājamahāvihāra in nearby Bentota, which was founded in the twelfth century and which, to this day, features a large recumbent image of Śākyamuni on his deathbed, and enshrines a tooth relic—not of the Buddha

35. Do Couto, for instance (1780, 10; Eng. trans., Ferguson 1909, 109–111), cites and criticizes Marco Polo by name in his discussion of Adam's Peak.

36. On Beruwala being Zheng He's favorite port of call in Sri Lanka, see Dreyer 2007, 71.

37. The Nicobar and Andaman Islands were also known as the country of the naked people. Ma Huan explains that long ago the Buddha visited these islands, but that when he took off his robes to go bathe, the local people stole his clothes and hid them. The Buddha then cursed them to always remain naked. See Mills 1970, 125.

but of his disciple Mahākassapa.[38] Alternatively, some scholars have placed this temple not at Beruwala but at Dondra (aka Devinuwara), the promontory that marks Sri Lanka's southernmost tip (Rockhill 1915, 375n1). This famous market town and landmark, also mentioned by Ma Huan and known to the Chinese as Fotang shan ("Buddha Hall Mountain") (Mills 1970, 125), was best known for its great temple to the Buddhist deity Upulvan (i.e., Viṣṇu) until its destruction by the Portuguese in 1587 (Holt 2004, 67–101). If this is the case, it is not impossible, given Ma Huan's casualness with distances and directions, that the temple he describes was none other than Mulgirigala which, as we shall see, was often confused with Adam's Peak, and also thought by some to be the final resting place of the Buddha because of the large image of the Buddha in parinirvāṇa there. It is located inland and east from Dondra.

Elsewhere, it should be said, Ma Huan also describes a "large mountain which penetrates high into the clouds" and is located "at the side of the king's residence" (presumably Kotte?). Though not really that close to Kotte, this can only be what we usually call Adam's Peak (Śrī Pada), for on its summit, he tells us, is to be found the footprint of "A-dan" [Adam], whom he identifies with the Chinese mythical ancestor Pangu. He further specifies that precious stones found in the region were considered to be the crystallized tears of the Buddha but makes no mention of a relic there or of the A-dan's footprint actually being the Buddha's (see Mills 1970, 127–128).

An Adam's Peak and a Tooth in the South

These scattered references to tooth relics and footprints on the southern part of the island serve as a backdrop, perhaps, to the accounts of those Dutch writers after Van Linschoten (e.g., Baldaeus and Valentijn and, following them, the German Heydt) who appear to confuse what we today identify as Adam's Peak (i.e., the mountain near Ratnapura, inland and southeast of Colombo) with the rocky mountain that they called "Adams Berg" located at Mulgirigala, in the far south of Sri Lanka. To keep the two mountains distinct in the discussion that follows, I shall refer to them as Adam's Peak-Śrī Pada and Adam's Peak-Mulgirigala.

Today, Mulgirigala is an important complex of Buddhist temples and caves on an isolated rock outcropping (it is sometimes called "the little

---

38. For a present-day account of the temple, see Anonymous 2018. For the story of Mahākassapa's tooth relic's arrival in Sri Lanka, see *Cūḷavaṃsa* 1980, 478; Eng. trans., Geiger 1929, 2: 166–167. See also Goloubew 1932, 460.

Sigiriya") about twenty kilometers inland from Tangalle (itself about thirty kilometers east of Dondra) on the southern coast of the island. Based on in situ inscriptions, the Buddhist caves at Mulgirigala date from the second century BCE (Ferguson 1911, 197–199; see also A. Mendis Guṇasékera, Appendix A to Ferguson 1911, 238–239).[39] In time, the monastery there became famous for its collection of manuscripts (it was there, for instance, that George Turnour came across the manuscript of the *Mahāvaṃsa* then extant nowhere else on the island).

The first Western notices of Mulgirigala need not concern us here, as they make no mention of a tooth relic and no clear reference to the footprint, confining themselves to viewing the mountain as the site of Adam's tomb.[40] The confusion with Adam's Peak-Śrī Pada is already somewhat evident in their accounts, but it becomes clearer in the work of Baldaeus, who was their near-contemporary. He makes several references to Adam's Peak, but at one point clearly locates it in the south: "Just by Belligamme [i.e., Weligama]," he tells us, "I saw the figure of a man at least six yards high, cut in a rock about half a yard deep, who used to be worshipped by the Cingaleses" (Baldaeus 1703, 820). This must be the great bas-relief image said to be of the bodhisattva Avalokiteśvara near Weligama, on the southern coast of the island, about twenty kilometers west of Dondra. The place is still known today as Kuṣṭharājagala.[41] "Near it," Baldaeus continues,

> is a high-peak'd Mountain, accounted the highest in the Indies [*sic*!], call'd *Pico de Adam* or *Adam's Peak* because they are of opinion that here stood formerly the Paradise,[42] where Adam was created. . . . Unto this Rock a vast number of People flock from distant places to see this sacred relick, tho the

---

39. For a modern account of the temple (which is classified as a *rājamahāvihāra*), see Wijesinghe 2016. Like Adam's Peak-Śrī Pada, Mulgirigala features steep ascents (sometimes by means of footsteps chiseled in the rock and attached iron chains). Its ancient Buddhist temples and caves are profusely decorated with paintings, on which see Bandaranayake 1986, 216–225.

40. These accounts are studied by Ferguson (1911, 199–201). To these should be added the report of François l'Estra (1677), on which see Strong forthcoming a.

41. For a photo, see Holt 1991, plate 8, and 232n2. Weligama is about thirty kilometers east of Galle.

42. The view not only that Sri Lanka was the site of Paradise but that Adam later lived on the island was common among the Portuguese, who attributed the island's prosperity to Adam's influence. Biedermann (2018, 97–98) quotes a letter from João Garcês (a sixteenth-century Portuguese official in Sri Lanka) as saying the island "was full of precious stones, and the mountains full of elephants, and hills full of cinnamon and the sea full of pearls, and all this was . . . thanks to Adam our father having been there and his footprint being there."

Mountain is of very difficult access . . . unless by means of certain iron chains[43] and iron spikes fastened to the rocks. (Baldaeus [1703] 2000, 820)

A bit further on, Baldaeus ([1703] 2000, 839) adds that on this Adam's Peak, in 1554, the Portuguese captured the monkey's tooth, a piece of information he must have gotten from Van Linschoten. His descriptions of the place, then, make it appear that he is referring to Adam's Peak-Śrī Pada, but his location of the place (nearby to Weligama) makes it seem like he is referring to Adam's Peak-Mulgirigala.

The same confusion is still present over fifty years later in Valentijn's work. He repeats at length Do Couto's description of Śrī Pada, to which he adds Van Linschoten's account of the capture of the monkey's tooth there by the Portuguese in 1554, but then, without indicating he is changing venues, finishes off his narrative with citations from two sources that clearly deal with Mulgirigala (Valentijn 1726, 376–378; Ferguson 1911, 202–204). These two texts, from which he quotes at length, are: an anonymous "Brief Description of the Images and Figures that are to be seen on the Mountain of Mookeregelle [Mulgirigala] otherwise named Adam's Mountain,"[44] and a letter describing the place written to the Dutch governor of Ceylon, Cornelis Simons, by one Govert (or possibly Gÿsbert) Helmont.[45]

In these texts, the association of Adam's Peak-Mulgirigala with Adamic mythology that was already present at Śrī-Pada (see Skeen [1870] 1997, 44; Percival 1803, 207; and Herbert [1634] 1638, 308) takes on a life of its own. No longer is the mountain just the site of Adam's tomb but, Valentijn and his informants claim, also that of Eve, and their images were to be found in side-by-side caves there. These are quite clearly Buddhist statues, but one—a large image of the Buddha in parinirvāṇa—is identified as the dying Adam, while the other—an image of the Buddha sitting under the nāga king Mucalinda—is said to be a statue of Eve being plagued by the snake from Genesis, extending along her back and over her head as though "it were pecking at her brains" (see Ferguson 1911, 204). In addition, other sites on the mountain are linked to the story of Adam and Eve's sons. For example, Westerners, as they climbed the peak, could retrace the steps of Abel as he

---

43. The iron chains on Adam's Peak-Śrī Pada are famous and were already mentioned by Ibn Battuta (see Gibb 1929, 258) in the fourteenth century, and by Barbosa (1866, 171) in the early sixteenth. See also Percival 1803, 207–208). However, they also exist on Adam's Peak-Mulgirigala (see Wijesinghe 2016).

44. "Korte Beschryving der Beelden, en Figuuren, welke op den Berg van Mockeregelle, anders Adams-Berg genaamd."

45. On his identity, see the entry by F. H. De Vos in Appendix B to Ferguson 1911, 239.

fled from his murderous brother Cain, culminating in the spot where he was killed high on the cliff face.[46]

The most extensive description of Mulgirigala from this period, however, comes to us from Johann Wolffgang Heydt, who, as mentioned, also confuses it with Adam's Peak-Śrī Pada, at least initially. Heydt does not actually visit either mountain, but he draws pictures of both from a distance—Śrī Pada from the outskirts of Colombo, and Mulgirigala from near Galle—amazingly, without apparently realizing they are two different mountains.[47] The initial result of this seems to be a compound description of the two sites: "Adam's Peak," he tells us, "[is where] Budu, the first man, as they call Adam, is said to have remained a long time, and . . . [where] the golden ape's-tooth which the Portuguese took away with them was also preserved. . . . On top of the peak, there is said to be a hugely large foot impressed in a rock, which they hold to be the foot of the Budu and reverence as such" (Heydt 1744, 203; Eng. trans. in Heydt 1952, 44). Once again, the tooth and the footprint seem to be together.

The Tooth in Jaffna

If the Dutch and German sources just surveyed appear to be somewhat confused about the location of the mountain on which or near which they claim the tooth was found, the Portuguese sources, by and large, are much clearer. They are virtually unanimous in declaring that the tooth was captured in Jaffna. They were not the only ones to state this, however; two of the French authors—Du Jarric and Le Blanc—do so as well. If we look at the totality of these sources, we can find a Franco-Portuguese lineage of traditions that consistently located the tooth in Jaffna over a period of a century (from 1610 to 1710), and this regardless of whether it was thought to be a monkey's tooth or the Buddha's. There, they declare, Dom Constantino's troops captured it in 1560.

Two background questions are important in considering the story of this capture of the tooth in Jaffna: What took the Portuguese to Jaffna in the first

---

46. See L'Estra 1677, 124–125; and the discussion in Strong forthcoming a. On Cain's murder of Abel, see Gen. 4:8–16. This story reminded Donald Stadtner (private communication, March 2, 2020) of the tale of the "Dhammasoṇḍa jātaka," in which the bodhisattva jumps into the jaw of a waiting monster (Indra in disguise) (see Gatellier 1881, 171).

47. See his plates 50 and 68 (Heydt 1744, 149 and 263; Eng. trans. in Heydt 1952, 7 and 44). It should be pointed out that as late as the early 1800s, the Anglican clergyman James Cordiner (1807, 1: 200) (who had a decent knowledge of Buddhism) was still confused about the identity of Adam's Peak and Mulgirigala, which he calls "a stupendous mountain of stone."

place? and, second, how is it that the tooth got there? For an answer to the first question, we must turn to Do Couto and Queiros, both of whom have lengthy descriptions of the events leading up to the Portuguese invasion of Jaffna in 1560. Their tale begins in 1542, when Martin Affonço de Souza arrives in Goa to take up his post as the new governor of Portuguese India. With him on board the same ship is Francis Xavier, co-founder of the Jesuit order, whom the king of Portugal himself (João III) has commissioned to help restore the Christian morals of the somewhat dissolute settlers of the colony, and to preach Roman Catholicism to the native populations in Goa and beyond.[48]

Intent upon his missionary work, Xavier soon turns his attention to the people of the "Fishery Coast"—the littoral lands along the southern tip of India just opposite the northern point of Sri Lanka. After about a year during which the future saint's fame as a charismatic teacher spreads all along the coast, he responds to a call from some people on the island of Mannar, just off the northwest shore of Sri Lanka (see fig. 1.1). There he preaches the gospel and quickly baptizes over six hundred people, grounding them in the fundamentals of the faith. Then, he moves on (Queiros 1930, 243).

In those days, conversion to Christianity, whether expedient or genuine, signaled cooperation with the Portuguese, who commonly used religion as a means of extending their sphere of influence, and their sphere of influence as a means of extending their religion. Thus when Cankili I (d. 1565), the Hindu king of nearby Jaffna, hears about Xavier's success on Mannar, he quickly becomes worried; Mannar is strategically important, controlling as it does the Palk Straits between Sri Lanka and South India, and it is not acceptable to him to let the Portuguese have it. So, Cankili assembles a large body of men, lands on the island, and massacres all those inhabitants who have converted to Christianity—men, women, and children. At the same time, he becomes suspicious of Christians within Jaffna and begins to persecute them (Queiros 1930, 243–244; see also Coleridge 1881, 1: 247).

Outraged and upset by this overt opposition to his proselytizing (and to Portuguese power), Xavier returns to Goa and demands that the governor immediately take action by attacking Jaffna. But Martin Affonço is a practical man, and his troops are already spread thin and engaged elsewhere. He gives Xavier some lukewarm assurances that he will see what he can do, but he makes no guarantees. In due time, he does send an expedition to punish

48. Xavier's departure from Lisbon and farewell to João III are depicted in a 1635 painting by José de Avelar Rebelo. See https://commons.wikimedia.org/wiki/File:Saint_Francis_Xavier_tak ing_leave_of_King_John_III_(1635)_-_Jos%C3%A9_Avelar_Rebelo.png.

Jaffna, but nothing comes of it; the fleet mustered in Goa is blown off course by storms and some ships are lost. Resigned, De Souza signs a peace treaty that effectively leaves Cankili in control of Jaffna and Mannar in exchange for a token acknowledgment of theoretical Portuguese sovereignty in the area. De Souza then goes back to Goa, and not long thereafter returns to Portugal (Queiros 1930, 250–253).

Not content with this situation and still eager to "regain" Mannar, Xavier decides to appeal directly to the king of Portugal, João III; he writes to him in distant Lisbon, in an effort to enlist his support (Queiros 1930, 246–250). Nothing happens, however, until after Xavier's death in southern China in 1552, and after João's death in Lisbon in 1557 (Gupta 2014, 51–60; Brockey 2015, 48). João is replaced on the throne by his grandson, Sebastião I, but since the new king is but a three-year-old boy, João's widow, Dona Catarina, acts as queen regent. The following year, Dom Constantino da Bragança is appointed as the new viceroy of Goa. As he is about to set sail from Lisbon, the Queen asks him "with special earnestness" to carry out the wishes of her late husband, and also those of the late (soon to be canonized) Francis Xavier—namely to punish the king of Jaffna for his massacre of Christians, and to reestablish a Christian community on the island of Mannar by resettling it with native converts from San Thome (Mylapore) in southern India (Ferguson [1908] 1993, 180; see also Queiros 1930, 351).[49] Accordingly, once in Goa, Dom Constantino spends the first part of 1560 assembling a great armada for an invasion of Jaffna. With the viceroy himself in command, the fleet sets sail in early September and by mid-October anchors just outside Jaffna (Do Couto 1783, 300–306; Eng. trans., Ferguson [1908] 1993, 181–184).[50]

In preparation for the attack on the city, the troops disembark on a small island in the bay. There, the muster roll is called, and a solemn mass is celebrated by Bishop Jorge Temudo, who preaches to the men a long exhortatory sermon and grants them the plenary indulgence that was originally decreed by Pope Leo X for all those "serving in the conquests of Africa, Ethiopia, Arabia, Persia, and India" (Ferguson [1908] 1993, 186n6).

At the muster, Dom Constantino finds he has only 1,200 men, although over 4,000 had enlisted in Goa. This, apparently, was not unusual; it was

49. On the plan to resettle Christians in Mannar and Jaffna, see Biedermann 2018, 149. On the community in Mylapore, see Sharan 1991. The plan ended more or less disastrously, when the Christians of San Thome made it clear they had no intention of moving to Sri Lanka, despite oppression in Mylapore by the king of Vijayanagara. See Ferguson [1908] 1993, 197.

50. On the greater context and possible strategy of the Jaffna invasion, see Biedermann 2018, 148–153.

customary—perhaps especially when viceroys set off on an expedition—to pad the rosters with names of persons who were encouraged to sign up but who never actually embarked. These lists were then later used to report expenses for salaries and the like, with the excess being pocketed by those in command—whether the viceroy himself or his underlings is not clear.[51]

In any case, undeterred by this discovery, at about two o'clock, the Portuguese forces cross the harbor in oared boats and run them up on a beach outside of town near Colombuthurai. After landing, they form into separate companies of two hundred men each, and begin to march on Jaffna city, the banner of Christ crucified held high in the air in front of them by a Dominican priest. Dom Constantino himself brings up the rear, with his own considerable retinue, in addition to various noblemen (*fidalgos*) interested in plunder or attracted by the thrill of being part of the action (Do Couto 1783, 308–309; Eng. trans., Ferguson [1908] 1993, 186–187).

The subsequent breaching of the city's defenses, and the fighting in the streets, are described in detail by Do Couto and Queiros and need not detain us here (Do Couto 1783, 309–316; Eng. trans., Ferguson [1908] 1993, 187–190; see also Queiros 1930, 357–61). Suffice it to say that the Portuguese initially have little trouble in taking over the town.[52] Once they do, they turn to looting, and it is then that, in Cankili's royal temple, they find the tooth.

But how did the tooth get there? Over the years, many Sri Lankan (and Western) scholars (e.g., Davids 1874, 340) have asked this question, in large part because they have viewed the presence of the Buddha's tooth in Jaffna as an unlikely anomaly, considering it to be a "Buddhist" relic and the town a "Hindu" city. How, they ask, is it possible for the Buddha's tooth—that palladium of Sinhalese sovereignty—to have ever ended up in the far northern point of the island, in the hands of the Āryacakravarti Dynasty of Tamil Śaivite kings?

As noted above, however, this thought—that Tamil rulers would be uninterested in possessing and honoring the tooth—is problematic. As we shall

---

51. As Aubrey Bell (1924, 49–50) points out: "dead men, prisoners, slaves, cripples maimed in street brawls, and infants in arms received a regular salary, or rather their names appeared on the pay list which the Captains presented to the Exchequer." On the routine nature of this corrupt practice, see Do Couto 2016, 62–63.

52. Eventually, however, the war ends in a stalemate. The Portuguese retake the island of Mannar, but Cankili gets to keep Jaffna. He, however, has to agree to no longer harass Christians in his kingdom, not to loot the cargo of vessels that happen to come aground on his shores, and to give up his son, the prince, as a hostage (the latter is taken to Goa where he, in time, converts to Christianity, and where he dies in 1571) (Queiros 1930, 370, 377).

see in part 2 of this book, some of the greatest sponsors of the cult of the tooth in Kandy were the Tamil Śaivite monarchs of the Nāyakkar Dynasty. More relevantly for now, perhaps, the Āryacakravarti Dynasty that ruled Jaffna had previously shown interest in the tooth when, in the thirteenth century, they had captured it and taken it to the Pāṇḍyan kingdom in South India. Moreover, as we have seen, the Hindu temple in Nallur where the tooth was found had actually been built by Sapumal Kumāraya, a member of the Kotte royal family that ruled Jaffna for a while in the fifteenth century (during a hiatus in the Āryacakravarti reign) and that was a great sponsor of a Sinhalese cultural golden age. Thus, the thought that it is inconceivable for the tooth to have ever been enshrined in Jaffna would seem to disregard the thoroughgoing religious and cultural syncretism of the times. It also assumes that the cult of the "Buddha's" tooth was exclusively "Buddhist," a point to which I shall return.

Nevertheless, it is true that no traditional Sinhala, Tamil, or Pali source ever mentions the tooth being in Jaffna during its many peregrinations. It was left to the Portuguese, therefore, to answer our second background question—how was it that the tooth got to Jaffna? This will involve a brief consideration of a tale featuring Vidiye Bandara (fl. 1546–1555). Vidiye was regent of Kotte during the infancy and youth of his son, João Dharmapala, whom the Portuguese Christianized as a young man, as we have seen.[53] Unlike his son, however, Vidiye was a charismatic and independently minded warrior who soon fell out with the Portuguese. In a major rebellion against their rule and the puppet status of his son—a rebellion that almost succeeded—he led armies of peasants in burning Portuguese settlements, destroying Catholic churches, executing priests, and killing all Christianized Sinhalese who refused to apostasize and return to whatever tradition (Buddhist or Hindu) they had previously been affiliated with (De Silva 1977, 25; Strathern 2007, 170–171). By 1555, however, Mayadunne, the king of Sītāwaka who had joined the rebellion, became anxious about Vidiye's ultimate ambitions, and double-crossed him by suddenly forming an alliance of convenience against him with the Portuguese. This led to Vidiye's defeat and his flight to Jaffna, where he sought the aid of the aforementioned Āryacakravarti king, Cankili I (De Silva 1981, 107).

It is by an elaboration on this story that the Portuguese seek to explain how the tooth got to Jaffna. For instance, Queiros (1930, 364) tells us

---

53. Vidiye's wife (Dharmapala's mother) was the daughter of Bhuvanekabāhu VII who died, sonless, passing on the throne to his infant grandson, João Dharmapala, whom the Portuguese first crowned in effigy in Lisbon.

that when Vidiye (whom he calls Tribule Pandar) fled north to Jaffna, he brought the relic with him from Kotte (along with some of the royal treasure). The Sinhalese warrior, he claims, had a "superstitious belief in the relic of Buddum [Buddha]," which he at all times kept with him on his person in a little golden box (apparently even when he was in prison) (Queiros 1930, 314).[54] He still had it when he was received by King Cankili in the Kandaswamy Nallur Temple in Jaffna, where they went to seal a new alliance against the Portuguese.[55] At that point, however, either by accident, or as a joke, or on purpose, a soldier in the crowded temple set fire to a bit of gunpowder that had spilled on the floor. Startled by the sudden flare-up and crackling of the powder, Vidiye feared he was being betrayed by Cankili and had been led into a trap, so he quickly drew his sword against the king. Cankili's bodyguards, seeing this aggressive action, responded immediately by cutting him down along with his men (Queiros 1930, 314–326).[56] In this way, we are left to suppose, the Buddha's tooth relic, which was on Vidiye's person, came into the possession of the Hindu Tamil king of Jaffna, along with some of the Kotte treasure. It was subsequently kept right there in the Nallur Temple, where the Portuguese ultimately found it when they looted the place. Elsewhere, Queiros (1930, 363) hypothesizes that when Cankili fled from the Portuguese in Jaffna, he took the Kotte treasure he had acquired with him, but somehow left the tooth relic behind in the temple.

We will probably never know whether Vidiye's death was an accident or a setup (historians have argued both sides). It should be said, however, that a number of Sri Lankan scholars have reworked this story to support an argument that what the Portuguese seized in Jaffna, and subsequently destroyed in Goa, was *not* the "genuine" tooth relic of the Buddha. This is the position adopted, for example, by the influential Sri Lankan historian P. E. Pieris who, in recalling Queiros's story of Vidiye Bandara's death, adds an interesting twist: "The Sinhalese sovereigns," he says,

> were accustomed to carry about their persons *a model* of the Danta Datu [the tooth relic] set in gems and gold, and such a model had accompanied the Prince [Vidiye] through all the tribulations he had been exposed to at the hands of the Portuguese. His last desperate throw had failed, but as he

54. Much the same tale is found in Courtenay (1900, 1: 207–208), who would not have known Queiros's work.
55. On Cankili's consistently anti-Portuguese stance, see Pathmanathan 2007, 33.
56. Do Couto, unlike Queiros, makes no mention of the tooth relic in this context. See Ferguson [1909] 1993, 176.

fled he still clung to the cherished object as the most precious of his treasures. (Pieris 1913, 136–137, italics added)

Pieris's claim, then, is that what the Portuguese captured in the Nallur Temple was not *the* tooth relic but merely a replica thereof. We have seen that replicas of the tooth, made either as gifts to foreign monarchs or as talismans to be carried by the king, were not uncommon,[57] so Pieris's scenario is readily imaginable. But it should be said that he presents no evidence—historical or storical—for his argument.

Queiros's account of how the tooth got located in Jaffna assumes that the relic in question was the (or a) tooth of the Buddha. Du Jarric, writing over seventy-five years before Queiros, seems to know the same tradition, although for him, it is the (or a) tooth of Hanumān that is brought from Kotte. He tells us that

This tooth had been for a long time in the keeping of the Emperor [*sic*] of Ceylon [i.e., the king of Kotte] the descendant of the fabulous race of the Sun.[58] It was to him and to all the pagans of the East, the most precious of treasures. When this Emperor [here apparently meaning Vidiye Bandara] had fled to the King of Jaffna, and had been by him treacherously put to death, the relic passed over to that tyrant. But when Dom Constantine seized his principal treasures, he found this tooth set with gold and numerous precious stones and took it with him to Goa with the rest of the booty. (Du Jarric 1610, 398; Gaspard 1918, 16–17)

There may be some echo of this in Le Blanc; for him, the tooth also belonged to Hanumān, and he prefaces his story of its capture by the Portuguese in Jaffna with a cryptic reference to the king of Kotte, "a descendant of the sun," who was put to death by the king of Jaffna. This presumably refers to Vidiye Bandara (Le Blanc 1648, 104).

As far as I know, there is no mention in any traditional Sri Lankan sources of any Sri Lankan king having a tooth relic of Hanumān. This is a topic that will be addressed more fully in the next chapter. But it should

---

57. See the story mentioned above of the clone of the tooth given to the Burmese king Anawrahta. See also Goloubew 1932, 454n; and Strong 2010, 189. Even in modern times, for security reasons, a facsimile of the tooth is sometimes used. This was the case, for example, during World War II in Kandy (see Herath 1994, 82). More recently a replica was sent to Thailand as a goodwill gesture for a celebration of a Kandy-style Esala Perahera (see Duangmee 2012).

58. The Sinhalese kings (of Kotte and later of Kandy) claimed descent from the mythical Indian solar dynasty (*sūryavaṃsa*).

be said here that the Portuguese sources that do refer to such a tooth were also used polemically by modern Sri Lankan authors. Thus, just as P. E. Pieris sought to belie the claim that what the Portuguese captured and destroyed in Jaffna was *the* Buddha's tooth (because it was a replica), a prominent modern scholar-monk—Kumburugamuwe Vajira—has argued that it was not the Buddha's tooth because (as, he tells us, we know from the Portuguese) *it was Hanumān's*—something Vajira deemed to be a far more appropriate and likely thing to find being worshipped in a Hindu temple in Jaffna (while the genuine tooth remained safe in Delgamuwa).[59]

Chapter Summary

The stories of the locations of the Portuguese tooth were, by and large, not shared by non-Westerners. They were indeed more or less irrelevant for Sri Lankans, who had their own traditions about the whereabouts of the tooth in different places historically, and, in the time of the Portuguese, in Kotte, Delgamuwa, and then Kandy.

Given the various confusions we have seen in this chapter, we will probably never know where the tooth was "actually" found by the Portuguese. Storically speaking, however, Adam's Peak (whether Śrī Pada or Mulgirigala) makes more sense than Jaffna. For one thing, it has narrative antecedents in the tales of Marco Polo and De Barros, both of whom spoke of a tooth relic on the mountain. For another, even for people who had never been to Sri Lanka, such as Van Linschoten, it was a famous place, perhaps the only significant site on the island he had heard of. Jaffna, on the other hand, came out of the blue—as a site for the tooth, it was a location with little pre-storical context (until the Portuguese made one up).

James Robson (2009, 23) reminds us that "[certain] places conjoin people, histories, thoughts, and memories. . . . This capacity for [them] to 'gather' is key to understanding how [they] become a repository for all kinds of mythical and actual histories." It is worth thinking of Adam's Peak and, to a lesser extent perhaps, Jaffna, as "gathering sites" (a term Robson borrows from Edward Casey) for multiple religious traditions, multiple identities, multiple stories. The footprint on Śrī Pada, as we have seen, brought together Muslim, Buddhist, and Hindu pilgrims and beliefs. It was, in the

---

59. See the review of K. Vajira's *Daladā Itihāsaya Saha Samsrititya* (Dehiwela: Tisara Press, 1983) in Pieris 1985, 67.

words of Strathern (2007, 151), "a truly cosmopolitan place of sacredness."[60] Such sites, of course, are not only repositories of traditions that already serve to define them; they are also places to which new traditions can be attached, about which new stories may be told. Thus, whether Van Linschoten had gotten the idea of a tooth on Adam's Peak from Marco Polo or not, it made sense for him to situate his tale of its capture there.

The cosmopolitanism of Adam's Peak was to a certain extent contagious and could affect any "new" traditions once they were implanted there. For instance, transferring to the tooth the model of the kind of things that were commonly said about the footprint, Father Peter Courtenay ([1913] 2005, 147), a Catholic missionary to Sri Lanka in the late nineteenth century, could state: "The Buddhist Sinhalese worshipped [the tooth relic] as the tooth of Buddha; the Hindu Tamils worshipped it as the tooth of the White Ape, their monkey god Hannumant [sic]; and the Moormen [i.e., Muslims] considered it as a tooth of Adam." To be sure, nowhere else have I seen anyone identify the tooth relic as being Adam's, but the ambience of Adam's Peak as its locale may have been one factor in its slippage of identity. And there was clearly such a slippage between the Buddha and Adam (and Eve) at Mulgirigala.

On the other hand, although conjunction (or even syncretism) may be one of the effects of contiguity in a given place, its flipside, as Robson (2009, 319) also makes clear, is the making of distinctions, the drawing of boundaries. Thus, the Sacred Footprint on Adam's Peak, with its converging identities, was also an object conducive to thinking about distinctions between traditions that might previously have been lumped together as "heathen." The same is true, as we shall see in the next chapter, about the tooth.

In the case of the temple at Nallur, in Jaffna, we have a somewhat different situation. Dedicated to the Śaivite god Murugan (aka Kārtikeya), it does not readily appear to have been a "shared space." Yet the cult of Murugan as Skanda or Kataragama in Sri Lanka is not without its syncretistic aspects.[61] In Kotte, for instance, Skanda was recognized as one of the four divine protectors of the island, and as such, his shrine was to be found in the complex of the Temple of the Tooth there. Moreover, as we have seen, the temple at Nallur in Jaffna was established as a royal temple next to the palace by Sapumal, the son of the king of Kotte, whose own religious orientation was utterly syncretistic.

---

60. Alternatively, it could be viewed as a "shared sacred place," like one of those studied by Yoginder Sikand (2003) in India.

61. This is true in modern times at the site of Kataragama in southern Sri Lanka (see Gombrich and Obeyesekere 1988, 411–444).

THREE

Whose Tooth Was It? Traditions about the Identity of the Relic

> Out of gratitude, after the death of the [white monkey], the king kept its tooth which he came to idolize, and erected altars for him which he caused others to worship. Other accounts relate that the tooth was that of a man and not of a monkey.
>
> —Manuel Faria e Souza (1666–1675, 2: 350–351)

Locality is not unrelated to identity, and some of the themes addressed in the last chapter will resurface in this one, as we turn to the matter of whose tooth it was that the Portuguese thought they had captured and destroyed. This is a question that often is not asked. Instead, there is a general assumption that, of course, the story is about the destruction of a relic that—rightly or wrongly—was identified as the *Buddha's* tooth, and other identities given to it are ignored or quickly cast aside as anomalies.

If, however, we look at table 3.1, which charts out the various answers to the question "Whose tooth was this?," we can see that only five of our fourteen sources (Do Couto, Trindade, Queiros, De Sousa, and Valentijn—see row 9) actually mention the Buddha. Moreover, in doing so, all five of these also raise the issue of other possible identities. Indeed, as row 5 of table 3.1 shows, *all* of our sources, without exception, at least refer to the view that the tooth was considered by some to be that of some sort of simian—either "an ape" or "a monkey,"[1] and/or "a white monkey," and/or Hanumān. Nine of them leave it at that; only the five mentioned above (four of them written

---

1. While recognizing that apes and monkeys are not the same, I will follow Lutgendorf (2007, 345n13) in using the two terms "interchangeably and unscientifically as has generally been the practice [in non-modern sources]."

Table 3.1 Synopsis of views about the identities of the Portuguese tooth

		Van Linschoten	Pimenta	Du Jarric	Texeira	Pyrard De Laval	Do Couto	Trindade	Le Blanc	Baldaeus	Faria e Souza	Queyros	De Sousa	Valentijn	Heydt
1	Source														
2	Date	1596	1605	1610	1610	1611	1616	1636	1648	1672	1674	1687	1710	1726	1744
3	Nationality of author	Du.	Por.	Fr.	Por.	Fr.	Por.	Por.	Fr.	Du.	Por	Por.	Por.	Du.	Ger.
4															
5	Tooth referred to as that of some sort of simian:	x	x	x	x	x	x	x	x	x	x	x	x	x	x
6	A monkey	x			x	x	x	x				x	x	x	x
7	A white monkey			x				x	x		x				
8	Hanumān		x	x	x				x	x				x	
9	Tooth referred to as that of the Buddha					x	x	x				x	x	x	

in Portuguese) go on to affirm, more or less strongly, the alternative belief that the tooth was that of the Buddha.

It can be concluded, therefore, on the basis of the Western sources we have surveyed, that the storical norm was to identify the tooth as being that of a simian figure, and that the understanding of the tooth as a Buddha relic was a Portuguese discovery, if not invention.[2] As can be seen in row 9 of table 3.1, it is Do Couto (1783, 316; Eng. trans., Tennent 1859, 2: 213) who first announces this as being the natives' actual view.[3] This recognition is then elaborated upon and extended by subsequent Portuguese historians, with a growing degree of affirmation. Trindade ([1630–1636] 1962–1967, 3: 181), for example, after identifying the relic as the tooth of a white monkey, adds that the local population "had it that this tooth was that of their Buddha whom they held to be a great saint." The same thing is mentioned by a source not in our table: João Ribeiro, a Portuguese soldier who served eighteen years in Ceylon (from 1640 to 1658) fighting the Dutch. In his *Fatalidade Historica da ilha de Ceilão* [Historical tragedy of the island of Ceylon], he states that there was in Jaffna "a tooth commonly said to be that of a monkey. . . . which the gentiles [i.e., non-Christians] believed [to be] the tooth of Budio" (Ribeiro [1685] 1899, 31; see also Ribeiro [1685] 1701, 118–119).[4] Queiros (1930, 364) is somewhat more emphatic. He blames "our [i.e., Portuguese] historians" for the view that this was a monkey's tooth and declares that to be "a manifest error." The natives rather always considered it to be "the tooth of Buddum . . . one of the most sacred objects of worship in the heathendom of the South and of Tartary." Finally, as we have seen, when we get to Francisco De Sousa's history, which dates to 1710, the tooth is, for the first time, definitively affirmed as being that of the Buddha (De Sousa 1710, 195). To be sure, the alternative—that it might be an ape's tooth—is mentioned, but only to be dismissed and ridiculed (De Sousa 1710, 200).

These post–Do Couto Portuguese sources, then, tend to blame their benighted uneducated "common" compatriots for the belief that the captured

2. This does not mean, however, that all the Portuguese sources mention this view. Some relatively early ones (i.e., Pimenta in 1605 and Texeira in 1610) simply accept the opinion that the tooth was that of a monkey or of Hanumān. The same is true of Faria e Souza who, in 1674, as seen in the epigraph to this chapter, refers to it first as the tooth of a white monkey, and only later admits that some say it is the tooth of a man without specifying who that man was.

3. It should be said that Do Couto is a bit ambiguous about his own beliefs. He at times seems to accept the belief that the tooth was the Buddha's, but then he reverts to calling it a monkey or white monkey's tooth (see Ferguson 1909, 191, 245).

4. On Ribeiro, see Boxer 1955, 2–6. For a modern edition of the Portuguese original of his work, see Ribeiro [1685] 1989.

relic was a monkey's tooth, and gradually agree instead with what they deem to be the "natives' view"—that it was that of the Buddha. The irony of all this, of course, is that no traditional indigenous sources have been found that make either of these assertions; Sri Lankans, by and large, do not know the tradition that it was a monkey's tooth, and they deny that the tooth the Portuguese captured (if they mention it at all) was actually the Buddha's. With all of this in mind, let us now turn to a more in-depth discussion of these various identities of the tooth.

Monkey's Tooth

The very first and very last of our sources (Van Linschoten and Heydt) make the simple single assertion that the tooth belonged to a monkey, without any further qualifications such as "white" or "whose name was Hanumān." At a purely physical level, this may make good sense. If the size of the tooth captured by the Portuguese was anything like that of the tooth relic presently in Kandy, it is not surprising that they might have thought it *not* to be the incisor of a human. Leonard Woolf, for instance, who, as part of his function as secretary to the British Resident in Kandy in the early twentieth century, viewed the tooth there "at close quarters three times," declares that "whatever else it may be, it has never been a human tooth . . . [since it] is a canine about three inches long and curved" (Woolf 1961, 144). Jonathan Forbes (1840, 1: 293), who saw the same tooth in Kandy in 1828, describes it as "a piece of discoloured ivory, slightly curved, nearly two inches in length."[5] The average human eyetooth is less than half as long as this from root to crown, but some monkeys (especially the gray langur [see below]) that abound in Sri Lanka and India, and with which the Portuguese would have been very familiar, do tend to have more pronounced fangs.

At a linguistic level, Hannah Wojciehowski (2011, 189) has suggested that there may have been some phonetic slippage between the Portuguese words *Budão*, sometimes rendered as *Budio* or *Buddum* (= "Buddha"), and *bugio* (= "monkey or ape"), and that this led to the confusion. This is something which, we have seen, was already put forward by De Sousa. For many Portuguese, such a phonetic slippage would perhaps have been readily seized upon as an opportunity to mock the worship of the tooth, since the word *bugio* was also a term of slander (Gray 1887, 2: 145n1). Wojciehowski (2011, 189n23), in a footnote, goes on to explore various pejorative con-

---

5. Davy (1821, 274), who viewed the tooth in 1818, gives a life-size drawing of it that is a little under two inches.

notations of Portuguese terms for monkey: like the other word for monkey, *macaco* (masc.) or *macaca* (fem.), *bugio* could have been a racial slur for dark-skinned people;[6] and the term also had sexual connotations.[7] Indeed, Faria e Souza (1666–1675, 2: 351) points out that the prime characteristic of monkeys is that they are deceptive and "lust itself."

Similarly, Philip Lutgendorf (2007, 334) has pointed to the colonial attitude toward monkeys as "diminutive primates whose names were often used as labels for despised human 'others' who unsuccessfully 'aped' the ways of their betters. The British themselves regularly jeered at their imperial subjects, from Ireland to Bengal, as 'apes.'"[8] And he goes on to quote the words of Horst Janson:

> [In the traditional Western view] apes were "man's poor relations," debased replicas of ourselves, just as men were the "poor relations" of the angels. The principle linking these three estates was that of devolution, not of evolution: man had been "demoted" from the level of a potential angel through an act of divine displeasure, while the ape had similarly forfeited his status as a human being. (Janson 1952, 13)[9]

It is also possible that the same appellation was meant to indicate a primitive and/or indigenous form of worship—a further way of belittling the native Sri Lankans who were thus portrayed as essentially being worshippers of an animal, and so less than animals themselves. Alternatively, the monkey's tooth might have been seen by them as a fetish (an originally Portuguese word—*feitiço*). It would, after all, not be too long before early theoreticians of religion would place "animal worship" and "fetish worship" at the most "primitive levels" of human cults (see Bosman 1705, 150–151; De Brosses 1760, 18–27). In part 2, we shall encounter other instances of this primitivization and indigenization of the tooth by the British. A. M. Hocart (1931, 4–5), for instance, believed that the origin of the worship of the

---

6. This is still true of *macaco/macaque/macaca* in French and in English; one recalls the political fate of US Senator George Allen who, on a campaign stop in 2006, called an Indian American employee of his opponent a "*macaca*."

7. Apparently, in Goan Portuguese, the feminine *bugia* meant prostitute (Wojciehowski 2011, 189n25).

8. "Monkey" was not only used as a term of slander by Europeans; the Japanese commonly used it to malign and demean outcastes and other marginals in their country. See Ohnuki-Tierney 1987, 128–159.

9. One might add "or as a god," given our sources' inclination to treat Hanumān as a deity who was chased out of heaven for some sin and condemned to live as a monkey.

Kandyan tooth could be found in the autochthonous cult of *yakṣas* (Sinhala, *yakka*, i.e., demons), who are commonly depicted as having "very large eye-teeth like a boar's tusk" (he might well have said "monkey's fang").

White Monkey's Tooth

A number of the sources in table 3.1, row 7 (Du Jarric, Trindade, Le Blanc, Faria e Souza), add a specification that the monkey in question was a "white monkey." In some cases, this appellation may suggest a further identification with Hanumān whether he is named or not. As Philip Lutgendorf (2007, 57) has pointed out, simianesque iconic representations of Hanumān can be divided into two categories—the so-called "macaque" and "langur" types. The designation "white monkey" may have been inspired by the latter. Indeed, gray langurs (*semnopithecus*) are striking for their black faces and generally long whitish hair, are commonly found throughout India and Sri Lanka, and are popularly known as "Hanumān langurs." Moreover, they also show prominent fangs when they bare their teeth.[10]

Faria e Souza, however, is primarily interested in the symbolic significance of the color white, and proceeds to comment on this. First, he proposes that whiteness, unusual in some animals, is considered to be admirable and even a mark of divinity, and he gives as an example the whiteness of the king of Siam's albino elephant (also much coveted, he adds [like the tooth], by the king of Pegu). But then he immediately suggests that whiteness is also a sign of blindness, like the whiteness of a blind eye. Thus idolaters, who worship white things, are in some sense blind. In this dual interpretation, there is a subtext perhaps more generally revelatory of Portuguese attitudes toward Sri Lankans and the tooth. The whiteness of the monkey is, in fact, evocative of a double demeaning. On the one hand, Faria e Souza is asserting that native dark-skinned people naturally admire and worship whites such as the Portuguese. On the other hand, he is suggesting that they are also blind and ignorant, because the object of their worship is a *monkey*.

These preliminaries aside, Faria e Souza (1666–1675, 2: 351) then tells a story about this white monkey which, he claims, he has found in several sources, though he does not specify which. An ancient Indian king had a wife whom he much loved but who ran away from him. The king sent out men to search for her, without success. But then he dispatched her favorite

10. For this reason and for their size, at the Commonwealth Games in Delhi in 2010, authorities deployed a troop of these Hanumān langurs to scare away smaller simians who were likely to pester tourists and sports fans and steal their food (Burridge 2010).

monkey, who was soon able to find her in her hiding place, and in this way, the king eventually got her back. Out of gratitude he then greatly regaled the monkey in life and, after it died, he kept its tooth and erected altars for it that he made others worship. The tooth captured by the Portuguese was that very tooth. In this story, however, the king turns out to be a fool and a cuck-old since, Faria e Souza implies, the monkey and the queen were actually lovers. For he promptly speaks of "bawdry behavior" and "lasciviousness," and he reinforces the suggestion of bestiality by likening the story to that of Leda, whom Jupiter approached in the guise of a swan, and of Amphitrite, whom Neptune seduced in the form of a dolphin.[11]

Hanumān's Tooth

It seems more or less obvious that, in his tale of the white monkey and the queen, Faria e Souza is reworking and mocking some version of the story of Rāma, Hanumān, and Sītā, even though he does not give names to any of his protagonists, and makes no reference either to Sri Lanka or to a de-mon figure such as Ravaṇa. The identification of the simian character as Ha-numān is explicitly made, however, in several other sources (Pimenta, Du Jarric, Texeira, Le Blanc, Baldaeus, and Valentijn), as may be seen in row 8 of table 3.1.[12]

The cult of Hanumān had an efflorescence in India in the early colo-nial period (Lutgendorf 2007, ch. 2). Vernacular *Rāmāyaṇas* started appear-ing in the twelfth century, particularly in the south, and would have been popular in Portuguese times (Lutgendorf 2007, 57), so it is not surprising to find that the authors cited above are aware of the gist of the Hanumān story. Hanumān would have been known in Goa, where the Portuguese de-stroyed several temples dedicated to him.[13] Hanumān would also have been well known in Jaffna in the sixteenth century, for the peninsula is close to Rāmasetu ("Rāma's Bridge," aka Adam's Bridge)—the "causeway" (now a

---

11. He adds that in some versions of the story, it is not a monkey who does these things but a man, but whether man or monkey, his critique remains the same.

12. In addition, Thomas Herbert (1606–1682), an Englishman who traveled in Persia, In-dia, and Ceylon in 1627–1629, makes mention ([1634] 1638, 307) of Dom Constantino's de-struction of "that infamous *Apis Hanimant,* or *Apes-tooth-god,* so highly, so generally resorted to by millions of Indians." On Herbert's life, see Davies 1870.

13. See, for example, the story of the Maruti temple in Mapusa (just north of Goa city), which was rebuilt in the nineteenth century on the site of a shop where, in Portuguese times, the local people continued surreptitiously to worship its image (see https://en.wikipedia.org/wiki/Mapusa).

line of islands and shoals separating Sri Lanka from the tip of India), said in the *Rāmāyana* to have been built by his monkey army, and in several of our sources to have been created by Hanumān when he hopped over the straits on his quest to find Sītā.[14] The Jaffna kings often used the "Setu" (bridge) as an emblem on their coinage (Rasanayagam [1926] 1984, 300–301). Moreover, the ruling Āryacakravarti Dynasty claimed close connections with the great Śaivite temple of Rāmanāthasvāmi at Rameśvaram, just on the Indian side of the straits, where Rāma worshipped Śiva after he invaded Sri Lanka, and where one of the main *lingams* is said to have been brought from the Himalayas by Hanumān.[15]

Be this as it may, we do not know whether Hanumān was actively worshipped in the temple in Nallur / Jaffna (along with its main deity, Murugan) when the Portuguese captured the place. Nor am I aware of a tooth ever being a symbolic object representing Hanumān (Murugan's emblem is the vel [spear]).[16] In short, I have found no support for the claim that the tooth was thought by *non-Portuguese* to be that of an ape or of Hanumān.

Why, then, did the Portuguese (and many other foreigners) keep mentioning that it was? We have already pointed to several possible explanations: there could have been a linguistic confusion between "Budao" and "*bugio*," and with that a desire to demean the Sri Lankans by saying they worshipped a monkey, and the only divine monkey they could think of was Hanumān. But there may be something else at work here.

14. In the *Rāmāyana*, Hanumān initially crosses the straits with a "great heroic leap" (Vālmīki 2006, 33–67) to go locate Sītā. Later on, at the time of the invasion of the island, the story is recounted of the building of Rāmasetu (in book six, the "Yuddha Kāṇḍa").

15. In recent times, Hanumān's popularity in Jaffna has been boosted by the dedication (in 2013) of a colossal (72 feet) standing image in imitation of a proliferation of other such modern giant Hanumān statues in India. But we should not be misled by this modern evidence. In an email message to a small group discussing this question, on February 14, 2018, Dennis McGilvray writes: "Just to interject an ethnographic footnote into this historical conversation, there has, until quite recently, been very little interest in Hanumān among modern Sri Lankan Tamils. Only in the last decade or so have conspicuous temples to Hanumān begun to appear. . . . [Some of these] have drawn criticism from high caste Tamil Śaivite Hindu traditionalists as dangerous and misguided. They don't even think Hanumān is a proper deity, only an animal servant of Rāma. . . . There must be good reasons for the new popularity of Hanumān, but they certainly do not come from the 16th century." According to Môhan Wijayaratna (1987, 297), there is even less interest in Hanumān and other figures in the *Rāmāyana* among the Sinhalese.

16. Very occasionally, in the *Rāmāyana* (e.g., when he first reveals his true form to Sītā [Vālmīki 2006, 309]), Hanumān's fangs are mentioned, but generally the epic associates teeth with the *rākṣasas* (demons).

Hanumān and Vijayanagara

Vincent Le Blanc who, perhaps most of all of our sources, seems to be familiar with the Hanumān tradition, declares that Hanumān came over to Sri Lanka from Vijayanagar (1648, 104). The same thing is already mentioned by Du Jarric (1610, 397), and reiterated by Valentijn eighty years later (1726, 383). We have also seen that several of our other sources (e.g., Van Linschoten) point out that Vijayanagar was one of the kingdoms interested in acquiring the tooth by ransoming it from the Portuguese, or, after its destruction, by buying a fake tooth from Kotte. Only later did Pegu come to the forefront of the ransomers.

Vijayanagara was a preeminent power in the South Indian region when the Portuguese first got there. Indeed, the Italian Nicolò De Conti, who traveled to South Asia in the first half of the fifteenth century, asserts that the king of Bizenegalia (i.e., Vijayanagar) was the most powerful (and wealthiest) monarch in the whole of India, and describes his capital city as being sixty miles in circumference (Bracciolini 1857, 6; see also Breazeale 2004, 113). Much of what he says is echoed by Ludovico Di Varthema ([1510] 1863, 125), at the start of the sixteenth century. Indeed, Vijayanagar had ports on both the Arabian Sea and the Bay of Bengal, and from these engaged in lively trade with merchants from as far away as China. Admiral Zheng He, for instance, traded with Vijayanagar, whose exports included cotton, spices, gems, ivory, rhinoceros horn, and the like (see Nilakanta Sastri [1955] 2002, 304).

The association of Hanumān with Vijayanagar is rooted in Hindu mythology, where Hanumān and the whole monkey clan of the *Rāmāyaṇa* are said to be from the land surrounding that city, the ancient kingdom of the *vanaras* ("monkeys") called Kiṣkindhā.[17] Ancient Vijayanagar, in fact, boasted many sites legendarily associated with Hanumān (e.g., the places where Rāma originally sought his (and the *vanara* king Sugriva's) aid, and where he reported to Rāma on his discovery of Sītā in Sri Lanka) (Verghese 1995, 43–53).[18] Even today, in Hampi, where the ruins of the ancient city are to be found, pilgrims and tourists can visit these sites, and popular tradition has it (or, at least, had it a hundred years ago) that "the tumbled masses of fallen

17. A whole section of the *Rāmāyaṇa* is called the "Kiṣkindhā Kāṇḍa" and recounts the saga of Rāma's dealings with the monkeys Sugrīva, Valli, and Hanumān (see Vālmīki 2005). Vijayanagara, it should be said, was not the only region of India to identify itself with Kiṣkindhā (see Verghese 1995, 43).

18. See also Ayyar 1920, 237; Fritz 1985, 265; Fritz 1986; and Malville 1994, 148.

boulders which encumber the site of Vijayanagar are the remains of the material collected by Hanumān's monkey hosts for the great causeway [across the rather distant Palk Straits]" (Longhurst 1917, 9).

In addition to these places associated with Hanumān, hundreds of images of him have been found at Hampi dating from Vijayanagar times (the fourteenth to sixteenth centuries). During this period, Hanumān "evidently enjoyed special veneration" in the region (Lutgendorf 2007, 60), for he was, in the words of one art historian, "the most ubiquitous of all the minor deities in Vijayanagar" (Verghese 1995, 90).[19]

More importantly, the Vijayanagar emperors, who thought of "their empire as the lands mentioned in the *Rāmāyana*," were viewed as incarnations of Rāma.[20] The artistically important Rāmacandra (aka Hazara Rama) Temple in Hampi, dedicated to Rāma and containing bas-relief depictions of the *Rāmāyana*, was the royal ceremonial temple of the Vijayanagar emperors, and at the epicenter of their capital (Verghese 1995, 47; Fritz 1986, 50–53; Lutgendorf 2007, 70). Every year, the king's suzerainty was ritually celebrated in a reenactment of Rāma's victory over Ravana at the end of the great Mahānavami Festival, "a grand public ritual that had political as well as socio-economic and military overtones."[21]

This identification of the emperor with Rāma is obviously supportive of the fact that Hanumān had a special place in Vijayanagar; just as the simian divinity was Rāma's faithful devotee and servant, so too was he a defender and representative of Vijayanagara sovereignty.[22] Thus, Hanumān's image was found everywhere in the city.[23] Moreover, his depiction was displayed on the royal standard of the early Vijayanagar kings who also stamped his image on some of their coins, together with their own names on the obverse sides.[24] An anecdote from the early history of Vijayanagara would seem to

19. Already a century ago, the archaeologist who first excavated Hampi, A. H. Longhurst (1917, 9), declared that the monkey god was "the most popular deity in the whole district."

20. Verghese 1995, 43. See also Walters 1996, 51. The kings of Vijayanagar were not the only ones to be so thought of. For a study and interpretation of the origins of claims of Indian rulers to be incarnations of Rāma, see Pollock 1993.

21. See Verghese 1995, 105–106; Karashima 2014, 214–218; Malville 1994, 152; Fritz 1986, 49; and, for a discussion of several early descriptions of the festival, see Stein 1980, 384–392.

22. Significantly, the Hanumān cult in Vijayanagara had virtually no existence until the foundation of the empire. See Verghese 1995, 91.

23. In the sixteenth century, Vyāsatīrtha, a saint of the Madhva sect that was dominant in Vijayanagara at the time, set up 733 images of Hanumān in various parts of the city. Today, thirty-nine statues and seventeen rock carvings of him may still be found in Hampi. See Malville 1994, 155–156; and Verghese 1995, 89.

24. Lutgendorf 2007, 61; Malville 1994, 153. See also Elliot 1886, 88–101, esp. 95 and 99.

reflect all of this. When the Bahmani sultan Mujahid Shah (r. 1375–1378) attacked the recently founded city, he managed to penetrate into the second line of its defenses but could get no farther. Before retreating, however, he came across an image of Hanumān that was being guarded by a number of brahmins. The sultan quickly disposed of these priests and then, "dismounting, struck the image in the face, mutilating its features" (Taylor 1879, 163). The message would seem to be clear: unable to get to the king of Vijayanagar, Mujahid Sultan lashed out at the image of Hanumān instead, his faithful servant and devotee, the symbol of his kingship.[25]

In the Sri Lankan context, Hanumān's role as protector of Vijayanagara recalls the case of another servant and devotee of Rāma—that of the demon Vibhīṣaṇa. In the *Rāmāyaṇa*, Vibhīṣaṇa is Rāvaṇa's "good," younger sibling, who turns against his demon brother and becomes a "paradigmatic vassal of Rāma" (Walters 1996, 51; see also Walters 1991/1992). As a recompense, after killing Rāvaṇa, Rāma appoints Vibhīṣaṇa as king of Sri Lanka to rule the island in his stead when he goes back to India with the rescued Sītā. In this way, Vibhīṣaṇa transforms his demon identity and comes to be recognized by Sri Lankans as one of the divine protectors of the island, and defenders of its kingship (Wijayaratna 1987, 149–152).[26]

Jonathan Walters has argued that the cult of Vibhīṣaṇa—as an autochthonous ruler-turned-protector whose loyalty was nonetheless to a South Indian invader (Rāma)—was the perfect vehicle for expressing the allegiance of certain fourteenth- and fifteenth-century Sri Lankan rulers to the Vijayanagara emperor (Walters 1991). The Vijayanagara Empire, as it expanded its territory to cover most of South India, came to take on the characteristics of a feudal "segmentary state" made up, outside its center (Vijayanagara proper), of relatively autonomous polities that were "structurally as well as morally coherent units in themselves" (Stein 1980, 23; see also Fritz 1986, 46). These were ruled by several hundred *nāyakas*, military leaders (some much more powerful than others) who annually had to renew their fealty to

25. Taylor (1879, 163) claims the mutilated image was still to be seen in his day. Presumably, this story is also a local attempt to explain the "puffed cheeks and lips" that are a feature of many Hanumān images. See also Sewell 1900, 46.

26. Vibhīṣaṇa was, in time, replaced as a protector god by Nātha. It should be said that the *Rāmāyaṇa* legend has always had a somewhat ambivalent status in Sri Lanka. On the one hand, as a great epic and piece of literature, it is respected and revered, especially by Hindus. On the other hand, it is a tale of invasion and conquest of the homeland, in which the "good guys" (Rāma, Hanumān, Sītā) are "foreigners," while the "bad guy" (Rāvaṇa) is the indigenous Lankan king. Vibhīṣaṇa, as a "good indigenous guy," was a solution to this dilemma. The cult of Vibhīṣaṇa is unknown in India (see Walters 1991, 130).

the emperor in the capital city (Karashima 2014, 194–203). There were no *nāyakas* outside of mainland South India,[27] but Vijayanagar's overlordship in the fourteenth and fifteenth centuries also extended, less formally, perhaps, to the petty kings of lowland Sri Lankan principalities such as Gampola, Kotte, Raigama, but most of all to Jaffna, where the Āryacakravartin kings were virtually vassals of Vijayanagar during this period (Walters 1991, 136; Nilakanta Sastri [1955] 2002, 686–690). Vijayanagaran forces invaded parts of the island as early as the 1370s (Rasanayagam [1926] 1984, 365) and, though they soon left, the kingdoms on the island nonetheless were obliged to continue paying tribute to their emperor (Sewell 1900, 302). For instance, in 1432, a general of King Devarāja II of Vijayanagar "crossed over to Ceylon . . . and evidently compelled the island to acknowledge the suzerainty of [the emperor]." Six years later one of Devarāja's inscriptions proclaimed that he had "recovered tribute from Ceylon" (Rasanayagam [1926] 1984, 366–367).[28]

In Kotte, and especially in nearby Kelaniya, the royal family expressed their loyalty to their overlord through the cult of Vibhīṣaṇa. Ritually speaking, according to Walters (1991, 141), this "was the index and icon of participation in the Vijayanagar empire." In fact, the heyday of the cult of Vibhīṣaṇa corresponds pretty much exactly to the period of Vijayanagar's ascendancy. It emerges seemingly out of nowhere in the early fourteenth century and soon a magnificent shrine is established for Vibhīṣaṇa in Kelaniya, where he is worshipped by the kings of nearby Kotte who, at the same time, venerated the tooth of the Buddha.[29] But his popularity and the importance of his cult soon fades, once Vijayanagara is defeated in 1565 and the Portuguese more fully replace Vijayanagar as the hegemonic power in the region.[30]

It is probable that, at first, the Portuguese did not understand the significance of the cult of Vibhīṣaṇa in Kelaniya, but they soon recognized its religious, political, and economic import, and once they did, they proceeded to destroy not only the Buddhist temple there, but also the shrine to Vibhīṣaṇa,

27. At least during Vijayanagara's ascendancy. After its defeat in 1565, several of the *nāyakas* declared independence, and they, in turn, became influential in Sri Lanka. As we shall see in part 2, they came to rule Kandy for a while.

28. For an account of repeated invasions of the Jaffna peninsula by Vijayanagara, aiming at putting down rebellions and restoring their overlordship, see Nilakanta Sastri 1959, 686–690.

29. During this period, Vibhīṣaṇa is also extolled in several Sinhalese "messenger poems," such as Toṭagamuve Śrī Rāhula's *Selalihini Sandesaya* (1462). See Walters 1996, 54; and Walters 1991, 133–137.

30. Today the diminished cult of Vibhīṣaṇa is found pretty much only in Kelaniya.

replacing them with churches (Walters 1996, 63–65).[31] To be sure, these were religious acts, motivated by a desire to eradicate idolatry, but they were also effective signals that the Portuguese were displacing Vijayanagar as the "foreign overlords."

Is it possible that something similar may be seen, in Jaffna, in the case of Hanumān who, like Vibhīṣaṇa, was symbolic of loyalty to Rāma and thus to his incarnation on earth, the emperor of Vijayanagara?[32] Jaffna, after all, was even more consistently under the aegis of Vijayanagara than Kotte, and Hanumān traditions were clearly known there. Could, then, the presence of a Hanumān tooth in the royal Āryacakravartin temple in Jaffna be a sign, not necessarily of popular devotion to the monkey god, but of an official recognition of Vijayanagara's suzerainty? We have no evidence of this, but the question is worth asking. In any case, whether the Jaffnans affirmed that the tooth was Hanumān's or not may not really matter. The Portuguese did and, aware themselves of the importance of Hanumān in Vijayanagara, initially identified the tooth they had captured as Hanumān's. By destroying it, they were thus making not just a religious but a political point: that they were ending the overlordship of the Vijayanagar emperors on the Jaffna peninsula and replacing them as the power to be reckoned with in the region. Another way of putting this is that in so far as they were replacing Vijayanagara, they were positioning themselves to be viewed as new Rāmas. Like the old Rāma, they were conquerors come from India, but unlike the old Rāma (and unlike Vijayanagar), they were conquerors who stayed on the island.

Mythologically, one of the aspects of Hanumān is that he was a link—a connector to the mainland. This was epitomized in the legend of Rāma Setu, the construction by Hanumān and the monkeys of the causeway or bridge across the Palk Straits. Interestingly, this is also what is most emphasized in our Portuguese and other sources (e.g., Pimenta, Du Jarric, Texeira), in their truncated accounts of Hanumān's skipping across that body of water and creating an island or sandbar at each step. By taking Hanumān's tooth back to Goa, and by destroying it there (and also by destroying Vibhīṣaṇa's shrine in Kelaniya), the Portuguese were eliminating several links to the

---

31. On the more general reasons for Portuguese destruction of temples or refurbishing them into churches, see Xavier and Županov 2015, 122–27.

32. As Mohan Wijayaratna (1987, 297–298) has shown, though Rāma, Sītā, and the like were not part of the Sri Lankan pantheon, the *Rāmāyaṇa* story was known and part of popular tradition (and, as such, sometimes maligned by Theravādin monks). Part of the epic was, in fact, reworked as early as the sixth century CE by Kumāradāsa, a Sinhalese author writing in Sanskrit. His work, the *Jānakīharaṇa* [The abduction of Jānakī (= Sītā)], was later (fifteenth century) denounced as frivolous by the aforementioned monk Toṭagamuve Śrī Rāhula.

mainland. This was not only because they were thereby declaring that they had replaced Vijayanagara, but because, as conquerors who had stayed, such a link was no longer needed.

The Buddha's Tooth

The empire of Vijayanagar officially lasted until 1646, but it lost much of its power in 1565, after a major military setback at the battle of Talicota with Muslim sultanates to the north (see Eaton 2006, 96–98). This was just five years after the tooth was captured in Jaffna, according to Do Couto. It took some time but, with the end of Vijayanagara's effective hegemony, Hanumān's symbolic importance waned, and the Portuguese searched for a new identity for the tooth. This they found in the Buddha.

As we have seen, the major post-1615 Portuguese historians (Do Couto, Queiros, De Sousa) all state, with increasing affirmation, that the tooth was the Buddha's, that the notion that it was Hanumān's or a monkey's was in error. As will be argued below, one of the reasons for this would seem to be the emergence in history and in the minds of the Portuguese, in the latter half of the sixteenth century, of the kingdom of Pegu, whose Buddhist *bona fides* were clear. More generally, however, during this period and later, three not unrelated factors emerged. The first was the growth of Portuguese knowledge of the life story of the Buddha, and more generally of Buddhism as something distinct from other traditions; the second was their increasing awareness of Buddhism as a pan-Asian religion; and the third was the Portuguese realization of the political importance of the *Buddha's* tooth, and their desire to undermine the claims of Southeast Asian and Sri Lankan rulers (in particular the kings of Pegu and of Kandy) to possess it by asserting that they (the Portuguese) had destroyed it. Each of these factors will be considered in turn.

Growth in the Knowledge of Buddhism and of the Buddha's Life Story

At one point in his *Itinerario*, Van Linschoten declares that in all of India and its surrounding lands, there are only four types of religionists: Heathens, Moors (i.e., Muslims), Jews, and Christians.[33] This amounts to saying that there are really two kinds of faith: monotheists (who are divided into vari-

---

33. On this very common early modern Western taxonomy of religions, see Masuzawa 2005, 46–64; and Lopez 2016, 7.

ous separate traditions), and all the others (including, for example, those engaged in what we would call Buddhist or Hindu practices) who are lumped together under the single rubric of "heathens," or "gentiles." Van Linschoten and many of his contemporaries make no real distinctions among these "others"—these "heathens"—and hence, for them, there is no such thing as identifiable Buddhists or Hindus. As he describes them, they all "have idoles and images, which they call pagodes, cut and formed most ugly, and like monstrous devils, to whom dayly they [make] offer[ings]" (Van Linschoten [1598] 1885, 1: 222–223).

It could be argued that Van Linschoten's ideological blinders and/or cultural ignorance led him to this kind of myopic lumping. In his defense, one might point out that the thoroughgoing religious syncretism in Sri Lanka at that time (and not only at the popular level)[34] might have made it harder for him to detect divides between traditions. Indeed, it is worth asking whether any observer, in sixteenth-century Sri Lanka, would or could have recognized a distinction between what we today think of as "Hinduism" and "Buddhism."

But this is also a time when outside observers *are* beginning to make differentiations. A generation after Van Linschoten, the Englishman Thomas Herbert ([1634] 1638, 306–307) expresses much the same sentiment as he does: "The Ile of Zeyloon," he declares, "is over-runne with stinking weeds of cursed Heythenisme." The population is "drunk with abominable demonomy and superstition . . . [and] scarce any Village or Mount [is] without its inanimate Pagod." But then he adds a curious sentence, pointing out that these idols, "being divers in shape, are therefore diversified, in that they relish [i.e., appeal to] the divers palats [tastes] of divers men."

The gradual Western "discovery" of the diversity of "heathenism," in particular of the dissimilarity between Buddhism and Hinduism, was a slow process, as were the realization of the Buddha's life story and the affirmation of his existence as a human being. It is commonly said not to have been completed in some circles until the mid-nineteenth century (App 2010, 133–253; Strong 2016, 144–145; Almond 1988, 13–16).[35] Yet when we look at Portuguese sources that identify the tooth as being the Buddha's (and not Hanumān's) and that simultaneously give us a bit of information

---

34. On this syncretism, see, for example, Gunawardana 1979, 222. See also Perera 1910, 16–17; and, for some good examples, Ilangasinha 1992, 65–66. How much this syncretism has continued into the present is an interesting question.

35. On this question specifically with regard to Sri Lanka, see also Scott 1994, 159–160.

about the Buddha, we can see that both of these processes were already underway two hundred to two hundred fifty years earlier.

In one of his studies of Portuguese historians of Asia, C. R. Boxer (1948,
18) points out that Do Couto "was clearly interested in Buddhism," and
had "a better appreciation and understanding of it" than his Portuguese
predecessors. This does not mean that his accounts of the religion, and
specifically of the life story of the Buddha, are not without their anomalies;
it just means that he seems to have a nascent awareness of the importance
of Buddhism *qua* Buddhism.

In his discussion of the footprint on the top of Adam's Peak, for instance,
Do Couto pauses to recount in some detail the first part of the legend of the
Buddha, according to the "natives whom he has questioned": his birth as
the son of a king "who reigned over the whole of the East"; the visit of the
soothsayers who declared he would become a great saint (rather than a great
king) should he be moved to wander forth on a religious quest; his father's
determination to prevent him from doing this by locking him up in luxuri-
ous palaces where "he was reared until the age of eighteen, without knowing
that there was sickness, death, or any other human misery"; the failure of
this scheme when, nonetheless, the bodhisattva encountered on separate
expeditions from the palace the signs of a sick man, an old man, and a corpse;
his subsequent meeting, in a vision, of a pilgrim "who persuaded him to
contemn the world and adopt a solitary life" (Ferguson [1908] 1993, 111–
112; original text in Do Couto 1780, 16–17).

Do Couto suspects that all this is a Sri Lankan reworking of the Christian
story of Saint Josaphat, who was converted by Barlaam.[36] In his view, the
"ancient heathens of these parts" must have known the tale of the Christian
saint's life and then added to it many fables to tell the life of Budaō. He then
further recalls his conversation with a very old man in the caves at Canará
(i.e., Kāṇherī [Yule and Burnell 1903, 477]), near Mumbai, who told him
the temples there were carved out of the rock "by order of the father of Saint
Josaphat." Do Couto surmises that the caves were later mistaken to have
been Buddhist sites (Do Couto 1780, 16–17; Eng. trans., Ferguson [1908]
1993, 114).[37]

36. In fact, the story of Barlaam and Josaphat is a Christianization of a biography of the
Buddha. Yule (in Polo 1993, 2: 325n) claims that Do Couto was the first to note this parallel,
even though he got the direction of influence wrong. On the place of the Barlaam and Josaphat
story in Western understandings of Buddhism, see Almond 1987; and Strong 2016, 142–143.

37. The Portuguese assumption that the Buddha (or at least his life story) must have a Christian basis was common. Do Couto (Ferguson [1908] 1993, 114–115) is of the opinion that the
footprint on Adam's Peak was that of Saint Thomas, and Ribeiro ([1685] 1899, 119) mentions

But Do Couto's account of the Buddha does not end with his great departure from home. Summarizing, he goes on to say:

> Omitting many fables that they [the local people] relate, both of his flight and his wanderings, after passing through many countries, they say that he came to Ceilaō [Ceylon], bringing with him a great concourse of disciples. There on that mountain [Adam's Peak] he led such a life for so many years that the natives worshipped him as [a] god; at which point his name was changed from Dramá Rajo [Dharmarāja] to Budaō [Buddha]. Then desiring to depart thence for other parts, his disciples who remained there begged him to leave them some memorial of him, that they might reverence it in his name; whereupon planting his foot upon that slab, he impressed that footprint, which continued to be held in much veneration. (Ferguson [1908] 1993, 113, slightly altered; original text in Do Couto 1780, 14–15)[38]

But Do Couto's account of the Buddha's life is also connected to the story of the tooth, for, as we have seen, he further declares that the Buddha was "a great saint [who], after visiting Ceylon, travelled over [to] Pegu and adjacent countries, converting the heathen and working miracles; and, death approaching, he wrenched this tooth from its socket, and sent it to Ceylon as the greatest of relics. So highly was it venerated by the Sinhalese and by all the people of the kingdom of Pegu, that they esteemed it above all other treasures" (Tennent 1859, 2: 213; original text in Do Couto 1783, 317).

Inklings of this tale, as we have seen, are already found in De Barros, and much the same thing is reiterated by subsequent Portuguese historians. Trindade ([1630–1636] 1962–1967, 3, 181), for example, tells us that:

> They [the Sri Lankans] had it that this tooth was that of their Buddha whom they held to be a great saint who, after leaving Ceylon where he had been doing great wonders for many years, went to the kingdom of Pegu, teaching

---

the view that the Buddha was actually none other than Saint Thomas, though the locals in their confusion failed to recognize this.

38. Other traditions speak of the Buddha at this time straddling the whole of Sri Lanka by planting his other foot north of Anurādhapura and leaving a second footprint there. See Legge [1886] 1965, 204. Queiros (1930, 38) tells us of a belief that the Buddha put one foot on the coast of southern India, near Thootukudi, and the other on Śrī Pada. Obeyesekere (1984, 307) refers to a Sinhalese folk belief that the Buddha "planted one of his footprints in the sands of Mecca and the other on Śrī Pada," and that there was a great stupa for his relic in Mecca called the "Makkama Mahā Vehera" [the Great Vihāra of Mecca], and that one of the Buddha's epithets was consequently "Makama Muni—the Sage of Mecca."

to all the true law that they have, and doing amazing miracles; and when he
was about to die, he took that tooth out of his mouth and sent it to Ceylon in
remembrance and as a memory of him, where he was so highly esteemed that
there was no object more holy and divine for all the Orientals.[39]

Similarly, Ribeiro ([1685] 1899, 31), the Portuguese soldier who was in
Ceylon from 1640 to 1658, declares that "the gentiles believed that this was
the tooth of Budão who had gone from Ceilão making converts and working miracles throughout Pegu and all the other kingdoms, and that when he
was at the point of death he had taken this tooth and sent it to Ceilão to be
preserved as a memorial of himself."

The generally accepted Portuguese view at this time, then, was that the
Buddha (a) spent quite a bit of time in Sri Lanka in the vicinity of Adam's
Peak; (b) eventually left Sri Lanka for Pegu; and (c) just before his death
there, extracted a tooth from his mouth and sent it back to the people of
Lanka. This was the tooth that the Portuguese captured. It is worth pausing
to consider each of these points in turn, and to ask where Do Couto and the
others may have gotten them.

The Portuguese were by no means the first to associate the Buddha with
Sri Lanka. From early on, accounts of his life connect him with the island.
For instance, as a preface to his description of Adam's Peak (which we touched
on in the last chapter), Marco Polo gives us a synopsis of the Buddha's early
life that is much the same as Do Couto's, with the difference that Polo locates it entirely in Ceylon and omits his travels to Pegu. For him, the Buddha
was a native Sri Lankan, the son of a local king, and his cult there is to be
explained in euhemeristic terms: after he died, his father was so aggrieved by
his son's death that he had a statue made of him, which he made his people
worship. In this way the prince (the Buddha) came to be divinized: "[The
people] do hold him for the greatest of all their gods. And they tell that the
aforesaid image of him was the first idol that the Idolaters ever had; and
from that have originated all the other idols. And this befell in the Island
of Seilan in India" (Polo 1993, 317–319). Polo then goes on (1993, 322),
as we have seen, to talk about the tooth and bowl relics of the Buddha on
Adam's Peak, though he makes no mention of a footprint there.

Do Couto (like De Barros before him) was familiar with Marco Polo's
account, but he disputes this view of the Buddha as a native Sri Lankan, for

---

39. See also De Sousa 1710, 199. It is noteworthy that the differently informed Queiros (see
below) makes no mention of any of this, though he gives a lengthy account of the life of the
Buddha.

he knows that the Buddha was born in India, at some point came to the island, and then left it (Do Couto 1780, 10; Eng. trans., Ferguson [1908] 1993, 109). Though he never mentions it, this view should ultimately be related to Pali and Sinhalese legends of the Buddha's three "apocryphal" visits to the island. According to the *Mahāvaṃsa*, on the first of these, after chasing away all the demons, the Blessed One converts, among other beings, Mahāsumana, the god of Adam's Peak, to whom he gives some hair relics. On his third and final journey, he actually visits Adam's Peak, marks the mountaintop with his footprint, and then spends the day in meditation at the foot of the mountain at a place that later came to be known as Divāguhā (Divine Cave) (*Mahāvaṃsa* 1908, 5–6, 10–11; Eng. trans., Geiger 1912, 3–9).[40]

Sri Lanka, however, was not the only place visited by the Buddha, according to Buddhist "apocryphal" traditions. Do Couto's tale of the Buddha going on to Pegu and extracting his tooth prior to his death also recalls a Mon tradition from Lower Burma, preserved, from the time of the Burmese King Dhammazedi (r. 1472–1492), in three virtually identical inscriptions at famous pagodas near Pegu.[41] The Mon legend states that in the eighth year of the Buddha's ministry (the same year in which, according to the *Mahāvaṃsa*, he made his third visit to Sri Lanka), he flew through the air from India to the kingdom of Lower Burma (Suvaṇṇabhūmi), at the invitation of his disciple Gavāmpati, who originally hailed from that region. There, he met the local Burmese king and preached to the people for seven days. When it came time for him to leave, the king asked him for a relic—that is, something that he could worship in the Buddha's stead after his departure. On that occasion, the Buddha turned down the king's request, but promised him that, at the time of his parinirvāṇa, he would oblige him by sending him one of his teeth. Thirty-seven years later, as the Buddha lay on his deathbed in India,

40. Both Adam's Peak and Divāguhā later came to be included in the Sinhalese list of the Sixteen Great Pilgrimage Places in Sri Lanka (see Gombrich 1971, 107–108). The present site of Divāguhā is disputed, though some identify it with the Batatotalena Cave in Sudagala. It should be noted that the tradition of the Buddha's visit to Adam's Peak on his third journey to Sri Lanka, though found in the *Mahāvaṃsa*, is not mentioned in the *Dīpavaṃsa* (see Oldenberg [1879] 1982, 128–129), the *Bāhiranidāna* (Jayawickrama 1962, 79), or the *Rājāvaliya*, although the latter text does say that on his third visit, the Buddha "stayed a minute at each of the sixteen sacred places" before returning to India (see Guṇasékara 1900, 14). Moreover, the *Mahāvaṃsa* itself was not at all widely known in Sri Lanka in Do Couto's time, though some of its traditions were (see Kemper 1991, 80–83). One wonders if it is a coincidence that the *Mahāvaṃsa* (the only ancient text to mention Adam's Peak by name in its account of the Buddha's voyages) was found in the monastery at Mulgirigala, which, some claimed, was that very mountain.

41. Dhammazedi was originally a monk who became ruler of Pegu and whose reign marked the start of Pegu's glory as a center of trade and of Theravāda Buddhism. On Dhammazedi's relations with Kotte, see Blackburn 2015, 247–251.

he remembered his promise, extracted a tooth from his mouth, and gave it to his disciple Gavāṃpati, who took it back with him to offer it to the king of Lower Burma (Shorto 1970, 16–17; see also Stadtner 2011, 147–148).[42]

Although I have seen no direct evidence of this, the Portuguese may well have been familiar with this legend from their extensive contacts with merchants and officials in Pegu, starting in 1519 and continuing throughout the sixteenth century, or from their countrymen or other foreigners who lived in Pegu at that time.[43] The only real change Do Couto makes to the story is to have the Buddha send the tooth to Sri Lanka rather than Pegu—a change obviously brought on by his desire to explain how the tooth got to the island in the first place.[44]

All this emphasis on Pegu may also help explain the growing Lusitanian awareness of the distinctiveness of Buddhism. Simply put, for the Portuguese in the time of Viceroy Dom Constantino, the king of Pegu was more obviously a Buddhist, in comparison, say, to Sri Lankan rulers. As Do Couto put it, Pegu was known, above all, as a kingdom "where they worship and venerate that idol called Budaõ" (Ferguson [1908] 1993, 108; original text in Do Couto 1780, 5–6)—something he never says about Sri Lanka.

This fits with the growing Portuguese assertion that it was primarily the king of Pegu in Burma (and not the Vijayanagara emperor) who actually made the offer to ransom the tooth. Simply put, after Do Couto, whenever the tooth is said to be the Buddha's, the ransom offerer is said to come from Pegu. This is not the case with earlier (pre–Do Couto) Portuguese sources, which are rather vague in identifying potential ransomers. Pimenta (see Purchas [1625] 1905, 208–209) states only that the "Ethnikes" (natives) offered 300,000 ducats for the tooth of Hanumān. Texeira (1715, 251; original text in Texeira 1610, 272) is even less precise, saying that a "vast treasure" was offered for the monkey's tooth, by the "neighboring infidels" around Goa. The same vagueness may be found in some early non-Portuguese sources. Pyrard de Laval (1619, 2: 152) simply states that "they" (unspecified indig-

42. This tooth then miraculously replicates itself into thirty-two relics that are then enshrined in the thirty-two provinces of the Pegu kingdom, with the original staying in the capital. See Shorto 1963.

43. For one foreigner's account of life in Pegu in the late sixteenth century, see Balbi 1590, 108ff (Eng. trans., Balbi 2003, 26–34). We will encounter another example below—the case of the merchant Martin Alfonso de Mello, who acted as a middleman for the king of Pegu in his negotiations over the tooth and who could have been familiar with this Gavāṃpati story.

44. If Do Couto had been more familiar with Sri Lankan traditions, he would have known that the tooth relic was not thought to have come to the island until the reign of Sirimeghavaṇṇa in the fourth century CE. See Strong 2004b, 194.

enous peoples) offered "great riches" for the tooth. Our earliest source, Van Linschoten (Van Linschoten 1885, 1: 292–294), does mention Pegu as one of the interested parties, along with Sion [= Mumbai], Bengala, and other countries, but then turns his attention to Vijayanagara, which, he says, "sent ambassadors to the Viceroy in Goa with offers of as much as 700,000 gold ducats."[45] Du Jarric (1610, 397–398; Gaspard 1918, 15–17) is a bit of an exception: while acknowledging that the loss of Hanumān's tooth was "deplored [by] the King of Jaffna and several other princes of India," he does affirm that it was the king of Pegu who "offered straight off 300,000 crowns [écus] . . . partly in gold and partly in kind, so ready was he to pay any price for it."

Generally speaking, though, the emphasis on the king of Pegu as the ransom-giver starts with Do Couto's identification of the tooth as the Buddha's; or conversely, perhaps, we should say that the emphasis on the tooth as the Buddha's starts with the identification of Pegu as the chief ransom-giver. We may well have a chicken-and-egg situation here: Pegu's perceived interest in the tooth could prompt the Portuguese to stress its Buddhist identity, while, in stressing the tooth's Buddhist identity, they might cause Pegu to be interested in it.

Do Couto, in fact, devotes a whole chapter to the account of the ransom offer, claiming it was arranged by a Portuguese intermediary:

> Martin Alfonso de Mello happened to be in Pegu with his ship on business, when the viceroy, Don Constantine, returned to Goa from Jaffna-patam, and the king [of Pegu], hearing that the "tooth" which was so profoundly revered by all Buddhists had been carried off, summoned Martin Alfonso to his presence, and besought him, on his return to India, to entreat the Viceroy to surrender it, offering to give in exchange whatever might be demanded for it. And those who know the Peguans, and the devotion with which they regard this relic of the devil, affirmed that the king would have given *three* or even *four hundred thousand cruzadoes* to obtain possession of it. On the advice of Martin Alfonso, the king dispatched ambassadors to accompany him to the Viceroy in this affair and empowered them to signify his readiness to ratify any agreement to which they might assent on his behalf. On reaching Goa, in April 1561, Martin Alfonso apprised the Viceroy of the arrival of the envoys, who . . . [formally] made a request for the tooth on behalf of their sovereign,

45. It is noteworthy that, in all of our sources, those vying for the tooth are "foreigners." The only account I know of that says otherwise is Herbert ([1634] 1638, 306), who declares that it was "the Zeylonians who proffered 300,000 duckets" for the tooth.

offering in return any terms that might be required, with a proposal for a perpetual alliance with Portugal, and an undertaking to provision the fortress of Malacca at all times when called upon; together with many other conditions and promises. (Tennent 1859, 2: 213–214; original text in De Couto 1783, 428–429; see also Ferguson [1908] 1993, 211–213)[46]

Arjun Appadurai (1986, 5) reminds us that value is embodied in commodities that are exchanged, that "even though from a *theoretical* point of view human actors encode things with significance, from a *methodological* point of view, it is the things-in-motion that illuminate their human and social context." Consequently, the destruction of a thing such as a relic represents not only a destruction of value but also a destruction of exchange. By destroying the Buddha's tooth, the Portuguese are refusing an exchange-relationship—with Pegu, but also, as we shall see, with Kandy.

Further Growth in the Knowledge of Buddhism and the Realization of Its Pan-Asian Nature

Do Couto's better (though still somewhat shaky) understanding of Buddhism, or at least the Buddha's life story, and of its importance to a place like Pegu, continued to grow among the Portuguese. When we get to Queiros's *Temporal and Spiritual Conquest of Ceylon* (1686), we find four full chapters dedicated to an explanation of the beliefs and practices of Buddhism, which is now explicitly distinguished from Hinduism. On this distinction, Queiros (1930, 118) is emphatic: "It is absolutely necessary not to confuse this sect [i.e., Buddhism] with that of the Veddaõs or of the Bramanes, a mistake into which some have fallen."[47]

In chapter 16 of book one, Queiros (1930, 118–119) asks outright, "Who are the Religious of the Sect of Buddum?" and he answers, first, with a de-

46. Much the same basic information is found in the works of subsequent Portuguese historians. Trindade ([1630–1636] 1962–1967, 3: 182) and Francisco de Sousa (1710, 195–196) basically repeat Do Couto, the former pointing out that, of all the monarchs in the area, it was the king of Pegu who worked the hardest at getting the tooth that he so longed for. Ribeiro ([1685] 1701, 118) ups the offer of the king of Pegu (and again changes the currency unit) to 800,000 pounds.

47. See also Queiros 1930, 78: "Though some writers confuse the Vedaõ with the sect of Buddum, Foe or Xaca (for he has all these names in different nations), they are certainly distinct, and both are received among all the nations of further India beyond Ceylon and the Ganges and in the Asiatic Tartary." On the other hand, as Strathern (2005, 55) points out, there are also examples of when Queiros *did* confuse these two traditions.

scription of Sri Lankan Buddhist monasteries, their place in society, the functions and hierarchy of their monks, and so forth. He then gives a not too inaccurate summary of the legend of the Buddha as "it is recorded in the Chingala (Sinhalese) scriptures": the tale of his birth in Delhi, of his father's desire for him to become a great king, of his life in the palace, of his seeing the four signs and wandering forth, and so on, not failing to mention the story of his coming to Adam's Peak, but omitting the tale of the Buddha's wrenching the tooth from his mouth on his deathbed. He contrasts Buddha images with "obscene and foul" and monstrous idols of the Hindus, and describes favorably the rites of Sinhalese devotees: "The worship they pay him is to prostrate themselves on the ground three times repeating the words *Buddum Sarnaõ Gachaõ* as if to say: Buddum, be Mindful of me."[48] To be sure, Queiros (1930, 120) is critical of Buddhist doctrine (e.g., the "transmigration of souls," which he likens to the views of Plato and Pythagoras), but he also concedes that though the Buddha is venerated in many countries, "it is doubtful whether he leads more to perdition than shameful Mahomet, whom he preceded by more than 1400 years."[49]

Queiros's views also reflect the gradual realization of the pan-Asian nature of Buddhism, extending beyond South and Southeast Asia, as did the reaches of the Portuguese. Specifically, he realizes that the Buddha's names in different places ("the Buddum of Ceylon, the Fô of China, the Xaka [Shaka] of Japan") all refer to one and the same figure,[50] and that the monks in various regions ("the Ganezes [*ganinanses*] of Ceylon, the Talpoys [talapoin] of Arracan, Pegu, Siam and other neighbouring realms, as well as the Lamazes [lamas] of Tartary and the Bonzes of China and Japan") all "agree in the essentials of their sect and profession" (Queiros 1930, 140–141).[51] This was a

48. The reference here is to the refuge formula "Buddham saraṇam gacchāmi" (I go to the Buddha for my refuge). See Strathern's comments on Queiros's translation (2005, 72).

49. Strathern (2005, 52) states that Queiros "had a bookish erudition regarding Sri Lankan culture and the version of Theravada Buddhism practiced there that was probably unrivalled in his time." He also points out (2005, 65), however, that although Queiros's views of Buddhism were not "comprehensively and consistently negative," they do "show a visceral disgust at all forms of 'idolatry' and it is not difficult to picture him serving in the Inquisition of Goa, an office that he discharged for 16 years."

50. This was also realized in 1690 by Engelbert Kaempfer, whose book, however, was not published until 1727 (see Lopez 2016, 1, 115–122). According to App (2012, 42; see also Lopez 2016, 237n1), the first person to make this realization was the Japan-based Jesuit Melchior Nunes Barreto.

51. Today, we may agree or disagree with such conclusions, but the realization of unity was important in its time. See Strong 2015, xix–xx.

realization that came much earlier to the Portuguese than it did to the British or French,[52] probably because of the pan-Asian nature of their empire and the stationing of Jesuit missionaries in all of these lands—Jesuits who tended to be in contact with one another, and very well informed about the languages, cultures, and religious beliefs in their area (Magone 2012, 270–271).[53]

Thus Queiros, being a Jesuit himself, and realizing that "the Buddum of Ceylon is the same as the Fô of China," simply writes to his confrère in Beijing, Father Thomas Pereira,[54] for more information. The latter replies by sending him a synopsis of an illustrated 190-chapter Chinese biography of the Buddha, which Queiros reproduces, with acknowledgment, as chapters 17, 18, and 19 of his book (Queiros 1930, 122–141). This constitutes what was for its day (1687) probably the most comprehensive and detailed account of the legend of Śākyamuni in any European language, and, had Queiros's manuscript not been confined for over two centuries to an archive, first in Lisbon and then in Rio, the history of the West's "discovery" of the life of the Buddha might have been quite different.[55] Chapter 17 covers "The Birth and Life of Fô up to the Thirtieth Year of Age," chapter 18, "The Life of Fô, from the Thirtieth Year Till he became Old," and chapter 19, "The Old Age and Death of Fô and what Happened after his Death." This latter

52. As Almond (1988, 9) points out, various British encyclopedias in the early nineteenth century still failed to make the connection between different names of the Buddha, while the 1777 edition of the *Dictionnaire historique des cultes religieux* gives separate entries (with no cross-references) for "Buddhu," "Chacabout" [Śākyamuni], and "Fo" (see Lubac 1952, 123). It will be remembered that Queiros's book was not published until 1916. The same point is made more generally in Masuzawa 2005, 122.

53. On the Jesuit acquisition of knowledge about "pagan" religions, see Xavier and Županov 2015, 119–157. For more on Queiros's understanding of the pan-Asian nature of Buddhism, see Županov 2010, 56.

54. Thomas Pereira (1645–1708) was a Portuguese Jesuit, mathematician, musician, and scholar of Chinese who spent over thirty years in China, most of it at the court of the emperor Kangxi of the Qing Dynasty. On his relationship and correspondence with Queiros, see Magone 2012; and Županov 2010.

55. On some of the reasons for the exclusion of such Jesuit materials from Orientalist discourse, see Županov 2010, 43–46. Pereira's text has affinities with the *Shijia rulai yinghua lu* [The account of the apparition on earth of the Buddha of the Śākyas] by the monk Baocheng (1368–1643), later translated by another Jesuit, Léon Wieger ([1913] 2002). Rui Magone (2012, 260–263), however, has argued that its actual source is more likely a text closely related to the *Shishiyuanliu yinghua shiji* [The origins, transformations and deeds of Buddha], a deluxe edition of the life of the Buddha, published at the imperial court in 1486. A facsimile of a somewhat later edition of the latter may be found in the Library of Congress's World Digital Library (see http://www.wdl.org/en/item/293). See also Lesbre 2002; Faure 2018, 279–282; and Strong (forthcoming a). On Queiros and Pereira's importance more generally, see Lopez 2013, 97–99; and Lopez 2016, 4.

part includes a description of the division of the Buddha's relics by Droṇa (between the devas, the nāgas, and the eight kings on earth), and then ends with a mention of their further distribution into 84,000 places by King Aśoka (Queiros 1930, 138–139).[56] Though Queiros makes no mention of the later Sri Lankan tradition that explains how the tooth relic got to the island in the fourth century CE, neither does he echo Do Couto's tale (which he clearly does not credit) that it was wrenched from the Buddha's mouth on his deathbed.

Indeed, Pereira's text in Queiros makes no mention of any tooth relics or of their going to Sri Lanka, nor does Queiros highlight this lack of reference. Instead, he comments on the similarity of Buddhist beliefs throughout Asia, and concludes by reasserting his view that if Buddhism and the Buddha seem attractive, it is because Satan has made them so to thwart missionary endeavors:

> If intelligent Europeans wonder, considering what it is that such intelligent people embrace as true, let them remember what heathen Europe so pertinaciously believed and worshipped. The fact is the Devil has forestalled everything. When we preach to the heathens [i.e., Hindus] in hither India, they reply that they also have a Trinity, and that their Vixnu incarnated himself times out of number; if we preach to those of further India [Southeast Asia] and of Ceylon (for this Sect [Buddhism] has disappeared from many parts of India wherein it began), they reply that their Buddum or their Fô or their Xaka also took the shape of a man, though he was an eternal being. And as the Religious of this Sect have a great reputation . . . it is a very difficult matter to convert any of his sectaries. (Queiros 1930, 141)

Though Queiros makes no mention of the Buddha's tooth relic in the context of his discussion of the pan-Asian nature of Buddhism, his list of those kingdoms willing to ransom the relic does reflect that realization, for he specifies (1930, 364–365) that it was not just the king of Pegu who was willing to offer the "greatest treasure" for the tooth but also the rulers of "Siam, Tartary, China, and Japan and in other smaller kingdoms where it is worshipped."

Francisco de Sousa, writing in 1710, picks up on this theme and does refer to tooth relics as a feature of Buddhism everywhere. In some ways, De Sousa is more informed than Queiros, but in others, he could have greatly

---

56. For a more easily accessible version of this text, see Lopez 2016, 75–94.

benefited from the latter's work, had it been available to him.[57] His account starts with a summary of the standard Portuguese understanding of the life of the Buddha, probably taken from De Barros: he was the son of a king of Delhi; he spread his false doctrines in India, and then in Ceylon, and then went to Pegu where, on his deathbed, "he took a tooth from his mouth and sent it to Ceylon as a pledge of his love [for the people of the island]. This is the tooth that the Peguans, belonging to the same Buddhist sect, wanted to recoup at whatever expense" (De Sousa 1710, 198). Then, however, he goes on as follows:

> This Budu of Pegu is the same as the Shaka of Japan, and in the city of Meaco [Miyako, i.e., Kyoto], the court of that empire, there is displayed a tooth of his with unbelievable solemnity, and when they want rain or sun, they take it out of the temple, and expose it to the air.[58] If Buddha preached to the Japanese, as some people write, it may be that he gave them another tooth as a testimony [just as he did for the people of Ceylon]. . . . According to the best information, an Emperor of China, in 605 AD, sent five very clever men to study the [Buddhist] doctrine which in the course of time, spread to Korea, and from there passed to Japan. By this same way went the tooth. (De Sousa 1710, 198–199)

De Sousa is here adding to the parallels between Sri Lankan and East Asian Buddhism, by pointing out that they both worship tooth relics of the same Buddha. The tooth De Sousa refers to as being venerated in Kyoto, then the imperial (though not the shogunal) capital of Japan, may be the same as that which was brought from China in the early thirteenth century during the reign of the shogun Sanetomo. First housed in Kamakura, at the end of the fourteenth century it was moved to the Shōkōkuji temple, north of the present-day imperial palace in Kyoto. Alternatively, it may be the tooth relic that was brought back from China (also in the thirteenth century) by the monk Tankai, and enshrined at the Sennyūji, a temple in Kyoto that later became the site of the tombs of virtually all the emperors during the Tokugawa period (Strong and Strong 1995, 6–8).[59]

---

57. De Sousa makes no mention of Queiros's magnum opus which, in his day, would have existed only in a single manuscript copy in Lisbon.

58. Relics in general were commonly used in rainmaking ceremonies in Japan (see Ruppert 2000, 234–235). On the use of the tooth relic for rainmaking in Sri Lanka, see Strong 2004b, 198–199.

59. The Sennyūji relic became the subject of a Nō play by the dramatist Zeami (1363–1443).

We have seen that Queiros emphasized the pan-Asian nature of the Buddhist tradition: here was a religion that had expanded to take over the whole continent—from Sri Lanka to Japan—that had, in other words, managed to do what the Portuguese themselves (or at least the Jesuits) had tried to do with Christianity, and that Queiros, for one, hoped they would do again. In this way, Queiros, at least, saw Buddhism as being in competition with Roman Catholicism for the hearts of all Asians.[60] Indeed, as we have seen above, he complains that it is the presence of Buddhists in "thither India" that makes Portuguese proselytizing difficult. Francisco de Sousa appears to take this one step further, realizing, in his own way, that the Buddha's tooth relic was symbolic of this expansion, since, just as Christian relics went with the Portuguese Empire wherever it advanced, so too had Buddhist ones.

Pamila Gupta, in an interesting study of the whole-body relic of Saint Francis Xavier entitled *The Relic State*, has argued that the saint's body that was enshrined in Goa in 1554 acted as a kind of somatic marker of the fortunes of the Portuguese Empire in Asia. At the beginning, both the saint and the state were "incorrupt," showing no signs of decay. By 1624, they both had suffered "amputations" (Xavier's arm was commandeered by the main Jesuit church in Rome, and the Portuguese were gradually losing Sri Lanka and other parts of East Asia to the Dutch); by 1782, the saint and the state were "dessicated"; by 1859, they were "shrinking"; by 1952, they were "in parts"; and by 1961, when India took over Goa, the Portuguese tried (without success) to move Xavier's body back to Portugal, as a "last colonial act" (Gupta 2004, 26–27).[61]

There is a similar sense, as we shall see, that the fortunes of the tooth relic were seen by the Portuguese (or at least were wishfully seen by them) as a kind of counter-marker of the health of Sri Lanka, and more broadly of Buddhism in general. In this light, we may perhaps better understand not only the Portuguese destruction of the tooth relic, but, more immediately, why it changed its identity.

60. More specifically, Queiros believed in the prophetic Christian destiny of Sri Lanka as the nation that would be regained from the Dutch and that would lead the way to the Portuguese establishment of Catholicism throughout the world. Interestingly, Strathern (2005, 52) compares this to the Theravāda view that the Buddha had consecrated Sri Lanka as the place where his true teachings would be preserved. This, he suggests, presented the Portuguese with "a further motivation to develop a Christian Providentialism, to compete with or colonise this long-standing Buddhist myth."

61. Many of the dates correspond to actual medical examinations of Xavier's relic-body, on which see also Gupta 2010. See also Gupta 2014.

As mentioned above, when the Portuguese first established themselves in Goa in 1510, their chief orientation and encounter was with other powers in the immediate Indian Ocean region (the empire of Vijayanagar, the Zamorin of Calicut, and the Near Eastern Muslim merchants who dominated the spice trade).[62] It was not long, however, before Portuguese horizons expanded farther east, to Southeast Asia (e.g., Pegu), and China and Japan, which they reached by 1543. Just as Buddhism had established a presence throughout the whole continent, so now the Portuguese were hoping to do so by showing themselves to be masters of the Buddha.

This sense of competition with Buddhism also came to be felt locally in Sri Lanka. This is best seen, perhaps, in the work of Dom Filipe Botelho, who, in his 1633 work, *Jornada de Uva* (Expedition to Uva), presents the conflicts in Sri Lanka as "the climax of a war of religion." For him, "Buddhism is the first enemy of Catholicism, much as Islam was the major threat to fifteenth-century Portugal" (Flores and Cruz 2007, 112). Botelho was a Sinhalese convert to Christianity from a family closely associated with King João Dharmapala that had followed him in adopting Roman Catholicism. Born in Colombo, he was educated by the Jesuits and became a Catholic priest. His main objective, in the face of increasing threats to Portuguese hegemony on the island, was to preserve the Catholic inheritance of the kingdom of Kotte "by denying political authority to the kingdom of Kandy as well as religious legitimacy to Buddhism" (Flores and Cruz 2007, 123).

The Portuguese Desire to Counter Rival Claims to the Tooth

The same sentiment can be found in two stories that several of our sources relate about the reappearance of tooth relics—fake ones, according to the Portuguese—after the destruction of the "original" one in Goa. The first of these tales concerns the king of Pegu, the second the king of Kandy. Together, they point to another reason for the Portuguese identifying the tooth as that of the Buddha: their realization that others were claiming to be in its possession and to thereby have legitimacy as rulers—and their desire to undermine those claims through these stories.

The appearance of "fake tooth relics" was actually a thematic thread from early on. As we have seen, Van Linschoten already states that, not long after the Portuguese destruction of the tooth of the monkey, a crafty Hindu

---

62. For a discussion of this context, see Mathew 1986.

merchant got another ape's tooth, and made the Indians and heathens believe that it was the same as that which the viceroy had captured—and that the Portuguese thought they had burned—because, actually, a god who had been there, invisible, had saved the tooth from destruction, by taking it away and substituting another, false one, in its place. All this, the merchant claimed, had been revealed to him in a vision by the god in question who, after orchestrating this operation, had delivered the true tooth to him, the merchant. This story, Linschoten adds, was believed by the king of Vijayanagar, who "desired the merchant to send the tooth to him, and with great joy received it, giving him a great sum of gold for it. And the tooth was then again [in Vijayanagar] held and kept in the same honor and esteem as it had been [in Ceylon]" (Van Linschoten 1885, 294).

Soon, however, probably with the gradual waning of the kingdom of Vijayanagar, it is no longer a crafty merchant who is panhandling a fake tooth, but João Dharmapala, the Christian monarch of Kotte, and it is no longer a monkey's tooth that is the subject of this subterfuge, but the Buddha's, and the duped king is no longer the ruler of Vijayanagar, but the king of Pegu, the very same monarch who was so eager to obtain the tooth by ransoming it from the Portuguese.

This king, whom Do Couto does not actually name but calls simply the Bramá king, was none other than Bayinnaung (1516–1581), one of the great sovereigns in Burmese history, who ruled an empire that extended far beyond the borders of present-day Myanmar. Do Couto first mentions the story of his being deceived in his initial account of the capture of the tooth in Decada VII, as evidence of the tooth's great value to the natives (Do Couto 1783, 317–318; Eng. trans., Ferguson [1908] 1993, 191–192). He then returns to it more fully in Decada VIII, after his account of the refusal of the ransom offer and of the destruction of the tooth in Goa. He describes at some length how King Bayinnaung, conscious of a prediction that he is destined to marry the daughter of the king of Ceylon, sends ambassadors to King João Dharmapala of Kotte to make inquiries. Dharmapala, eager to accept the offer, pretends to have a daughter (when in fact he does not) and goes forward with arrangements for the alliance, keeping them secret from the Portuguese. At the same time, he sees an opportunity to make money: having become aware of the Burmese interest in the tooth relic and their willingness to spend vast sums for it, he has a facsimile of the tooth fashioned out of a stag's horn and puts it in a costly gold reliquary adorned with all sorts of gems. He then has his chamberlain secretly let it be known to the Peguan ambassadors that what the Portuguese had captured and smashed was not the real tooth of the Buddha; rather, his master, the king of Kotte, has had it all along, though he can no longer worship it openly because he has become a Christian at the insistence of the Portuguese. Learning this, the Burmese envoys—both lay and monastic—express their fervent desire to see and venerate the relic. Accordingly, the chamberlain, with feigned excess of caution and repeated entreaties that they must tell no one about this—for the Portuguese must be kept in the dark!—takes the ambassadors at night to worship the staghorn tooth on a decorated altar set up for the purpose in his own house. Having thus viewed and worshipped the tooth, and believing it to be the genuine item, the envoys beg the chamberlain to let them take it back with them to Pegu, as a further enhancement of the wedding and the alliance. In exchange, they are willing to give the king of Kotte a million in gold and, every year, a ship laden with rice (Do Couto 1786, 76–77; Eng. trans., Ferguson [1908] 1993, 244–246; and Tennent 1859, 2: 217–218).

The chamberlain makes a great show of reluctance and only pretends gradually to be convinced. But eventually, it is arranged: the fake bride is sent first and is received in Pegu with great pomp and circumstance. The ambassadors then return with the promised boatload of treasure, and, in exchange, get the fake tooth, whose subsequent reception in Burma, Do Couto spends several pages in describing. In due time, according to Do Couto, the king of Pegu comes to find out that he has been doubly duped—that neither his new wife nor the relic is "genuine"—but by then the Sinhalese "princess" has already become his queen, and the tooth has been received by his people with such fervor and enshrined in a new pagoda especially built for it that he resolves to cover up the affair so as to avoid losing face.[63] All this, Do Couto says, he knows from his friend Antonio Toscano, who was at the time in Pegu and was an eyewitness to these events, and who subsequently became his (Do Couto's) neighbor in Goa (Do Couto 1786, 78–88; Eng. trans., Ferguson [1908] 1993, 250–253; and Tennent 1859, 2: 219–221).[64]

It is, of course, possible that this "fake" relic was actually the "genuine" one that had originally been in Kotte and that what the Portuguese destroyed was a replica.[65] Of this, we shall never be sure, but we do know, from

---

63. It is unclear whether Bayinnaung himself initially thought his tooth relic was "genuine" or not, but his subjects clearly did (Phayre [1883] 1967, 117–118). Do Couto (see Ferguson [1908] 1993, 249) claims he found out his new queen was not actually Dom Joaõ's daughter from some Chinese merchants who had been told by the Portuguese envoy who had accompanied her to Pegu.

64. This whole episode is recounted in a lively manner in Collis 1943, 192–205.

65. It has been argued that the king of Kotte would never have given away or sold the tooth. However, as Maung Htin Aung (1967, 126) points out, Joaõ Dharmapala was a Christian (and

Burmese stories, that Bayinnaung, the ruler of Pegu at this time, did obtain a tooth relic from Kotte that (whether "genuine" or not) he enshrined in the Mahazedi in his capital.[66] This supposedly took place between 1574 and 1576,[67] and marked the culmination of Bayinnaung's ambition to possess the relic. In this, he apparently wanted to outdo his great eleventh-century predecessor, King Anawrahta, who had tried to get the Sri Lankan tooth relic for enshrinement in his Shwezigon Pagoda, but only managed to obtain a miraculously emanated clone of the original (Pe Maung Tin and Luce [1923] 1960, 88–91). The Portuguese themselves seem to have been aware of Bayinnaung's infatuation, since, as Trindade ([1630–1636] 1962–1967, 3, 181) put it, they knew that "each year, the king of Pegu used to send his ambassadors to Ceilão with rich gifts to let him get an imprint, as a wax seal, of the precious tooth [in Kotte], in a mass of amber, civet, musk and other aromatic confections that they brought in a pot of gold." Along these same lines, in 1555, distressed by news that the Portuguese had despoiled the temple of the tooth in Kotte, Bayinnaung sent to it many offerings and the wherewithal for beautifying its sanctuary,[68] and, famously, a broom made of his own hair and one from that of his chief queen for sweeping its steps.[69]

The Portuguese, not only those living in Burma but in Goa as well, would certainly have been aware of the presence of this Buddha relic in Pegu, and of the prestige and legitimacy it granted to the Peguan king. The story that it was a fake, if not their own whole-cloth invention, seems at least to have been retold and embellished by them, in an effort to undermine that prestige

---

so presumably no longer devoted to the tooth), and was in need of money, while his chamberlain was a Buddhist, who may well have wanted the tooth to be secure in a Buddhist land (while making a bit of money at the same time).

66. The Burmese claim that he also got the bowl relic at this time. When Pegu was destroyed, the relics were taken to Toungoo. Thence, the tooth was transferred to Ava, and finally, in the seventeenth century, to Sagaing, where it supposedly remains today. For an account and a description of the modern Kaung Hmu Daw pagoda in Sagaing where the tooth and bowl are thought to be enshrined today, see Stadtner 2011, 234–239. See also Htin Aung 1997.

67. See Harvey's ([1925] 1967, 344) reference to the *Hmannan Yazawin*—the so-called *Glass Palace Chronicle*. See also Phayre [1883] 1967, 117. Ferguson (1908, 244n1) disputes this dating and claims erroneously that the story does "not appear to be recorded in the native annals of Burma." Do Couto first wrote Decada VIII in 1613 (Bell 1924, 35). If his informant, Antonio Toscano, was alive then, he would have been an old man—thirty-eight years after 1574–1575—and even older and perhaps dead if, as Ferguson claims, the events he witnessed took place in 1562 or 1563.

68. Harvey ([1925] 1967, 172) states erroneously that Bayinnaung's presents were sent to the tooth in Kandy, but this makes no sense since, in 1555, the tooth had not yet been enshrined there.

69. This is mentioned in Bayinnaung's Shwezigon Bell Inscription. See Tun Aung Chain 2004, 108—I would like to thank Donald Stadtner for this reference. See also Htin Aung 1997.

and authority. At the same time, the story weakened any possible claim by persons in Kotte to still be in possession of the tooth, and so suggests an awareness of rumors that the tooth might have been hidden away in that kingdom and never sent to Jaffna in the first place. Reflected in all this is a new realization of the function of the tooth as a palladium of power for its possessor, and this the Portuguese could not allow. For them, their tooth alone was "genuine," and that is what they had destroyed.

Much the same reasoning most probably lies behind their story of yet another "fake" tooth—the one in Kandy. According to Do Couto, the tooth sent to Bayinnaung was not the only relic to reappear in Sri Lanka. In an addendum to the tale just told, he further claims that the king of Kandy, Dom João da Austria (aka Konappu Bandara, aka Vimaladharmasuriya I), gets wind of the saga of the king of Kotte duping the Burmese, and decides he too should get into the act. He sends his own embassy to Pegu, announcing that neither the tooth the Portuguese destroyed nor that sent by the king of Kotte was genuine; that actually, he, the king of Kandy, has had the real tooth of the Buddha all along (and that he also has a real daughter!), and that he is now willing to send them both to Burma, for a price, of course.[70] Bayinnaung, however, refuses the offer—having been duped once, he is understandably wary of being duped again—and so the tooth remains in Kandy (Do Couto 1786, 87–88; Eng. trans., Ferguson [1908] 1993, 251–252; Tennent 1859, 2: 220–221).[71]

There are some problems of chronology with this story. As we have seen, Vimaladharmasuriya did not build his temple for the tooth relic in Kandy or even claim to be in possession of it until after his defeat of Rājasinha I of Sītāwaka in 1591, as well as his great victory over the Portuguese at Danture in 1594, and his marriage (in a further effort to legitimize his usurpation of the throne) to a royal princess (Kusumasana devi, aka Dona Catarina) shortly thereafter (Holt 2007, 166–167). By then, Bayinnaung had been dead for thirteen years. It would not have been possible, therefore, for the Kandyan monarch to have ever offered him the tooth. What this tale reflects, rather, is, again, the Portuguese realization (probably sometime after 1600)

---

70. Interestingly, the word used for "Buddha" here is Quiay (or Quiar)—a term that Ferguson (1908, 246n1) says is equivalent to the Mon "kyâik," meaning Lord or Buddha.

71. This story is also told by the Reverend P. Thomas (1919, 34), who adds a unique twist, claiming that the king of Kandy, after being turned down by Bayinnaung, was worried that his attempted trickery might come to light, and so decided to start worshipping his fake tooth himself, inventing the story that it was the original tooth reconstituted in a lotus blossom after its "destruction" by the Portuguese. I would like to thank Steven Kemper for sending me a copy of Thomas's article.

of the political importance of the tooth, and their desire to undermine Kandy's claim to possess it by inventing stories to prove it was fake, while theirs—though now destroyed—was genuine.

Francisco De Sousa (1710, 199) gives a slightly different version of this story. He tells us that

> The Sinhalese pretend that Buddha's tooth sailed through the bottom of the mortar when Dom Constantino was asked to destroy it, and it proceeded to Kandy to rest on top of a beautiful rose[72] [lotus blossom?] where it was given a famous temple called Dalidagis [Daḷadā-Ge] which means the house of the sacred tooth. They invented this fable to give the Peguans to understand that the tooth was still in Ceylon.[73]

On the other hand, Queiros (1930, 1: 60) eschews such fanciful tales. As we have seen, he seems quite knowledgeable about the Temple of the Tooth in Kandy, describing it and the tooth's seven nesting reliquaries in some detail. His way of undermining the authenticity of this tooth is to clearly differentiate it from the one found in Jaffna and destroyed by Dom Constantino, which he accepts as having been the Buddha's. The Kandyan relic, he declares, was simply the tooth of a buffalo (Queiros 1930, 1: 59–60).

Chapter Summary

Throughout all of this chapter, the Portuguese tooth has remained a tooth. In other words, its nature as a material object has had primacy over its identity; the tooth comes first, and only then is it given definition—a definition which, I have argued, varies and gradually changes from one storyteller to another, generally moving over time from being a relic of a monkey to one

---

72. Ribeiro ([1685] 1701, 119) and William Hurd (1780, 94) also specify that the flower was a rose.

73. Echoes of this story may still be found late in the nineteenth century. George Skeen (1903, 21) reports that "one tradition amongst the Kandyans is that the Portuguese ground the tooth to powder, and then threw the powder into the Mahaveli-ganga [sic!], where next morning the tooth, miraculously re-united, was found floating on a lotus plant. Hence it is now placed in the centre of a golden lotus." Around the same time, Jean Baptiste Van der Aa (1899, 263), a Belgian Jesuit teaching at the Catholic seminary in Kandy, reports much the same story, but locates it in Goa: the burned ashes of the ground-up tooth floated out to sea, where a lotus, emerging from the depths, opened up its calyx to enclose it. Within the ashes reconstituted themselves into the tooth, and the flower, detaching itself from its stem, "swam" all the way to Ceylon. It will be remembered that the Dāṭhāvaṃsa (see above) also has the tooth floating on a lotus after the heretics in India try unsuccessfully to destroy it.

of Hanumān to one of the Buddha. This change in identity reflects what Tambiah (1984, 336) calls the "cycle of transactions," in which charismatic objects reflect political, commercial, or other "secular" purposes. At the same time, it is part and parcel with the Portuguese "discovery" of Buddhism, that is, with their realization of Buddhism as a distinct religion, to be differentiated from "Hinduism," and the two of them no longer to be lumped together in "heathenism."

This realization was a result not primarily of the study of texts, but of the evolving transactional ways in which the Portuguese answered the questions "What is this object? Whose Tooth was this?" The identities the Portuguese gave to the tooth centered around an awareness at some level of the relic as a hegemonic symbol in the region. As a tooth of Hanumān, it connected the island to the Hindu powers of Vijayanagar, which the Portuguese sought to displace. As the geopolitical influence of that empire waned, it became a tooth of the Buddha, reflecting a growing Portuguese realization of the power of places like Pegu and of the pan-Asian importance of Buddhism as a competing ideology to Catholicism. Either way, its capture and destruction by the Portuguese may be seen as their attempt to sever the links of other powers with Sri Lanka and to reassert the fact that they are the new hegemons over the island.

Those other powers, however, both those outside Sri Lanka like Pegu, and within it like Kandy, were mostly deaf to this Portuguese assertion, at least in so far as the tooth was concerned. Indeed, they now claimed themselves to be in possession of the Buddha's relic. This necessitated, on the part of the Portuguese, the telling of stories about the fake nature of their claims—that their tooth relics were not *truly* the Buddha's but sculpted from the horn of a stag or the tooth of a buffalo. At the same time, this denunciation of their rivals' relics as "false" forced them to assert that their own tooth (though now destroyed) was "genuine"—an interesting claim for people who believed that the only "true" relics were their own Roman Catholic ones.

All of this is reinforced by the stories (also characteristic of the cycle of transactions) of the Portuguese keen awareness of the potential monetary value of the tooth and what it could do for them as individuals and for the cash flow of the empire. Thus, the "details" of the lists of the kingdoms that were interested in ransoming the tooth from the Portuguese also reflect how pride of place is first given to Vijayanagara as the party most interested in regaining ownership of the relic. Then, however, Vijayanagara drops out of the picture and it is the king of Pegu who is now willing to pay huge sums to buy the tooth back.

Geopolitical factors, however, were not the only elements involved in the Portuguese definition and destruction of the tooth. There were also religious considerations—Tambiah's first dimension of the fetishism of objects. These, more than the underlying questions of geopolitical hegemony, came to the fore in the debate the Portuguese held in Goa just prior to their destruction of the tooth, and to this we must now turn.

FOUR

The Trial of the Tooth

The Devil was in that Little Bone.

—A Franciscan Father in Jaffna, 1560 (see Queiros 1930, 1: 365)

In the previous chapter, I touched on accounts of the offers made by various principalities to ransom the tooth after the news broke that the Portuguese had captured it. These offers, as we have seen, are ultimately rejected by the viceroy, Dom Constantino da Bragança, but that was not a decision that came easily.

The debate that is held in Goa about what to do with the captured tooth is interesting because, before being resolved in favor of destruction, it reflects an additional range of Portuguese attitudes toward the tooth relic. Some of our sources (Pimenta, Pyrard, and Le Blanc) make no mention of it at all. Queiros (1930, 1: 365) likewise passes it over, referring only to Faria e Souza's account for the particulars.[1] The other sources recount it with various degrees of detail.

Early Accounts

The first hint at a discussion in Goa about the tooth (of a monkey) comes from Van Linschoten ([1598] 1885, 293) who states that, initially, Dom Constantino

---

1. This may be because Queiros's book focuses on what happened in Sri Lanka, and so does not touch much on events in Goa. Interestingly, though, Queiros does mention that there was a debate, of sorts, about the tooth already in Jaffna, for he says that, after the Portuguese victory there, Bishop D. Jorge Temudo preached a sermon, taking as his text the words of Genesis 14:21 ("Give me souls, take the other things for yourself"). This sermon, Queiros declares, had three points "all in allusion to the idol": the effects of ambition, contempt for riches, and the obligation of seeking the interests of God. We shall see that, in other sources, a similar sermon is said to be preached in Goa by Archbishop Dom Gaspar.

was inclined to accept the offer of the king of Pegu, but the archbishop, Dom Gaspar, "dissuaded him from it, saying [that] being Christians, they ought not to give it [back to] them again, because it would encourage idolatry."

Du Jarric, however, is the first to mention a formal debate on the question. Writing in 1610, he tells us that "there was a great diversity of opinion on the matter," and, not wanting to take responsibility for deciding one way or the other, the viceroy opted to bring the issue to an open council for further discussion and joint resolution. To this council, in addition to its ordinary members, he invited a great number of Portuguese nobles, and, on the clerical side, the archbishop of Goa (Dom Gaspar), and the prelates and superiors of the three locally established religious orders (the Dominicans, the Franciscans, and the Jesuits) (Du Jarric 1610, 399; Gaspard 1918, 17).

In this assembly, some *fidalgos* pointed to the state's urgent need for revenue, which would be alleviated by the ransom money.[2] Others were more blatantly self-interested; one captain, for instance, proposed that, "with the Viceroy's permission," he would personally take the tooth to Pegu, but exhibit it at various places along the way so as "to collect the offerings that people would give in order to be able to see and kiss it."[3] In this way, he opined, he could amass "more money than the revenue from the best of settlements, and more booty than there was to be had in [all of] India" (Du Jarric 1610, 400; Gaspard 1918, 18). Dom Gaspar and the "learned theologians," however, argue that the tooth could not be sold to the idolators without participating in the sin of their idolatry. Interestingly, in taking this position, they also appear to grant the tooth the status of a relic, which they understand from their own Roman Catholic perspective; they argue that "since the Barbarians esteem this tooth as something holy and sacred, it follows that it would be unlawful for them to buy it or for the Portuguese to sell it" (Du Jarric 1610, 400; Gaspard 1918, 18). Apparently, here (without perhaps realizing it) they are invoking Canon Law 1190.1, which forbids all trafficking in relics, and applying it to the Buddhists![4]

2. This need was genuine. As Diffie and Winius (1977, 431) put it: "The crown's deficit in its Asian operation before 1571 probably ran to at least 25,000 cruzados per year in relatively quiet years. . . . One can be sure that in years of campaigning like 1560 (when Viceroy Constantino de Bragança invaded Jaffnapatam) or siege like 1570 (the Muslim grand assault), the deficit increased many fold."

3. Though the practice of raising money by special exhibitions of relics and taking them on tour is known in the Buddhist tradition, the kissing of relics on such occasions is not. That is clearly informed by Roman Catholic relic practices.

4. See http://www.vatican.va/archive/ENG1104/_P4D.HTM. See also, however, Geary 1990, 40, 43.

Do Couto paints a slightly different picture. He says that Dom Constantino, convinced by "some old captains and fidalgos," at first thought they *should* accept the Peguan ransom offer, as it would help the state, "which was in debt and in want" (Ferguson [1908] 1993, 212; original text in Do Couto 1783, 430). He is about to give his approval, when the archbishop Dom Gaspar gets wind of this and intervenes, preaching against the sale in church, in front of the viceroy and the whole court. At that, Dom Constantino has second thoughts. As Do Couto put it, "[since] he was a very devout Catholic, and God-fearing, and obedient to the prelates, he [the viceroy] did not care to go forward with that business, or to do anything without a general council" (Ferguson [1908] 1993, 213; original text in Do Couto 1783, 430).

Participating in this council are all of the groups of churchmen mentioned above (Do Couto even gives us their names), with the addition of two other individuals not specified by Du Jarric but placed at the head of the list by Do Couto, right after the archbishop: the inquisitors, Aleixo Dias Falcão and Francisco Marques Botelho (Ferguson [1908] 1993, 213; original text in Do Couto 1783, 431).[5] We shall deal with the question of the Inquisition in Goa and its relationship to the burning of the tooth in chapter 5 below. For now, suffice it to quote Wojciehowski's statement (2011, 209) that "the destruction of the [tooth] in 1561 coincided with the arrival of the Portuguese Inquisition in Goa. . . . In this context, we might wonder whether the Viceroy capitulated not so much to the purportedly superior arguments of the Archbishop and his camp, as to the superior force of the Inquisition that was then establishing its rule by intimidation."

Do Couto does not say as much; instead, he merely indicates that the viceroy was quickly convinced by the argument of the prelates that "the tooth could not be given up [for ransom] because it would give occasion to great idolatries and insult to God our Lord; and that that was a sin that could not be committed, even at the risk of the state and the whole world" (Ferguson [1908] 1993, 213; original text in Do Couto 1783, 431).[6] But surely Do Couto's placing the inquisitors at the top of the list of those attending the debate is significant, and it is interesting that he makes little

---

5. Do Couto does not actually give the inquisitors' names here, since he has already done so at 1783, 335.

6. Do Couto adds that a written agreement to this was drawn up and signed by all present—a copy of which, he says, was still to be found in his day in the archives in Goa (the Torre do Tombo of which he, Do Couto, was in charge). According to Da Cunha (1875, 44n), this document no longer exists.

mention of any of the arguments used against the Church's position at the debate. It is possible that he may have been hesitant to do so for personal reasons, worried about crossing the Inquisition himself in his own writings, or about getting others in trouble, posthumously or not.[7]

Faria e Souza's Account

Faria e Souza, however, writing in the 1670s, does present the arguments of both sides in this council, and gives us a most detailed and dramatic account of the debate. He first portrays a situation in which everyone squabbles chaotically until silence is called for and an orderly discussion is arranged. In it, extended eloquent speeches are given by representatives of both sides—those for selling the tooth, and those against it. Faria e Souza "quotes" these speeches at length, but it is not clear where he is getting this material. Not naming the speakers in question, it is likely that he is writing the speeches for them, on the grounds, perhaps, of indications in the historical record of what was generally said on that occasion, but with the purpose, probably, of telling a dramatic story. On the other hand, with the Goan Inquisition still active in his day, it is possible that Faria e Souza did not want to get certain individuals—or, more likely, their descendants—in trouble by naming them (though, unlike Do Couto, he makes no mention of any inquisitors being present at the debate).

All we are told about the first speaker is that he is a military man—a captain. This officer begins by proclaiming his own and the army's religious *bona fides*:

> No one doubts that all of us who exercise our weapons in the shadow of Catholic flags (and none so Catholic as ours!) care less for the profits of war than for the respectability of religion. . . . But, on this occasion, I am persuaded that without obtaining the former, we let the latter fall from our fingers. . . .
>
> If the Author and Founder of our kingdom [i.e., God] who is the General of our conquests, allowed us to have this idol, was it not done so that we could obtain this ransom money in order to raise many Christian altars where the sovereign sacrifice can be made repeatedly? . . . I concede that the Devil in this tooth may bite many souls if we sell it and place it where the Gentiles . . . can seek it out, but, with the money given for it, we will be able to lift up, in many provinces, many Catholic souls, so much so that this fruit would exceed

---

any damage brought on by this idol. . . . This is all the more so the case when we realize that in denying this tooth to the Gentiles, we take away from them neither the facsimiles that they have of it (which they adore as much as the original),[8] nor their innumerable other remaining idols. But with the sum offered to us for this single idol, we will be able to remove many of those others. . . . It is very clear that [without the sale of this tooth] we will remain unable to develop our evangelical culture. But with this influx of cash, if we accept it, we will indubitably be able to send to the bottom of these waters many Gentile tribes, each of which is a pagoda of idolatries. We must raise up new fortresses, for they are temples of our teachings. We must increase our power for it is our religion's most singular advocate. One cannot muzzle barbaric souls and the mouth of idolatry by means of [destroying] a minor tooth! . . . How little would we stop the profane and abominable rites by opposing this sale! It should be sold for Christ himself [not] for profane purposes. . . . This idol has the capacity of defeating many idols, and of being the architect of many images of His only-begotten Son and His sacrosanct Virgin Mother, and of being the means of new and glorious triumphs of the cross, the banner of our armies. How confused will be the barbarians, whom we dominate and intend to put under our yoke, when they see their most beloved idol turned into swords, muskets, and torments of war that will penetrate their doors and their eyes! The sale of unclean and foul things can help build fragrant things. If we can make things for heaven by selling this heinousness of hell, why should we have any doubts? . . . Selling the tooth will lead to certain gain and two assured losses: the loss [to the King of Pegu] of the money he gives us, and the ruin we will make of him by means of the money received. . . . [It is true] that, in the Book of Judges (this, you theologians know better than I), God questions those who stop serving him in order to serve idols; but here we are trying to sell idols, so that we can make their number less and so serve Him more. . . . I surrender to the doctrines of our sacred books which are understood better by our teachers, but I believe that, with this income, we will much advance the interests of our true religion and so diminish those of the Gentiles. (Faria e Souza 1666–1675, 2: 353–357)

At the end of his speech, the captain is vehemently cheered by his fellow officers, and even, according to Faria e Souza, some ecclesiastics applaud him. But then it is the turn of the other side to speak—the churchmen who

---

8. This is apparently a reference to the story, touched on above, of King Bayinnaung getting (in the 1550s) imprints of the tooth relic made in amber that he could worship back in Pegu.

oppose the sale. One "theologian" (we are not told who) gets up and responds in this way:

> If the idols do not fear the swords of solid theology more than the theologies of strong swords . . . they will continue to exist throughout Asia. Of course, we know that it is better to cut down this idol and its cultivators with weapons made of iron, [but] this sale has just been supported with rhetoric. At least the Church, in order to explain its sentiments in opposition to it, will speak [directly] to God: "My Lord, thou art my only Lord and Treasure . . . outside of you there can be no other help in this predicament . . . you who brought prosperity to our Catholic family, as you promised you would to our leader, our undefeated, heroic, and saintly King Don Alfonso Enriquez.[9] O solely powerful God, weaken, snuff out, and completely extinguish the will of those who, finding themselves the owners of this idol . . . would place it again in its most heinous pagodas, silencing those who praise and spread your true worship, and giving reason for those idolaters to exaggerate from this day forward the strength of their idols, seeing that they could regain them after their being captive in our hands. Lord, give me confidence in this: may the supporters of this sale, by virtue of the words from my lips, apply themselves to the total destruction of this abominable part of a beast in which the cunning Lucifer is disguised!

> I can say it no better than Jeremiah: "Wash, o my people, your stained hearts of this horrible greed, so that you may be exalted with great glory."[10] "For how long?" [the prophet asks.] For as long as there remains in you these cowardly thoughts to make this idol once more an authority for its followers. "For how long?" [For as long as] it seems to me I am hearing, from the mouth of the secular state, those words of a person referred to by Hosea: "I see myself rich, because I have found an idol for myself."[11] But if the Divine Scriptures teach us that idols are nothing, exactly less than nothing will come from their sale. All this treasure imagined from this sale will have the quality usually experienced by dreamers: big with the eyes closed, nothing at all with them open. . . .

> The result of this crime, even when it is committed with the good intention of making new altars at which the true God is venerated, will be ruinous.

9. Afonso I, the Conqueror (O Conquistador) (twelfth century CE), was the founding king of Portugal.

10. Jeremiah 4:14: "O Jerusalem, wash your heart from wickedness, that you may be saved. How long shall your evil thoughts lodge within you?"

11. Hosea 12:8: "Ephraim has said, 'Ah, but I am rich, I have gained wealth for myself'; but all his riches can never offset the guilt he has incurred."

This can be seen from Leviticus, where God affirms that He does not want the sacrifices of those who consent to idolatry (however Catholic they may be), but that He will overthrow their sanctuaries and cities.[12] God does not sell his obeisances for a price, because to buy them is . . . an offense against Him. The Devil, yes, he is the one who buys adorations at such prices. . . .

What would one [usually] expect God to do to Rachel after she steals some of her father Laban's estate and leaves him?[13] She robs him of his idols, but God not only does *not* punish her [for stealing], but favors her, and makes it so that the old man [Laban], when he sets out to look for her in anger, in no way [actually] annoys her. She sees that he is full of anger, but *does not give back* the idols, though in fear for her life.[14] He is left without them, and they are later buried. Here, gentlemen, we come to our case in point: if we deny this [tooth] to the Gentiles, [it is true] there would be no shortage of others; but Laban did not lack other [idols], and when those taken by Rachel were not returned, that was deemed to be so much a service to God that He let pass some singularly offensive things, such as her [stealing] and lying and disobeying her parents (because Rachel did not speak the truth to him in what she said, nor was she obedient in what she denied him). . . .

If our king were to send us a resolute order for proper execution, would it be acceptable that we should deliberate whether it was right? Surely not! Thus, if God, by means of the beautiful and most zealous Rachel and her beloved and most faithful Jacob, enjoins us to bury this idol, [we should do so]. How can human intentions be brought into consideration about that which is demanded by God?

How can the King of Pegu regard us as truly being Christians when he sees that we make his idol so precious? Because, without a doubt, we will make this tooth more estimable to the idolaters if we sell it to them at such a price. Already, the king offers us three hundred thousand escudos, and now we want to ask a million? So, this demon is worth more in our opinion than it is to him? The greatest idolater is the one who values the idol the most! Therefore, gentlemen, in the presence of God, we should affirm with Jeremiah: "there has been established by Me a people by whom idols will be vanquished,

12. Leviticus 26:30–31: [If you walk contrary to me] I will destroy your high places, and cut down your incense altars, and cast your dead bodies upon the dead bodies of your idols; and my soul will abhor you. And I will lay your cities waste, and will make your sanctuaries desolate, and I will not smell your pleasing odors."
13. Genesis 31:19–21.
14. When Laban enters Rachel's tent to search for the idols, Rachel hides them in a saddlebag and sits on top of them; Laban looks everywhere and would like Rachel to move, but she says she cannot get up, as she is having her period. Laban desists and goes away. See Genesis 31:34–35.

overthrown and made extinct beyond the ends of the earth; and there will be no room for reverence for any other name than Mine."[15] And with Ezekiel: "I will lay my sword upon the idolaters . . . to scatter all idols and eliminate them from the altars of all idolaters, whose bones I will turn to dust."[16] To dust, then, this bone must be reduced, and exhaled in smoke over live coals. This is what God himself celebrated, according to his own Josiah when he gave the bones of the idolaters to the fire.[17] No doubt, he was teaching what our most faithful king, now represented in the Viceroy before us, should do with this bone. Here, the Divine Scripture will be fulfilled, for it assures us the infernal Dragon will be assailed and burnt for a second time in that Other Fire. And there is nothing that burns better than the fire of Portuguese faith which, for many years, has burnt as much as the fire of the Abyss. (Faria e Souza 1666–1675, 2: 357–363)

This speech, according to Faria e Souza, "quieted the tongues of those who originally favored a sale," and the viceroy immediately determined to get rid of the tooth. He had it brought, and,

witnessed by all that noble audience, he threw it with his own hand into a mortar, where it was quickly reduced to powder; he then poured the powder onto burning embers, the smoke from which resulted in an excessively bad odor, exceeding that which one would naturally expect from a bone when it burns. It was, in the end, a pill from Hell. (Faria e Souza 1666–1675, 2: 364)

The two sets of arguments in this debate—for and against the sale of the tooth—are noteworthy expressions of Portuguese attitudes toward this relic. The captain's point is basically a this-worldly transactional one. Roman Catholicism will thrive where the Empire is best able to establish itself, but that takes money. Therefore, the ransom offer for the tooth should be accepted; by selling this idol, the Portuguese will be able not only to destroy other idols, but to erect more Christian places of worship throughout Asia. This, of course, masks a subtext that everyone present must have been aware of, that, given the corruption and greed rampant at the time in the

15. See Jeremiah 50.
16. Ezekiel 6:3–4. "Thus says the Lord God . . . Behold I, even I, will bring a sword upon you, and I will destroy your high places. Your altars shall become desolate, and your incense altars shall be broken; and I will cast down your slain before your idols."
17. 2 Kings 23:16: "And as Josiah turned, he saw the tombs there on the mount; and he sent and took the bones out of the tombs, and burned them upon the altar [to the goddess Asherah], and defiled it."

administration of the Portuguese Empire, very little of this money would end up serving that purpose, for most of it would disappear into the pockets of those in power. Faria e Souza, in fact, hints at this when, in an aside not translated above, he says of the captain that he "must have been one in whom greed dominated and who wished to take the tooth to the buyers out of appetite for profit," but who was wise enough not to let his avarice show. The prelate, of course, knows this, and refers to it directly when he quotes Jeremiah ("Wash, O my people, your stained hearts of this horrible greed") and when he declares that his opponents want to sell the tooth "for their own particular interests." It is likely, of course, that some of these funds would have enabled military expeditions that would have "destroyed more idols," but, as we have seen in the case of Jaffna, the sacking of "heathen" places of worship had, as another of its primary aims, the appropriation of treasure.

The prelate's arguments in this debate are somewhat more complex, but basically raise otherworldly religious concerns. First, he adopts a clever tactic of not directly opposing the reasoning of the captain, but instead praying for him—asking that he and all his opponents be led by God to see and change the error of their ways. He then, as we have seen, goes on to quote extensively from Old Testament prophets and other biblical stories justifying the destruction of idols. He especially uses the story of Rachel and Laban to hint that God is willing to overlook lying and disobedience and especially theft when they are in the service of combating idolatry, the greater sin. Like Rachel, who hid stolen idols from her father, the Portuguese have stolen the tooth from the temple in Jaffna; like Rachel, they should not give it back to its owners but destroy it. More generally, there is an affirmation that the Portuguese are heirs to the People of Israel; they are God's chosen people (but on a global scale) for the maintenance and spread of his worship. The prelate also makes the point that to receive payment for an idol is to participate in idolatry; the higher the price, the greater the participation. Finally, he chooses to demonize the tooth by portraying it as belonging to Satan himself. This is a theme that needs a bit more explication.

The Tooth Relic as a Demonic Force

In chapter 3 above, I examined various identities assigned to the tooth by its capturers. It is striking that in the debate in Goa—the "trial" of the tooth—no mention is made of these. It is as though whether the tooth belonged to a monkey or Hanumān or the Buddha is irrelevant, for all these figures are subsumed under the view that the tooth being destroyed has another identity: it is the Devil's own. It is as though some sort of other-worldly myopia prevents them from seeing anything but Satan in the tooth. This is important, for if, as we will suggest, the overall tale of the tooth has its origins with the storical events of the debate about it and its destruction in Goa, the identifications of it as Hanumān's or the Buddha's are second-ary. In other words, the records of the debate suggest that the Portuguese destruction of the tooth was not primarily motivated by any particular an-tagonism toward Hinduism or Buddhism, but by fear of demonic forces, and a desire to express triumphalism over Satan.

Focusing on the Spanish in the Western hemisphere, Fernando Cervantes (1994) has pointed to the importance of demonology for our understand-ing of sixteenth-century colonial encounters. The same may be said of the Portuguese in Asia: underlying much of their treatment of the tooth is a worldview that saw them engaged in a great battle between the forces of good and the forces of evil—between God and Satan. This opposition was given a very specific focus in the object of the tooth. Among our sources, Faria e Souza was perhaps the most emphatic in identifying the tooth as belonging to the Devil himself,[18] but he was by no means alone in doing so. Do Couto (1783, 429 and 82; Eng. trans., Ferguson [1908] 1993, 212 and 249) calls it at one point a "relic of the Demon" (*reliquia do demonio*) and, at another, a "tooth of the Devil" (*dente do diabo*), while Queiros (1930, 1: 364–365) reports that already in Jaffna, immediately after the tooth's cap-ture, Bishop Temudo had urged Dom Constantino to burn the thing right away, and that Franciscans at that time feared it would bring harm to the Portuguese forces because "the Demon was in that little bone and where he was there would be no good." Courtenay ([1913] 2005, 139) adds that Father Melchior, a missionary present on the same occasion, indignantly protested that to take the tooth back to Goa would only give it more impor-tance, and he prophesied that, "having preferred sordid lucre to the glory of God, the expedition would fail."

At the end of his account of the debate, Faria e Souza (1666–1675, 2: 354) introduces the image of the Devil using this tooth "to bite many souls." Furthermore, he has his theologian conclude his presentation by de-claring that "We will torment the infernal dragon, [i.e., Satan] mightily if, indeed, we break this, his tooth, in his very mouth" (Faria e Souza 1666–1675, 2: 363). The notion that the tooth is the Devil's own is then rein-forced in his account of its burning, when it emits a foul odor "exceeding

---

18. For a discussion of the "demonic" category in the context of the Goan Inquisition, see Rodrigues da Silva Tavim 2016.

that which naturally one expects from a bone when it burns" (a point mentioned by several of our sources), causing Faria e Souza to conclude that "it was, finally, a pill [*pastilla*] from Hell" (Faria e Souza 1666–1675, 2: 364).

But Faria e Souza does not stop his exploration of this vivid theme here. A bit further on, he expands on his comments when he compares the two "fake" teeth—the one created by Dharmapala of Kotte and sold to the king of Pegu, and the other by Vimaladharmasuriya of Kandy—to new canine implants in the mouth of Satan. But then, realizing perhaps that this simile might undermine his advocacy for destroying the tooth, since it might be seen as resulting in the Devil replacing one lost tooth with two new ones (thus mushrooming the number of idols rather than reducing it), he quickly assures his readers that it does not matter if "the devil replaced a real tooth of his with two others, [for] he would always chew less with them, because, in the end, they were false. [Moreover], he had to endure the constant pain of having had in his mouth the pliers of Portuguese faith, which most skillfully acted as the Devil's dentist when extracting his tooth." And, he concludes: "With the gift of an apple, [Satan] already did much [bad] business in the cradle of human kind [i.e., the Garden of Eden], but I hear that, with this treasure [i.e., the tooth] thrown back in his face, he came to lose much of what he had hoped to gain in all of India" (Faria e Souza 1666–1675, 2: 364–365).

Theologically, in terms of a doctrine of evil, this argument is a bit convoluted, but interesting, for it distinguishes between demonic teeth that are genuine, and demonic teeth that are fake. To be sure, both types of teeth are of the Devil, but the first are worse than the latter, for the Devil can chew more sinners, that is, do more works of evil, with his real than with his false teeth.[19] In the end, then, the Portuguese identification of the tooth they captured in Jaffna as being of the Devil put a new premium on their argument for its authenticity vis-à-vis the other tooth relics they encountered. If they were uncertain whether or not it was a "true tooth" of Hanumān, or a "true tooth" of the Buddha, they could still affirm it was a "true tooth" of Satan.

In a passage entitled "The Devil and His Dentist," Wojciehowski (2011, 198–201) gives a noteworthy analysis of Faria e Souza's foray into demonology, from a generally psychological perspective. She states that in his

---

19. Though false teeth had been around since the time of the Etruscans, they began to reappear in Western culture in the seventeenth century. It is likely that Faria e Souza's comments are based on the fact that, in his day, false teeth were definitively inferior to real ones in looks and in chewing ability, and that they were at times painful. One wonders whether Faria e Souza is writing based on personal experience of seventeenth-century dentures.

account, we can recognize that "the Portuguese colonials defined themselves against the foreign body represented metonymically by the tooth,"
adding in a footnote that "for Freud, this type of imagery would evoke the
perennial phobia of the 'Vagina dentata,' here racialized as well as gendered"
(Wojciehowski 2011, 200). More specifically, she refers to the "oral element"
in various "colonial fantasies of the epoch," portraying the Portuguese as
the "sadistic . . . dentist of Christendom torturing the devil," and equating
the Devil with "the devouring mouth of pagan Asia . . . that threatens to
eat, dismember, destroy, digest, and implicitly, excrete all those who stand
it its way" (Wojciehowski 2011, 200–201). It should be pointed out, however, that the notion of hell being a devouring mouth has a more directly
Christian reference. As Caroline Bynum (1995, 192–193, and plates 12 and
31) has made clear, a common portrayal, starting in late medieval times,
shows Satan actually crunching sinners between his teeth, only to be forced
to regurgitate them by Christ at the second coming. Here a new significance
of the tooth emerges: it was a ready symbol of the Devil, and of a fate that
could be avoided by its elimination.

Addendum: Paths Taken and Not Taken

All in all, this chapter shows that the Portuguese, in debating what to do
about the tooth, reject the this-worldly potential of the charismatic object
they had captured (Tambiah's "cycle of transactions") and emphasize instead its religious import. In doing so, though, it seems that they are unable
to break out of their own worldview; no mention is made of the Buddha or
Hanumān or even a monkey idol, but only of the familiar idols of the Old
Testament and the all-too-real presence of the Devil. Scholars dealing with
the clash of Western and non-Western cultures in early colonial times have
occasionally invoked the notions of "cultural incommensurability" to de-
note an inability to bridge an epistemological gap.[20] Subrahmanyam (2017,
xv), however, in his study of the Portuguese in India, rejects the utility of
this concept at least for his particular topic. He prefers instead the notion of
"epistemological deficit" (by which he means the inability of the Portuguese
to distinguish between different types of heathens or "gentiles" [gentios]).
But he limits its application to the very early period of Portuguese presence in Asia, and cautions that the degree of such inabilities varies widely

20. The notion is a social-sciences application of the concept of "incommensurability" between scientific paradigms developed by Thomas Kuhn and others. See Subrahmanyam 2012,
4–7.

from person to person, situation to situation, and time period to time period (Subrahmanyam 2017, 103). In my own thinking, I find the sixteenth- and seventeenth-century Portuguese in India and Sri Lanka to have often been quite attuned (this does not mean sympathetic) to the this-worldly concerns of the cultures they encountered, but (depending on the person, situation, and time period) less so to their otherworldly interests. In the case of the debate about the tooth in Goa, I am particularly interested in the "otherworldly myopia" of the prelate (as well as the archbishop Dom Gaspar, and eventually Dom Constantino)—their inability to recognize any non-Christian referents (e.g., Hanumān, the Buddha) for the tooth, even if it were only to condemn them. It is as though they are nearsighted when it comes to the transcendent, that they have blinders on in their arguments against the tooth, and so can only see it in terms of their own Christian mythology of evil.

This myopia, of course, was not permanent and not suffered by everyone. In chapter 3 above, we saw how the Portuguese did come to "put on some glasses" and recognize the otherworldly identities of the tooth relic, albeit primarily for this-worldly political reasons. The ecclesiasts at the debate in Goa, however, still have their blinders on. Lest it be thought, however, that this was the *only* solution available to them at the time, I would like to finish this chapter by speculatively exploring some other possible arguments that could have been made in this debate. Not all Roman Catholic prelates and missionaries in sixteenth-century India were quite so forceful as the prelate or Archbishop Gaspar or the other ecclesiastics in Goa in their assertion that there could be no possible salvation outside the Church (*"extra ecclesiam nulla salus"*) and that preserving such a thing as the tooth was an act of evil.

About the same time that Do Couto was writing his account of the debate over the tooth, the Italian Jesuit father Roberto de Nobili (1577–1656) arrived in Goa.[21] He soon proceeded to Cochin and then to Madurai and quickly mastered Tamil, Telugu, and Sanskrit. In part because he was not living in a Portuguese settlement, and in part because he became thoroughly versed in classical Indian schools of thought, he came to believe that the best method of proselytizing native Hindus was by means of what he called "accommodation." This involved allowing converts to retain what were deemed (by De Nobili) to be merely cultural (and not finally religious) traditions (such as wearing the sacred thread, observing dietary preferences, and participating in certain festivals). In this way, a distinction was made

---

21. For a biography of De Nobili, see Županov 1999, 1–16; and Cronin 1959.

between *"civility* [which encompassed] customs, habits, and rituals, and *religion* [which referred] principally to beliefs" (Xavier and Županov 2015, 149–153).[22] Realizing the low esteem Brahmins and other Hindus had for the Portuguese, De Nobili claimed not to be a *parangi* [Tamil pejorative for Portuguese and other Europeans] but a "Roman Brahmin" (Xavier and Županov 2015, 152). Alternatively, he allowed himself to be identified as a *"muni"* (a sage, as in Śākyamuni) by the small Buddhist community in Madurai (see Cronin 1959, 126). He shaved his head, went barefoot, dressed in a *dhoti*, and wore a sacred thread around his left shoulder (whose three strands he maintained signified not just Brahmā, Viṣṇu, and Śiva, but God the Father, the Son, and the Holy Spirit). He used Tamil or Sanskrit words to designate Christian things (e.g., *"kovil"* [for church], *"guru"* [for Catholic priest], *"Veda"* [for Bible], and *"pūjā"* [for mass]). In general, he presented Christianity as though it were a culmination or new rendition of the Brahmanical tradition (Xavier and Županov 2015, 149–153).

De Nobili was not without his predecessors. He may have been influenced by a fellow English Jesuit, Thomas Stephens (1549–1619), who had arrived in Goa in 1579, and remained there until his death forty years later. Stephens became fluent in both Konkani and Marathi and composed, in those languages, the *Kristapurāṇa*, an epic poem recounting the story of creation and the life of Jesus in the traditional form of a Hindu *purāṇa*, which became very popular among local converts.[23] The same effort to "indigenize" the Christian story appeared later in the *Ezourvedam* (the "Jesus-Veda"), a composition in Sanskrit that pretended to be a long-lost Vedic text. When it first appeared, De Nobili was suspected of having been its author, though this was later shown not to be the case.[24]

Both Stephens and De Nobili, moreover, would likely have been aware of the issues that were deliberated at the so-called Valladolid Debate, held in Spain in 1550–1551. At this conclave, theologians assembled to discuss the moral and human rights of colonized peoples (especially in Latin America),

22. De Nobili was fiercely opposed by his fellow Jesuit in Madurai, Gonçalo Fernandes Trancoso, for whom such accommodation was equivalent to permitting the perpetuation of paganism. As Xavier and Županov put it, for Fernandes Trancoso, "being Catholic basically meant becoming Portuguese." Their dispute was eventually formalized in what came to be known as the "Malabar Rites Controversy," which lasted for some time (see Brucker 1913). A similar debate arose in Jesuit circles in China (e.g., the "Chinese Rites Controversy"), although the cultural particulars differed in the two cases, as did their eventual treatment by the Vatican.

23. For a study of the *Kristapurāṇa*, see Falcao 3003.

24. The *Ezourveda* was probably written by one of DeNobili's French disciples. See Rocher 1984.

their status as rational human beings, as well as the propriety of various techniques used to convert them. Prominent at the debate was a Dominican friar, Bartolomé de las Casas (1484–1566), who was known as a defender of the indigenous rights (and rites) of the Incas and other Indians. Las Casas pointed to what he saw as the positive rational aspects of idolatry, going so far as to define idols as anything that inspires persons to honor whatever they define as goodness or excellence, affirming at the same time that such goodness is ultimately a reflection of God's goodness. This led him to come to what Sabine MacCormack (2006, 632–633) has called "a radical new conclusion about the nature of idolatrous worship." "No difference," Las Casas declared, "exists between offering sacrifice to the true God or a false one if he is held and understood to be the true God. The reason is that conscience that is in error binds as much [to the good] as does the conscience that is not in error."[25] Las Casas was even willing to accept human sacrifice and supposed cannibalism as legitimate and rational cultural expressions of the faith of the Indians.[26]

Given all these options, it is interesting that there were no such liberal views among the ecclesiastics who debated the fate of the tooth in Goa.[27] In part, this may have been due to the presence of the inquisitors in the colony at the time, but, as we shall see in the next chapter, there were other contextual factors involved as well.

25. On the potential importance of Las Casas in the development of the study of religion, see Bernand and Gruzinski 1988.

26. Needless to say, such views were controversial and had important implications for the question of the treatment and forced Christianization of natives in the Americas by the Spaniards. And Las Casas made the matter more acute by opining that in his view, the Spanish were greater idolaters than the Incas, for "their idol was the riches of the Indies" (MacCormack 2006, 634).

27. It should be said that Stuart Schwartz (2008, 4–5) has argued that when sixteenth-century Iberian Catholic attitudes toward other religions are studied "from the bottom up" and not through the educated elite's perspective, a rather different, and more accepting and tolerant, viewpoint emerges.

FIVE

The Destruction of the Tooth

The Portuguese, more zealous in religion than in the politics of governing a newly conquered people, had [the tooth] burned in the presence of the ambassadors so as not to foment the idolatry of the Hindus; at the same time, they deprived themselves of being able to take a part of the wealth of the Indies.

—François De la Boullaye-Le-Gouz (1653, 179)

[And when Moses had come down from the mountain], he took the [golden] calf which they had made, and burnt it with fire, and ground it to powder, and scattered it upon the water.

—Exodus 32:20

We come now to the episode of the actual destruction of the tooth by Dom Constantino and the archbishop. In terms of narrative, this is one of the concluding events to be considered, but I suspect that it was actually one of the first stories to be told. Faria e Souza, as we have seen, does not give many details about it, somewhat curiously after his extended treatment of the debate leading up to it. Similarly, some other sources (Van Linschoten, Pimenta, Pyrard, Le Blanc) just mention the destruction in passing. Du Jarric (1610) is the first to provide us with some details, so much so that it is hard to remember that he was not an eyewitness to these events but sitting in his study in Bordeaux fifty years afterward. According to him, once the decision is made to destroy the tooth, the viceroy has it brought and shows it to all those who are present to assure them that this is the very same relic as that which was taken in Jaffna, so as "to prevent people from saying later on that it was some other" (Gaspard 1918, 19; Du Jarric 1610, 399). He then has all the jewels removed from it. The relic, he specifies, was "set all round with a great many rubies and sapphires, not very big, but very precious and of great value," and "too rich and precious for such a vile and hateful object" (Gaspard 1918, 19; Du Jarric 1610, 399). Dom Constantino next calls for a brazier with hot coals to be brought forward, along with a bronze mortar. He puts the tooth in the mortar with his own hands, and orders it pounded and reduced to powder "in the presence of the whole assembly." He then throws the powder into the brazier "in the view of all," and then "the stench it gave forth was so horrid that, unable to stand it, they all of them held their noses" (Gaspard 1918, 19; Du Jarric 1610, 399).

According to this account, at each step, care is taken to make sure that the destructive actions are public and evident to everyone present. Dom Constantino holds up the tooth to show it to the crowd, and after placing it in the mortar, has it pounded, and then burned for all to see. This not only gives the whole thing a ritual quality, but it shows that there is no sleight of hand going on. Generally speaking, when such precautions are specified in a story, it means that the very thing warned about is, in fact, already happening. It may well be that Du Jarric here wants to counter the Sinhalese claims, already mentioned by Van Linschoten ([1598] 1885, 1: 292–294), that, at the final moment, the tooth magically slipped through the bottom of the mortar, or was secretly ferreted away by an invisible deity, only to reappear in Sri Lanka. Alternatively, it may mean that accusations were being made that what the Portuguese destroyed was not the "real" tooth. Here the assertion is not only that the tooth is real, but that its destruction is real, confirmed by the bad smell of the smoke (which, as we have seen, is later taken to confirm that this was a satanic object).

More immediately and more explicitly, however, Du Jarric claims that this public ceremony was the culmination of the punishment of King Cankili of Jaffna for having put to death the Christians on the island of Mannar (see chapter 1 above). "Such was the chastisement," he concludes,

> which Divine Justice visited on the wicked King of Jaffna. . . . He was punished, first of all, in his dominions, by the loss of that isle of Mannar and by becoming a tributary to the Portuguese; second, by the capture of his eldest son [who was taken as hostage to Goa]; third, by the destruction of the capital city of his kingdom; and lastly, by the loss of his treasure [both] lawfully and wrongfully amassed, in particular, by the loss of this monkey's tooth. (Gaspard 1918, 19; original text in Du Jarric 1610, 399)

Texeira, writing at the same time (1610) as Du Jarric, similarly emphasizes the public nature of the destruction of the tooth, but for him, it is for a different audience. He tells us that, after the Council concludes its deliberations, the *"neighbouring infidels"* in the region of Goa, who have come in their effort to ransom the tooth, are summoned to

> the open place before the viceroy's palace, which they call *Terreiro de Visorey* [the Viceroy's Terrace]. There, in the presence of a vast multitude of people and all the principal persons in the city, the tooth is shown to them and they are asked whether it is the very same tooth as that which they demanded and offered to ransom? They answer with most respectful awe and submission that it is. Then immediately before their faces, it was cast into the fire . . . where it was burnt; then taken out again in their presence, put into a mortar, and pounded to fine dust, which they then cast into the river that runs close by. . . . Thus, [the ambassadors were] "given to understand what sort of gods they worshipped, as well as the uncorrupted zeal of the Christian religion." (Texeira 1715, 251–252, slightly altered; original text in Texeira 1610, 271–272)

In addition to the difference in intended audience, there is one other detail in Texeira's account that is worth noting. Unlike Du Jarric, he adds a third method of disposal of the tooth: throwing the pulverized remains of the tooth into the river, something which, we have seen, is also mentioned by several other sources.[1] I will try to make some sense of the importance of this detail in the discussion below.

First, however, mention needs to be made of Do Couto's account of the destruction of the tooth. There is nothing particularly original about his description of the immediate events: after the decision of the council is put down on paper and signed by all present, we are told that the viceroy orders the treasurer to bring the tooth. It is then handed over to the archbishop, Dom Gaspar, who pounds it in a mortar, "with his own hand, in the presence of all," incinerates the fragments on a brazier, and then has "the ashes and cinders . . . thrown into the midst of the river in the sight of all, who witnessed it from the verandas and windows that looked on to the sea" (Ferguson [1908] 1993, 213; original text in Do Couto 1783, 432–433).

What is different about Do Couto's account is the postscript with which he ends this episode. Alone among all our other sources, he tells us that, soon after these events, in Portugal, some of Dom Constantino's supporters

---

1. It should be noted that, in Texeira's account (1610, 272), the order of the first two destruction methods is different: he says the tooth was put in the brazier first and then crushed in the mortar. All other sources that mention this (including Du Jarric) have it crushed first and then burned in the fire.

(apparently wanting to counter critics who thought he should have sold the tooth for the good of the empire's finances) had an escutcheon or plaque (Port., *tarja*) made on which they depicted the viceroy and the archbishop at a table, surrounded by the prelates and divines who had been present at the council, and in the midst of all of them, some Gentiles with purses in their hands full of money, which they are laying on a great brazier, and the letter C, repeated five times—to wit: C C C C C—underneath which were the words: *Constantinus, coeli, cupidine, cremavit, crumenas*. Do Couto states that the meaning of this ("ignoring the Latin construction") is "Constantino, devoted to heaven, rejected the treasures of the earth" (Tennent 1859, 2, 433; original text in Do Couto 1783, 433; see also Ferguson [1908] 1993, 213–214). This, however, does not quite do justice to the fact that this medallion depicts the bags of money being burned (along with the tooth, presumably). A better rendition would be: "Constantino, in a passion for heaven, spurned and burned the money bags," or, more colloquially, "Constantino, craving celestial-compensation, cooked [the] cash."[2]

This addendum by Do Couto is interesting for a number of reasons. First, it shows how the tooth has become symbolic of lucre; in burning the relic, Dom Constantino is, of course, rejecting corruption and greed, but he is also shown here as "burning the money bags," as though he had received the ransom and then destroyed it. Second, it appears to reflect the fact that the viceroy, even during his own lifetime, had become somewhat of a controversial figure in Goa (and perhaps also in Portugal), who stood in need of support and justification. As one authority, the French priest and scholar Denis L. Cottineau de Kloguen (1831, 33), was to put it, "[Dom Constantino] was firm, wise, mild, polite and benevolent; but he nevertheless incurred the hatred [of a number of people]." The latter included not only persons who thought that, for the good of the State, he should have accepted the ransom money, but also many in Goa, such as his successor as viceroy, Dom Francisco Coutinho, who objected to his having befriended and protected the controversial poet Luís de Camões (1524–1580). Though today considered one of the greatest literary figures in Portuguese history, Camões was, in his time, notoriously given to alienating figures in authority by virtue of his actions as well as his writings.[3] Dom Constantino, who

2. I would like to thank my colleague Margaret Imber, professor of classics at Bates College, for suggesting these two translations.

3. See Mickle n.d. for an account of his embellished life story. For a biographical chronology of his life, and an English translation (by Landeg White) of his major work, see also Camões 1997.

admired his genius as a man of letters, was much maligned for backing him. In the time of the Inquisition, it was always dangerous to have enemies, so there appears to have developed a countermovement among Dom Constantino's supporters (such as Do Couto and several other of our sources) to confirm his good reputation.

The Destruction of the Tooth and Hindu Funerals

The stories of the Portuguese destruction of the tooth need to be viewed in a number of different and complexly interwoven contexts. For simplicity's sake, in what follows, I will present some of these by portraying the tooth in four different ways: as a dead body needing disposal, as a pagan idol, as an auto-da-fé victim, and as a relic.

It is well known that cremation is one of the most common ways of disposing of a corpse in India—at present as in the time of the Portuguese. In so far as the tooth is a part of a once-living body, it may be possible to see the Portuguese use of fire in destroying it as referencing a funeral by cremation. But burning is not the only thing that destroys a body in Hindu funerary rites. In a typical cremation, after the flesh of the body has burned away, and the flames, having died down somewhat, are attacking the bones, the chief mourner approaches, and with a stick breaks open the skull of the deceased (to release the *ātman*). This can be done literally or symbolically (e.g., by breaking a clay pot) and marks an important ritual moment. A third "disposal" comes a few days later: after the pyre has cooled, some close relatives come back, sift through the ashes, and collect any remaining charred bones. These, together with some of the ashes, are pulverized and put in a pot and then scattered in a nearby river.[4] In other words, the full destruction of the Hindu corpse—a ritual that seeks to assure that the deceased will definitely not remain in this world but pass on to another—involves not only the use of fire, but also the breaking up of bones, and the sinking of any cremains in water.[5]

It is interesting that the Portuguese, in their treatment of the tooth, employ all three of these methods. It could be argued that, in most accounts, from the perspective of a Hindu funeral, the order in which they carry out

4. For a meticulous description of Hindu cremation rites not too distant from the time of the Portuguese in India, see Dubois [1807] 1906, 482–500. See also Parry 1994, 172–178.

5. It might be noted that not all Hindus are cremated. Certain kinds of corpses (generally those not fit for being "sacrificed" in the fire, or not needing such sacrifice, such as *sannyāsins*) are immersed; others may be buried (see Parry 1994, 184, 260–261).

the first two steps of this process is "wrong": crushing the bone of the tooth is said to precede, rather than follow, the burning of it. That is not universally true, however. Texeira, for example (see above), gets the order "right," describing how the tooth is first burned, then broken up and pounded, then thrown into the river. It may be that Texeira, who lived in Goa several times and did business there, was familiar with Hindu funerary practices and sought to reference those in his account. Indeed, it is noteworthy that he portrays the whole ritual destruction of the tooth as a spectacle intended for the "neighboring infidels," that is, the largely Hindu population of Goa. Was the Portuguese message to the assembled crowds thus meant to be "your monkey god is fully dead and gone, cremated according to your own rites"?[6] Perhaps not, but the coincidence is nonetheless noteworthy.

The order of the acts in which the tooth was destroyed, however, is perhaps not so important as the conjunction in a single ceremony of the three methods. It is noteworthy that the Portuguese decide, here, not to use their own, Christian, method of disposing of a dead body, that is, burial. They want, rather, a complete destruction of the tooth, and in this, again, there is a parallelism with Hindu funerals, which also seek a complete elimination of the body, in part out of fear that otherwise the deceased may be tempted to hang around and haunt the world of the living, and in part out of a desire to guarantee their passage onward in the realms of rebirth. Hindu mourners do not want the dead to remain *here*, and cremation, coupled with crushing the remains and throwing them in a river, it has been said, is one of the best ways of ensuring that they do not (Parry 1994, 179). Similarly, the Portuguese clearly did not want the tooth to remain in this world and took the same steps as Hindus to make sure that did not happen.

The Destruction of the Tooth and Portuguese Iconoclasm in Goa

The triple method of disposal, however, also has another referent. As is clear in the epigraph at the start of this chapter, it was employed in the paradigmatic biblical destruction of an idol instantiated by the story of Moses and the Golden Calf. Moses destroys the Calf by first burning it and then pulverizing it before disposing of the fragments in water.[7] Though the Golden Calf was not mentioned in the debate that preceded the destruction of the

---

6. This would have been especially ironic, since by this time, as we shall see, Hindus in Goa were no longer permitted to cremate their dead inside the city.

7. It is possible that Texeira had this in mind, instead of (or in addition to) the example of the Hindu funeral.

tooth (see above, chapter 4), we should recall here the many references made on that occasion to idolatry in the Old Testament, and it is clear that, in addition to thinking of the tooth as part of a dead body, we also need to consider it as an idol.[8]

In fact, idols—in particular Hindu images and objects of worship—were very much on the minds of the Portuguese Catholics in Goa in the middle of the sixteenth century. This was a time of a sustained and thoroughgoing iconoclastic campaign against all aspects of Hindu culture, expressed most clearly in the destruction of countless Hindu temples and shrines in the colony.[9] The first hint of what was to come may be found as early as 1522 in a letter from Bishop Duarte Nunez to King João III. In it, he proposes that the territory of Goa be made into a completely Christian place—that all local pagan landholders be forced to either convert or leave, and, specifically, that all Hindu temples be destroyed and replaced with churches.[10] No immediate steps on this recommendation were taken, however, until 1542, with the arrival of Governor Martin Afonso de Sousa along with Francis Xavier. It was under him and subsequent viceroys that these oppressive measures were first implemented (Henn 2014, 41). Then, in 1550, the campaign was expanded, by direct order of King João III, to include not only temples but all statues and images of Hindu deities, whether in public places or in private homes.[11] Moreover, no public "Gentile festivals" or funerals were to be permitted on the island, and no brahmin priests could live there or be brought over from the mainland (Henn 2014, 42). This order was repeated in 1559, by João III's successor, the queen regent Dona Catarina, who was just as specific as her late husband:

> in the island of Goa and its other annexed territories, there should be no more idols, nor images within nor outside of any house and all those found should be burned and disfigured. . . . Nor should it be possible to make them from wood, nor stone, nor any metal, nor any other materials, nor should

8. It should be noted that, according to Xavier and Županov (2015, 126), the threefold "Mosaic method" of disposal was meted out to images of gods in Goan temples in the iconoclasm of the 1560s.

9. Interestingly, Henn (2014, 48) speculates that the campaign in Goa might, in part, have been a reaction to Protestant destruction of images in Europe at the time, the Protestants being one of the targets of the Counter Reformation (also happening then).

10. For a description of the systematic way in which the materials of the Hindu temples were reused in Christian shrines and churches, see Xavier and Županov 2015, 126.

11. On royal orders in this period, see Whiteway 1899, 60–63; and Shirodkar 1998, 2: 36–42.

it be allowed to have any public Gentile festival indoors or outside, nor should Brahmanical Gentile priests be allowed . . . nor [temple] pools for the Gentiles, nor should they be allowed to burn [their dead]. (quoted in Henn 2014, 43)[12]

Alexander Henn (2014, 45) has pointed out that such orders, issued in Lisbon, were not necessarily always fully carried out on the ground in Goa, where local corruption and the ongoing influence of rich crypto-Hindus created various exceptions or found certain loopholes. Moreover, as was discussed above, there were various viewpoints on idols in Portuguese Goa, such as those of Thomas Stephens and Roberto De Nobili. Nonetheless, within a few decades, the campaign was more or less successful. Virtually all Hindus who had not at least nominally agreed to convert had left the city, the performance of non-Christian rituals or customs was ended, and all Hindu images had been replaced with Catholic ones. When Luís de Camões wrote his *Lusíads* in 1572, he characterized the Portuguese in Goa as "[ruling] with an iron fist the idol-worshiping Hindus and everyone throughout that land [who had] thoughts of rebellion" (Camões 1997, 35).

It is worth speculating how this ongoing iconoclastic campaign may have affected the debate about what to do with the tooth. Dom Constantino was under not only ecclesiastical but also royal pressure to destroy idols, since Queen Regent Catarina's order to do so was issued during the time of his vice regency, and he was thus the one expected to carry it out (Wojciehowski 2011, 210). But the tooth did not readily fit into the normal category of local "idols." Unlike the Hindu images of gods that were being burned or melted down, the tooth was not anthropomorphic or even theomorphic. Nor was it something that had been found in a temple or shrine in Goa. Nor was it particularly "Hindu." Nonetheless, the context of the times might have influenced the Portuguese to categorize the tooth as being, generically, an idol, and not mentioning, in doing so, its confusing Buddhist identity.

In their study of Buddhism and iconoclasm in East Asia, Rambelli and Reinders (2012, 171–203) distinguish between three related dimensions of acts of religiously inspired destruction: iconoclasm per se, which targets material entities; "semioclasm," which destroys or changes the meaning of

12. At about the same time, the self-immolation of widows (*sati*) was forbidden (see Shirodkar 1998, 2: 37). The aims of the persecution were also economic. Laws were passed allowing the confiscation of temple lands, as well as the appropriation of the wealth of Hindus who died by their Christian relatives, and, lacking any, by the Church. For a description of the full extent of the campaign, see Whiteway 1899, 60–67.

the object; and "hieroclasm," the destruction of its sacrality. In their consideration of the tooth as an icon, and in their destruction of it in Goa, the Portuguese would seem to have engaged in all three of these acts: they completely obliterated the object; they redefined its meaning as a tooth of the Devil; and in so doing, they erased whatever sacrality it might have had in Sri Lanka.

The Destruction of the Tooth and the Portuguese Inquisition in Goa

Non-Christian objects, such as temples and images, were not the only things being destroyed in sixteenth-century Goa; non-Christian persons were as well. Just about the same time as the iconoclastic movement was reaching its culmination in Goa, the Portuguese Inquisition was introduced there.[13] It quickly set about targeting suspected heretics—Jews, Protestants, Hindu converts who were deemed backsliders, and so on—by subjecting them to the ordeal of the auto-da-fé, and confiscating their wealth and property, whether they were dead or alive. As mentioned, the Goanese branch of the Inquisition was officially established in 1560, and though it did not hold its first auto-da-fé until 1562, the two first inquisitors, Aleixo Dias Falcão and Francisco Marques Botelho, were, according to Do Couto, present at the debate about the tooth, and presumably also at its ceremonial destruction in 1561 (Saraiva 2001, 345).

The word "auto-da-fé" (Portuguese for the Latin *actus de fide* ["act of faith"]) has popularly come to signify its harshest sentence of burning at the stake, though in fact, most of the condemned were not executed but received lesser punishments. These often involved assigned penances of various sorts, exile and/or prison, and, usually, confiscation of wealth. Also, as we shall see, many—indeed, in Goa, a slight majority—of the "executed" victims were, in fact, already dead when they were burned, having died in prison from sickness or torture, or having passed away at home even before being—posthumously—accused and tried. They were usually burned in effigy, along with their bones, which were exhumed for the occasion.[14]

---

13. Prior to 1560, prisoners of the Inquisition in India had to be sent back to Portugal for trial.

14. According to one listing, of the 4,046 persons sentenced at seventy-one autos-da-fé held in Goa between 1600 and 1773, fifty-seven were burned alive at the stake, while sixty-four were burned in effigy, along with their bones. See Saraiva 2001, 345. (By way of contrast, in Lisbon, between 1540 and 1794, out of a total of 7,666 persons tried, 461 were executed in person and only 181 in effigy.) For an engraving showing effigies of the dead in Goa, and the small coffers containing their bones, see Amiel and Lima 1997, 256.

The victims in Goa included, first and foremost, "New Christians," of which, in India, there were two kinds: recently converted Hindus and Muslims (or their descendants) who were suspected of backsliding;[15] and recently converted Jews, or, more commonly as time went on, the descendants of long-ago Jewish converts, who were nonetheless still suspect and stigmatized.[16] In addition, there were people who were deemed to be practicing witchcraft or sorcery, natives caught observing Hindu religious practices in Goan territory (where such things were outlawed), and anyone not liked enough by anyone else nasty enough and in a position to make accusations.[17]

Autos-da-fé were great public ecclesiastical rituals—the grand joint culmination of the trials of many individuals whose secret separate interrogations had been going on for some time. They were important occasions in the religious and social life of Goa and were held periodically every two to three years.[18] Meticulous records and transcripts of the trials were kept, but in the case of the Inquisition at Goa, most of the latter were burned by the Church after the final abolishment of the Inquisition there in 1812, when it was decided to archive only the inventories and catalogs and not the full files (Saraiva 2001, 345–346). We do have, however, a graphic firsthand description of the whole process by an eyewitness, Charles Gabriel Dellon, a French physician from Agde in Languedoc who went out to India in 1667 and was arrested six years later on trumped-up charges. He was held and interrogated by the Inquisition in Goa for two years before going through his auto-da-fé ceremony, at the end of which he was excommunicated (this was later rescinded), deprived of all his worldly wealth, forbidden to remain

15. It has been estimated that, during Dom Constantino's three-year tenure as viceroy (1558–1561), around 36,000 Indians were baptized in Goa (Disney 2009, 2: 165; cited in Wojciehowski 2011, 210n77).

16. As Hannah Wojciehowski (2011, 209–212) remarks, there were many such formerly Jewish "New Christians" in the Portuguese colonies in Asia, since a lot of them had fled from Portugal when the danger to them increased with the establishment of the Inquisition there. The presence of these "crypto-Jews" throughout the Portuguese territories so infuriated Francis Xavier that he called for sending the Inquisition to Goa as early as 1546. For a seventeenth-century account of "New Christians" and the Inquisition, see Dellon 1688, 158–173. Nevertheless, the Jews, even unconverted, were crucial to Goa's economy (see De Souza 1979, 120–124).

17. Over the duration of the Inquisition in Goa, 71 percent of the accused were considered to be "crypto-Hindus." "Crypto-Jews" represented only 9 percent of the accused, but they made up 71 percent of those actually condemned to death (see Amiel and Lima 1997, 72).

18. How long one spent in prison being interrogated thus depended on how long before or after an auto-da-fé one had been arrested. Dellon (1688, 310) complains that he was deliberately sent to Goa just after the auto-da-fé of 1673, and so had to languish in prison for another two years before his case could be resolved.

in India, and condemned to five years of service in "La Galère"—not a ship, but an eponymously named prison in Lisbon, called "the Galley" (Dellon 1688, 280–281).[19] When he was finally freed, and made it back to Paris, he wrote an account of his experiences. In what follows, I will depend on his relation for its description of the final auto-da-fé ceremony.[20]

On the day chosen for the auto-da-fé ritual, Dellon is removed from his cell in the middle of the night and taken outside, where he joins a cohort of about two hundred other accused heretics and apostates (only a dozen of whom are Europeans, himself included).[21] At dawn, the people of the city are summoned, by the ringing of church bells, to gather outside their homes for the hour-long spectacle of the parade of the prisoners, who are then all marched, each accompanied by a citizen of Goa who has been chosen to act as his or her "sponsor" for the Act of Faith. They are forced to walk barefoot (Dellon mentions his feet being badly cut by stones), and are dressed in black garments, over which they are made to wear a yellow sackcloth cloak, marked in front and back with a red Saint Andrew's cross, and sometimes emblems of their crimes. At the head of the procession goes an elevated image of Saint Dominic, the putative founder of the Inquisition, bearing a sword in one hand and an olive branch in the other, over the inscription "Justitia et Misericordia" [Justice and compassion] (Dellon 1688, 266–267).[22]

Once the procession arrives at the Church of Saint Francis, all the prisoners enter the nave and are seated on benches. The crowd of townspeople follow along and fill the rest of the building, before the inquisitors and the viceroy and his officials make their entrance and take their seats to either

19. The prison was so-called because, as Dellon explains (1688, 395), Portugal did not then have a system of condemning prisoners to a servitude of rowing on actual galleys (boats). In the Galley Prison, in Lisbon, convicts were chained in pairs and taken out to work in a factory every day from dawn to dusk. They did labor in building ships and other things. Though condemned to five years, Dellon managed to have his sentence commuted after seven months through the appeal of his parents in France and the intervention of influential aristocrats in France and church authorities in Lisbon. He was freed in June 1677, having first been arrested in India in August 1673 (Dellon 1688, 417–418). For a biography of Dellon, see Amiel and Lima 1997, 41–53. On Dellon's importance in the study of Indian religion, see Subrahmanyam 2017, 124–125.

20. A number of works in the nineteenth and early twentieth centuries claimed, wrongly, that Dellon's account was a forgery. On this, see Amiel and Lima 1997, 75–76. A much briefer but earlier firsthand description of the Inquisition in Goa may be found in Pyrard de Laval 1619, 2: 94–97.

21. Dellon 1688, 153. According to surviving records, the number of accused in his cohort was actually 141. See Amiel and Lima 1997, 79.

22. For an illustration, see Amiel and Lima 1997, 30 and 192.

side of the High Altar, which has been draped in black for the occasion. The ritual per se begins with a sermon by the superior of the local Augustinians. This is followed by the calling forth of the prisoners, one at a time, to hear lengthy readings of their individual crimes and sentences, following which they are forced to kneel and repeat the confession of faith. It is on this occasion that Dellon finally learns of his actual offenses: (1) doubting the validity of the doctrine of Baptism by Desire; (2) blaspheming by calling an ivory crucifix "a piece of ivory"; and (3) maligning the Inquisition and its ministers. For these crimes, he is excommunicated, has all his goods confiscated by the king, and is banished from the Indies, condemned to five years of prison and hard labor in Lisbon, and given a large number of religious penances (Dellon 1688, 276–279).

Once all the prisoners not guilty of capital offenses have been sentenced and have confessed their sins and their faith anew, the inquisitors finally turn their attention to the sentencing of those who are condemned to die. Seated separately at the back of the church, they (including the effigies of those who are already dead) are dressed in special gray costumes graphically painted with devils and flaming pieces of wood. On the occasion of Dellon's auto-da-fé, there are two living persons—a man and a woman— both Indian Christians who were deemed to have apostatized and become sorcerers. In addition, there are four deceased individuals represented by their life-size likenesses as well as their bones contained in small caskets, all of which are to be ceremonially burned on separate pyres at the same time as those condemned to die while still living.

Once this final sentencing is finished, those condemned to die, as well as the bones and statues of those so condemned but already dead, are immediately taken to the riverbank, where the viceroy and his court have reassembled and where the pyres have already been prepared. There the living are given one last chance to say whether they wish to die as Christians, in which case they are killed by strangulation before having their bodies burned; if they refuse, they are burned alive (Dellon 1688, 290–291).

As we have seen, Hannah Wojciehowski (2011, 184) has stated that "the burning of the tooth must be considered a precursor to the thousands of autos-da-fé that would be conducted in Goa over the next two and a half centuries." Indeed, there are some striking parallels. Both the destruction of the tooth and the autos-da-fé involving execution were grand, public events, held in an open space (the same one?) by the riverside, featuring destruction by incineration, and designed to condemn heresy, warn potential backsliders, and make clear the power of the Church. What interests me here, however, are some of the more detailed parallels, as well as some of the differences.

It is noteworthy that in Goa, it was as common to see the effigies and bones of dead persons burned on the pyres of the Inquisition as it was to witness the burning at the stake of actual live victims. In an era when burial in consecrated ground was the accepted Christian norm and cremation was viewed with horror, the burning of a person's bones, of course, had severe eschatological and soteriological implications, condemning victims not only in this life, but in the life to come, by barring them from eventual bodily resurrection. Dellon, in his account, is quite focused on these bones, and distinguishes two types of situations. On the one hand, the inquisitors could order the exhumation of the bones of persons who had died even before they were accused of any crime, and were only posthumously accused of wrongdoing, tried, and sentenced.[23] (Dellon remarks, wryly, that such persons, who could have been dead for years, often happened to have been wealthy, but, being dead, were no longer powerful.) On the other hand, there were those prisoners who happened to die (of illness or under torture) while being interrogated. They were quickly interred without ceremony in the prison itself, so that their bodies would remain accessible and could be "deboned" ("*désossé*"), once they were posthumously found guilty and condemned to death (Dellon 1688, 139). Either way, their skeletal remains were broken up and placed in small casket-cases made especially for the purpose, which were then carried to the pyres. It is clear that it was thought better to burn bones at an auto-da-fé than to burn (dead) bodies. The emphasis here on the bones—rather than on the whole corpses—of the dead is interesting, for it means that the burning of the tooth, itself a bone, and itself brought in a small casket to the place of public execution, would not have been that great an anomaly in sixteenth-century Goa.

Mention should be made, however, of one detail in the description of the destruction of the tooth, which differentiates it from a typical auto-da-fé. As Dellon makes clear repeatedly in his book, one of the motivating factors of the Inquisition was not only the combating of perceived heresies, but also the acquisition of money. Those arrested found themselves stripped of

---

23. This apparently was fairly common. Perhaps the most famous case of someone being burned posthumously at the stake is that of the auto-da-fé of the renowned Goan botanist Garcia de Orta, whose effigy and exhumed remains were burned in 1580. He had died in 1569 but was later accused of having backslid and secretly "judaized." See Saraiva 2001, 346–347n5. On de Orta more generally, see Subrahmanyam 2017, 19–20.

all of their worldly goods, and thus rich, but not particularly powerful or well-connected persons, such as the generally economically successful "new Christians," were favored targets. With the auto-da-fé, the Church and the Portuguese had figured out a way for combining religious and monetary pursuits. With the burning of the tooth, however, they (as we saw in the accounts of the debate above) reasserted that divide, since it involved the giving up (for the sake of "religion") a fortune that was being offered as ransom money. To be sure, the destruction of the tooth was not completely without gain. As we have seen above, one of our earliest sources, that of the French Jesuit Du Jarric, specifies that Dom Constantino had all the precious stones set around the coffer containing the tooth removed prior to its burning. These, he says, "were of great value" (Gaspard 1918, 19; Du Jarric 1610, 399), but they could hardly have been worth as much as the great sums mentioned as a potential ransom payment. Indeed, more generally, Du Jarric is tuned in to the fact that the tooth was pretty much the only thing the Portuguese got from Jaffna. In that sense, it may be seen as symbolic not only of the Portuguese giving up on the ransom money (something graphically illustrated in the Dom Constantino's CCCCC medallion), but also of their *loss* of the great royal treasure which King Cankili was said to possess, but which they never managed to capture (see Gaspard 1918, 19; Du Jarric 1610, 399).

Much the same point is made in the accounts of finding the tooth on Adam's Peak: the Portuguese ransacked everything, looking for booty, but the relic was the only thing they found (see Van Linschoten 1598, 81). The destruction of the tooth thus has a double significance: it is symbolic of putting an end not only to idolatry, but to the quest for material gain, and in this, it was rather different than the auto-da-fé.

Relics, the Destruction of the Tooth, and the Body of Francis Xavier

There is one final context to be considered in understanding Portuguese attitudes toward the tooth at this time in Goa. Though no mention is made of this being the tooth of the Buddha in the debates leading up to its destruction, there are references elsewhere to its being thought of as a relic. Do Couto, for instance, at one point, calls it a "relic"—indeed, a "very great relic" (*mui grande reliquio*) (Do Couto 1783, 17: 317)—and not an idol (*idolo*) or a fetish (*feitiço*).

He would, of course, have been familiar with relics from his own Roman Catholic tradition. Indeed, elsewhere, Do Couto (1786, 18: 82; Eng. trans.,

Tennent 1859, 2: 218–219) tells us that the king of Pegu venerated the Buddha's tooth, "even as we esteem the tooth of Saint Apollonia,"[24] and he even praises him for his fervent desire to get it back, unlike (he adds critically) "certain kings of Christendom" who allowed several important Christian relics to "remain so long in the hands of the Turks".[25]

More immediately, in Do Couto's time, relics of Christian saints were, even in Asia, ubiquitous. Ines Županov (n.d., 6), who has studied the use of Catholic relics in Portuguese imperialism and colonialism, concludes that if we put together the relics that accompanied missionaries, Portuguese ecclesiastics, and pious laypersons, "we have potentially millions [sic?] of tiny little bones, pieces of cloth or writing, splinters of the true cross and many other varieties constantly moving into, through, and out of Asia." Do Couto's recognition of the tooth as a "relic" indicates his own realization that the Buddha was not only a human being, but a saintly one, albeit of a different tradition. Indeed, he calls the Buddha their "great saint" (grande santo) (Do Couto 1783, 17, 317).

Patrick Geary (1986, 169) has pointed out that relics, like slaves, "belong to that category, unusual in Western Society, of objects that are both persons and things." Like slaves, they have commercial worth, and though, according to canon law, they should not technically be bought or sold, they effectively were. They certainly were thought to have value. As Geary (1986, 184) puts it: "When, in the course of raids on neighboring nobles, an enemy's property was pillaged, relics were normally included in the spoils." When captured, they were not typically (or at least not immediately) destroyed (unlike "idols," which the Portuguese on raids commonly shattered and/or burned right away).

More importantly, the assumption that the tooth was viewed as a relic (albeit a heathen one) placed it in a very specific context. In 1554, just six years prior to the capture of the tooth and seven years prior to its destruction, the whole-body relic of the not-yet-beatified Francis Xavier was enshrined in Goa, in the Church of São Paulo.[26]

---

24. Apollonia was a virgin saint whose martyrdom included having all her teeth violently pulled out. She is accordingly the patron saint of dentistry and can be prayed to for dental problems. A tooth relic of hers was enshrined in the Cathedral of Porto, in northern Portugal.

25. Specifically, Do Couto refers here to "the nail which fastened our Savior to the Cross; the thorns which encircled his most sacred head; [and] the spear which pierced his blessed side."

26. Some decades later it was placed in the Basilica do Bom Jesus, also in Goa (its construction was finished in 1605). There, in the words of one authority, "Xavier's tomb [was] walled into a central part of the edifice, almost reminiscent of the garbha grha of a Hindu temple" (Županov n.d., 22). His full-body relic remains there to this day, apart from an arm requested

Xavier passed away on an island off the south China coast, not far from Macao, in December 1552. The following year, his body was taken to Malacca, where it was reburied on March 22. Almost a year later, remarkably still in a perfect state of preservation, it was exhumed and translated to Goa, where it arrived just before Holy Week, on March 16, 1554. There it was received not only by the local Jesuit hierarchs, but by the viceroy, Dom Afonso de Noronha (Dom Constantino's predecessor), by all the *fidalgos* of his court, and by all the clergy and all the people of the city (Brockey 2015, 48–49; Gupta 2004, 104).

According to the Jesuit priest Melchior Nunes Barreto, who was an eyewitness to the event, once Xavier's coffin had reached the church, the crowd had grown to about 6,000 people who refused to leave until they had been shown the body. "And so," Barreto later wrote to Ignatius of Loyola, the Jesuit superior general, "we showed it to them" (Wicki 1954, 3: 77). Moved by devotion and curiosity, the crowd then pressed forward, threatening to break the altar bar behind which the now-opened coffin had been placed. Some people cried out, some beat their breasts, all tried to kiss the dead holy man's feet and hands. As Barreto put it, "If we had not been there with him, I greatly fear that everyone would have taken a piece [of him] as a relic, such was the great fervor of the people" (Brockey 2015, 49; original Spanish text in Wicki 1954, 3: 77).[27]

Despite the fact that Xavier was not yet a saint, the fear of devotees taking pieces of his clothing or body was a real one. Indeed, during his beatification hearings in 1616, two old women who had been present on the occasion of the arrival of his body in Goa over sixty years earlier testified that at that time they had seen someone try to bite off one of his toes, while kissing his feet. That, however, was not what impressed them: they were more interested in the fact that, miraculously, blood had flowed from the wound, a full two years after his death![28]

---

by the Pope in 1614, which was sent to Rome. For a view of that arm during its tour of Canada in January 2018, see https://www.youtube.com/watch?v=K7YjkGMGI-Q (last accessed April 19, 2019).

27. Such tumultuous scenes of devotional frenzy at the exposition of relics were by no means uncommon. For a good example from a few decades later in Lisbon, see Brockey 2005, 22–25. In the case of Xavier in Goa, the body remained on display for three days (Gupta 2004, 116).

28. Brockey 2015, 50. Such attempted thefts by biting relic-kissers were likewise by no means uncommon. For a number of Christian examples in late antiquity and the Middle Ages, see Strong 2004a, 29–38. At least one miracle needs to be certified for beatification. Later, Catholics would claim that vast numbers of miracles occurred when Saint Francis's body was first taken to Saint Paul's in Goa: the blind recovered their sight, the paralyzed got up and walked, the

Xavier died at the time of the Council of Trent (1545–1563), which was formulating Roman Catholic responses to the rise of Protestantism. Among these was a careful reassertion of the sanctity of relics in the face of attacks on them by figures such as Martin Bucer (1491–1551) and John Calvin (1509–1564).[29] In this context, the body of Francis Xavier, miraculously incorrupt, was seen, especially in Jesuit circles, as a kind of showpiece of a "good" and "proper" relic, which could be contrasted with the dead bodies of non-Catholics. For instance, the Jesuit cardinal Roberto Bellarmino (1542–1621), who became an important spokesperson for Counter Reformation theology, engaged in a bit of post-mortem comparison, contrasting the state of Xavier's body to that (in his opinion) of Martin Luther (1483–1546), who predeceased him by six years. As a sign of God's favor, he states, Xavier's body relic was miraculously preserved after his death, while Luther's corpse had begun to decay: "It rotted such that the bad smell could not keep from leaking out of the tin box in which that miserable body was placed . . . and this . . . in the middle of winter when everything was frozen by the cold" (quoted in Brockey 2015, 56).

Such messages were clear: as concretely marked by the relics of its saints, Catholicism was pure and did not decay; other religions were not and did. In this context alone, the citizens of Goa must have been struck by the contrast between the body of their great saint Xavier and the tooth of the Gentiles, especially when the latter, upon burning, emitted a foul odor, as several of our sources testify (see Faria e Souza 1666–1675, 2: 364).

This contrast, moreover, must have been reinforced by a further factor at play in our consideration of the treatment of the tooth. This was the belief that, although they could be stolen and divided and translated from place to place, relics were, generally speaking, thought to be indestructible. This was true in both Christianity and Buddhism. In Roman Catholicism, for instance, a number of techniques developed for ascertaining the authenticity of a relic by showing it to be indestructible. One of these, beginning in the Middle Ages, was a trial by fire. This was a recognized ceremony with its own established liturgy, whereby the relic was placed in a specially prepared charcoal brazier; if the flames died down and went out and the relic remained intact, its genuineness was confirmed; if not, its counterfeit nature was exposed.[30]

---

deaf could hear, the dumb could speak, lepers were made clean. See *Catholic Messenger and the Western World* 1932.

29. See Eire 1986, 91; and Calvin 1970.

30. On the ritual and its usage, see Dooley 1931, 26–27; Snoek 1995, 329–332; and Head 1993. See also Geary 1986, 178.

There are obvious echoes here with the ceremony of the destruction of the tooth, with the difference, of course, that the latter *did* get burned and was destroyed by the fire. Whatever other connotations this act may have had, at least for some of the Portuguese present, and for Christians hearing about it, it was sending the message that this tooth had failed the traditional test of genuineness: it was not a true relic.

Interestingly, much the same conclusion may have been reached by some Buddhists, for they too believed in the indestructibility of genuine relics. Thus, in their eyes as well, the fact that this tooth had been smashed and burned could be seen as an indication that it was *not* the true tooth of the Buddha, but merely a facsimile. In fact, for Buddhists, 1561 was not the first time that some non-Buddhists had tried to smash, burn, and sink the Buddha's tooth. As we have seen, according to the thirteenth-century *Dāṭhāvaṃsa* [The chronicle of the tooth], much the same thing had happened long ago in Kalinga, before the tooth was even brought to Sri Lanka. The Indian ruler at that time was Paṇḍu, who objected to the Kalingans worshipping a "dead person's bone," and so had it brought to his capital, where he tried to destroy it (see fig. 2.1 above). First, a charcoal pit was prepared, and the tooth was thrown into it; instantly, the flames were cooled, and the relic was seen to rest, unburned, on a lotus blossom. Then the relic was placed on a chopping block and smashed with a hammer; un-fractured, the tooth merely slipped into the anvil, intact. Then, attempts were made to sink it in a moat and to bury it and have it trampled by elephants. In each case, it resurfaced unscathed (Law 1925, 18–22 [text], 23–30 [trans.]). Giving up, Paṇḍu converted to Buddhism, and the tooth was returned to Kalinga, whence it was eventually sent to Sri Lanka.

The destruction of the tooth by the Portuguese, especially when contrasted with the nearby intact and indestructible body of Francis Xavier, may be seen as part of a greater cultural war that used relics to score ideological victories. Županov (n.d., 23) has stated in this regard that

> there is no doubt that Christian sacred relics were an important part of the joint venture of Iberian and Catholic imperial expansion in the early modern period. They marked the spaces of actual territorial conquest, especially in the Americas, and of newly opened spiritual markets, in Asia in particular.

Pamila Gupta (2004, 137), in a passage of her dissertation that seems not to have made it into her book by the same title, is even more specific:

> The Portuguese destruction of the Buddha's tooth suggests their continuing encroachment upon new territories in Portuguese Asia, their investment in

expanding the practice of relic translation to new contexts and with regard to new religions and publics, and their investment in increasing the (exchange) value of Xavier's corpse. . . . [The] Portuguese and "native" forces were using these religious relics as symbols of territorial power as well as to expand the jurisdiction of saint and state.[31]

As a postscript to all this, it may be said that such relic warfare, in some ways, still goes on to this day. Indeed, in recent times, some Sri Lankan Buddhists have claimed that the incorrupt body of Saint Francis Xavier in Goa is not really his, but that of their own famed Buddhist monk and scholar Toṭagāmuwa Sri Rahula (1408–1491). Because of his ascetic lifestyle, and because of his masterful knowledge of powerful Ayurvedic drugs (so goes the story), Toṭagāmuwa's body did not decompose after his death at a cave near Indurigiri. Consequently, he was not cremated. The following century, however, a Portuguese captain named Pereira managed to find Toṭagāmuwa's body (the villagers had been hiding it), and had it shipped to Goa. It arrived there in 1554, at the same time as Xavier's body. Somehow the two corpses were mixed up, and Xavier's was thrown overboard (the Sri Lankan implication was that it was beginning to rot) and Rahula's was enshrined in Goa, where it has lain ever since.[32]

---

31. She adds the interesting datum that Emperor Akbar, the newly appointed ruler of the Mughal Dynasty after 1556, sent an emissary to Goa during his tenure to pay his respects to Xavier's relic.

32. There are various conflicting versions of this story. See Himbutana 2006; Holt 1991, 236n9; and Gupta 2004, 102n239. In recent times, some Sri Lankan activists have demanded that DNA tests be done and that the body be returned to Sri Lanka if it proves to be that of a Sri Lankan. They claim that the body in Goa is short and dark-skinned, but that Xavier was fair-skinned and tall, since he was a Basque and "[all] Basques are tall" (*sic*) (see Waduge 2014). For an outraged Goan response to this demand, see https://www.youtube.com/watch?v=AmckPSGCkZo. Also, on the Indian side, some have lobbied for the return of the body to Europe, claiming that a man who inflicted atrocities on Indians should not be honored in India. See Anonymous n.d.

The Storical Evolution of the Tales of the Portuguese Tooth

Before passing on to a consideration of British dealings with the tooth relic, it may be useful to recap some of what we have learned so far about the Portuguese case. In the paragraphs that follow, I will try to sum up the findings of part 1 by spelling out more precisely what I have been calling the "storical" evolution—a genealogy of sorts—of the development of the overall narrative of the Portuguese discovery and destruction of the tooth.

In my opinion, our story begins not in Sri Lanka, but in Portuguese Goa. There, in the mid- to late sixteenth century, a tale was told of a remembered, public event—the ceremonial burning of a pagan tooth by either the viceroy or the archbishop or both. I am, in fact, willing to assert that this starting point, this *storical* event, was also an actual *historical* event—something that really happened to a real object. As we have seen, there are many contextual factors that help explain the occurrence of this event in Goa at this time: the ongoing Portuguese iconoclastic campaign in the city and environs, the advent of the Inquisition to the colony, the arrival there of the whole-body relic of Francis Xavier, and the preponderance of demonological anxieties at the time. It is also one of the few things on which virtually all of our fourteen sources—despite their divergences on other matters—are in agreement.

I am less certain about the historicity of the debate in Goa preceding the destruction of the tooth. This strikes me, rather, as the point at which our storical evolution starts. One of the things that made the historical event of the destruction of the tooth story-worthy was the fact that it implied the rejection—not just by the Church but also by the State represented by the viceroy—of the supposed vast sums of money being proffered by the would-be ransomers. In the context of the rampant corruption of the times in Goa, this tale truly was remarkable, and it is quite possible that without it, the story of the tooth might have died out altogether. In other words, in its early stages, the tale of the tooth had as much to do with the glorification of religious faith over secular greeds and needs, as it did with scoring points against Buddhism or Hinduism, Pegu or Vijayanagara, or Sri Lanka.

In this, the figure of Dom Constantino da Braganza was central. Indeed, it is possible that one of the primary aims of the story of the debate was upholding the reputation of the viceroy as a paradigm of virtue and pious propriety, and thereby to defend him from his maligners both during his lifetime and posthumously. This, as we have seen, was epitomized in Do Couto's account of the "CCCCC medallion" that was struck to commemorate the occasion and glorify Dom Constantino, but the theme is also found in the other narratives of the discussions about what to do with the tooth. That these were written in the shadow of the Inquisition seems likely.

Two important questions—where did this tooth come from, and whose tooth was it?—do not seem to have been at the forefront of the minds of the debaters and tooth-burners in Goa. But they rapidly came to preoccupy the storytellers, and in time, multiple answers to both were given, although sometimes these were kept separate and sometimes combined.

There was general agreement from the start that the tooth came from Sri Lanka, but as we have seen, there was some disagreement as to where on the island it was found. Starting with our oldest source, Van Linschoten, we can see the development of a story that was remarkably persistent in Dutch circles. This was that the tooth was found on Adam's Peak, and was somehow connected to the fame of the renowned footprint embedded in the rock on top of that mountain. This view may have originated most immediately in João de Barros's account of a tooth on Adam's Peak, most likely written prior to the 1560 Jaffna invasion (De Barros [1563] 1777, 116; Ferguson 1909, 36). Marco Polo too, we have seen, was cognizant of a similar tradition. At a general level, this association may simply have been due to the fact that for foreigners, Adam's Peak, at that time and for centuries prior to it, was the single most famous site in Sri Lanka. If one were looking to locate the tooth somewhere on the island, it might be the only place one (or one's readers) had heard of. On the other hand, the cosmopolitan, multicultural, multireligious nature of the footprint on Adam's Peak may have served to facilitate the multiple identities given to the tooth.

There was, however, another, rival (and in the end apparently victorious) version of the tale that placed the tooth's capture in Jaffna. In its origin, this location may simply have been due to the association of the destruction of the tooth with the viceroy, Dom Constantino—something that could be connected to the belief that it was taken during the just-completed expedition to Jaffna that he had personally led. In time, though, especially among those claiming the tooth was the Buddha's, there appears to have been a realization that there was something odd about its location in Jaffna, and this spawned the explanatory story that it was taken there by Vidiye Bandara, when he fled north from Kotte, and that it was left there after he was killed. This explanation must reflect some degree of Portuguese awareness, at this point in time, of the Sri Lankan tradition of a tooth of relic in Kotte.

The second question—whose tooth was this?—was similarly given multiple answers, and here we can see our genealogy develop two lineages of tradition—one focusing on simian identities, the other on the Buddha.

The "simian lineage" came first. That it was the earliest is reflected not only in its exclusive appearance in the first five of our sources (according to publication date), but also, more importantly, in the fact that all of the later (post–Do Couto) sources that propose that the tooth was the Buddha's do so only after trying to correct or add to the simian theory. They were thus clearly well aware of its existence as a tale.

Very quickly, however, within the simian lineage, there arose several sub-lineages: the monkey's tooth sub-lineage, the white monkey's tooth sub-lineage, and the Hanumān sub-lineage. The first two of these may have developed for a variety of reasons, among them a desire to mock and malign those pagans who honored the tooth. The Hanumān sub-lineage clearly picked up on the legend of the divine figure of Hanumān of *Rāmāyaṇa* fame. At the same time, I suggested that Hanumān may have been the equivalent in Jaffna to the figure of Vibhīṣaṇa in Kotte. In other words, he may have been a symbol of South Indian—specifically Vijayanagaran—hegemony, something the Portuguese were eager to displace.

As their perception of the geopolitical configuration of powers changed, however, the Portuguese found themselves more inclined to find another identity for the tooth. The view that the tooth was the Buddha's appears to have been the latest to have developed, and came about not only from a better realization of the legend of the Buddha (and his dealings with Sri Lanka), but also from a growing awareness (rightly or wrongly) of the pan-Asian importance of Buddhism as a religious rival to Roman Catholicism in the Portuguese domains. At the same time, the evolving geopolitical significance of the identity of the tooth was underlined by growing Portuguese awareness that others (e.g., King Bayinnaung of Pegu; King Vimaladharmas-uriya of Kandy) claimed to be in possession of the Buddha's tooth relic. This was reflected in two further storical developments that seemed aimed at undermining these claims. First, there was Do Couto's tale that Bayinnaung's tooth was a fake that the king of Kotte had had carved out of staghorn and sold to him as the genuine relic. Second, there was the closely related tale of the king of Kandy trying (but failing) to execute the same chicanery with a different fake relic, one later said to be nothing but a buffalo's tooth. The origin of these two tales of trickery can be traced back to Van Linschoten, who mentions a clever merchant carving a new tooth and selling it to the emperor of Vijayanagara. But in any case, their intent seems the same: to recognize the fact that both Pegu and Kandy claimed to be in possession of *the* tooth, but to undermine those assertions, by explaining them away, and maintaining that the genuine tooth of the Buddha was the one the Portuguese destroyed in Goa.

Finally, there is one more general point to be made in this storical survey to the tale of the tooth. That is the realization, virtually from the start, that whether the tooth was Hanumān's or the Buddha's, it was an "object from away"—something that was imported to Sri Lanka from abroad, and that retained its transnational connections. The Portuguese were well aware that both Hanumān and the Buddha came from India. In Sri Lanka, mythologically, Hanumān was an illustration of a complex and paradoxical trope: the liberating invader. But so was the Buddha. Rāma was not the only one to conquer the demons of the island; the Buddha did so as well. The Sri Lankan chronicles make this clear in their story of the Buddha's various visits to the island (which read like conquests over indigenous forces). On one of those visits, the Buddha in fact sets fire to Sri Lanka in order to chase off the demons (*Mahāvaṃsa* 1908, 5; Eng. trans., Geiger 1912, 4), in a way not dissimilar to Hanumān who, in the *Rāmāyaṇa* (see Vālmīki 2006, ch. 5), burns the whole island with his tail, become a torch after Rāvaṇa sets it on fire.[1] More generally, Rāma, Hanumān, and the Buddha all served to make Sri Lanka part and parcel of South (and Southeast) Asian culture, religion, and politics. In this context, it is interesting to note that the German Jesuit Athanasius Kircher (1602–1680), sometimes called the "last man who knew everything" (Lopez 2017, 64), tells us that, though the Chinese refer to the Buddha as Xe Cian and the Japanese as Xaca, "the Indians call him Rāma" (Kircher [1667] 1987, 141).

I suggested in chapter 3 that Hanumān's tooth was a symbol of Indian (specifically Vijayanagaran) hegemonic power over the island, that the Portuguese would naturally seek to break and replace. We shall find, in part 2 below, that the same may be said of the Kandyan tooth, with the difference that the foreign hegemons (first the Nāyakkar kings of Kandy and then the

---

1. De la Boullaye-Le-Gouz (1653, 165–166) recounts a popular seventeenth-century version of this story about Hanumān (whom he calls Hermand) before telling (179) the story of the Portuguese capture of his tooth relic.

British) did not reside in India, but in Sri Lanka itself. Indeed, as we shall see, Victor Goloubew has argued that precisely because the Hindu Nāyakkar kings were "foreigners" from South India, they felt the "foreign" object of the tooth to be a good symbol for their sovereignty, and helped them maintain the political notion of a greater empire "uniting the royalty of [Sri Lanka] to those of the [South Indian] Dravidian dynasties" (Goloubew 1932, 457).

Do Couto and the Portuguese historians following him argued that the tooth captured by Dom Constantino in Jaffna was not that of a monkey or of Hanumān, but that of the Buddha. In the end, however, there is a sense in which the tooth retained its multiple identities. It did not perhaps do so as overtly and explicitly as the footprint on Adam's Peak, with its simulta- neous general acceptance of multiple religious affiliations, but, as we shall see, in its cult and in its symbolism, the tooth was able to bring together elements of Buddhist and Hindu culture, as well as powers both indigenous and "foreign."

PART TWO

The British and the Tooth Relic

SIX

The Cosmopolitan Tooth: The Relic in Kandy before the British Became Aware of It

What seems more or less certain is that the cult of the Sacred Tooth developed, so
to speak, in a double milieu and that, despite its Buddhistic appearances, it kept
some solid connections to the Dravidian world. This, perhaps, makes us understand why, among Ceylonese kings of Indian descent, there were so many fervent
venerators of the Daḷadā.

—Victor Goloubew (1932, 456–457)

By and large, except for a few scholars, Sri Lankans did not participate in
telling stories about the destruction of the Portuguese tooth. They were, in
fact, more or less oblivious to it. They were very much aware, however, of
their own tooth—the one in Kotte that was taken to Delgamuwa and thence
to Kandy—and had their own tales to tell about it. This accounts for a difference between the narratives we will consider in the chapters that follow
and those we looked at in part 1. The Portuguese had almost carte blanche
to say what they wanted about the tooth they captured, especially after its
destruction. The British, on the other hand, had to build their story on a pre-
existing Sri Lankan narrative about a relic that had already been esteemed
and venerated in Kandy for over two centuries, and, in Sri Lanka, for much
longer than that. With this in mind, this first chapter of part 2 will be largely
introductory. In it, I will present my understanding of the status and nature
of the Kandyan tooth prior to the advent of the British, or rather prior to
1815, when they first became aware of its importance.

The Kandyan kingdom was the last remaining part of Ceylon to come
under the control of a Western colonial power. As we have seen, the island's
coastal regions had long been occupied—first by the Portuguese, starting
early in the sixteenth century, and then by the Dutch, from c. 1650 on, and

finally, by the British, beginning in 1796. But neither the Portuguese nor the Dutch nor the British (prior to 1815) had ever definitively conquered the center of the island, though they had all attacked the town of Kandy and briefly held it at different times (see De Silva 1981, 113–129, 161–187).

Located at an altitude of roughly 450 meters, on the side of an artificial lake (dug by corvée labor in 1807), and further surrounded by forested hills and mountains, the town of Kandy occupies the heart of the island's central highlands. Doctor John Davy, a physician who accompanied the 1815 British expedition there, describes the town as he saw it. In his estimation, its situation is "beautiful and romantic," but he is little impressed by the houses of the people which, he tells us, "are all of clay, of one story . . . [and] thatched, with the exception of the dwellings of the chiefs, which are tiled" (Davy 1821, 365). He does, however, take note of the palace, various Buddhist monasteries (the Malwatta and Asgiriya *vihāras*), and the temples (*devales*) of the four protector gods of the city—in his day, Nātha, Viṣṇu, Kataragama, and Pattini. "The palace," he admits,

> did occupy a considerable space of ground. Its front, about 200 yards long, made rather an imposing appearance: it looked towards the principal temples [the *devales*] and rose above a handsome moat, the walls of which were pierced with triangular cavities for purposes of illumination. At one extremity, it was terminated by an hexagonal building of two stories [the Patthirippuwa—more commonly thought of as octagonal] . . . in which the king, on great occasions, appeared to the people, assembled in the square below. At the other extremity, it was bounded by the women's apartments . . . The intermediate space was occupied chiefly by the great entrance to the palace, and by the temple (the Dalada Maligawa) a little in the rear. . . . [This] was the domestic temple of the king, and is the most venerated of any in the country, as it contains the relic, the tooth of Boodhoo, to which the whole island was dedicated, and which is considered by good Boodhists as the most precious thing in the world. The temple is small, of two stories, built in the Chinese [*sic*] style of architecture. The sanctum is an inner room, about twelve feet square, on the upper story, without windows, and to which a ray of natural light never penetrates. You enter it by folding doors, with polished brass panels, before and behind which is a curtain. The splendour of the place is very striking; the roof and walls are lined with gold brocade; and nothing scarcely is to be seen but gold, gems, and sweet-smelling flowers. (Davy 1821, 365–367, slightly altered)

Davy makes no mention of the Hindu-Buddhist cosmo-political symbolism of the layout of the city. In fact, the Kandy he describes—to a large

Figure 6.1. The Temple of the Tooth c. 1820. From Davy 1821, front end insert.

Figure 6.2. The Temple of the Tooth in 2007. Photo courtesy Donald Stadtner.

extent the re-creation of its last king, Śrī Vikrama (r. 1798–1815)—reflected various Indian modes of kingship (see Duncan 1990, 88). Like the ancient cities that Paul Wheatley (1971) called "pivots of the four quarters," Kandy (in cosmological imagination) had four quarters, with four gates, and four shrines to the gods, and four ferries across the Mahaweli river (see Duncan 1990, 92).[1] It was further and differently divided into a total of twenty-one blocks,[2] corresponding to the number of provinces surrounding Kandy in Śrī Vikrama's theoretical realm of the whole of the island: the circle of nine counties (*ratas*) immediately around Kandy town plus an outer ring of twelve provinces (*disas*).[3] At the symbolic center of all of this—the *axis mundi*—stood the palace, understood to represent Śakra's (i.e., Indra's) heaven on the top of Mount Meru, and thus reinforcing the image of Śrī Vikrama as an earthly embodiment of the king of the gods himself. Attached to the palace, the Temple of the Tooth (more literally, the "Palace of the Tooth" [Sinhala, Dalada Maligawa]), was thought to represent the magnificent building in Śakra's abode in which the tooth relic of the Buddha was originally enshrined.[4] Reinforcing all this cosmic symbolism was the Patthirippuwa (the Octagon), and the nearby Kandy Lake that was said to represent the Ocean of Milk which, in Hindu mythology, was churned by the gods and the asuras in order to create the world.[5] Indeed, the "wave-swell" pattern (Sinhala, *diyareli bemma*) of the famous wall around the lake is said to reflect the turbulence at the time of its churning (Duncan 1990, 101; and Silva 2017, 147–148).[6] (See the map of Kandy c. 1820 in fig. 6.3.)

1. Silva (2017, 148–149) has a useful map that shows "the imaginary boundary of the square shape of the city."

2. Originally, the town had sixteen blocks. Śrī Vikrama, however, had five additional blocks built to bring the number up to twenty-one. See Duncan 1990, 93.

3. In theory, the twenty-one blocks were each the site of the mansions (*walauwa*) of the twenty-one governors of those twenty-one provinces, in which "the families of the nobles were kept hostage as guarantors of their patriarch's loyalty" (Duncan 1990, 94). This model resembles what Stanley Tambiah (1976, 102–131) has called a "galactic polity," but it is Sri Lanka–specific. As Strathern and Biedermann (2017, 9) have pointed out, "in late medieval Sri Lanka . . . to be a *cakravarti* came to mean to have conquered the four quarters of the island."

4. This claim is pointed out by Duncan (1990, 109). It would seem to contradict, however, the well-established Buddhist tradition that, of the four original tooth relics of the Buddha, the one that ended up in Sri Lanka was *not* the one that first went to Indra's heaven, but the one that went to the land of Kalinga (see Strong 2004b, 190–191).

5. The actual name of the lake is the "Ocean of Milk" (Sinhala, Kiri Muhuda).

6. On the construction of Kandy Lake and the "cosmic city," see also Obeyesekere 2017, 126–133.

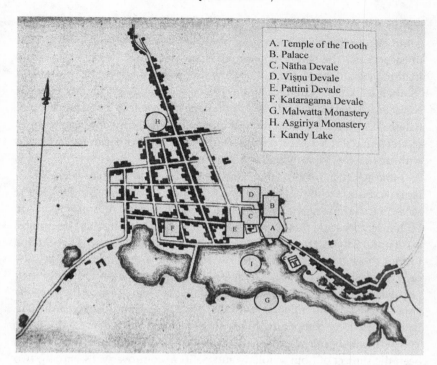

Figure 6.3. Map of Kandy c. 1820. From Davy 1821, front end insert. Relabeled by John Strong.

Nāyakkar Rule

Śrī Vikrama, the king who built the Kandy that the British took over in 1815, was the last of a line of monarchs who, since 1739, had ruled over the kingdom. These sovereigns were not originally from Sri Lanka but hailed from Madurai, in what is today Tamil Nadu in South India. Collectively known as the Nāyakkars (aka Nayaks), their dynasty traced its roots to a community of Telugu speakers from the Vijayanagara Empire, who long ago had moved south to Madurai, where they were known as "Northerners" (Tamil, *vatukas*). The first three of the Sri Lankan Nāyakkar rulers were actually born in Madurai, while the last, Śrī Vikrama, was born in Kandy (Gunawardana 1994, 198).

The origins of the dynasty may be quickly told. For generations, primarily for reasons of caste, but also pedigree and prestige,[7] Kandyan kings had

7. And perhaps also to counter the maritime powers of Portugal and then Holland (Dewaraja 1972, 198–200).

habitually taken Nāyakkar princesses as their chief queens. In this way, they could ensure that their successors would be seen as *kṣatriyas* of the "solar lineage," since the Nāyakkars were of that caste either "in reality or imagination" (Seneviratne 1978, 9).[8] However, when the last of the so-called "Sinhalese" kings, Narendra Sinha, passed away in 1739, he and his chief Nāyakkar queen were childless. Although he had a son by a non-*kṣatriya* Sinhalese concubine, the latter did not qualify for the throne for caste reasons, so Narendra Sinha was succeeded by his Nāyakkar brother-in-law, who was enthroned as Śrī Vijaya Rājasinha.

Although it is not clear that contemporaries perceived it as such, Śrī Vijaya's accession to the throne marked the start of a new "dynasty," in the sense that the king of Kandy was now a person who was "fully Nāyakkar" on both his father's and mother's side, and whose family's religious background was Hindu Śaivite. Subsequent rulers reinforced this identity by continuing to find their queens in Madurai. The royal family, however, were not the only South Indians in town. Gradually, over the generations, many of their Nāyakkar relatives and associates followed them to Kandy, where they steadily amassed wealth and influence with the king, "at least in the eyes of the Sinhalese aristocracy competing for the king's favours" (Dewaraja 1972, 59).[9]

The posited "otherness" of the Nāyakkar rulers and their relatives has been the subject of both scholarly and political controversy. Essentially, two views—two stories—may be discerned. The first basically assumes that "Nāyakkar" should be understood as an ethnic category, and that because their ethnic affiliations put them at odds with the traditional Kandyan aristocracy and the Sinhalese people over whom they ruled, the Nāyakkars were perceived and resented as foreigners. As Lorna Dewaraja put it, "Kandy [came to be ruled by kings who] were aliens, not only in race, but in language, religion and culture as well" (1972, 20). In order to compensate for this perceived foreignness, so goes the theory, they officially embraced Buddhism, as much, if not more so, than their Sinhalese predecessors. Thus, if only for political reasons, they "displayed an intense devotion to the faith and became lavish benefactors of the sangha . . . even when their relatives in the court remained openly Hindu" (Dewaraja 1972, 121). In this way, somewhat ironically but understandably, it was under Nāyakkar rulers such

8. At this time, apart from the royal family, there were no other *kṣatriyas* in Sri Lanka. Thus, in an exogamous system, the only place men of the royal family could find *kṣatriya* spouses was abroad. See Rogers 2004, 627. The practice of taking princesses from South India had ancient roots but was revived by Rājasinha II (1635–1687). See Dewaraja 1972, 28.

9. Obeyesekere (2017, 201) disputes this view that the king brought his Nāyakkar relatives in to dominate Kandy.

as Kīrti Śrī Rājasiṃha (r. 1747–1782) that a veritable renewal of Buddhist institutions in Kandy took place: the higher ordination of monks (which had lapsed in the 1720s) was restored (with the help of Siamese Buddhists) in 1753; the tooth relic, as we shall see, was for the first time featured in the annual festival known as the Esala Perahera; the king himself visited important Buddhist pilgrimage sites in different parts of the realm, and founded or restored several great monasteries (see Holt 1996; and Blackburn 2001, 60–62).

The second view suggests that the claim that the Nāyakkars were "aliens" in Kandy is anachronistic, based more on post-British concepts of ethnicity than on eighteenth- and early nineteenth-century historical realities. As John Rogers (2004, 631) put it, "there was no sense that the king needed to be 'racially' or 'ethnically' Sinhalese—such a notion, in fact, did not exist." Similarly, H. L. Seneviratne has questioned just how foreign, culturally speaking, the Nāyakkars actually were. He points out that all of the kings of the dynasty were brought up in Kandy and educated by Buddhist monks; if the Tamil language was used at court, it was because it was culturally prestigious, somewhat like French at the court of the Romanovs in Russia; moreover, all of the Nāyakkars (except perhaps for the very last of them toward the end of his rule) were popular among the people; and their support and sponsorship of Buddhism and the tooth relic, rather than being aimed at countering their "otherness," was actually a continuation of the political support given to the religion by their Sinhalese predecessors. What was important in kingship was caste purity and not ethnicity, so that the decision to use the system of succession by one's brother-in-law that brought the first Nāyakkar to the throne made perfect sense; it was the only way to guarantee the *kṣatriya* status of the ruler. Indeed, the greater scandal would have been for Narendra Siṃha to have been succeeded by the son of a lesser wife who lacked that status (Seneviratne 1976, 58).[10]

Concomitant to this view goes the argument that it was first the Dutch, and then the British, who tried to divide (and conquer) Kandy by seeking to alienate the "Sinhalese" from their "foreign" Nāyakkar kings. It should be said that the British were somewhat slow in adopting this approach. As we shall see, when they first unsuccessfully invaded Kandy in 1803, they sought to replace the last Nāyakkar with a puppet of their own, Muttusāmi, who, however, was himself also a Nāyakkar! It was not until their successful invasion of 1815 that the British, in their propaganda, began to argue that the

---

10. See also Bechert 1963; and Strathern 2007, 153.

Nāyakkars were a "foreign" dynasty (Rogers 2004, 637).[11] They reinforced this in the so-called Kandyan Convention (see chapter 7), which proclaimed that "Malabars" (i.e., Nāyakkars) were no longer allowed to reside in the Kandyan kingdom, and indeed, soon thereafter, the British sought to repatriate Malabars to India. By the 1830s, a liberal age of reform (embodied in the report of the Colebrooke-Cameron Commission) sought to minimize caste difference as "the prevalent form of colonial social organization" on the island, and to replace that with ethnicity and perceived foreign origins (Sivasundaram 2013, 18).[12] This view was then perpetuated and reinforced in the twentieth and twenty-first centuries by ongoing ethnic tensions.

Which of these two views is correct? Sujit Sivasundaram has argued, essentially, that we should adopt both of them, and I am inclined to agree. As he puts it (2013, 33), "it is useful to see the Nayaks as being both excluded from and included by what it meant to be Sinhala and Buddhist, where the sense of these categories is taken to indicate the period's meanings." He goes on to catalog points in favor of each view. On one hand, the Nāyakkars certainly presented themselves as pious Buddhists and were taught Sinhala and Pali by Buddhist monk tutors, "while overseeing a period of cultural [and religious] renaissance." On the other hand, Buddhist monks were involved in an unsuccessful 1760 plot to assassinate the then Nāyakkar king, Kīrti Śrī, giving as one of his "outrages" his "Hindu" habit of plastering his body with ash. In addition, there is some anti-Tamil language that appears in some Sinhala literature at this time (Sivasundaram 2013, 45).

Sivasundaram further argues that Nāyakkar rule is best described as a "transregional kingship" (2013, 31), that "despite the discourse of Sinhalaness, the Kandyan kingdom was cosmopolitan" (2013, 41). And he points to the number of foreigners, including Europeans, who resided in Kandy during this period, where they often worked for the king. In 1810, for instance, a considerable number of mercenaries were in the ranks of the Kandyan royal army. These included 250–300 Malays, 200 Kaffirs (from Africa), 20 sepoys from India, 250 Muslims, 100 Malabars (from South India), and a British

11. See below for the initial "Proclamation" of reasons for the 1815 invasion by Governor Brownrigg. For a cogent tracing of the different stages in Sri Lankan and Western views of the ethnic identity of the last Kandyan kings, see Gunawardana 1994.

12. See also Rogers 2004, 640. Dharmadasa 1976 argues that anti-Tamil "racialist" propaganda against Śrī Vikrama can be found in both Sinhalese and British sources, but see Gunawardana 1994, 214–216, for a sharp critique of Dharmadasa. Roberts (2003) also argues that the emergence of distinct identities in Sri Lanka was not due solely to the impact of colonial rule and consequent modernization. On the Report of the Colebrooke-Cameron Commission, see Mendis 1956.

artilleryman who had defected to Kandy in 1803 and was in charge of the production of gunpowder for the kingdom.[13] Muslims, locally known as Moors, who had fled up-country when the Portuguese occupied the coast-lands in the sixteenth century, were dominant in matters of trade in Kandy (especially the commerce in areca nuts with South India). Moors were also responsible for cleaning and polishing the silver and gold vessels used in rit-uals in the Temple of the Tooth (see Sivasundaram 2013, 42; and Dewaraja 2018, 46). Moreover, Sinhalese Buddhists themselves maintained periodic but significant relations with co-religionists in Southeast Asia, which they traveled to on Dutch ships. The notion that Kandy was an entirely isolated kingdom, completely cut off from the rest of the world, should, therefore, be corrected.

Cosmopolitanism, Transregionality, and the Tooth Relic

All of this, I would argue, is significant for understanding the place of the tooth relic at this time in Kandy. Generally speaking, as has been men-tioned, the tooth has been viewed as an emblem—a palladium—of Sin-halese Buddhist sovereignty, a "symbol of nationalism which unified the Sinhalese against foreign rulers" (Herath 1994, 163). There is undoubtedly some truth in this. At the same time, however, it should be said that by the mid-eighteenth century, the tooth had become an ideal symbol for mul-ticultural rule, a potent legitimator of a sovereignty that could help unite multiple nations and ethnicities. It was, in brief, a "cosmopolitan object."[14]

This may well have been the case, however, long before the mid-eighteenth century. Indeed, it can be argued that the tooth had always had in Sri Lanka somewhat of a cosmopolitan status, with links to the mainland and to "other" cultures. Like the Nāyakkar kings, it came from India, arriving sometime in the fourth century CE during the reign of King Sirimeghavaṇṇa, who belonged to the Lambakaṇṇa Dynasty which, like the Nāyakkars, traced its origins to Tamil connections. The tooth seems then to have been associated with the Abhayagiri sect of Buddhism, which was sponsored by some Lambakaṇṇa rulers. Curiously, there is little mention of it during its first six centuries in Sri Lanka, in the chronicles of the period written, for the

13. For an account of this man, whose name was Benson, see Pieris 1950, 689–694.

14. In this it was similar to the footprint on Adam's Peak, which has been called "a truly cosmopolitan site of sacredness. . . . One of the most important holy sites in Asia" (Strathern 2007, 151). For a wide array of essays on the theme of cosmopolitanism in Sri Lankan history, see Biedermann and Strathern 2017.

most part, by monks of the rival Mahānikāya sect (see Strong 2004b, 194). Subsequently, however, in Sri Lankan history, the tooth definitely served as the palladium for the early kings of Kotte. For instance, as we have seen, Parākramabāhu VI (1412–1467), whose reign marks one of the apogees of Sinhala literature, built a magnificent "palace" for the tooth in his capital. Parākramabāhu VI, however, was most likely a Hindu in his own personal inclinations (see Perera 1910, 16).

Moreover, if one looks at the veneration of the tooth in its temple in Kandy—as it is carried out today and was during Nāyakkar times—it is clear that, cultically speaking, the tooth represents far more than just the Buddha. As I have argued elsewhere, it was also treated as a king and as a god (Strong 2004b, 199). For one thing, the building it is housed in is not called a monastery or even a temple (though I have been using that word); rather, it is called a "palace" (māligāwa) and in it, like a king, the tooth "necessitates the constant presence . . . of numerous servants and lay officials, administrators, secretaries, musicians, cooks, night watchmen, shoulder-pole carriers, torch bearers—a whole personnel . . . that is approximately the same as the entourage of a sovereign" (Goloubew 1932, 460–461). At the same time, its actual daily veneration (which is quite different from that accorded to other, more generic, Buddha relics in Sri Lanka) resembles nothing so much as the pūjā commonly performed for Hindu deities. Each day, at dawn, the tooth is awakened, and offered water with which to wash its hands, a toothstick, water for a bath, a towel to dry the face, another towel for the body, fresh robes, a seat, a fan, a fly-whisk, and so on, and then a full meal, consisting of gruel, rice, curry, and sweetmeats. Then, after a pause during which the relic is left alone to "eat," the meal is cleared away and a chew of betel is offered. Granted, there are Buddhist aspects to the cult—the tooth, after all, was thought to be the Buddha's, and monks were among the chief promoters and officiants of its veneration—but cultically speaking, the relic was an amalgamation of identities (see Strong 2004b, 199–200; Seneviratne 1978, 38–60; Hocart 1931, 18–33).

This syncretism, I would argue, was further encouraged by the Nāyakkar kings and, once promoted, was one of the things that allowed them so readily to support the worship and defense of the tooth. Two examples of this may be given. The first concerns Śrī Vijaya, the founding monarch of the new Nāyakkar Dynasty. According to a story preserved in the Cūḷavaṃsa, soon after his coronation, Śrī Vijaya decided to further decorate and rededicate the new Temple of the Tooth that had been built by his Sinhalese predecessor and to newly enshrine the tooth relic therein. But some of his Nāyakkar advisers told him that bad things might happen were he to do that himself—that he should leave the ceremony to others, to native Kandyans. In this, we have a recognition of the theme of his "foreignness." So, he left the capital and told the Sinhalese temple caretakers to re-enshrine the relic in his absence. But they were unsuccessful: they tried as hard as they could to open the reliquary, working at it the whole night through, but they were unable to unlock it; some mysterious force prevented them. The next morning, they went to the king to let him know of their failure. Śrī Vijaya then decided he would try to do it himself despite his ministers' forebodings, and when he got back to the temple, the reliquary opened with no difficulty whatsoever as soon as he touched the lock. He then proceeded to open each of the caskets inside until he laid his eyes on the tooth itself. Transported with devotion, he made great offerings to the tooth and decided to hold a public exhibition of it. He had the whole capital purified and decorated, and, announcing that he would sponsor a festival comparable to that celebrated by Indra in the city of the gods, he invited members of the sangha, laypersons, and the whole population of the capital and kingdom to gather. Then, publicly prostrating himself before the tooth, he took it in his hand, marched outside to the great pavilion set up in front of the temple, and, holding the tooth aloft, displayed it to the assembled multitude. That night, a great festival of lamps was held in honor of the tooth throughout the kingdom (*Cūḷavaṃsa* 1980, 546–548; Eng. trans., Geiger 1929, 2: 248–251).[15]

In this story, the tooth itself, through its own supernatural resistance to being moved by anyone other than Śrī Vijaya, seems to be making two points: first, it takes a king to access a relic;[16] and second, that king's "foreignness" makes no difference. Indeed, it might even be said that in this case, the tooth itself has temporarily become a "foreign" object, needing a "foreign" (i.e., Nāyakkar) monarch to restore its full indigeneity by making it available once again to the people.

A second, perhaps more historical, example may be found in the case of Śrī Vijaya's successor, King Kīrti Śrī. It was under his rule in 1775 that Kandy's premier annual festival, the so-called Esala Perahera, was redefined to include not only the procession of the insignia of the four protector gods of Kandy—Viṣṇu, Nātha, Kataragama, and Pattini—but also the Buddha's tooth relic, which, previously, had been paraded separately.[17] This is

---

15. We shall see that the British governor of Ceylon holds a somewhat similar celebration in 1828.

16. Much the same point has been made more generally, from the perspective of a different context, by Wyatt 2001.

17. This is not quite accurate. When the tooth was at Delgamuwa (where it had been taken to safeguard it from the Portuguese in Kotte), King Rājasinha I instituted a *perahera* for it and the

generally said to have been instituted by the king in order to please some visiting Siamese monks who were shocked that the Buddha was not given a place in this most important celebration (Malalgoda 1976, 64), but it may also be viewed as an instance of amalgamation that clearly suited the needs of the Nāyakkar monarch. It has remained a feature of the Esala Perahera ever since.[18]

In an extensive review of A. M. Hocart's (1931) classic monograph—*The Temple of the Tooth in Kandy*—Victor Goloubew has argued that Sri Lankan kings of South Indian origin were fervent devotees of the Dalada precisely because it, like them, had a "foreign" provenance, coming as it did from India. Moreover, its cult in Kandy, mixing as it did Hindu and Buddhist elements, was ideal for maintaining the political "concept of a vast empire half-Tamil, half-Sinhalese, uniting the royalty of Ceylon to those of the Dravidian dynasties established on the Coromandel Coast" (Goloubew 1932, 457). The tooth, in other words, was the ideal object of worship and legitimation for the Nāyakkar monarchs, in its multicultural, cosmopolitan context. All of this may well serve as background to the British takeover of the tooth and of responsibility for its cult after 1815. Like the Nāyakkars, they too were "foreigners," ruling over Kandy, but also governing a multicultural, multireligious South Asia. In a curious ironic way, it was only when the British started in 1815 pushing the story that Śrī Vikrama was a barbaric foreigner that they began to realize that the tooth could be a useful tool for them, as foreigners, to legitimately rule Kandy.

Goloubew's theory, it should be said, was drawn up in opposition to the view of Hocart (1931, 4–5), who thought of the Kandyan tooth as a representation of the fang of a *yakṣa* (demon),[19] and thereby sought to argue that the cult of the relic had autochthonous roots in the religion of the people, both the indigenous Veddas and the Sinhalese. This does not strike me, however, as being counter to Goloubew's view; rather, it expands cosmopolitanism to include another layer of Sri Lankan identity.

---

four guardian gods from Delgamuwa to Ratnapura. For a short history of the *perahera*, see Perera 1984; and Dewaraja 2018, 29–50.

18. As John Holt (2007, 162; and 2017, 67–130) has pointed out, the religious syncretism involved in the Esala Perahera may be more complex than this. The tooth relic can be posited to represent Theravāda Buddhism, while the four deities and their *devales* (shrines) can be associated with the other "major trajectories of religion in South India," with Viṣṇu representing Vaiṣṇavism, Kataragama (Skanda/Murukan) representing Śaivism, the goddess Pattini representing goddess worship, and Nātha (Avalokiteśvara) representing Mahāyāna Buddhism. For what appears to be a pre-1775 description of the *perahera* in Kandy, see Hurd 1780, 96.

19. *Yakṣas* (Sinhala, *yakku*), still today venerated in Sri Lanka, are commonly represented as having long, curved eyeteeth like those of a wild boar. On their cult, see Kapferer 1983.

Possession and veneration of the cosmopolitan tooth relic, however, made for prestige not just among Nāyakkars and the Sinhalese; it also enabled foreign contacts of a different sort—with other Asian Buddhists. We have already seen that, in the time of the Portuguese and before, Sri Lanka's possession of the tooth was recognized throughout the Buddhist world. It comes as no surprise, then, to read in the *Cūḷavaṃsa* (1980, 576; Eng. trans., Geiger 1929, 2: 284) that, in addition to instituting a new style of amalgamated Esala Perahera, Kīrti Śrī arranged a special exhibition of the tooth relic for the Siamese monks who had been invited to restore the higher ordination in Lanka. As we shall see, the British were to sponsor much the same ceremony when they subsequently received a delegation of monks from that country. Moreover, Kīrti Śrī sent to the king of Siam, as a return gift, a jeweled replica of the tooth itself, which the Siamese responded to not only by worshipping it but by sending back to Sri Lanka many offerings for the tooth, including golden canopies to cover it (*Cūḷavaṃsa* 1980, 579; Eng. trans., Geiger 1929, 2: 287). The "cosmopolitan tooth" thus became one of the foci for exchange among nations.

Protection and Preservation of the Tooth

The Nāyakkars, of course, were not only great venerators of the Dalada; they were also, like the Sinhalese monarchs before them, its steadfast guardians. Whenever the kingdom was threatened, the first things kings would do would be to ensure that the tooth (and usually also the royal treasure) was taken away from the capital to a place of safety in the hinterlands. This had been true historically in various internecine conflicts in Sri Lanka, and it remained the case when the attackers were foreign colonial powers. Often the king, and sometimes the whole population, would leave the city, and the invaders would find the capital deserted and empty and realize that, though they had captured the town, they had failed to defeat the enemy.

It should be said that the town of Kandy itself was somewhat of a "fortress," not because of its walls or fortifications, but because of its natural location.[20] Situated in the central highlands of Sri Lanka, it is surrounded on three sides by the Mahaweli Ganga, a major river that, at certain times of the year, can be much swollen by monsoon rains. Today the city is easily reachable by road or by rail, but in the early nineteenth century, it was

---

20. Interestingly, John Davy (1821, 365) states that from a military point of view, the site of Kandy was "ill chosen and insecure, and hardly admitting of defence." But that may be because there was little resistance to the British in 1815.

difficult to access. There were several routes to it from the western or eastern littorals (i.e., from the Colombo or the Trincomalee or Batticaloa regions), but all of these involved climbing up steep and narrow defiles through thickly forested territory. Allegedly, these paths were deliberately kept undeveloped and difficult by the Kandyans, for protection purposes. As Robert Knox ([1681] 1966, 4), an English merchant who was captured in Sri Lanka and spent nineteen years as a prisoner in Kandy in the seventeenth century, put it: "the King careth not to make his country easie to travel, but desires to keep it intricate." Moreover, to the northeast and south, the town of Kandy was surrounded by vast tracts of mountainous jungle that were deemed impassable by those who did not know their way. It was to these regions that the kings of Kandy typically retreated when their first line of defense (the passes) were breached. Indeed, over the centuries, several "refuge palaces" were built in remote areas (e.g., at Medamahanuwara and Hanguranketa) for the king to use when fleeing the capital. Many of these mountain fortresses had buildings attached to them for housing the tooth relic where its daily cult could be continued (Hamilton 1888).

For example, when the Portuguese invade Kandy in 1611, it takes them fifteen days to capture the strongpoint at Balana Pass (several miles from the town). When they finally get to Kandy city, it is more or less empty, and they realize that during the time they were delayed, the Kandyans "carried away whatever they could to the woods" (including the tooth relic and the royal treasure). There are thus "scanty spoils" to be had, and the Portuguese, disappointed, resign themselves to setting fire to the "pagodes" (temples) and the palace, before having to leave (Queiros 1930, 2, 613–615).[21]

The same thing happens in 1638. General Diogo De Mello, seeking to punish the king of Kandy, invades the capital. This time he meets no resistance whatsoever, for the king and the whole population have already fled to the rocky escarpments. Again, the Portuguese find nothing to loot—all treasures, including the tooth, have been taken away. Again, they set fire to the city, the palaces, and "the pagoda of the king" (i.e., the Temple of the Tooth). They then proceed to withdraw, but soon find they have been lured into a trap, for their way out of Kandy is now blocked by a force of 16,000 men, and after a fierce battle, most of the Portuguese, including De Mello, are killed (Queiros 1930, 2, 804–805).[22]

21. On this expedition and a subsequent battle in 1617, see also Perniola 1989, 2: 328, and 2: 412–424.

22. While this has been described by some as the basic Kandyan strategy for dealing with invaders, Wickremesekera (2004, 131) objects that this is too simplistic.

The Kandyan strategy is made even more explicit in stories about the Dutch invasion led by Governor Van Eck in 1765. On February 19 of that year, the Dutch march into the deserted city completely unopposed. Van Eck gives orders to prevent chaotic looting (so as to control the apportionment of booty), but these are futile; the soldiers ignore the official seals their commanders have affixed to the doors of the palace and break in. Finally, the officers give up and open the place for plunder, but there is little to be had; the most precious items were already removed by the king before fleeing, so that what is left consists "chiefly of linen, stuffs, furniture, some silver-gilt articles, curiosities, and copper coins" (Raven-Hart 1954, 99; see also Buultjens 1899, 44 and 59).

Similarly, at the Temple of the Tooth, where things appear to have been somewhat less chaotic, relatively little is found, except that Van Eck himself appropriates two precious items that got left behind by the fleeing king, presumably because they were too awkward to transport: the relic's large outermost silver dagoba (the tooth itself was not in it), and the golden canopy that shelters it during its public processions. These two items very nearly get melted down for repartition as booty. According to official Dutch correspondence between Batavia and Holland on November 8, 1765:

> Van Eck took possession of a large silver-gilt machine [sic] like a bell but closed below and in two pieces of which the upper can be removed, weighing 210 lbs, which served to contain their holiest relic, the famous Tooth of Boedoe [i.e., Buddha] in a gold and jeweled chest. And van Eck . . . presented this to the troops, to be distributed among them in addition to the 100,000 florins promised. We request Your Excellencies' orders, adding that we feel that this promise can hardly now be cancelled, and that it were best fulfilled by melting and sale, and distributing its value in the form of minor articles of equipment. (See Raven-Hart 1954, 135.)

In fact, the tooth's largest reliquary is not melted down. As Wagenaar (2016, 121) makes clear, Batavia turns down Van Eck's request (posthumously—he soon dies) but agrees to compensate the men for their loss. The reliquary is then ordered to be returned to the king of Kandy as part of a peace treaty agreement, if he wants it back. If he does not, the booty is to go to Van Eck's heirs. In the event, as we shall see, the reliquary is later restored intact and remains in Kandy today.[23]

23. For a Sri Lankan account of this whole episode, see *Cūḷavaṃsa* 1980, 562–565; Eng. trans., Geiger 1929, 2: 267–270.

Dutch Lack of Awareness of the Tooth

Despite these accounts, the Dutch seem to have been more or less oblivious to the political and religious importance of the tooth. Indeed, prior to Van Eck's expedition in 1765, they may not even have been aware of its presence in Kandy.

The Dutch first arrived on the east coast of Sri Lanka in 1602. By 1658, they had completely overthrown the Portuguese and replaced them as rulers of all the littoral regions of the island. Almost from the start, they entered into trade talks with the kings of Kandy, who still occupied the uplands and center of the country. These principally involved negotiations over obtaining cinnamon, various spices, and elephants from Kandyan lands. In time, the Dutch regularly sent an embassy to the court in Kandy to renew contacts and iron out relations. There they were formally received by the king in his audience chamber, where the Dutch envoys, laden with gifts, were expected to kneel down and proffer their letter from their governor-general. The first such embassy occurred in 1602, when Admiral Joris van Spilbergen traveled to Kandy from Batticaloa and where he was cordially received by King Vimaladharmasuriya, who saw in the Dutch possible allies against the Portuguese (Weinman 1963, 6).

Other embassies followed in 1612, 1640, 1656, 1671, 1672, and 1721, when a succession of envoys made the journey and were variously treated by different Kandyan monarchs. In the accounts of these missions, no mention is made of the tooth relic or the Temple of the Tooth, despite the fact that these envoys were being received by the king in the adjacent palace's audience chamber (Weinman 1963, 7–9). There would seem to be a number of reasons for this.

First, the Dutch were primarily, if not exclusively, interested in trade negotiations with the Kandyans. If one reads, for instance, the copy of the peace treaty that the Dutch imposed on the Kandyans in 1766, there is no mention in it of culture, religion, or politics—it is primarily concerned with clarifying issues of sovereignty over certain territories, guaranteeing Kandyans the right to harvest salt from the littoral and the Dutch the right to peel cinnamon from the interior, mutually agreeing to the capture and return of runaway slaves, and so on (Bell 1888–1889). In this, it is strikingly different from the Convention of 1815 that the British signed with the Kandyans (on which see below). In general, then, the Dutch, while vaguely aware of the story of a tooth relic's capture by the Portuguese, do not appear to have been particularly attuned to its importance as a palladium of rule.

Second, it may be that the Dutch, prior to Van Eck, were simply unaware of the presence of the tooth in Kandy and so were not looking to find it there. The Kandyans had a pretty consistent policy of closely curtailing the movements of any ambassadors or envoys who made it to their capital. They were housed in a rest house well outside town, which they were not allowed to leave, except when conducting their business with the king.

Johann Wolffgang Heydt, who accompanied Daniel Aggreen's embassy to Kandy in 1736 in part to draw maps of it, complains that he could only make hurried and surreptitious sketches of the palace and environs, trying to fill them in later from memory, because Sinhalese officials forbade such things. As Heydt (1744, 270; Eng. trans., Heydt 1952, 93–94) puts it:

> It is a pity that the Sinhalese are so obstinate and will not allow that all this might be drawn exactly from nature, with time and patience; but the King fears, lest his land be spied out: for this reason also the Ambassadors of the Company are brought here and taken back again by night, and must pass the rest of the time in . . . a rest-place built for them [that] lies 2 hours from Candea [Kandy]. The Ambassadors, both coming and going are always accompanied by many Court officials.

Heydt, however, comes close. He does manage to put together, in plate 90 of his book, a drawing/plan of the royal palace, which actually shows the temple of the tooth, but his accompanying description betrays the fact that he had no idea what this building housed, and the Kandyans were not about to tell him:

> Further is to be seen a small towerlet which was visible both from without and within the courtyard. To the right is a long and high building, on the outside of which were painted all sorts of dragons and foliage in yellow and red colours, and which is also provided with an entrance. To the question, what [is] this? the answer was given through the interpreter, [only] that it was a pagoda [pagodé], in which many Bramins dwelt and made their prayers. (Heydt 1744, 270; Eng. trans., Heydt 1952, 934–994, slightly altered)

Much the same situation of ignorance seems to have existed in 1762—just three years before Van Eck's expedition—when John Pybus was sent by the British on a sort of spy mission to Kandy, in order to explore the possibilities of an alliance with the Sinhalese and to try to gauge what the Dutch were up to. In his report to his superiors in the British government in Madras, he notes (by way of explaining the dearth of information he was able to gather) that he was unable to leave the house where he lodged, except at night when he was taken to the palace on business, and that none of his Malabar servants were allowed to converse with anyone but the translator appointed by the king. He consequently was unable to get a sense even of the layout of the buildings of the palace (Pybus 1862, 12, 73–82). He makes no mention of the tooth or its temple.

The same is true, it should be pointed out, of other early British visitors to the city. Robert Percival (Percival 1803, 206), for instance, who was also on the embassy to Kandy in 1800, makes no mention whatsoever either of the Temple of the Tooth or of the relic, even though he does note the importance of the Esala Perahera in Kandy as a great ceremony that the king attends. Similarly, James Cordiner (Cordiner 1807, 2, 182), who was chaplain for the garrison in Colombo and who, for his day, had a decent knowledge of Sinhalese Buddhism, makes no mention of the tooth or its temple in his description of Kandy in 1803, limiting himself to describing the palace and a few (unspecified) temples dedicated to the Buddha as the only buildings of any consequence.

The Ignorance Continues: The British Debacle of 1803

The Portuguese and Dutch experiences in taking Kandy are, in many ways, a preview of the British experience in 1803. The English too march unopposed into an empty city; they too are then plagued by guerrilla warfare and disease and supply problems; they too leave a small garrison behind which is defeated and which, when it tries to negotiate free passage out of Kandy, is massacred almost to a man; and they too seem to be unaware of the importance of the tooth.

The British aim, in fact, is to capture or kill the Kandyan king, Śrī Vikrama, and to replace him with a puppet of their own. This is Muttusāmi (aka Buddhasāmi), a brother-in-law of the previous king with some claim to the throne. Upon the death of the previous monarch, Muttusāmi was arrested by the first *adikar* (chief minister) Pilimatalawa, who was very much a mover, shaker, and kingmaker in Kandyan politics of the time. Pilimatalawa had engineered the selection of Śrī Vikrama as the new monarch and wanted potential rivals eliminated or at least imprisoned. Subsequently, however, Pilimatalawa escaped and fled to British territory, where he was welcomed and given a small pension by colonial authorities, because they thought he might someday be useful to their cause.[24]

---

24. As Obeyesekere (2017, 31–33) has shown, the British plan to take Kandy was in the works almost from the very moment their portion of Ceylon became a crown colony in 1798.

Indeed, in 1803, Governor Frederick North (in office 1798–1805) finally decides the time has come to use him. In January of that year, he orders an armed expeditionary force to be sent up to Kandy under the command of General Hay MacDowall. All told, there are about 3,200 fighting men, most of whom are Malay mercenaries, with a few companies of British soldiers and of Tamils from South India, some lowland Sinhalese support troops, and some Bengali artillerymen. General MacDowall is worried; he knows that once the rainy season starts in earnest, supplying his troops from the coasts will be very difficult. Governor North, however, is convinced that supplies will come from the local population, who will welcome and support Muttusāmi as their new king (Methley 1918, 104).[25] Developments would prove him wrong.

Crossing the Mahaweli river on February 22, MacDowall's troops march into Kandy and find the town, "like a second Moscow," entirely deserted, the storehouses empty, and "the Palace and several of the Boodoo Temples in flames" (Methley 1918, 105; see also Powell [1973] 1984, 92).[26] Once again, the Kandyans have deserted their capital and retreated to the hinterlands.

Sinhalese lore, both written and oral, tells a story recounting more precisely what happened: King Śrī Vikrama, receiving reports that the British are advancing, resolves, in consultation with his ministers, to evacuate the city, as his predecessors had done in similar situations. Indeed, such a thing had become almost routine. As Punchibandara Dolapihilla (1959, 117) explains:

In Senkadagala [Kandy], evacuation of the capital was by no means a rare occurrence. Court astrologers had [already] fixed a propitious hour for the retreat. A line of tuskers was led into the Paragaha Maluwa [the courtyard south of the Dalada Maligawa] and loads of temple treasures [were] strung across their backs. At their head was a caparisoned animal and astride it the new guardian of the Dalada in his state costume. A cannon went off; and from every corner of the city rose a tremendous cry of *saadu*. It was the *nekata* [propitious moment] fixed by the astrologers. Priests waiting for the signal took the Dalada out of its inner sanctuary. At the same moment the king stepped out of the palace building in which he resided. He then walked to the relic shrine to honour it before its journey. When he had worshipped, the

25. On Governor North see also, however, Wickremeratne 1973.
26. Methley's mention of Moscow is, of course, a reference to Napoleon's invasion of that city in 1812, albeit an anachronistic one; the British in 1803 would not have thought of Kandy as a "second" Moscow.

Maha Nayaka of the Malwatta brought the relic in its innermost casket to the chieftain on the caparisoned tusker; and the cavalcade started off. . . . Behind went tuskers with the ran-awuda [golden insignia] of the devale temples.[27]

As soon as the tooth has left, it is the turn of the nobility and the people. One by one, courtiers and their wives and children and servants and slaves depart in palanquins while elephants loaded with their movable valuables follow behind. From the palace, the queens and the women of the harem leave with their escorts, while in the king's treasure house, officials and their peons pack up "regalia and heaps of priceless treasure." Secretarial officials "record the articles that go into each package, the destination to which it will go, and names of those who would be in charge." At the same time, other officials in the armory see to the dispatch of muskets and other weapons, of gunpowder and musket balls (Dolapihilla 1959, 118, slightly altered).[28]

The king, however, does not go with them but remains in his palace, sort of like a captain on a foundering ship. At long last, when most everyone has departed, he calls sixty men from his guard and orders them to burn the manor houses [walauwa] of his courtiers, declaring that they will not want to live in those homes again after "filthy beef-eating Englishmen" have stayed in them (Dolapihilla 1959, 116). So too he orders parts of his own palace set on fire, so that Muttusāmi will not be able to enjoy it. The only buildings that he spares are the Audience Hall and the Temple of the Tooth.[29] Only then does the king mount his tusker and make his way to his refuge palace at Hanguranketa (in remote mountains about thirty-two kilometers southeast of Kandy) (Dolapihilla 1959, 119).

27. This chapter of Dolapihilla's book is partly based on the *Ingirisi Hatana* [The English war], a Sinhalese poem written in 1812 and describing the events of 1803 as well as praising the Kandyan king for his victory. For more on the poem, see Sivasundaram 2013, 39. For a partial translation by Uddaya Meddegama, see Obeyesekere 2017, 345–367. According to a different text, the *Daladāvittiya*, probably written by a monk from the Asgiriya monastery, a group of monks volunteered to take charge of the relic and take it away from the capital for safekeeping. See Gunawardana 1994, 202.

28. It is interesting to note what the Kandyans do leave behind. The British later find "rooms full of antiquated weapons, immense brass lamps 'shaped like elephants' . . . Dutch paintings, mirrors, chandeliers . . . and Dutch glassware in cases which had never been opened" (Methley 1918, 105–106).

29. By all accounts, the royal Audience Hall (where the king received petitioners and ambassadors from away) was the architectural gem of the palace complex. For reproductions of several drawings, see De Silva and Beumer 1988, 341, 343. Obeyesekere (2017, 66n43) vehemently disagrees with Dolapihilla's claim that Śrī Vikrama sets all these fires, calling it "nonsense." He suspects the British did so.

Had the British been aware of this emphasis placed by Śrī Vikrama and his court on getting the tooth and its treasures—but first and foremost the tooth—out of Kandy to safety, they might have paid more attention to its importance as an object, and made some effort to recapture it. In fact, when they enter the deserted town, their focus is on proclaiming Muttusāmi (himself a Nāyakkar) as king. Within the month, with considerable pomp and ceremony, they go ahead and anoint him as the new ruler. Only then do they reveal the terms of his coronation: the Kandyan territory is to be greatly reduced in size, and Muttusāmi is to swear allegiance to King George III; in other words, he is to become a token, subservient king with limited authority over a small principality. His vassal status is thus made clear (Methley 1918, 106). Given this and given that the real king—Śrī Vikrama—is still at large, very few Sinhalese are willing to affirm Muttusāmi's enthronement (Powell [1973] 1984, 95).[30] Moreover, he lacks the one thing that might grant him legitimacy: the tooth relic.

In time, the situation for the British in Kandy becomes untenable. The monsoon season starts in earnest, and the troops, who are unable to capture the fugitive king, are plagued by heavy rains, by disease ("jungle fever" and beriberi), and by harassment from Kandyan guerillas (Methley 1918, 106–107). More specifically, the Kandyans attack the long lines of unarmed and poorly guarded porters employed to provision the forces, mostly low-country villagers. Increasingly, these "coolies" are killed or caused to quit and go home. Food and supplies in the city become scarce. So too does the opium that was ordinarily rationed out to the Malay troops (*London Quarterly Review* 1840, 295–296). Sickness increases. A makeshift hospital for native troops is set up in the Malwatta Monastery (which was then across paddy fields from the palace and the Temple of the Tooth—Kandy Lake having not yet been dug) (Turner 1918, 78). Another hospital for English troops is set up in a long hallway in the palace formerly used as a refectory for feeding monks. In both places, men are dying at a rate of about ten a day (Powell [1973] 1984, 120; see also Cordiner 1807, 2: 206).

In addition, supplies of money are running low. When MacDowall is asked by Muttusāmi for 300 gold pagodas [a coin minted in South Asia] to cover his own expenses and those of his "court," the general finds he does not have that sum. So, he commandeers some Kandyan coiners to make cash out of the metal obtained from vessels left behind at the Temple of the Tooth; they strike a few pieces but then will proceed no further, appearing to

---

30. By Governor North's own admission, in a month's time, "scarcely one adherent had appeared to pay homage to the new King" (Methley 1918, 106–107).

be ill or under a charm, and declaring that "the vessels they had demolished and profaned had driven them out of their senses" (Pieris 1939, 59).

MacDowall decides to solve his provisioning problems by withdrawing the bulk of his troops to Colombo,[31] opting to remain in Kandy with but a small garrison (thus repeating the mistakes of the Portuguese and the Dutch before him). He also orders all the sick to be evacuated to Trincomalee, but of the one hundred fifty or so in the hospital, only twenty-three are able to walk, and there are not enough coolies and doolies [a kind of sedan chair] left to transport the others (Methley 1918, 107–108, 113).

Then, MacDowall himself gets ill. He is treated with doses of James powder (a mixture of antimony and calcium pyrophosphate—a "medicine" patented by the English physician Robert James [1703–1776]), taken with rhubarb every two hours and followed by a hot bath. That seems to help for a while, but does not fully cure him, so he is given massive doses of mercury (a treatment for yellow fever) (Pieris 1939, 61). This apparently controls the fever but leaves his bowels and mouth ravaged with sores. Too sick to function, on June 11, MacDowall has himself carried to Colombo, leaving the troops behind under the command of Major Adam Davie, a "well-disposed [and] inoffensive" Scot from Edinburgh who has only been in Sri Lanka for about a year and has never seen any real military action in his life (Marshall 1846, 108n).[32]

The whole saga of the calamity that follows need not be recounted in detail here. Suffice it to say that: (1) the Malay mercenaries, who form the bulk of the British forces, start going over to the enemy, being encouraged to defect by fellow Malays in the service of the Kandyan king (Cordiner 1807, 2: 204);[33] (2) when the few remaining still functional British troops, barricaded in the palace, are finally attacked by an overwhelming number of Kandyans, they are forced to surrender; (3) Major Davie agrees to give up all their weapons in exchange for an escorted retreat out of Kandy (together with Muttusāmi), but they are unable to cross the torrent of the Mahaweli

31. The retreat to Colombo does not, however, free the men from sickness; of those who withdraw to the coast, 75 percent are dead of the fever within three months. See Powell [1973] 1984, 108.

32. On Davie, see also Knighton 1845, 317; and Fellowes 1817, 163, both of whom decry his inexperience. However, for an example of the impossible situation Davie had been left in, see his own letter to a friend in Anderson 1809, 189.

33. The brother of the chief Malay officer on the British side (who did not desert) was, in fact, a chief officer on the Kandyan side. On the ultimate fate of one of these deserters, the Malay drum major, see Saldin 2003.

River;[34] (4) there, the next day, they are forced to give up Muttusāmi to the Kandyans, who promptly have him executed;[35] and (5) all the white British soldiers (effectively, now, prisoners) are then separated from the Asian ones; the latter are permitted to join the Kandyan forces, the former are decapitated by the river,[36] except for a few who miraculously escape,[37] and for Davie and his second-in-command, Captain Rumley, who are spared by order of the king.

The ultimate fate of Rumley is unknown, but Davie stays on in Kandy under various forms of house arrest and actual incarceration for almost a decade. At various points, he manages to get brief pathetic messages (written in invisible ink, i.e., lime juice) smuggled out to British authorities, who send spies trying to contact him (see Fortescue 1921, 163–164).[38] These notes later serve the purposes of British propaganda eager to portray the king of Kandy as a ruthless tyrant; in fact, Davie seems to have lived a rollercoaster life in Kandy, under various degrees of confinement and types of treatment. He is even said to have gotten married there and had a son (Powell [1973] 1984, 128–129).

The defeat of the British in Kandy, and the serious depletion of their forces due to desertion and disease, leave them potentially vulnerable on the island as a whole; there is a very real chance that the Kandyans will seize the opportunity to invade the coastal areas and try to end colonial rule altogether. Worried, Governor North sends emergency requests for more

34. They spend a miserable night in the rain in Watapuluwa (now an affluent suburb of Kandy) near a great bo-tree that later came to be known as Davie's Tree and still marked the spot into the twentieth century (Methley 1918, 120).

35. His kinsmen, too, are beheaded. The servants have their ears and nose cut off and are released. For an eyewitness account by one of the servants, see Pieris 1950, 674–683. See also Powell [1973] 1984, 119–120; and, for a slightly different account of all these events, Fellowes 1817, 162–163.

36. According to John Gimlette (2016, 171–172), this is said to have taken place near the village of Lewella ("Blood Sand"), now a suburb of Kandy not far from Watapuluwa. Obeyesekere (2017, 46 and 67n53) argues that Śrī Vikrama did not order the killing of the English soldiers, but that it was the work of the first *adikar*. This is also the view of Pieris 1939, 67.

37. The Dutch assistant surgeon, Greeving, together with a man named Humphreys, manage to roll down the hillside while no one is looking and hide out for a number of days. They are later recaptured and brought before the king, where they are spared, and allowed to live in Kandy under house arrest. Humphreys soon dies, but Greeving manages to escape to the coast a year later (see Kriekenbeek 1918). Other survivors include Corporal George X. Barnsley, whose extraordinary escape is recounted in Alexander 1830, 112; and Sergeant Jan Egbertus Thoen—whose tale can be found in Powell [1973] 1984, 120–121. On him, see also Obeyesekere 2017, 203–210.

38. In one of these messages, he asks that he be sent some opium or laudanum to ease his pain, or, barring that, a pair of pistols to put an end to his life.

troops to India; some are sent but not many can be spared, the British then being in the midst of fighting the second Maratha War. Moreover, Britain is also fighting in Europe, where the Napoleonic Wars—which are not without their effect in South Asia—have just broken out. North, in despair, seeks to get more troops by buying African slaves, who had been used for warfare in the West Indies. In the end, with a force of under two thousand men, comprising "British, Bengalis, Madrasis, Cingalese, Malays, and Africans" (Fortescue 1921, 158),[39] the British are successful in repelling the Kandyan attacks on Colombo and other coastal areas. And North, seeking revenge, even begins planning another invasion of Kandy for 1804 (Fortescue 1921, 157–159). His plans are thwarted, however, by the lack of transport coolies, and he sends out orders calling off the attack. However, one column of sixty British and two hundred native troops, under the command of Major Arthur Johnston, misunderstanding the rescinding order, proceeds boldly on to Kandy by a difficult route through over two hundred miles of mountain and jungle. Once again, they find the city has been deserted. Unbeleaguered by the Kandyans, Johnston installs himself in the palace until such time as he realizes that the other columns are not going to come, at which point he decides to go back to the coast. Now, however, the Kandyans are waiting for him; Johnston's forces are ambushed and suffer heavy casualties on their way out. All told, it is another fiasco.[40]

Obeyesekere (2017, 52) claims that the "palace" that Johnston stayed in in Kandy was, unbeknownst to him, actually the Temple of the Tooth, and his "refuge" in that place was the actual reason he was not attacked in the city. Whether true or not, this story reflects once again the fact that, in 1803–1804, the British remain innocent and ignorant of the importance of the tooth relic. Instead, their focus is on replacing the king with their own candidate, Muttusāmi, without realizing that his sovereignty would be in dire need of legitimation by such a thing as the palladial relic. Simply put, the British do not know enough at this point about Kandy and its kingship to even be aware of the importance of what, in any case, they were not finding in their conquest of the city.

---

39. On how the British purchased 700 African slaves from Portuguese Goa, and made them into soldiers, see Cordiner 1807, 1: 65–66.

40. For an account of this expedition, see Johnston 1810. Obeyesekere (2017, 50–52) emphasizes the wanton destruction and pillaging carried out by Johnston on his way into Kandy.

SEVEN

The British Takeover of 1815 and the Kandyan Convention

His Royal Highness has commanded me to signify to you his general approval of the principles of liberal policy by which you have been guided in acceding to the Convention as proposed for the annexation of the Kingdom of Kandy to His Majesty's dominions, but I cannot conceal from you that the satisfaction of His Royal Highness would have been more complete if the 5th Article in the Convention which relates to the superstition of Boodhoo had been couched in terms less liable to misconstruction.

—Lord Bathurst to Governor Robert Brownrigg, August 30, 1815

J. W. Fortescue, in his voluminous *History of the British Army*, devotes a whole chapter to the Kandyan debacle of 1803, which he calls "a forgotten little war" (1921, 138), justifying the space given over to it because, in his view, it is something that "may serve as a warning of the mischief that may be done by a foolish Governor [i.e., North] seconded by a foolish General [i.e., MacDowall]" (1921, 165). He devotes virtually no space to the campaign of 1815, probably because it was not much of a war,[1] though, in terms of its significance for Sri Lankan history, it was infinitely more important than the conflict of 1803.

Once again, in 1815, the Kandyans repeat their time-honored strategy for dealing with invaders; they offer virtually no resistance to the British multi-pronged advance into their territory, preferring to abandon their capital and bide their time. Thus, the city of Kandy is empty when the British get there

1. Dewaraja (1972, 5) points out that not a single British soldier was killed in the taking of Kandy in 1815. On some of the reasons for this, see below and see Wickremesekera 2004, 199–200.

in February 1815; Śrī Vikrama and all his people have fled, having sent the tooth relic and the greater part of the royal treasure off to various places in the countryside well in advance.[2] This time, however, the dénouement is different. Several of the Kandyan chiefs switch allegiance to the British side and offer their support; within a week, the king is captured (he is quickly sent to Colombo and, in time, exiled to South India); a fortnight later, the British governor signs a treaty with the principal Kandyan chiefs, agreeing, among other things, to "maintain and protect" the Buddhist religion (including its places of worship) which, within the Kandyan provinces, is declared to be "inviolable"; six weeks later, at the request of the British, the tooth relic is re-enshrined in the Dalada Maligawa with great ceremony.

Why 1815 Differed from 1803

It should be said that between 1803 and 1815, at least two things happen that make this relatively easy victory possible: first, some Kandyans become more and more disaffected with their king, in part because the king is portrayed as becoming more and more autocratic and oppressive in his relations with his ministers, with the rest of the Kandyan aristocracy, and with the people.[3] This makes Kandy more ripe for a coup d'état than it was in 1803. And second, the British are better informed and better prepared this time around.

Let me start with stories that show rising disaffection with the king. Shortly after his victories over the British in 1803–1804, Śrī Vikrama decides to vaunt and enhance his power and prestige in a number of ways. First, he undertakes several massive construction projects in Kandy. These entail the forced participation in corvée labor of large numbers of ordinary people not only from the capital but from the surrounding provinces. As we have seen, Śrī Vikrama's vision involved architecturally making the city into a microcosmic replica of the heaven of Indra (Śakra), the king of the gods. Symbolically, this scheme is intended to set his own palace at the top of Mount Meru, and himself as "god-king-bodhisattva" within it. Physically,

---

2. A deposition made by the former king's chief servant, who was responsible for packing up and inventorying the royal treasure to be sent off, reveals that this was done about three months before the 1815 invasion. Specific written records were made and enclosed by him in each sealed box—the king's personal ornaments, the state dresses, and the regalia (including, presumably, the tooth relic)—were, however, not sent away until the invasion was actually underway and the British were drawing close. See Somasunderam 2008, 346–347. (This dissertation was subsequently made into a book—Somasunderam 2015—which I have not seen.)

3. On the general reasons for what some Sri Lankan scholars refer to as the "Rebellion of 1815" (as though the British had little to do with it), see Dharmadasa 1976, 5–11.

this entails making additions to the palace and to the Temple of the Tooth; extending several streets in town to create new blocks to fill out a grid so as to better reflect the cosmic mandala-scheme informing the structure of the kingdom as a whole; and, most onerously, digging an artificial lake, over two miles in circumference, and as much as sixty feet deep. Today, this body of water—Kandy Lake—is one of the charming features of the town. As mentioned, however, its original name was "Kiri Muhuda"—the "Ocean of Milk"—whose churning in Hindu mythology is symbolic of the creation of new order, the establishment of the kingship of the gods, and their victory over the demons.[4] The lake was thus part of an overall attempt to more greatly glorify the figure of the king. In the popular mind, however, the labor spent on excavating it came to be greatly resented.

Such construction projects were not new. One of Śrī Vikrama's Sinhalese predecessors, Rājasiṃha II (1629–1687), had used corvée labor for great building undertakings around his palace, and also a different lake (now filled in), symbolic of Lake Anotatta (Skt., Anavatapta), a mythological body of water near Mount Meru, said, in Buddhist legend, to have been visited by the Buddha.[5]

Gananath Obeyesekere (1984, 333) has pointed out that these attempts to architecturally equate microcosms with macrocosms and the labor they required were *not* uncritically accepted by the masses, especially when they could not be justified as public works but were seen purely as ways to magnify the prestige of the king. For evidence, he points to popular traditions embodied in certain rituals and stories associated with a legendary evil king named Pāṇḍi. In particular, in the mythic scenario entitled "Pataka" ("tank" or "pond" or "pit"), the people's protest may be seen in their accusations that he causes them to suffer by forcing them to carry large baskets of dirt in order to dig out the pond (Obeyesekere 1984, 329–330). This village drama originally must have been inspired by the case of Rājasiṃha II's Anotatta-like lake, but it continued to be popular for several centuries, and Obeyesekere (1984, 338–346) sees its sentiments as precedents for popular objections to Śrī Vikrama's lake.[6]

---

4. Duncan 1990, 87–153. More generally on overlapping symbolisms in the layout of Kandy, see Silva 2011. See also Obeyesekere 2017, 136–140.

5. It is often depicted in Sri Lankan art as the source of four major rivers (see, e.g., Bandaranaike 1986, plate 92).

6. In his 2017 work, however, Obeyesekere (2017, 213) denies that this drama had Rājasiṃha as its referent (he admits to having been "erroneous" about that in 1984), and he questions its applicability to Śrī Vikrama. Instead, he has nothing but praise for the grandness of Śrī Vikrama's construction projects, including the lake, and emphasizes his popularity among the people.

In the case of the Nāyakkar monarchs (e.g., Śrī Vikrama), some people, resenting this corvée labor as more than the usual obligations of *rājakariya* ("duties to the king"), turn also to emphasize the "foreignness," that is, the Tamil identity, of the oppressor.[7] The "Ocean of Milk," though certainly familiar to Buddhist cosmology, is something more involved in emphasizing a Hindu rather than a Buddhist notion of divine kingship. Perhaps in conjunction with this, rumors spread that part of Śrī Vikrama's scheme involves a "Hinduization of the capital." For instance, it is said that he wants to move the Asgiriya and Malwatta monasteries out of town to Peradeniya (six kilometers away);[8] to transfer the four *devales* there as well (so as to make room for a new palace yard in the temple square); and that the king's Tamil relatives are already practicing the Hindu custom of goat sacrifice, right in front of the Dalada Maligawa. Moreover, the king himself is said to have vastly increased the size of his harem, importing Tamil girls from South India and demanding the daughters of Kandyan nobles, and, in his paranoia, bringing in seventy Malabar soldiers a month to be trained by French and Dutch officers and act as his personal praetorian guard.[9]

How much of all of this is true and how much of it is propaganda remains an important question. However, in addition to growing popular resentment of the king in the early nineteenth century, the relationship between Śrī Vikrama and the Kandyan chiefs who are his ministers and the rulers of his provinces becomes increasingly discordant. This leads some of the ministers to plot rebellions and to turn to the British for potential support. This restlessness culminates in 1814 with the revolt in one of the provinces led by the first *adikar* (prime minister), Ehelepola. The king responds by replacing Ehelepola with another *adikar*, Molligoda, whom he sends to quash the uprising—something he accomplishes effectively. Ehelepola flees to Colombo, where he is given safe haven by the British.[10]

Śrī Vikrama's reactions to this rebellion are violently extreme, or at least they come to be depicted as such in stories recounted by both the British

7. For other evidence of this "ethnicization" of accusations against Śrī Vikrama, see the poem "Kiralasandesaya" ("The Lapwing's Message"), written in praise of Ehelepola and in accusation of the "evil, ungrateful and lowly Tamil [the king] who began to ruin this Lanka" (Sivasundaram 2013, 45–46). For a different interpretation of this text, see Obeyesekere 2017, 91–101.

8. Indeed, the original plan for Kandy Lake entailed flooding the land occupied by the Malwatta Monastery (see Dewaraja 1972, 134).

9. Gooneratne and Gooneratne 1999, 119. Obeyesekere (2017, 215–217) is highly critical of the Gooneratnes on this and other points. See also Vimalananda and Jayasuriya 1966, 11.

10. For Ehelepola's own personal recollection of these events from the place of his later exile in Mauritius, in 1828 (and written in an attempt to get clemency from the British), see CO 416/20, 34Aff.

and some Sri Lankans. The king, it is said, had not always been a cruel tyrant; he had, in fact, often shown signs of generosity and compassion in administering justice in the past. But after Ehelepola's rebellion, something snaps: "Surrounded by hostile courtiers and alienated priests, he [i]s now isolated on his throne, able to trust only a handful of his Malabar relations" (Powell [1973] 1984, 204).[11] When Molligoda brings prisoners back to Kandy, the king instantly condemns forty-seven of them to death by impalement, a cruel punishment that is almost without precedent in Kandyan law (D'Oyly 1929, 56). When a chief who had corresponded with Ehelepola is arrested, he is found guilty of treason, is dismembered, and has his eyes plucked out before being beheaded. More shockingly, a Buddhist priest suspected of being part of the conspiracy is also executed. Furthermore, almost seventy acting village headmen from the Seven Korales—the province that had rebelled—are summoned to the capital; they are "tried," and condemned to death by flogging (Pieris 1939, Appendix H).[12]

The king then turns his wrath on members of Ehelepola's family who are still in Kandy. The tradition of the Kandyan court was that the relatives of *adikars* and other rulers of provinces should reside in the capital as hostages of a sort—guarantors of their husband's or father's loyalty. Thus, Ehelepola's wife (Kumarihami) and their children were arrested the moment he rebelled. But now the king decides they are to be executed. According to a tradition that has been disputed by some (see Pieris 1939, Appendix H; and especially Obeyesekere 2017, 76–101 and 197–208) but that quickly passes into popular lore, the mother is made to watch as her sons—the oldest of whom is eleven—are one by one beheaded, the last being an infant torn from her arms. The severed heads are then placed in a large mortar, and she is forced to pound them with a pestle. Then she herself is taken away and drowned.[13] Whatever the factual truth of this scenario, the story itself is

11. See also Somadunderam 2008, 151. This is also the view expressed in the *Sulu Rājāvaliya*, on which see Obeyesekere 2017, 270–275.

12. Obeyesekere (2017, 218) raises doubts about most of these atrocities.

13. The story is told in many places; the first published English version (apparently based largely on the account of Thomas Thoen—a Dutchman, who had been captured in Kandy in 1803, and was still alive in 1815—seems to be that of William Tolfrey (1815, 4 and 21–24; see also Fellowes 1817, 172; Davy 1821, 321–323; and Obeyesekere 2017, 203–208). But Governor Brownrigg early on knew the details of the story that he reported to the secretary of state for the colonies, Lord Bathurst, in a letter from Kandy on February 25, 1815 (see CO 54/55, 97 recto). A more or less contemporary Sinhalese account was the *Ehelepola Daruwan Marawima* [The killing of Ehelepola's children], translated in Vimalananda and Jayasura 1966, 15–17. It includes such shocking details as the milk trickling out of the mouth of the decapitated baby who was torn from Kumarihami's breast, and the threat to have Kumarihami raped by a *rodiya* (untouchable)

symptomatic of Śrī Vikrama's growing reputation for vindictive viciousness and tyranny—among the British, and among his subjects (both ordinary people and the Kandyan chiefs). The net effect of this was to turn some of the Kandyans, at least, against their ruler, and to make them more open and welcoming than they had been in 1803 of a British putsch.

A second factor that distinguishes the 1815 invasion of Kandy from that in 1803 was the sheer degree of preparation on the part of the British. Indeed, under the leadership of the new governor of Ceylon, Lieutenant-General Robert Brownrigg, they take great care to lay the groundwork for their takeover. Determined to avoid the mistakes of their predecessors, they study accounts of the Portuguese and the Dutch expeditions, and of their own failed British incursions in 1803 and 1804. They choose to invade during the cool season and not in the midst of the monsoon. They make accurate maps of all the Kandyan highlands, so as not to be dependent on dubious and possibly duplicitous local guides.[14] They lay plans for a five-pronged attack, coming at Kandy from all sides of the island. They divest their troops of cumbersome baggage, and develop a strategy for a quick offensive, including a secret plan for intercepting and rapidly capturing the king before he has a chance to escape fully into the hinterland (D'Oyly 1917, 200). Most of all, with the help of Ehelepola and a host of other informants, they acquire a good knowledge of the enemy's forces, and engage

---

if she refused to pound the heads. (The latter point was used by the British in their propaganda against the "barbarity" of Kandyan policy—see Somasunderam 2008, 152.) It also features her nine-year-old boy, Madduma Bandara, who, we are told, bravely volunteered to be executed first in place of his cringing older brother. The child has remained to this day a folk hero (see Vimalananda and Jayasuriya 1966; and see Obeyesekere 2017, 268–269). In recent decades, the story has been revived as an example of Sinhalese resistance to perceived Tamil threats, with Vimalananda and Jayasuriya (1966, i), for instance, calling Śrī Vikrama "a wicked raving Tamil tyrant." Another Sinhala poem, *Āhālepola Haṭanē* [Ehelepola's war], also dwells on the story of the execution of his children and wife, emphasizing the reaction of the people (see De Silva 1915–1916, 57). In 2014, the tale was featured in a Sinhala film drama, *Ehelepola Kumarihami*. Obeyesekere (2017, 75–101, 279–284) believes that Kumarihami and her children were killed on orders of the king, but that the story of the manner of their execution was a piece of British propaganda that then influenced certain Sri Lankans. He points to other Sinhalese poems, such as the "Āhālepola varnanāva" [In praise of Ehelepola], which say virtually nothing about this execution, despite their being virulently anti-Tamil and anti–Śrī Vikrama works. He also shows (2017, 199–200) that the trope of punishment-by-pounding-children-in-a-mortar was a common formulaic story among Sinhalese and Westerners dating at least as far back as Robert Knox (seventeenth century). Ehelepola himself (see CO 416/20) merely states that his wife and family were killed (after saying he had assumed they would not be) but says nothing of the details of their execution.

14. On the problems stemming from dependence on local guides (in 1803), see Sivasundaram 2013, 92.

in secret negotiations with some of the disaffected Kandyan chiefs, whom they convince to join forces with them (Somasunderam 2008, 154–165).[15]

John D'Oyly

Key to all of this is the role played by a remarkable civil servant named John D'Oyly, who later becomes the first British Resident in Kandy, and who, for his accomplishments, is eventually awarded the hereditary title of "1st baronet, of Kandy." Born in Sussex in 1774, he is educated at Westminster School and then at Cambridge University, which he enters in 1792. There he excels academically, particularly in the study of classical languages, taking several scholarships and first prizes. At the age of twenty-eight, in 1802, he joins the Ceylon Civil Service under Governor North, and works for some years as agent of revenue, first in Colombo and then in Matara. During this time, he achieves an impressive knowledge of Sinhala, becoming able to speak, read, and write it with confidence. More importantly, he becomes familiar with Sinhalese culture, traditions, and religious beliefs and practices, which he absorbs in part from language study with an erudite and elderly Buddhist monk in Matara. In Matara, he also forms a relationship of uncertain nature and extent with the brilliant, witty, and formidable Sinhala poetess Gajaman Nona (1748–1815), whose patron he becomes, and with whom he exchanges verses.[16] His intelligence and abilities do not go unnoticed, and he is quickly made "Chief Translator to the British Government of Ceylon"—a title that belies the considerably greater and more influential role he comes to play.[17]

Such familiarity with the local language and culture was rare for an Englishman in the colonies in those days, so much so that, later in his career, D'Oyly was accused of "going native" and of having become a Buddhist (Gooneratne and Gooneratne 1999, 153–154). But in the years leading up to 1815, D'Oyly puts his knowledge to use in building a network of spies and informants who keep him fully apprised of developments in Kandy. Through them, he exchanges *olas* (messages or letters written on palm leaf) with Kandyan chiefs and bribes sources for information or for coming over to the British side.[18] A list of persons whom he used as spies and informants

15. For Ehelepola's own account of the help he rendered the British during their invasion, see CO 416/20.

16. On Gajaman Nona and D'Oyly, see Obeyesekere 2017, 255–258.

17. For a biography of D'Oyly, see Gooneratne and Gooneratne 1999. Obeyesekere (2017, 56) claims that "chief translator" is a pseudonym for "master spy."

18. For an interesting account of D'Oyly's spy network, see Obeyesekere 2017, 109–126.

between 1810 and 1815 includes the names of twenty-four ordinary persons or minor headmen, six Buddhist monks, six Kandyan chiefs, three lowland chiefs, and two disaffected relatives of the king (Somasunderam 2008, 324).

D'Oyly uses his contacts not only to gain information, but to spread pieces of misinformation—such as the widespread rumor that the British have no intention of actually ruling Kandy, but are merely trying to help Ehelepola gain the throne, thereby establishing a new, properly Sinhalese dynasty and getting rid of a cruel Tamil tyrant. The overall intent is to present their conquest of Kandy not as a foreign invasion but as merely rendering assistance to a native revolution. To this end, D'Oyly and Governor Brownrigg encourage the spread of some of the negative stories reviewed earlier in this chapter. Specifically, they work together in crafting, publishing, and distributing, on the eve of the incursion, a "Proclamation"—in English and Sinhala—portraying the British not as invaders but as liberators of the Kandyan people from the yoke of foreign (i.e., Nāyakkar) rule. Among other things, this document declares that the British "could not hear with indifference the prayers of the inhabitants [of the Kandyan provinces] who, with one unanimous voice raised against the tyranny and oppression of their ruler . . . and his acts of atrocious barbarity . . . implored the protection of the British government." It adds that British troops, in the course of their invasion, would observe "the most rigorous discipline," that "peaceable inhabitants will be protected from all injury . . . [that] payment will scrupulously be made for every article of provisions which they furnish. . . . [and that] their religion shall be [held] sacred and their temples respected" (Powell [1973] 1984, 281–282).[19]

It should be said that at this point, Governor Brownrigg does not actually have permission from London to go to war against Kandy. In fact, such a venture is specifically discouraged. The Napoleonic Wars are still going on, and there are many, in Britain, who have no interest in their country's getting involved in yet another distant and potentially costly conflict. In his correspondence with Lord Bathurst, therefore, Governor Brownrigg is careful to lay the groundwork for what he wants to do. He consistently vilifies the figure of Śrī Vikrama, portraying him as a cruel, vicious, and uncivilized oriental despot who needs to be taken out, but he presents all his plans and

---

19. For the text of the "Proclamation," see Marshall 1846, 207–210. This, of course, is not exactly what happened. In areas removed from Kandy, British troops plundered a number of monasteries and *devales*, just as earlier, in 1803, they had demolished the Aluvihāra in Matale (famous as the place where the Buddhist canon was first put into writing), and pillaged the Saman Devale in Sabaragamuwa (see Malalgoda 1976, 108–109).

preparations for an intervention as merely provisional—"for an eventual expedition," if needed. At the same time, he makes it clear to Bathurst that this time, should war become necessary, they will be ready; that is, there will be no repeat of 1803 (CO 54/53, 190). But he is still waiting for a clear-cut provocation—an "excuse" that he can use to justify invasion. The king's cruelty toward his own people is not enough; the governor needs to be seen as responding to aggression against Britain and its territories (Gooneratne and Gooneratne 1999, 109).

The needed "excuse" comes late in October 1814. D'Oyly sends Brownrigg a report of the robbing and mutilation by Kandyan troops of ten lowland Sinhalese traders who had ventured into Kandyan territory but who were technically British subjects (CO 54/53, 220–231; CO 54/58, 184A). When this is followed, a few weeks later, by the burning of a village by Kandyan troops just over the border in British territory, Brownrigg has all that he needs. Not only have Kandyans killed British subjects (albeit lowland Sri Lankans), but they have encroached (although temporarily) onto British lands. Such things cannot go uncontested! They must be avenged! So, without waiting for a reply or instructions from London (which would have taken five months or so), Brownrigg launches, in mid-January 1815, his multipronged attack against Kandy as an act of "self-defense" (Powell [1973] 1984, 212).

Actual fighting is minimal. Local chiefs quickly come over to the British side, thanks, in part, to D'Oyly's propaganda and machinations. Moreover, D'Oyly, in secret negotiations, has even won over the acting *adikar*, Molligoda, although the latter dares not openly join the British for fear of what the king will do to his family in Kandy. Instead, he and D'Oyly agree that for the time being, Molligoda's forces will make a token show of resistance, but then quickly surrender or retreat—until such time as his family can get to safety.

By February 11, the British march unopposed into Kandy town. Again, the place has been deserted. The king and all members of the court have fled, and all portable items of significant value are gone, at least from the palace and the Temple of the Tooth, including the relic. As Captain De Bussche, Brownrigg's Swiss aide-de-camp, was to recollect in a letter home:

When we took possession of the palace all the treasures we found in it were a great number of empty boxes, some hundred earthen pots which had been in use, half a dozen broken down couches, with some paddy stampers and whips: every valuable was removed, and little has been discovered since, at least by the army. Our prize money, of which you say so much, will turn out to be a mere trifle, compared to what every person expected from the great riches the Kings of Kandy had amassed by oppression during several preceding centuries. (De Bussche 1817, 83)

Most importantly, however, the king has fled, and this is of primary concern to D'Oyly. Anxious to avoid a repeat of the 1803 situation in which the capital has been captured, but not its ruler, he wastes no time. He wants to intercept Śrī Vikrama before the latter has a chance to get to truly impenetrable jungle regions. Without delay, and aided by his network of informants, he sends out patrols to scour the area east of the capital to look for the king. He himself proceeds in that direction to Teldeniya (see fig. 8.1 below) to direct operations. More and more, with the strong backing of Ehelepola, who has eyes on the throne for himself, he gets local villagers to come over to the British side, sometimes by threats, sometimes by bribes. As he writes to Brownrigg in Kandy: "The Time being arrived when Gold may probably be employed with Success, I beg leave to request that some Pagodas [a form of gold coin] may be sent to me, with Authority to dispose of them on account of Secret Service for the Object of discovering & securing the King's Person" (D'Oyly 1917, 208). Initially, more and more news comes in about sightings of various members of the king's court, many of whom are actually captured. D'Oyly's diary (1917, 205–207) contains lists of "Malabar prisoners" arrested in various villages east of Kandy on various days; these include members of the extended royal family (the king's mothers-in-law, some of his cousins, nephews and nieces), and some of their servants and coolies. There is a sense that they are getting close.

Finally, on February 18, 1815, in a postscript to a letter to Brownrigg in Kandy, D'Oyly (1917, 211) announces: "PS. 6½ PM. 5 Men have arrived with Intelligence, that the King is in a Forest about 6 Quarter Leagues from hence. Tho' I cannot altogether rely upon it as certain, it comes with such an Appearance of Credit, that according to their Request, a Detachment will be sent, with the View of attempting to intercept him, & at once terminating the War."

The lead proves to be a good one. That very evening, the king (along with his wives and close attendants) is captured in the district of Udadumbara (about forty kilometers from Kandy). The next day, D'Oyly (1917, 211–212) writes to Brownrigg: "Dear Sir, I have the sincerest Joy in reporting to Yr. Excellency that the Object of your anxious Wishes is accomplished & the King of Kandy a Captive in our Hands." And he goes on to describe briefly how some native troops he sent out located the king and some of his entourage hiding in a house. They surrounded the place. A few of the king's attendants made a show of resistance but quickly fled, and the king then surrendered without a fight. As soon as he got the news, he (d'Oyly) sent palanquins and had the king and his queens brought to him at his camp at Teldeniya.

Upon receipt of this news, while dining in Kandy with a small group of his officers, Governor Brownrigg is moved to tears, overcome by the historical importance of the event. Going around the table, he shakes the hand of each man present, and thanks them all for accomplishing what had been "vainly attempted for nearly three centuries by three European powers in succession" (Marshall 1846, 157–158). "From that day," as one observer later remarked, "we may date the extinction of Ceylonese independence, an independence which had continued, without any material interruption, for 2357 years—*Sic transit Gloria mundi*" (Knighton 1845, 325).

In time, stories were to embellish the account of the king's capture with details and drama and controversy.[20] Though interesting, these need not detain us here; the tooth relic was not with the king, and it is likely that at that point, he himself had no good idea of where exactly it was, or at least he was not about to tell the British. D'Oyly treats his royal prisoner with respect; he avoids taking him back to Kandy and, instead, has him escorted (on a palanquin) directly to Colombo. There, eventually, the king and his family are sent into exile to the fort at Vellore near Madras (now Chennai) in India. The choice of South India makes good sense given the Nāyakkar identity of Śrī Vikrama and the British desire to portray him as a foreigner (who was thus simply being repatriated to his true home) (see Sivasundaram 2013, 31–33).[21]

The Kandyan Convention, Article Five

On March 2, 1815, a mere two weeks after the king is captured, Governor Brownrigg assembles all the Kandyan chiefs who have come over to the British side in the audience hall of the royal palace. Again, D'Oyly and Brownrigg are conscious of decorum and symbolism. They screen off the elevated part of the hall where, previously, the Kandyan monarch used to place himself on a high throne. Brownrigg then sits at the head of the lower chamber, in closer proximity to where the chiefs will stand. Ehelepola, who

---

20. For an early account, see Tolfrey 1815. For one instance of how the tale was told forty years later, see Pohath 1896. See also Obeyesekere 2017, 171–173.

21. For an eyewitness account of the king's embarkation for Madras on HMS *Cornwallis* (on January 24, 1816), see *Asiatic Journal and Monthly Register* 1816c, 102. See also Obeyesekere 2017, 331–341.

has refused all appointments from the British (since he really wants them to make him king), arrives first, followed by the *adikar* Molligoda. They are preceded by their whip-cracking lictors—which they are due by virtue of their rank—and they enter the hall, after passing between two mounted lines of soldiers from the Ceylon Light Dragoons drawn up in the square outside. They are followed by the rest of the chiefs, while the British officers line the sides of the hall (Tolfrey 1815, 46).[22]

The meeting starts with mutual complimentary inquiries from both the governor and the chiefs, with Brownrigg telling them how pleased he is at their support and his delight at being able to have been "the means of their deliverance," and assuring them "of full protection in their persons, their property, and all their rights." He then announces to them that a document has been drawn up, which he hopes they will be pleased to sign (Marshall 1846, 123).

This document, or treaty, in both English and Sinhala, was authored principally by D'Oyly and is generally known as the Kandyan Convention. It is read out in the two languages and is then unanimously approved by all present. It is then taken outside the hall and is proclaimed to lesser head-men and all those who could not get into the proceedings.[23]

The Kandyan Convention makes clear a number of things. First, it states not only that Śrī Vikrama has been deposed, but that all of his relatives "whether in the ascending, descending, or collateral line, and whether by affinity or blood, are also forever excluded from the throne; and that all claim and title of the Malabar race to the dominion of the Kandyan provinces is abolished and extinguished" (Powell [1973] 1984, 283). In other words, all the South Indian Nāyakkar aristocrats who have come in the past half century to so dominate the Kandyan court are now "declared enemies to the government of the Kandyan provinces, and . . . prohibited from entering those provinces, on any pretence whatever, without a written permission for the purpose, by the authority of the British government" (Powell [1973]

22. The account in Marshall 1846, 123, appears to be largely plagiarized from Tolfrey.

23. Preliminary to the Convention per se, the British also issued (in English but not in Sinhala) an "Official Declaration of the Settlement of the Kandyan Provinces," in which they reasserted that the British conquest of Kandyan territory was something that was "led by the invitation of the [Kandyan] chiefs, and welcomed by the acclamation of the people" (Marshall 1846, 210). This was followed by a recollection in detail of all the horrible deeds (starting in 1803) of Śrī Vikrama not only toward the British but also toward his own people. This seems to have been aimed at British consumption both in Ceylon and in England (Marshall 1846, 212). For a copy of this "preface," see Tolfrey 1815, 39–43.

1984, 284). This is rather striking, given the fact that just twelve years earlier, the British had tried to install a Nāyakkar (Muttusāmi) on the throne.

Lest, however, this declaration lead to expectations that the deposed Nāyakkar ruler would be replaced by a fully Sinhalese king (e.g., Ehelepola), the very next article of the Convention makes it clear that the new king of Kandy is His Majesty George III, acting through the prince regent, George, Prince of Wales, acting in turn through the governor and lieutenant governors of Ceylon.[24] This does not mean a change of government structure at the lower echelons. That is to be preserved: Sinhalese *adikars* (ministers), *dissaves* (district governors), and other chieftains and headmen will retain the "rights, privileges, and powers of their respective offices," provided they are reappointed to them by their new British sovereigns (Powell [1973] 1984, 284). But there is to be no Kandyan king, at least "for the time being" (Powell [1973] 1984, 284)—a direct contradiction to the expectation, promoted by D'Oyly in his propaganda and attractive to Ehelepola, that there would be one.

Many Kandyan chiefs fear that this new structure will simply not work for the preservation of Buddhism which, after all, the British monarchical system was not geared to maintain. Traditional Buddhist polity in Sri Lanka depended, in many ways, on an active, authoritative, involved, and *present* monarch, which the distant British sovereign was clearly not.[25] Perhaps sensing this, and feeling a need to reassure not only the Kandyan chiefs but also the leading Buddhist monks, D'Oyly and Brownrigg insist on the inclusion in the Convention of "Article Five," which states: "The religion of Boodhoo, professed by the chiefs and inhabitants of these provinces, is declared inviolable; and its rites, ministers, and places of worship, are to be maintained and protected" (Powell [1973] 1984, 284).[26]

24. George the Prince of Wales became regent in 1811, since by then his father's mental illness was so pronounced that it was impossible for him to actually govern the empire.

25. D'Oyly was a keen student of traditional Kandyan modes of governance and later wrote a study of such (which was published posthumously). In it, the very first sentence reads: "The Power of the King is Supreme and absolute. The Ministers advise, but cannot control his Will" (D'Oyly 1929, 1). For an original draft of D'Oyly's book, see CO 416/19, 2A-82A.

26. Powell [1973] 1984, 284, uses the word "rights," which I have here corrected to "rites." Powell is copying the mistaken text found in Marshall 1846, 274, which reflects the reading in Davy 1821, 501, and this wording led to some confusion, especially among missionaries who did not see Buddhism as having any "rights" at all. The original handwritten text of the Convention, however, a facsimile of which may be seen at https://en.wikipedia.org/wiki/Kandyan_Convention, clearly has "rites," as does the first printed version of the text in *Asiatic Journal and Monthly Register* 1816b, 230. So too does Bathurst's letter to Brownrigg in August 1815 (see CO 54/55, 118).

In his report to Lord Bathurst, Governor Brownrigg, worried that this paragraph might well be controversial (as indeed it became), comments on it in this way:

The 5th [article] confirms the superstition of Boodhoo in a manner more Emphatical than would have been my choice. But as the reverence felt towards it at present by all classes of the inhabitants is unbounded and mixed with a strong shade of jealousy and doubt about its future protection—and that in truth our secure possession of the country hinged upon this point, I found it necessary to quiet all uneasiness respecting it by an article of guarantee coached in the most unqualified terms. (CO 54/55, 118 verso)

William Tolfrey (1815, 44–45) echoes this sentiment. In a private letter dated March 2, 1815, he admits that the document is "carefully adapted to the wishes of the chiefs and people, and with a more particular degree of attention to some prejudices, the indulgence of which was plainly understood to be a sine qua non of their voluntary submission to an European power." And then he lists two of these "prejudices": the "preservation of the religion of Boodho [and] . . . the recognition and continuance of their local institutions."[27]

At the meeting of his Governing Council, held in Colombo on April 1, 1815, Brownrigg feels obligated to return to this proviso:

The 5th Clause which recognizes and protects the religion of Boodho and the 8th clause which continues the administration of justice on its former footing are no other than practical applications of the general principle held out by the Manifesto of the War and merely amount to a fair and faithful performance of the promise solemnly pledged in his Majesty's name by the concluding clause of the Proclamation alluded to. (CO 54/55, 195)[28]

It would seem, then, at this point, that official British attitudes toward Buddhism are governed by two things: a practical desire not to give Sri Lankan Buddhists religious cause for nonacceptance of their rule, and a general ideology of tolerance (or at least of non-oppression) stemming from

27. In this light, Obeyesekere (2017, 226) declares that Article Five "is D'Oyly's triumph because he realized that the Kandyans would never accept British rule without [it]."

28. For that Manifesto (i.e., the "Proclamation"), see above. Brownrigg's point here is that it (and its final clause guaranteeing that the "religion [of the Sinhalese] shall be sacred and their temples respected") had already previously been approved by the Council; hence the Convention represents no new departure of policy.

the Enlightenment. These two factors, however, are soon undermined by the rise, in Britain and elsewhere, of Christian evangelical missionary sentiments that saw Buddhism on the island not as a pawn to be used for governing but as an opponent to be destroyed. As Barcroft Boake (1854, 3) put it, "when so vague and ungarded [*sic*] a promise, to maintain and protect a false religion, came to be known in England, it excited no small animadversion."

Indeed, reactions to Article Five of the Convention from missionary societies and others interested in the promotion of Christianity in Sri Lanka are not slow in coming. Lord Bathurst, who originally responded with worry about the term "inviolable" in his reply to Brownrigg, writes to him again on August 30, 1815, to communicate the opinion of none other than the prince regent, the future George IV (as we have seen in the epigraph to this chapter). His Majesty was worried about misunderstandings that might arise from Article Five's guarantee to support the "Religion of Boodhoo." After communicating the prince regent's view to Brownrigg, Bathurst goes on to assure the governor of his support (because he is "well aware that [the latter's true] feelings on these subjects are . . . in perfect accord with those of His Majesty's Government"). But he also issues a caveat:

> If the term "inviolable" in the first clause of the Article is . . . understood as precluding the efforts which [we] are making to disseminate Christianity in Ceylon by the propagation of the Scriptures, or by the fair and discreet preaching of its Ministers, it would be very much at variance with the principles upon which His Majesty's Government have uniformly acted for guarding against so great an evil. (quoted in Pieris 1950, 596)

In other words, here we have one of the first statements, couched, to be sure, very diplomatically, of the view that will surface repeatedly over the next several decades, that "inviolable" should signify only that Buddhism is not to be outlawed and Buddhists are not to be openly persecuted, and should not be taken to mean that Christianity cannot be allowed to proselytize and offer an alternative faith system that could undermine Buddhism.

At the same time, it should be said that some objectors in London and elsewhere had, at this time, mixed feelings about "the religion of Boodhoo." Indeed, British understanding of Buddhism and of its relationship to Hinduism and to "demon-worship" was just in its infancy in 1815. Generally speaking, all three traditions were thought of as idolatrous, but they were placed on a sort of "spectrum of decency," with Buddhism at one end, "devil-worship" at the other, and Hinduism somewhere in between (though it was often seen as more akin to devil-worship and liable to depravity than the former) (Harris 2006, 55). There was thus a tendency among some to feel better about Buddhism.[29] The following comment of William Martin Harvard (1790–1857) (himself a Wesleyan missionary who spent several years in Ceylon) is typical, at least of this one view:

> Compared with the prevailing religion of the Hindoos, Buddhism wears an aspect amiable and humane. Unlike the worship of *Juggernaut* (to instance one Hindoo deity only) for whom rubric prescribes impurity and blood as acceptable and even essential *acts of worship*, the worship of Buddhu is simple and inoffensive. The sacred books of this system forbid cruelty, dishonesty, unchastity, and falsehood; and inculcate kindness, sympathy, and subordination in civil society. The system tends to correct the inveterate prejudices of *caste*; and has even produced institutions of benevolence and mercy in different parts of the island. (Harvard 1823, lxi, slightly altered)

In this context, it is interesting to note that the Kandyan Convention, in its English version, makes mention *only* of the "Religion of Boodhoo" and omits references to other religious traditions in Kandy. This appears to have been a deliberate choice on the part of D'Oyly and is in marked contrast to the Sinhala version of Article Five that was intended to reassure the Kandyan chiefs. Equally important to them was not only "the Buddha"—symbolized primarily for them by the tooth relic—but also the worship of the devas—the four protector gods of Kandy—Viṣṇu, Nātha, Kataragama, and Pattini. Aware of this, D'Oyly, in the Sinhala version of Article Five (which is the version that many of the chiefs would have gone by), phrases things rather differently:

> The Sāsana [religion] of Buddha *and the Āgama of the Dēvas* [tradition of the gods] in which the Officials and Inhabitants of the aforesaid Raṭaval [lands] have faith, must be so maintained that they cannot be broken, and their ceremonies, Sangha, Vihārasthānas [monastic dwellings] *and Dēvālayas* [shrines of the gods] maintained and protected.[30]

29. David Scott (1994, 159–160) has remarked with regard to this issue that "the question of the relation between Buddhism and Hinduism, though by no means resolved, gave way to a concern with the relation between Buddhism and demonism."

30. Pieris 1950, 17 (italics added) and 591–593. I'd like to thank Steven Berkwitz (personal communication, September 4, 2016) for his comments on this Sinhala version, the original handwritten text of which may be found at https://en.wikipedia.org/wiki/Kandyan_Convention. See also De Silva 1965a, 64n2; and Obeyesekere 2017, 226–229, who offers his own translation of this Sinhala version of Article Five.

As P. E. Pieris points out, "Th[is] omission of all reference to the Dēvas cannot have been accidental" (Pieris 1950, 17). Indeed, if those who worried about the word "inviolable" in the English version of Article Five had known what was being promised in the Sinhala version, their objections might have carried the day. It was one thing for the government to support the "mild" presence of Buddhism, but quite another to protect the worship of "depraved deities." On the other hand, D'Oyly knew that, for the Kandyan chiefs and people, the well-being of Buddhism—specifically, the cult of the Buddha's tooth—depended on the support of its protector of its guardian devas. Thus, both needed to be guaranteed.[31]

It is not clear to me that Governor Brownrigg was ever really aware of what was in the Sinhala version of Article Five. Certainly, Lord Bathurst and the missionary societies in London were not. But D'Oyly, in his subsequent actions, shows himself repeatedly concerned with keeping the guarantees of that Sinhala version in mind. As we shall see, he participates not only in the return of the Buddha's tooth to its temple, but also in the return of the emblems of the protector gods to their *devales*, and he himself takes part in rituals at those *devales*.

Meeting with the Monks

On the same day that the Kandyan Convention is signed,[32] Governor Brownrigg appoints D'Oyly as accredited agent of the British government in the Kandyan Provinces. D'Oyly formally accepts the position three days later (D'Oyly 1917, 228). He then promptly comes down with dysentery and fever, which he treats with tincture of rhubarb, salts, and castor oil, before trying laudanum, "which stops the Disease, I think, too suddenly, & brings on Head Ache" (1917, 229).

On March 10, somewhat recovered, he attends the meeting that Governor Brownrigg decides to have with the monks of the two chief Buddhist temples in Kandy—the Malwatta and Asgiriya monasteries—in order to officially reappoint them to their posts, and to reassure them further of Britain's intention with regard to the Buddhist religion.

31. On this, see also Obeyesekere 2017, 228.
32. Most of the Kandyan chiefs signed on March 10, except for Ehelepola, who is said to have signed later, although there is some modern Sri Lankan speculation about whether or not his signature was forged by D'Oyly. On this rumor, see the remarks by Anura Manatunga of Kelaniya University in March 2015 (http://lankanworldview.blogspot.com/2015/03/dynamics -of-national-struggles-1815-1848_1.html).

At 6:00 p.m., the monks arrive at the Temple of the Tooth and then proceed from there to the nearby Hall of Audience where Brownrigg and D'Oyly await them. The Malwatta bhikkhus, headed by their aged elder, line up on the right side, while those from Asgiriya go to the left.[33] After some initial formalities in which Brownrigg inquires as to the health and well-being of the monks, the conversation goes like this, according to D'Oyly's diary entry (1917, 230):

> His Excellency [i.e., Brownrigg]: "I beg the Priests will rest assured that they will receive under the British Government full Protection & Security—Their Temples will be held sacred, & their Religion respected." [Here D'Oyly notes that this statement is much amplified to the priests by the Adikar Ehelepola.]
>
> Priest: "Since the time of Vijaya[34] the Religion of Buddha has been aided & supported in this Island by the Sovereigns who have successively reigned. By means of this Religion the Sovereigns & the People of Ceylon have flourished, & the World maintained in Security & Welfare. It is by the Increase & Prosperity of Religion that Disease & other Calamities are averted from the Land & Good attends the World. Therefore, we are highly gratified to hear that it is His Excellency's Intention to protect & promote the Interests of Religion."

Brownrigg then repeats his assurances that Buddhism will receive his fullest protection. These formalities over, the monks retire to the Dalada Maligawa, where they are joined by D'Oyly, Ehelepola, and other Kandyan chiefs, and here they get into the nitty-gritty of negotiation. Three topics are of concern: the reappointment by the new regime of monastic leaders; the protection of property and return of valuables belonging to various monasteries and specifically to the Temple of the Tooth; and, last but not least, the return of the emblems of the *devales* and of the tooth relic itself to Kandy. I will deal with the first two of these in the remainder of this chapter, and with the third in chapter 8.

The first issue is quickly (if only temporarily) dealt with later that evening: back in the Hall of Audience, Brownrigg, taking upon himself, as governor, the prerogatives and authority that formerly belonged to the king, formally (re)-appoints to their posts the *mahānāyakas* and *anunāyakas* of both the Malwatta and Asgiriya monasteries, as well as the *basnāyaka nilames* of the Nātha and Viṣṇu *devales* (D'Oyly 1917, 229). Similarly, over the next

---

33. For an eyewitness account of the scene, see De Bussche 1817, 43–46.
34. The legendary first king of Sri Lanka, said to have arrived on the island on the day of the Buddha's parinirvana.

week, in line with the provisions of the Kandyan Convention, he reaffirms traditional Sinhalese political structures by officially conferring government offices upon former Kandyan aristocrats. Molligoda is reappointed as first *adikar*. Ehelepola's brother-in-law Kapuwatte is made second *adikar* as well as Diyawadana Nilame (the layman in charge of the Temple of the Tooth and its properties). Ehelepola himself refuses all appointments (since he is still hoping to become king) but instead accepts the new title of "Friend of the British Government," with the understanding that with this new honor he would still retain precedence over all other chiefs (Powell [1973] 1984, 234).[35] It is clear, however, that his authority is utterly dependent on his subservience to the British. As J. W. Bennett (1843, 411) wryly remarks, Brownrigg and D'Oyly, for their actions, got baronetcies, but Ehelepola, who wanted to be king, "was honored with the Prince Regent's portrait set with brilliants, to be worn round his neck, suspended from a magnificent gold chain!"[36]

The second issue proves to be more complicated. Brownrigg and D'Oyly seek to assure the monks that the villages and properties belonging to the monasteries and to the four *devales* that the king had, during the late emergency, taken over for his own use or assigned to loyal subordinates will be "fully restored to the temples" (D'Oyly 1917, 231). But such things are not always straightforward, since some of these villages are also claimed as the traditional fiefdoms of dispossessed Kandyan chiefs, and others have complicated histories. Still, Brownrigg shows signs of being quite willing to cut through "red tape." For instance, on March 19, 1815, on the day before his return to Colombo, Brownrigg gathers the Malwatta and Asgiriya elders to bid them good-bye and reassure them of his ongoing support. They take the opportunity to state that there is a field in the village of Yatiwawala [across the Mahaweli river just north of Kandy], "which in the time of [King] Kirti Śrī [seventeenth century] was offered to the Temple [of the Tooth], but which was [then] possessed by the late Moratota Nayaka Unnanse, next by Paranatela, & after his Death, given to the Gabadawa [the royal storehouse], and granted to a Malabar, who is now sent Prisoner to Colombo. . . ." Could

---

35. The full list of appointments at this time may be found in D'Oyly 1917, 235–238.

36. There were some Englishmen who eventually came to think that maybe Ehelepola *should* have become king. As Archibald Lawrie (1896, 203), who was later a district judge in Kandy, put it: "it may be that [Ehelepola] was a more able stateman than the Englishmen with whom he had to deal. If [he] had been raised to the throne as a king dependent on England, with a resident English garrison at once to support and to control him, the Kandyans might possibly have been spared the horrors of the insurrection of 1818 and the cruelty of its suppression by the English."

something be done about this? Brownrigg responds by immediately restoring the field to the temple (D'Oyly 1917, 239).

Then, in a further gesture of goodwill to the monks, he states: "A new Pavilion [the famous octagonal hall (the Patthirippuwa) attached to the Temple of the Tooth] has lately been erected by the King near [the] Dalada Maligawa. Having no particular Occasion for this Pavilion, I present it to the Temple for the use of the Priests."[37] All of this, according to D'Oyly, greatly pleases the high monks: "We receive with the greatest Joy this Proof of His Excellency's Intention to promote & increase the Prosperity of Religion—& we consider, that from this Day Religion is beginning to flourish. . . . Religion is under the Protection of the Gods, & those who support Religion will receive their Favour—as His Excellency the Governor in this manner protects & promotes the Prosperity of Religion, so will the Gods forever afford him Protection" (D'Oyly 1917, 239–240). After Brownrigg's departure for Colombo, it falls to D'Oyly to handle these kinds of situations (see D'Oyly 1917, 243–244).

Land, however, is not the only thing belonging to the Temple of the Tooth (or the king, or the chiefs, or the monasteries, or the *devales*). There is also the matter of the treasures (gems, jewelry, gold, precious artifacts, etc.) that were carried off to various places in the countryside for safekeeping at the time of the king's flight. The question of these properties—their locations, and how to recover them—comes up almost as soon as the king is captured. D'Oyly, through his network of informants, is quick to locate some of them. On February 22, 1815, just four days after the capture of the king, he writes in his diary: "The Royal Property concealed in different Parts of the Country, have been placed under the Charge of responsible Persons, and if we can only preserve them from the Depredations of our own Soldiers and Followers, and the plundering Inhabitants of other Kandyan Provinces, I do not think there is Danger of losing it" (D'Oyly 1917, 217). On the same day, he adds:

> I have sent people this morning to bring away some boxes and other property at [the villages of] Giddawa [about thirty-one kilometers from Kandy] and Henagehuwala [about twenty-three kilometers from Kandy], which the persons in charge render no difficulty in delivering, when demanded. In the same manner, the other chiefs in charge will doubtless in a few days produce the

---

37. Obeyesekere (2017, 229) contextualizes this act of largesse by pointing out that Brownrigg had previously been using the Octagon as his command center (scandalous in itself) but would now be returning to Colombo.

other concealed treasures, when called upon by the proper authority. (D'Oyly 1917, 218)

This is not to say everything is being recovered; around the same time, D'Oyly also writes to Brownrigg (1917, 218) that the king, one night, asked to see him, and, in a confidential manner, took him by the hand, and told him that he was willing to reveal to him various places, known only to himself, where royal treasures had been hidden. D'Oyly understood this to be a "douceur" (a bribe) aimed at obtaining unspecified advantages, so he told the king outright that he would immediately communicate any information about concealed properties to Governor Brownrigg and that the treasures recovered would be turned over to the government.[38]

Nevertheless, it is clear that over the next several weeks, more and more hidden treasures are discovered, or are voluntarily turned in not only to the British but to the Kandyan *adikars*. As William Tolfrey (1815, 35, slightly altered) puts it: "Scarcely a day now passes, without bringing in accounts to Kandy of the discovery of money and jewels, and the army has begun to look with some confidence to a handsome remuneration for their labors."[39]

However, complications about such treasures quickly arise because not everything hidden away actually belonged to the king. As mentioned, at the time of the invasion, properties of the Temple of the Tooth, of various monasteries and *devales*, and of some of the Kandyan nobles were all taken away for safekeeping, in addition to royal treasures. Upon their recovery, however, it is not always clear what belonged to whom, and sorting things out proves to be difficult. The British military is clearly inclined to declare as many items as possible to have belonged to the king, so they can be appropriated as "spoils of war." Brownrigg and D'Oyly, however, have mixed inclinations, since they want to use some of this wealth in their diplomatic dealings with the monks and the Kandyan chiefs.

Given this situation, a "Prize Committee" is set up by the military, chaired by one Major MacKay, to inquire into the provenance of the properties taken or found by troops or turned in by villagers, and to dispose of them

38. Ultimately, the king does turn over a written list of such hidden items, but not so much, it is argued (see Tolfrey 1815, 34; Fellowes 1817, 181), for a return of favor, but because he got so mad at the overall betrayal of some of his subjects that he did not want them to enjoy the treasures for themselves.

39. There are various possible reasons for keepers of such treasures to return them: honest belief that the items were not theirs and should be returned; fear of getting found holding what, in effect, were now "hot properties"; and desire for rewards or favors, either from the *adikars*, or from the British as new rulers.

accordingly. One of the specified tasks of this board is to investigate various claims of the Dalada Maligawa and of the monasteries to "property seized as prize," with the understanding that items determined to have belonged to religious institutions will go to them and *not* to the Crown. For the next few weeks, D'Oyly, among his many other duties, attends these committee meetings, which seem to take place almost daily from 11:00 a.m. to 5 p.m.[40]

The transcripts of some of these sessions have been preserved in the records of the Colonial Office (CO 5456, 214a–215a). For example, on one day in March 1815, the following questions and answers between British Committee members and an unidentified monk take place. It is clear from the first part of this exchange that the military interrogator is trying to disprove that such wealth could belong to Buddhist monks, and interestingly, he even refers to a rule of the Vinaya—the monastic code—to try to bolster his argument:

Q. "Is it customary to present gold and silver, money, jewels and precious stones to temples?"
A. "It is customary."
Q. "Are not the priests of Bhudda [sic] prohibited from the use of all these things?"
A. "The use of gold, silver and precious stones is prohibited."
Q. "What then do the Priests do with such valuables?"
A. "They adorn the relicks of Bhudda with these ornaments."
Q. "Are there ever gifts of arms, such as swords, knives and creeses [krisses] made of Iron or steel?"
A. "No never."
Q. "Are ever such things kept in their temples?"
A. "Guns only to fire on rejoicing days; all other description of weapons are prohibited."
Q. "Who ordered the property of the temple [of the tooth] to be removed, and where was it taken to on its removal?"
A. "The property was removed to the villages belonging to the temple, namely Pelligoda and Palogama, and it was deposited there by order of the king by the servants of the temple."
Q. "Was it not known to the people and the priesthood that the English government protected the temples and were they not considered a place of greater security than villages?"

40. See, for example, D'Oyly 1917, 243ff, where he records attending meetings on March 21, 22, 23, 24, 25, 27, 28, 29, 30, and so on.

A. "They did not know that property would be safe in the temples and it is customary in times of commotion to remove property from the temple."

Q. "When was the property in question removed?"

A. "Some of it thirty days before the British entered Kandy and a part of it before that." . . .

[Later, in questioning a lay official of the Dalada Maligawa (perhaps the Diyawadana Nilame, though this is not stated), the inquiry goes as follows:]

Q. "Do you have a list of objects removed?"

A. "Yes."

Q. "Does this book belong to yourself, to the defeated king or to the temple?"

A. "It is my book, it is the register of the property of the temple, kept by me in virtue of my office which has descended to me from my ancestors." (CO 54/56, 221B)

There then follows a catalog of several pages of various sorts of precious items and gems such as rubies, emeralds, diamonds, amethysts . . . . But even with such a list in hand, identifying particular objects returned and sorting out the question of their actual ownership remains difficult. One modus operandi of the committee seems to have been to hold up individual pieces of jewelry and various gems and to simply ask the monks, *adikars*, and temple attendants assembled as witnesses to whom the items in question belonged. In this way, they eventually developed a new catalog of captured treasures in which each item is listed and it is recorded who recognizes it. The process is a slow one, for with each item there often goes a story. For example, here is one of D'Oyly's diary entries (1917, 246) for March 25:

Attended Committee of Enquiry from 10 till 5. The 2nd adikar [Kapuwatte] is present. He recognizes a gold elegant ornament set with emeralds, [a large] diamond and rubies in imitation of a bird, and informs that it was made and offered to the Temple [of the Tooth] by [King] Kīrti Śrī [r. 1747–1782]. His father, Kapuwatte, Disave of Saffragam, had gone as ambassador to Batavia [in Java, then capital of the Dutch East Indies] and received as presents a gold chain and a diamond ring. He died on his passage home but before his death, desired that these ornaments be presented to the king. He himself [the 2nd *adikar* Kapuwatte], then eleven years of age, presented them, and the king observed: "I bore great love for the disave, may good merit attend him. This diamond shall be set in the forehead of the bird which is now being made for dedication to the Dalada Maligawa." It was set accordingly and it now bears that very diamond.

This item, which had belonged to the king, but had been given by him to the Tooth Relic, is now to be retained by the temple.[41] Unfortunately, however, cases are not always so clear. The identifiers are not always in agreement, and sometimes, no one seems to recognize the objects in question. One possible reason for this is that some of the treasures recaptured and returned in March 1815 had actually been taken away—not on this latest flight of the king—but on the occasion of previous evacuations of Kandy by previous monarchs, some as far back as the time of the Dutch invasions in the seventeenth century. Apparently, some earlier caches of treasures sent by former kings to the traditional places of hiding were never returned to Kandy, and then got mixed up with the new caches established by Śrī Vikrāma. Thus, in some cases, witnesses are being asked to identify items that no one has seen for decades or as much as a century. Another complication is that treasures are sometimes found to have been the property of a particular past king but offered by him to the Dalada upon his deathbed—a rather common merit-making gesture—or loaned by him to the temple for a particular ritual or festival. Did such gifts represent a transfer of ownership?

Coupled with this, of course, is the problem of the deliberate or mistaken identification of items by individuals seeking to preserve them for the temple or to ingratiate themselves to the British Army. For example, D'Oyly (1917, 244) mentions in his diary that one "servant of the temple" who had been most helpful in leading troops to a particular cache of treasure, "asserting it at that time to be the Property of the King" (and hence now of the British crown), changes his mind and now declares it to belong to the temple, perhaps in a desire to make merit by "offering" it in this way to the relic. Frustrated and suspicious of the motivations of their witnesses, at one point the committee actually plants a gold ring belonging to one of its own members—a certain Mr. Wilson—among the items being examined. The 1st *adikar*, Molligoda, and the monks, to their credit, say they do not recognize the item, but the 2nd *adikar* Kapuwatte and Ehelepola both claim it as belonging to the temple . . . (D'Oyly 1917, 248).

It is apparent, however, that D'Oyly and Brownrigg want to get the process over and done with fast. The reason for this is clear: they want to bring back the tooth relic itself, and the monks are insisting that this cannot and will not happen until the temple is sufficiently adorned with the gems and jewels and treasures befitting its re-enshrinement there. To this Brownrigg agrees. On March 29, 1815, a list is drawn up by the monks and temple

41. The bird ornament still adorns the reliquary—see figure 11.2 below.

officials as to what items will be wanted. These include chains of gold of various kinds, gold sheets (*patra*) covered with inscriptions, plates set with precious stones, three miniature reliquary stupas, and so on. Over the following days, additional articles, mainly gold and silver vessels, are added to the list, all with the explication that they too are absolutely necessary for the festival of bringing back the relic (D'Oyly 1917, 248–250).

And here a problem develops: many of the items being claimed by the monks as needed for the festival are among those whose ownership has not been established by the army committee of inquiry, and the latter is balking at turning all these precious things over to the temple, insisting that the burden of proof of ownership lies with the monks, and "claiming a right to retain [for the army] all that has not been recorded to their satisfaction to be church property" (CO 54/56, 128A). A compromise solution, however, is soon reached. Brownrigg intervenes and issues an order that disputed treasures needed by the temple for the return of the tooth should be handed over immediately to the priests, with, however, the stipulation that the two *adikars* would guarantee that these items would later be returned to the army if it made good on its claim to ownership with the Prize Committee (CO 54/56, 127B–128A).

In fact, even this compromise runs into difficulties, for the very next day, the *adikars* demur on their promise to actually sign a paper "pledging themselves to redeliver the property [to the army] in 10 days, if so required" (D'Oyly 1917, 248). The reason is clear: after giving their oral assurances to the agreement, the *adikars* consulted with the monks who, while reaffirming that they will arrange for the relic to be brought back as soon as the precious items listed are delivered up to the temple, add the caveat that "ornaments, after being placed round the relic, cannot be returned [to their donors]" (D'Oyly 1917, 248). Thus, from their perspective, there can be no such thing as what Brownrigg envisages, that is, a "temporary loan" to the Temple of the Tooth, for ritual purposes, of treasures that may later be found to belong to the government. In other words, if the British want the relic returned to the capital, they are essentially going to have to be willing to pay for that.

It is not clear what D'Oyly's immediate reaction is to this hiccough, but he keeps negotiations open. He knows the *adikars* are also anxious to get the tooth relic back, and, four days later, he convinces them to sign the pledge, which they do "without consulting the Priests" (D'Oyly 1917, 250).

EIGHT

The Relic Returns: The Tooth and Its Properties Restored to the Temple

The Kandyans attach as much importance to the possession of a sacred relic called
Delada . . . as the Trojans of old did to their statue of Pallas. It was therefore, considered sound policy to show that we were equally as conscious of the political value
of the relic as the Kandyans themselves; and an imposing ceremonial was ordered
for restoring the Palladium . . . to the Delada Malagawa, or Palace of the Tooth,
from which it had been removed during the army's advance upon the capital.

—John Whitchurch Bennett (1843, 411–412)

Besides their insistence on the return of what they viewed as the jewels necessary for ensuring the continuation of the cult of the tooth, the monks, in
their discussions with D'Oyly, make clear another request: that not only the
Buddha's tooth relic, but also the emblems of the protector deities must be
honored. This comes as no surprise to D'Oyly, who, after all, was well aware
of the Sinhala version of Article Five of the Kandyan Convention, guaranteeing essentially that. He starts making arrangements, therefore, not only for
the return of the tooth, but also for what he consistently calls "the return
of the gods." The hope is originally to have the two events on the same day,
but in the course of things they occur separately, and since the "return of
the gods" happens first, I shall turn to it here and deal with the return of
the tooth later.

The Return of the Gods

The date for the return of the gods to their *devales* is originally set for March 27,
2015. On March 23, however, a bullock accidentally drowns in the pool of
one of the *devales*, causing the *kapurale* (priest) to declare that at least seven

days of purification will be needed before being able to bring the gods back. The new date is set for April 7. At the same time, precautions are taken to remove a "Malabar madman" who is lying in the street, lest he die there, incurring further pollution (D'Oyly 1917, 245).

By April 6, the insignia of the gods, which had been evacuated to the hinterlands west of the capital for safekeeping, are reported to have arrived at the village of Gannoruwa, about seven kilometers from Kandy, just over the Mahaweli River (see fig. 8.1 below). The next day, Molligoda and various other Kandyan chiefs go out to meet the gods who are being escorted into town from the west. Just outside the Kandy city limits, they wait for D'Oyly, who comes out to join them there in the early afternoon so he can be part of the procession. The parade then forms as follows: first come people bearing banners, accompanied by tom-tom players from the different provinces, along with their respective provincial governors. They are followed by lesser provincial headmen and an English military band. Then come the elephants bearing, in bejeweled howdahs, the golden weapons (ranāyudha) of the four gods, each tusker flanked by two others. The god Nātha comes first, followed by Viṣṇu and Kataragama, with Pattini bringing up the rear. Each elephant is followed by the chief officer (basnāyaka nilame) of the devale in question and various other attendants. Then come four palanquins—one for each of the gods—bearing other arms and vessels belonging to them and escorted by attendant women waving yak tails. Finally, last but definitely not least, comes John D'Oyly, walking with Molligoda Adikar and other Kandyan chiefs (D'Oyly 1917, 253).

Shortly after the procession takes off, the "Friend of the British Government," Ehelepola, arrives on horseback. The parade stops, and D'Oyly invites him to dismount and join them. Ehelepola claims that he has a sore foot and cannot walk, but everyone in the crowd knows that traditionally, on such occasions, the horse is a mount ridden by the king, at the rear of the procession, and murmurs start to buzz among the other chiefs. Abruptly, Ehelepola decides not to join the procession and rides off. He later sends a message to D'Oyly claiming to be feeling unwell (D'Oyly 1917, 254).[1]

The procession enters the main square of the city, where the chiefs all stand in rank order while the elephants veer off, each to the gate of its respective devale, to await the firing of a cannon that will mark the auspicious moment (nekata) for their return. As soon as they hear the signal, the elephants instantly and simultaneously enter the gates of their temples to the

1. On Ehelepola's riding a horse, see Obeyesekere 2017, 94.

further roar of gunfire and a salute of nine guns fired by the British artillery. The gods have come home. The two priests of the Nātha and Viṣṇu *devales* inform D'Oyly that the next day will be the proper time for him to make the usual monetary offerings (*pandura*) to the various gods (D'Oyly 1917, 253–254).

Indeed, the next day, April 8, D'Oyly goes with Molligoda to the Temple of the Tooth, where the presents for each of the *devales* have been prepared "with great purity." D'Oyly takes up each of the bundles, handing them in turn to official governmental envoy-messengers for delivery to the gods. The rest is best described by D'Oyly himself:

> The four kapuralla [priests] stand on the left, myself with the 1st adikar on [the] right, 2nd adikar on the left, and the other chiefs on each side in the veranda of the Temple. I address them saying: "We are not come to this country to destroy the religion of Buddha and the gods, which have prevailed from ancient times in this country, but to protect and to promote it. I desire you to pray to the gods to bestow favour on us and all the inhabitants of this island." . . . The kapurale replies at length, stating that Buddha delivered charge of this island and religion to Sakra [Indra], who committed it to Vishnu, who from the time of King Vijaya has protected them during a long succession of kings, and whilst reverence has been paid to the gods, the world and religion have prospered. Now since they have heard from the chiefs that the English Government rules the country and that religion will be protected and promoted, they are ready to perform their service and to pray for the welfare and prosperity of all the inhabitants of Ceylon. But it will be difficult to perform their services without our assistance. . . . I assure them that they will receive every assistance for the due performance of their religious ceremonies and worship. (D'Oyly 1917, 255, slightly altered)

The messenger-envoys then take the offerings, borne under canopies each held up by four men on poles, to the various *devales*, accompanied by tom-tom beaters and by different chiefs (D'Oyly 1917, 255). We can see, in these accounts, the extent to which D'Oyly, at least, was willing to go (participating in rituals, making offerings on behalf of the government, etc.) to fulfill the promise of Article Five of the Sinhala Kandyan Convention.

The Return of the Tooth

Unlike General MacDowall who, as we have seen, in 1803, seemed to have been more or less oblivious to the importance of recapturing the tooth,

Brownrigg and D'Oyly have had the relic much on their minds from the very start of their invasion in 1815. Rather than go out and search for it, however, they wish to have it voluntarily returned to the temple by the Kandyans, as a recognition of their legitimacy. As Brownrigg later put it to Lord Bathurst: "It was deemed by Mr. D'Oyly as well as myself an object of the first importance and occupied our earliest attention to prevail on the chiefs and priests to have . . . a certain relick of Buddha of great celebrity brought back to the temple in Kandy" (CO 54/56, 127B).

This is important, for it is sometimes thought that the British *capture* the tooth in 1815 the way they capture the king. Nothing could be further from the truth. Instead, they have to negotiate carefully with the Kandyans and make considerable concessions to them for its return. In any case, they have no other choice, since they do not actually know where the tooth is.

If the return of the gods happens, as we have seen, more or less without a hitch, the same is not true for the return of the tooth. Given some of the difficulties outlined above, a new target date is set for April 10. Apparently, however, some of the monks are still said to have cold feet, and to now again express fears that if they bring back the Dalada, it will be carried away by the British to Colombo and maybe beyond and not retained in Kandy (CO 54/56, 128A).

This is not an illegitimate concern. As we have seen, the Dutch had taken the canopy and outermost relic casket to Colombo when they had invaded in 1765. Moreover, various regalia, captured by the British around the time of Śrī Vikrama's arrest, had already, in fact, been taken off and sent as victory prizes to the king of England. These included the state sword of the king, and his golden throne and footstool originally fashioned for Rājasimha II or his successor in the seventeenth century.[2] These Brownrigg charged his son, Major Brownrigg, to take back to England "and lay at the feet of his Royal Highness, the Prince Regent," assuring Lord Bathurst, at the same time, that "all other insignia of royalty that can be recovered, will be forwarded for the gracious acceptance of his royal highness" (CO 54/55, 103B–104A).[3] Indeed, soon the "royal standard of Kandy"[4] was sent for display in Whitehall

2. For a detailed description of the throne and footstool, see Tolfrey 1815, 5–38; and Pearson 1929.

3. For over a century, the throne was kept at Windsor Castle, where it was used during investiture ceremonies for the Order of the Garter. Along with the sword of state, however, it was returned to Ceylon in 1934 by the Duke of Gloucester and is presently housed in the Colombo National Museum. For a firsthand account of its return, see *Straits Times* 1934, 13; on controversies surrounding the throne after its return to the island, see Wickramasinghe 2006, 106–111.

4. On this flag, see the discussion in Obeyesekere 2017, 240–245.

Chapel, where it joined the Imperial eagles and colors that were taken at Waterloo (Bennett 1843, 411). Other Kandyan regalia dispatched to the king of England were eventually sold at auction "for the benefit of the captors." These included a crown, a complete suit of embossed armor, and a golden necklace 23.5 feet in length, all "richly studded with diamonds, emeralds, rubies, sapphires, Pearls, &c."[5] More enigmatic is a chest of Kandyan jewels (valued at six thousand pounds) that was sent to the Bank of England in 1818 for deposit in the personal account of Lord Bathurst, the secretary of state for the colonies.[6] And Brownrigg himself was not altogether beyond suspicion in such things: a magnificent gilded eighth-century Sri Lankan image of the goddess Tārā, acquired at some point by the governor, was eventually donated to the British Museum, where it remains today. A museum catalog (see Zwalf 1985, 150) says it was "found" at an unknown place between Trincomalee and Batticaloa, but popular tradition, at least in Sri Lanka, claims it was one of the items taken from the last king of Kandy in 1815.[7]

All told, then, the suspicions of the Kandyan monks in 1815 that the tooth relic, once returned to its temple, might not long remain enshrined there are quite understandable. However, the two *adikars*, Molligoda and Kapuwatte, seek to reassure the monks that the relic *will* stay in Kandy, as does D'Oyly himself. They are all anxious not to have the return of the tooth postponed any further, and a decision is made to go ahead with the preparations for that event (D'Oyly 1917, 250). In the following days, a series of actions take place:

On April 4, the properties designated as essential "adornments" for the occasion are physically given over by the Prize Committee to the guardians of the temple, so that the re-enshrinement of the tooth will be able to take place.

On April 5, a party headed by Kapuwatte—the 2nd *adikar*, who is also the Diyawadana nilame—sets off for the village of Piṭigoda, where the tooth relic is reputed to be, in order to bring it back to Kandy.

On April 6, Molligoda takes D'Oyly to the temple to show him the preparations and ornamentations that have been readied for the reception of the relic, and plans are made for D'Oyly to give a *danaya* (a food offering)

---

5. See Auction House of Mr. Thomas King 1820; Gooneratne and Gooneratne 1999, 16; Pieris 1939, Appendix M; and Powell [1973] 1984, 228.

6. A bill asking Lord Bathurst to pay the transport and docking fees, plus a half percent commission on the value of the chest, may be found in CO 54/72, 19A.

7. See https://joyofmuseums.com/museums/united-kingdom-museums/london-museums /british-museum/highlights-of-the-british-museum/statue-of-tara-british-museum/.

to the monks on the morning after the relic is re-enshrined (D'Oyly 1917, 251). Everything seems all set. But then, at 8:00 p.m., a messenger arrives from Kapuwatte saying that the Dalada is actually not at Pitigoda but farther away at Mediwaka (about forty-eight kilometers east of Kandy), and that it cannot possibly be brought to Kandy in time for the *nekata* (the astrologically auspicious moment) set for its entrance into the city. So, Kapuwatte plans to have the relic brought the next day only as far as Kundasale (about ten kilometers east of Kandy), and there wait for another auspicious *nekata* day and time to be determined (D'Oyly 1917, 251–252). D'Oyly is upset, but he adjusts to the new circumstances: he immediately sends a message to the Venerable Kobbekaduwa, the chief monk of the Malwatta Monastery, asking him how the relic should be brought to Kandy from Kundasale. The elder replies that he will leave early the next morning to go to Kundasale; there he will take the relic in his own hand and ride with it in a palanquin as far as the eastern entrance to the city. From there he will proceed around the southern side of the lake by the Malwatta Monastery, where the relic will be mounted on an elephant and brought to the Temple of the Tooth via the bund and the street. This somewhat circuitous route is necessary, he explains, because a corpse has recently been interred near the Kumaruppe approach road on the other side of the lake, and the resulting impurity makes that more direct road inauspicious. Although he does not mention it, at the same time, it is clear that Kobbekaduwa is eager to have his monastery (the Malwatta) have the prestige and honor of being visited—if only briefly—by the relic. In any case, D'Oyly goes to bed, thinking that all has been set for the following day (D'Oyly 1917, 252).

The next morning, April 7, however, he receives a message from the Venerable Kobbekaduwa, supposedly on his way to Kundasale. The elder tells him that he has just met a monk on the road who informed him that the relic is not at Kundasale, and that he does not know its present location. In addition, Kobbekaduwa makes it clear that he is miffed at Kapuwatte, who is taking actions without consulting him, thereby neglecting the respect and attention due to the monks. He (Kobbekaduwa) is still willing to have the Dalada brought back to Kandy, but it should be done in a proper manner, "on the first favourable Day after the New Year" (in 1815 celebrated on April 11) (D'Oyly 1917, 253). Reading between the lines of D'Oyly's somewhat telegraphic diary entries, it becomes clear that the Malwatta elder has known all along the true location of the relic (although he is not revealing it), and that he has effectively been leading Kapuwatte (and through him, D'Oyly) on a wild goose chase. It is also evident that he wants to have complete control of the return of the tooth. He does not think it appropriate for a

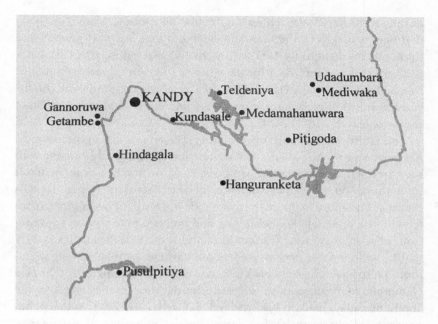

Figure 8.1. Map of sites in the Kandyan area relevant to the return of the tooth in 1815.

lay official (even the Diyawadana Nilame) to be in charge or even partially involved.

On the evening of April 7, Kapuwatte comes back to Kandy, not only empty-handed, but repeating his admission that he has no idea where the relic is now located. He had heard it was in Piṭigoda, but when he sent messengers to inquire there, they were told it had gone to Pallewela, but others said it had been sent away five or six days earlier, perhaps to Kitulpe. . . . [8]

On the following day, April 8, immediately after sending off the offerings to the *devales*, D'Oyly has an impromptu discussion about the tooth relic, in front of the Dalada Maligawa, with Kapuwatte and several Kandyan chiefs, including Molligoda and Ratwatte (the governor of Matale province). Soon a heated argument breaks out; Molligoda asks Kapuwatte rather sharply how can it be that he, as Diyawadana Nilame, is ignorant of the location

8. Piṭigoda and Kitulpe were among the ten villages whose inhabitants had hereditary duties of service to the Temple of the Tooth (see Seneviratne 1978, 35). It makes sense, therefore, that they might be thought of as sites for the sheltering of the relic. On Kitulpe's duties to the temple, see Pieris 1956, 76.

of the tooth? Kapuwatte replies angrily that he is not to blame, implying that he was tricked by the Malwatta elder, but then Ratwatte joins in and further recriminations fly. D'Oyly puts an end to it, telling them all that it is disgraceful and improper for the chiefs to be seen bickering in public, especially in front of the Dalada Maligawa, and he peremptorily calls on the two *adikars* (Molligoda and Kapuwatte) to adjourn with him to the Hall of Audience (D'Oyly 1917, 256).

This is rather remarkable; up until now, D'Oyly, as British agent in Kandy, has been acting with patience and diplomacy, engagingly negotiating with the chiefs whose cooperation he needs. Here, for the first time, he flexes his authority. In the Hall of Audience, he takes Kapuwatte to task. He tells him that his failure to locate the tooth relic is a result of his failure to confer with the Venerable Kobbekaduwa, and orders him to consult with him from now on. Kapuwatte is humiliated and apologetic; he assures D'Oyly that he will send out persons to determine where the relic actually is and promises to have it brought back to Kandy before the celebration of the next Nānumura Mangallaya (a weekly rite of purification at the Temple of the Tooth, nowadays held on Wednesdays)[9] (D'Oyly 1917, 256). At this point, however, D'Oyly clearly has lost patience with Kapuwatte and realizes that, if he wants the return of the tooth, he himself should deal with the Malwatta elder.

On the morning of April 9, he sends two trusted Sinhalese aristocrats whom he has known and worked with since 1812 to see the Venerable Kobbekaduwa. In conciliatory tones, they explain the mess-up with Kapuwatte, and express D'Oyly's hope that the sacred relic can now be brought back. The elder, in reply, apologizes for having deceived D'Oyly, and declares he will now inquire as to the first favorable *nekata* for returning the relic and let him know when that can happen. Encouragingly, he further specifies that the road from Hindagala to Getambe to Kandy should be cleansed and decorated in preparation for its coming (D'Oyly 1917, 257). These villages are to the southwest of the capital, so it would appear the relic had once again been moved or had been in a completely different location in a different direction all along.

In the following days, D'Oyly is busy supervising arrangements for the upcoming celebration of the Sinhalese New Year. At 5 p.m. on April 10, he meets the two *adikars* in the Hall of Audience and makes arrangements for the ornamental New Year's decoration of the palace (his residence). At

9. On the Nānumura Mangallaya ceremony, see Seneviratne 1978, 56–60.

9 p.m., he goes to the Nātha Devale, where the two *adikars* and the other chiefs have gathered, to attend the preparation of the medicinal waters, which the chief of the medicinal department and his assistants are busy making, pounding out the drugs in a mortar, boiling them down, and straining them into earthenware pots. There is no news of the relic.

On New Year's morning, April 11, two small pots of these medicinal waters are sent, along with drummers and great ceremony, to each of the temples in Kandy, including the Temple of the Tooth, some temples in the countryside, and the residences of the *adikars*. Six pots are also sent to D'Oyly. That evening, he participates in the ceremony in the Hall of Audience, in which Ehelepola and the two *adikars* and all the other chiefs, according to their rank, use the medicinal waters to ceremonially anoint their foreheads (D'Oyly 1917, 258–259).[10] A new year is breaking.

The next few days are celebratory days for the people, but D'Oyly is hard at work dealing with various crises. There is no further news about the tooth's whereabouts, but he continues to make preparations for its arrival. On April 13, he spends the entire day along with Ehelepola, the two *adikars*, and five monks from the two Kandyan temples (three from Malwatta and two from Asgiriya) trying to identify various new items of jewelry that have just been brought in but, with the tooth relic not yet returned, the British prize agents are in no position to argue for the interests of the Crown. D'Oyly arranges to have items claimed for the temple "unconditionally surrendered" to it. At the same time, he is particularly respectful of the monks in other ways. As he puts it (1917, 261, slightly altered):

> As the priests were called early to the palace, I caused a danaya [meritorious offering of food] to be prepared and given to them at the Pattrippuwa [Octagonal Pavilion] in the best Kandyan manner, with four kinds of rice, thirty-one of curry, and twelve of cakes, etc. And I sent some of it to the Venerable Kobbekaduwa [at the Malwatta Monastery] who is unable, from sickness, to attend.

The next day, April 14, the identification of properties continues and now becomes even easier. The parties involved start making deals; the *adikars* and monks are willing to give up "some broken pieces of gold and silver vessels . . . on consideration of appropriating to the Temple five golden

---

10. Ceremonies in the *devales* are canceled, however, since, as D'Oyly explains, two dogs were shot in the street between the Nātha and Pattini *devales*, which were then shut down for three days, along with the Viṣṇu devale.

cups, doubtful property, and a large silver plate admitted to be the king's."
And the prize agents, perhaps encouraged or goaded by D'Oyly, now show
themselves to be more generous: "A fine image of Buddha carved of crystal,
which neither *adikars* nor priests recognize, is presented to the temple by the
Committee, and it is received with much satisfaction" (D'Oyly 1917, 261).

Finally, on April 22, there is news of the tooth. Kapuwatte comes to see
D'Oyly, along with the governor of the province of Uva (to the southeast of
Kandy), and they announce that the tooth is being brought that very day
to Hindagala from the Puhulpitiya Monastery (about fifty-five kilometers
south of Kandy). Apparently, that had been its hiding place all along—or
at least its final hiding place. Today, the somewhat dilapidated site (on the
other side of the Kotmale Reservoir from the town of Morape) is known as
the Pusulpitiya Rāja Mahā Vihāra, and visitors to it are still shown an old
michelia (*campaka*) tree, in a hollow of which, so a sign declares, the sacred
tooth relic was hidden during a time of unrest, in the days of British colonial
rule (https://savanij.wordpress.com/tag/temple/).[11]

Hindagala, just south of the present-day campus of the University of
Peradeniya, is about ten kilometers from Kandy. The Diyawadana Nilame
recommends bringing the tooth the next day from there to Huduhumpola
(aka Suduhumpola) Monastery, located within present-day Kandy about
two kilometers from downtown, where it can be poised for return to the
Temple of the Tooth at 10:00 a.m. the following day, April 24 (10:00 to
10:45 a.m. having been determined by the astrologers to be an auspicious
nekata and hence a window of opportunity for the ritual) (D'Oyly 1917,
265–266).

Given all of this mix-up about the relic's location, and the delays and
other shenanigans in arranging for its return (which, as we shall soon see,
are not yet quite ended), it should be stated that there was some suspicion
as to the authenticity of the tooth being brought back on this occasion.
Simply put, was it the "real relic"—the very same one that had been taken
away prior to the English invasion—and how would anyone know that?
Indeed, the 1st *adikar*, Molligoda, who is cooperating with the British, has
his suspicions in this regard, and expresses to D'Oyly and others his own
worry that Ehelepola (working with the Venerable Kobbekaduwa?) may

11. See also Herath 1994, 178–179n107; and http://kandycity.lk/places/pusulpitiya-raja
-maha-viharaya/. The temple has an ancient history and is legendarily associated with the great
Sinhalese king Duṭṭhagāmaṇī. It is also said to have been one of the thirty-two places that
received a Bodhi-tree sapling from the original Bo-tree in Anurādhapura. According to local
tradition, it was also used as a hiding place for the tooth relic in the thirteenth century during
the Chola invasion from South India, before it was taken to Dambadeniya by Vijayabāhu III.

have substituted a replica of the tooth in its stead, saving the real one to be revealed later for his own purposes of taking the throne (Pieris 1950, 323). The difficulty, of course, is that, apart from some of the monks involved in its cult, very few people (including Molligoda and D'Oyly) have actually ever seen the relic, the last time it was publicly displayed being in 1775, thus making authentication problematic. As Brownrigg realizes, the only persons who might have correct knowledge of what the tooth actually looks like are likely to be the very parties involved in any deceit on that matter (Pieris 1950, 323). Given this uncertainty and given also his recognition of Molligoda's own jealous dislike and suspicion of Ehelepola, D'Oyly chooses to ignore all this and go ahead with the return and re-enshrinement of the tooth.

Agreeing to the plan to bring the tooth from Huduhumpola on April 24, he starts issuing orders to decorate the Temple of the Tooth, and to purify the town in preparation for the occasion. Not only are all Kandyans told to clean the streets in front of their doors, but so are non-Kandyans—Malays, and lowland inhabitants of the city (D'Oyly 1917, 267). He also writes to the Venerable Kobbekaduwa at the Malwatta Monastery that, in his view, the *Mahāparinibbāna sutta* should be the subject for the abbot's sermon on the night of the twenty-fourth. This text, which recounts the final days and death of the Buddha, including the initial distribution of his relics, makes perfectly good sense as a topic for the return of the tooth, but it is not clear whether D'Oyly is here responding to an inquiry from Kobbekaduwa, or whether D'Oyly is suggesting this topic at his own initiative. In any case, Kobbekaduwa replies that there may not be time enough for him to go over the text and prepare a sermon on it by that date (D'Oyly 1917, 266).

This, in fact, is perhaps a hint from him of his desire to slow things down further. Indeed, when, on April 23, the Venerable Elder goes to Hindagala to welcome the relic and take charge of its conveyance to Kandy, he immediately writes to D'Oyly that it will not be possible to bring it to the temple by the *nekata* (10:00 a.m.) on the twenty-fourth, because there will be other rituals going on there that morning, it being *poya* day (the day of the full moon). He proposes instead that the relic leave Hindagala not on the twenty-third but on the twenty-fourth, and not until 10:00 a.m. It could then enter the temple at some auspicious hour in the afternoon. The *poya* day beating of tom-toms will then go on all night and the following day until noon. Since he (Kobbekaduwa) needs to be present at the preaching of the Dharma (*bana*), and since he will be very tired from traveling on Monday (the twenty-fourth), he proposes deferring his sermon until Tuesday evening, April 25 (D'Oyly 1917, 267).

It is noteworthy that all of this is in the form of a request for D'Oyly's permission to do this, thus treating the British Resident effectively as though he were king of Kandy, that is, having final authority in the matter. At the same time, the monk is aware that D'Oyly may well be ignorant of all of the parameters of the moment. What Kobbekaduwa does *not* say here, but what he apparently implies, is that by delaying the relic's departure from Hindagala, and by personally bringing it directly to Kandy from there (on the twenty-fourth), he will bypass the stop for one night at the Huduhumpola Monastery. Reading between the lines, we can see here the ongoing rivalry between the monk Kobbekaduwa and Kapuwatte, the lay *adikar* and Diyawadana Nilame in charge of the temple. The plan to have it stop at the Huduhumpola Monastery for the night was Kapuwatte's idea; Kobbekaduwa, once again, wants to assert control by imposing his own schedule by scrapping that proposal. In addition, it should be said that the Huduhumpola Monastery belongs to the Asgiriya chapter of the Siyam Nikāya, while Kobbekaduwa is the chief monk of the Malwatta Monastery, so it may be that we also have here the surfacing of another instance of the Malwatta-Asgiriya rivalry (D'Oyly 1917, 267). In the end, as we shall see, Kobbekaduwa appears to get his way, since the relic is not brought in by the 10:00 a.m. *nekata* and does not get to Kandy until late in the afternoon of the twenty-fourth, and D'Oyly makes no mention, in his diary, of it being at Huduhumpola.

D'Oyly and the Re-Enshrinement of the Dalada

In fact, rather shockingly, and for reasons that are unclear, D'Oyly's diary ends at this point! It is not known whether he stopped writing his diary altogether, for want of time or whatever reason, or whether this was the end of the notebook he was using and subsequent volumes were lost. Storically speaking, I have toyed with the idea that this moment—when the return of the relic is assured—provided a logical ending point for D'Oyly in his narrative, but in fact the tale goes on. For its continuation and true culmination, therefore, I will turn to an account written on April 28, 1815, by an anonymous author in the *Asiatic Journal and Monthly Register for British India and Its Dependencies*, who was present on the occasion in Kandy, and who has been identified as Lieutenant W. H. Lyttleton (Malalgoda 1976, 118n53). It is worth quoting large sections of it:

> To give splendor to this event, preparations were made for many days previous. On Sunday [April 23], the high-priest left Kandy, for the purpose of

escorting it [the tooth relic] in, attended by a numerous body of priests. About one o'clock [the next day], it was intimated to Mr. D'Oyly that the procession was approaching [and] he, attended by Mr. Wright and myself, left the palace on foot, and proceeded toward the entrance of the town, to join it. On our arrival, we were met by the high-priest and chiefs who appeared delighted at this mark of respect to their religion. Complimentary congratulations detained the procession for a short period. (*Asiatic Journal and Monthly Register* 1816a, 91)[12]

There then follows a detailed account of the procession, which extended for over a mile in length, and was drawn up as follows:

(1) Eight large elephants, with white tusks, with rich coverings, accompanied by numerous attendants;

(2) High Priest [Kobbekaduwa], supported by two young priests;

(3) One hundred and fifty priests;

(4) A SACRED IMAGE [of the Buddha] covered with gold brocade, carried in a muncheal [palanquin] with a canopy over it;

(5) Sixty flags of different colours;

(6) Trumpets and tom-toms;

(7) Dancing girls [i.e., *alatti* women waving yak tails];

(8) Whip crackers;

(9) Molligoda, 1st *adikar*, attended by numerous chiefs;

(10) Two hundred headmen;

(11) Gingals [large muskets] of the temple;

(12) Tom-toms;

(13) Drums of His Majesty's 3rd Ceylon regiment;

(14) Five most beautiful tusked elephants abreast, the centre one carrying THE SACRED RELIC. This elephant was highly ornamented, tusks cased in gold; the rest carried attendants holding silver and gilt umbrellas and fans, etc.;

(15) Whip crackers;

(16) Kapuwatte, 2nd *adikar*, in charge of the temple, attended by many chiefs, and accompanied by:

(17) Mr. Doyly, Mr. Wright, and myself;

(18) Some hundred headmen and followers;

(19) Six large tusked elephants followed separately next, each carrying a sacred image;

---

12. A somewhat different version of this and the following descriptions may be found in Bennett 1843, 412–413.

(20) Some hundreds of natives. (*Asiatic Journal and Monthly Register* 1816a, 91, slightly altered)

Thus arrayed, the *perahera* makes its way through streets strewn with white cloth (as a symbol of purity), by houses decorated with young plantain trees. "The procession," reports Lyttleton, "which was most magnificent, was conducted with the greatest regularity; not the smallest disorder was observable" (*Asiatic Journal and Monthly Register* 1816a, 91).

This, however, is not quite true. It will be noticed that Ehelepola, who, hoping to be king, had refused an appointment from the British—in exchange for their recognizing him as a prominent leader and friend of the British government—does not appear in the order of march given above, claiming, as before, that his health would not permit him to walk on foot. After the official formation passes by, however, at the tail end of things, he once again suddenly appears on horseback, accompanied by many attendants. As mentioned above, this was the traditional mode of *perahera* participation for the Kandyan king, so Ehelepola is sending a clear political message here, by acting in the role of monarch. He had thought of doing this at the time of the return of the gods, but now, at the return of the tooth, he actually carries through with it. D'Oyly, as far as we can tell, ignores him (*Asiatic Journal and Monthly Register* 1816a, 91).

When the *perehera* reaches the Temple of the Tooth at 4:00 p.m., it is a little early for the newly established *nekata* set for its entrance into the building, so it uses up some more time by moving once around the square in front of the palace. Finally, the auspicious moment arrives, signaled by the firing of gingal guns from the temple, answered by one boom from the English artillery. Two temple servants, their mouths covered with cloth so as not to pollute it, take the relic down from the tusker that bore it, and the chiefs and monks and the three Englishmen (D'Oyly, Wright, and Lyttleton) all follow the tooth into the Temple, pausing to take off their shoes on the way in (*Asiatic Journal and Monthly Register* 1816a, 91).

As we shall see, this detail—the customary respectful act of taking off one's shoes upon entering a sacred place—is one of the things that came to shock some of D'Oyly's contemporaries, and that was pounced on by his detractors. That an Englishman should ever go shoeless in public was bad enough; but that he should remove his footwear out of respect for a "heathen idol," and do so as representative of the British government, was outrageous and unchristian. Even more shocking (to some), however, was what came next. As Lyttleton describes it:

After a few complimentary words, Mr. D'Oyly intimated that he wished to make an offering to the temple in the name of his Excellency the Governor and would retire to bring it. After a short interval, he returned, and presented as an offering to the temple, a most beautiful musical clock.[13] . . . The burst of applause which continued for some minutes, upon this beautiful work being produced (which so fully showed the superiority of our countrymen as mechanics), proved the high estimation they put upon the present; but, when, as if by magic, this little machine was put in motion, the expressions of delight, by both priests and chiefs, exceeded all belief. Several other smaller customary offerings were [also] made. (*Asiatic Journal and Monthly Register* 1816a, 91)[14]

This action, too, almost immediately drew the ire of Christian critics, who saw in it official approbation and support of Buddhism. For instance, in a letter from Kandy on April 29, 1815, to the *Ceylon Government Gazette*, a person signing himself "Clericus Damnoniensis" (1815, May 3) vents his outrage: "We can no longer be surprised," he exclaims,

that men should be found who are hostile to the propagation of the Christian religion in India. We have here an account of Englishmen, servants of the crown, not only sanctioning idolatrous processions and worship by their presence, but actually *joining in an act of idolatry by presenting an offering in a heathen temple . . . in the name of his Excellency the Governor*. Now, however expedient it may be to guarantee to conquered nations the possession of their religion and laws, it can never be necessary to join an idolatrous people in their acts of worship, in order further to gain their good will; and surely no other motive can be assigned for such conduct, unless we suppose that our countrymen have indeed renounced their religion.[15]

13. The clock had been sent to Colombo from England during the governorship of Thomas Maitland (1805–1811) for possible use, in negotiations, as a gift to the Kandyan king (CO 54/56, 127b).

14. Interestingly, eight years later D'Oyly requested guidance on how to repair a musical clock from his brother Thomas in England. Thomas complied by sending him what amounted to a whole manual of elaborate instructions on the topic. We are not told, however, whether this was for the clock offered to the tooth, nor even whether the latter was in need of repair. See Pieris 1938, 114.

15. The letter was reprinted in the *General Evening Post* of November 12, 1815, before being taken up by the *Christian Observer* (Boston) 15, no. 169 (January 1816): 26. "Clericus Damnionensis" then goes on to speculate that the choice of a clock "to a superstitious people" was especially "ill-judged . . . [for] we cannot but wonder if, in their ignorant state, the clock itself should be made an additional object of adoration."

Much the same sentiments are expressed by one "Moderator" (1816, 221) who writes a bit later to the editor of the *Asiatic Journal and Monthly Register*, bemoaning "the monstrous spectacle of a Christian government joining in the idolatrous rites of a heathen temple," which, he specifies in a footnote, took place on a Sunday, and adding his "hope that the superior authorities at home, will feel it incumbent upon them to take proper notice of this impolitic and disgraceful proceeding."

Not everyone, however, shares these sentiments. The "Moderator's" letter just cited was, in part, a response to one "Mythologus" (1816a, 19) who writes approvingly of "the pleasing account which we have had of the attentions paid by the British Government in Ceylon, on [the] occasion of the restoration of that form of divine worship in Candy."[16]

And in the same issue of the *Asiatic Journal*, another person, calling himself "Candidus," is quite critical of "Clericus Damnoniensis." He suggests, first, that British support of Buddhism has nothing to do with the demeaning of Christianity, but is an important statement of the support of Sinhalese traditions against the Hindu legacy of the Nāyakkar rulers. Second, moving to an ad hominem argument, he states that the view that the Kandyans might "add the clock to their objects of worship" is ridiculous and merely reflects the ignorance and prejudices of its proposer, adding that "to judge uncharitably of the understanding, as well as the virtues, of such as profess a different religion from our own, is one of the common failings of ill-informed persons. . . . [A] national religion is everywhere entitled to the respect of the rulers" (Candidus 1816, 225–226).

Another writer, who dubs himself "An Old English Politician" (1816, 213), similarly praises D'Oyly for his action, and echoes the first point made by "Candidus":

> The restoration and proffered protection of the religion of Buddha in Candy was an act which every consideration of sound policy, to say nothing of humanity, concurred in dictating. The disciples of Buddha had been oppressed by the Brahminical dynasty on the throne. It belonged to the cunning, as well as to the benevolence, of the conqueror, to raise up this ancient worship; he could have no motive for giving the religion of Brahma the preference; and

---

16. Mythologus (1816a, 21) then goes on to discourse on various etymologies and identities of the name "Buddha," ending up preferring the one that equates him with the god Odin, and flippantly concluding that "in protecting the religion of Buddha in Ceylon, we are but protecting the religion of our ancestors."

the protection he promised was a protection only against the ministers of the latter.

This variety of responses to D'Oyly's actions (and through him to the British policy toward the tooth enacted by Brownrigg) is noteworthy. As we shall see, the success of subsequent missionary objections to such a policy sometimes gives an impression of general British intolerance toward any support of Buddhism whatsoever, so it is important to note that, from the start, attitudes were, in fact, more mixed than they sometimes are said to be.

It is likely, however, that D'Oyly saw his offering of the clock and his other acts of respect with regard to the tooth as merely part and parcel of his job which, in his mind, involved ritually taking on some of the roles formerly held by the king of Kandy. In other words, for him, it was engagement in what Tambiah would view as a transactional this-worldly relation with the tooth as a charismatic object. In his view, it was an extension of the government's responsibility vis-à-vis Buddhism as spelled out in the Kandyan Convention—that its "rites, ministers, and places of worship be maintained and protected." In the same vein, as we have seen above, he takes on various other monarchical functions: he supervises the return of the gods, and makes donations to the *devales*; he makes offerings of food to the monks; he observes local customs with regard to concerns for purity and astrology; he participates in New Year's celebrations; and he makes appointments not only to government offices but to monastic and priestly posts.

In D'Oyly's eyes, the re-enshrinement of the tooth and the enthusiastic receipt of his offering of the clock are a great success. As he writes the very next morning to Governor Brownrigg:

> The whole ceremony I believe has been satisfactory both to the priests and people. It is apparently a mere matter of religion, but is in truth of the highest political importance; regarding which I had felt considerable anxiety, and I may here repeat the sentiment which I before expressed, that we have this day obtained the surest proof of the confidence of the Kandyan Nation and their acquiescence in the dominion of the British government. (CO 54/56, 129B)

The Tooth Back in Kandy: The Perahera of 1817

It is sometimes stated that the British takeover of 1815 marked a radical change in the status of the tooth. In fact, with the relic back in its temple, and British officials such as D'Oyly in control, things in Kandy gradually return to a semblance of normal. Apparently, at the quotidian level, the

British interpret their responsibilities for the tooth relic as meaning non-interference in its daily cult and veneration. In other words, they let the Kandyans pretty much perpetuate their old traditions, though in a different context, of course.[17]

For example, they reinstitute the annual Esala Perahera in the summer of 1817. This festival, in which the tooth, together with the sacred emblems of the four *devales*, is paraded through the streets of the city, is witnessed by Governor Brownrigg and his wife and a host of guests from Colombo, come up for the special occasion.

A detailed account of the ceremony was written for and presented to the governor on August 19, 1817, by Millāva, the provincial chief of Vellassa (to the southeast of Kandy) (Pieris 1956, 135–138). This individual was an articulate, perceptive, and dignified Kandyan chief, whose description of the *perahera* has been called "most valuable and authentic" and has been used by historians and anthropologists interested in early nineteenth-century iterations of the festival (Seneviratne 1978, 108–114, and 178n12). What is of note here, however, is not so much the detailed account he presents of the history of the festival and the variations in its rituals over its two-week period, but the place he assigns to Governor Brownrigg in the proceedings.

It is clear that Brownrigg is there as more than just a tourist. For instance, Millāva describes how, each day, before the start of the procession, tight-rope dancers and other performers gather in the street near the Viṣṇu and Nātha Devales, just beneath the windows where the king of Kandy used to view such entertainment and where, now, Governor and Lady Brownrigg station themselves to witness the same (Millāva 1817, 22). In other words, Brownrigg here is consciously or unconsciously agreeing to play the ritual role of a Kandyan monarch *qua* spectator. To be sure, the governor does not process in the actual *perahera* the way the former kings of Kandy sometimes did. He thus does not engage in the ritual circumambulation that had the purpose of "summoning the aid of the Sacred Tooth Relic and the insignia of the gods in the Perahera in an attempt at 'capturing' (or recapturing) the city . . . and the kingdom" (Seneviratne 1978, 85, slightly altered).

He does, however, participate in the final dénouement of the festival. In Kandyan times, "the chief functionaries . . . ceremonially reported to the king that the Perahera was successfully completed" (Seneviratne 1978,

17. Thus, in 1816, when a delegation of Siamese monks is allowed to make a visit to the tooth, they remark that little has changed at the temple since the last time they were in Kandy, when the kingdom was still independent. See Malalgoda 2002, 15; and Dhaninivat 1965, 139–140.

88). So too, in 1817, all the chiefs who had participated in the *perahera* go "to the hall of audience to pay their respects to His Excellency the Governor, and to report the successful termination and happy omens of the great festival" (Millāva 1817, 22). And here Millāva (1817, 23) expounds with some degree of pride upon the dignified demeanor of the chiefs (himself presumably among them), and the magnificence of their dress: "Their richly embroidered velvet caps, with elegant gold flowers on the top so various (for no two were alike) . . . their large plaited tippets fringed with gold over their splendid brocade full sleeved jackets, with the immense folds of gold muslin which composed their lower garments, etc." Millāva, however, is quick to note that in this final ritual, one thing has changed since the days of Śrī Vikrama: the governor is receiving the obeisance of the Kandyan chiefs in the company of his wife, Lady Brownrigg! Being the dignified gentlemen that they are, the chiefs take this in stride. As Millāva (1817, 23) puts it, "the elegance and the courtliness of the Kandyan chiefs were never more strikingly displayed than by the polite and graceful manner with which they advanced to make their obeisance to her Ladyship, who with her usual kindness and condescension received their respectful salutations." But he cannot help but note that this is remarkable for these chiefs, who "must have hitherto held the female character, however exalted in rank, to be entitled to no share of public consideration or exalted mark of respect." The proceedings end, however, with a return to things "more agreeable to Kandyan custom": a formal pronouncement by a representative of the chiefs who not only extolls and thanks the governor, but "attribute[s] the unprecedented productiveness of the soil, and the extraordinary general prosperity of the country, since it came under the rule of the English, to the famed good fortune of His Excellency" (Millāva 1817, 23). Generally speaking, then, in this Perahera of 1817, we can find some differences due to the imposition of the new regime, but, on the whole, the continuity with older pre-British traditions is what is most striking.

NINE

The Relic Lost and Recaptured:
The Tooth and the Rebellion of 1817–1818

No sooner was it made known that the Dalada was in the possession of the British, than the followers of Buddha returned to their allegiance; district after district laid down their arms and acknowledged the sovereignty of Great Britain.

—Henry Charles Sirr (1850, 1: 341)

The British bloodless conquest of Kandy in 1815—which they presented as a liberation from tyrannical rule—did not go uncontested for long. Despite the Kandyan Convention's promise to uphold Buddhism, despite the reestablishment of the tooth in its temple and the resumption of the Perahera, many Kandyans—chiefs, monks, provincial headmen, and other people—remained discontent. On the one hand, they were resentful of the English presence that undermined Kandyan ways. Though the likes of D'Oyly and Brownrigg were decorous and polite in their treatment of Kandyan aristocrats and monks, minor British officials and low-ranking military officers were not. They paid little attention to distinctions of caste or privilege and were not deferential to chiefs when they met them in the streets (Davy 1821, 326). On the other hand, there was general disappointment that the English had failed to install a Sinhalese king, whether Ehelepola or not. The Kandyans "had no notion of a king ruling over them at the distance of thousands of miles . . . they wanted a king whom they could see, and before whom they could prostrate and obtain summary justice" (Davy 1821, 327). According to Henry Marshall (1846, 134–135), Kandyan aristocrats used to ask him when the English intended to return to the maritime provinces. "You have now," they would say, "deposed the king and nothing more is required—you may leave us. . . . The British rule in the Kandyan country [is] as incompatible as yoking a buffalo and a cow to the same plough."

Such sentiments quickly boil over into the so-called rebellion of 1817–1818 in which the tooth relic, as we shall see in this chapter, plays a central role. The spark that starts the actual insurrection is the appearance in the jungles of Vellassa, southeast of Kandy, in September 1817, of "a mysterious stranger," dressed sometimes as a Malabar and on other occasions in yellow robes, attended by a coterie of eight monks (Powell [1973] 1984, 240). This man is actually an ex-monk named Vilbave, but he claims to be Doraisami—a Nāyakkar relative of the exiled king Śrī Vikrama. He further declares that not only does he have royal blood, but he has been personally chosen by the god Kataragama at his shrine in the south to reclaim the Kandyan throne (De Silva 1981, 232–233).[1] The British promptly dub him "the Pretender," and eventually seek to expose him as a fraud. In the jungles of Uva and Vellassa, however, this charismatic individual soon recruits a following of Veddas (Sri Lanka's so-called indigenous people) and Sinhalese villagers, and begins to engage in guerilla warfare against the colonial powers.[2] The rebellion has many of the markings of a millenarian movement or cargo cult. Vilbave's followers proclaim: "The island has been in darkness, but like the Sun who gives light to and shines upon all, a king has arisen!" (Malalgoda 1970, 434–435). And they do not hesitate to tell the British authorities that "We have received a King for this country by the favor of Gods from the four parts of the world and from the God Kandasāmi of Kataragama. . . . It is known to all . . . that the 18 [English] forts shall be taken by him. . . . The English will never have any success" (CO 54/71; see also Malalgoda 1970, 435).

In the beginning, the British do not take the uprising all that seriously, but then two things happen: first, the rebels ambush and kill Silvester Wilson, the British agent at Badulla, in October 2017 (Powell [1973] 1984, 240–244).[3]

1. See also Malalgoda 1970, 436. The priests of the Kataragama shrine supposedly handed over to Vilbave the shrine's insignia of the god.

2. On the Veddas' involvement in the uprising, see Obeyesekere 2002. This was not the only movement featuring a "pretender" to the throne claiming kinship with the exiled royal family. According to Malalgoda (1970), there were no fewer than eight such persons between 1817 and 1858. Vilbave's movement, however, was the most long-lived and widespread.

3. A memorial stone to Wilson was erected in 1912 near the spot where he was killed (along with a few Muslim soldiers). It reads: "In Memory of Silvester Douglas Wilson, Assistant Resident and Agent of the British Government in the Province of Uva, who was killed near this spot at the outbreak of the Kandyan Rebellion, 16th September, 1817" (see Brohier 1933, 3, where the text is recorded slightly erroneously). The stone may still be seen today at Kilometer 186 of the A5 highway from Peradeniya to Batticaloa. See https://www.youtube.com/watch?v=_-9uyCwUq_4, a video in which the narrator claims that the heads of those killed on the occasion were nailed to the wall of the local *devale* as an offering to the god Bandara. On the stone in the video, Wilson's name has been partly chiseled out, an apparent act of defacement. The

This catches the government's attention, and troops are sent out from Kandy to put down the troublemakers.[4] Second, and more importantly, some of the Kandyan chiefs decide to join the movement. Foremost among them is the provincial chief (*dissava*) of Uva, Keppetipola (the brother of Ehelepola's wife Kumarihami). With the blessing of the British in Kandy, he volunteers to go back to his home province, ostensibly to restore order. Once there, however, he joins the rebels and effectively becomes their leader, giving the uprising the imprimatur of his respectability. He thereby inspires other Kandyan chiefs—most notably Madugalle[5] and the younger Pilimatalawa—to take up the cause of the movement, and the rebellion quickly spreads to other provinces. What was a relatively minor and isolated disturbance quickly becomes a major revolt with military significance. To be sure, some chiefs, such as the 1st *adikar* Molligoda, remain loyal to the British, but by April–May 1818, the insurrection has developed into a veritable war and colonial forces have their hands full and are getting very worried.[6] Indeed, at one point, they even contemplate withdrawing all their forces from the interior of the island (De Silva 1981, 231–232; see also Davy 1821, 329).[7]

---

identity of Wilson's killer is still a matter of dispute in the region. As Obeyesekere (2002) points out, "who shot Douglas Sylvester Wilson is as much of a point of honor for Sinhala people in the area just as who killed Captain Cook was for Hawaiians. To this day various Sinhala families in Vellassa vie with each other for that somewhat dubious honor."

4. By November 1817, Brownrigg realizes he should have sent more troops. On the seventh of that month, he writes to London: "If, as I am convinced from what is now passing, it will be necessary to maintain a larger military force in the interior than has hitherto been the case, and our principal deficiency being in Black or Native troops, I venture to suggest for H.R.H. consideration, the expediency of one of the West India regiments being sent to this island; as no troops are so well adapted to the service of this county as Negroes or Caffrees—they do not assimilate to or associate with the Kandyans who consider them with dread, and they have always proved faithful, obedient and courageous soldiers when trained. . . . If this suggestion is favorably received, I would humbly recommend that no time should be lost in forwarding such a reinforcement" (CO 54/72, 106A).

5. Ironically, Governor Brownrigg had just, some months earlier, pardoned Madugalle for being, in 1816, convicted as a participant in a suspected plot to revolt against the English government. See Powell [1973] 1984, 243.

6. For a contemporary account of the insurrection focusing on British troop movements, see *Asiatic Journal and Monthly Miscellany* 1818. For a personal account of one soldier's experience during this war, see Calladine 1924, 49–77.

7. A measure of the government's alarm may be seen in the fact that it starts arresting chiefs who have not yet joined the rebellion, on suspicion that they might do so. This includes Ehelepola, the "Friend of the British Government," who is never actually charged with disloyalty, but who is sent to Colombo and kept in custody there as a preventative measure. Ehelepola, in fact, is still distrusted even after the rebellion is quelled and, though never charged or tried for anything, is exiled to Mauritius, where he passes away in 1829. See Hewavissenti 2010; and Burrun 2015.

There is a sense in which Keppetipola and the chiefs have usurped the movement, effectively taking it over from Vilbave for their own purposes, but they nonetheless keep him as a figurehead. Indeed, to further Vilbave's legitimacy, in May 1818, Keppetipola stages an actual enthronement ceremony at Wellaweya in the province of Uva during which Vilbave is formally consecrated as King Vīrakrama Śrī Kīrti. This grand ceremony further worries the British.

The Theft of the Tooth

Vilbave's enthronement sets the stage for the movement's acquisition of further palladia. The new king and Keppetipola already had, from the shrine at Kataragama, the insignia of that god (his vel or spear-like emblem) as one symbol of legitimacy (Malalgoda 1970, 436). Soon, however, they publicly add to that nothing less than the tooth relic of the Buddha. On July 5, 1818, in Hanguranketa (thirty-one kilometers southeast of Kandy), Keppetipola puts on display, under a canopy on a flower-covered stand, what he claims to be the tooth, brought from the temple in Kandy by a village headman and two native troops in British uniform, who stand on guard nearby. With the relic in their possession, he proclaims that no enemy can now defeat them. The crowd rejoices, and the three heroes who have brought the tooth are taken into the presence of the recently crowned "king," who grants each of them a village as a recompense. The news is not long in reaching D'Oyly and Brownrigg, who are much alarmed; they were not even aware that the tooth was missing! (Pieris 1950, 322).

Brownrigg realizes that they are losing the politics of display. As he writes to Lord Bathurst in London, "The public coronation of the pretender was resorted to in order to dazzle the minds of the people who certainly do not think highly of the unostentatious and little ceremonious manner in which the British government is conducted, and, as a preparatory measure to a great attack on our posts, the exhibition of the sacred relic was made an instrument to give confidence in the protection of the gods" (CO 54/71, 260A–B). At the same time, he worries anew that the relic returned in 1815 might indeed have been a fake, engineered by Ehelepola, and that the rebels are now in possession of the "real" tooth (CO 54/71, 261A).

The tooth relic itself, kept under multiple locks and keys inside multiple nesting reliquaries all set within a closed golden dagoba inside the locked sanctuary in the temple, is not commonly visible, so its presence or absence would not generally be felt. Moreover, the door to the sanctuary is guarded night and day by an armed sentry. How could it possibly be that the relic had been taken? Brownrigg publicly denies the theft, calling the story the product of rumors, and thereby implying that Keppetipola's relic is a fake. He might, of course, have simply opened all the reliquaries and shown the tooth to be inside, safe and sound, but D'Oyly, who perhaps suspects something is amiss, advises against this, pointing out that "uncertainty [i]s preferable to unwelcome knowledge" (Pieris 1950, 323; see also CO 54/71, 262A). If it should happen that the relic is *not* there, the results would be disastrous for them. Better simply to dismiss Keppetipola's claim that it had been stolen as so ridiculous as to not even merit verification.

Beneath this façade of confidence, however, some British officials remain uncertain. George Lusignan, the secretary for the Kandyan provinces, jocularly proposes that just in case, "D'Oyly ought to set to work and fabricate [a replica of the relic] to introduce into the casket . . . [for] it [would] surely serve the purpose of deceiving as well as a real one" (Pieris 1950, 323–324). Such a suggestion, of course, would be totally impracticable, given the fact that even D'Oyly can hardly open the reliquary alone without the presence of multiple Sinhalese attendants.

In the end, it turns out that the relic *has* been stolen. According to Rambukpota, one of the chiefs who joined the rebellion but surrendered to the British on July 22, 1818, the heist was carried out by the Venerable Wāriyapola Sumangala, the *anunāyaka* (second monk in charge) of the Asgiriya Monastery. As one of the monks appointed to serve the shrine, he had access to the inner sanctuary. His confederates were all from a village that belonged to the temple and consequently owed regular corvée service to the tooth. One of them was in charge of the vessels in which the daily food offerings were brought to the tooth, so he, by virtue of his responsibilities, also had access to the shrine room. On the evening set for the heist, the conspirators arrive just before closing time, expressing their wish to make an offering to the relic. All other worshippers have left. Since no more fresh flowers are available in the shrine room, Wāriyapola, as monk in charge, asks the lascarin (Sri Lankan soldier) on guard in the room to be so kind as to fetch a tray of flowers from outside. Not willing to disobey the venerable monk, he leaves on that mission, and as soon as he is gone, Wāriyapola lets the conspirators into the sanctuary and then locks the door behind them, explaining to the guard when he returns that the men could not wait for the flowers and had left, and that he had just closed things up for the night. Inside the sanctuary, the thieves remain hidden until dawn, careful not to make any noise. The next day, however, under the cover of the loud drumming marking the start of the first morning pūjā, they force open the lock on the outer dagoba and remove the smaller caskets from within, including the one containing the tooth. When the sanctuary is opened by Wāriyapola, they hide behind the dagoba (which they had reclosed) and subsequently are able to abscond with their prize. They promptly take it to Hanguranketa, where Wāriyapola joins them, and they present it to Keppetipola (Pieris 1950, 325).[8]

There is some evidence that possession of the relic inspired the rebels in their battles against colonial forces, but in time, their cause is doomed by the British policy that crushes the rebellion with an overwhelming use of force and brutality (Obeyesekere 2002). This features a scorched-earth policy of burning villages, destroying crops, cutting down palm trees, breaking up levees around irrigation tanks, and summarily hanging all those deemed to be disloyal. Davy estimates that, all in all, ten thousand Sri Lankan "rebels" are killed, many of them actually innocent villagers (Davy 1821, 330).[9] The rebels are also seriously outgunned, many of their numbers still using bows and arrows as their main weapons. Eventually, the British close in on the movement's leaders. On October 28, 1818, a British patrol receives intelligence as to their whereabouts, southeast of Anurādhapura; after a forced march of sixteen miles, they catch a man who, under threat, leads them to a house where Keppetipola, Pilimatalawa, Madugalle, and several others are hiding. The first two are immediately captured, but Madugalle escapes in the confusion, only to be tracked down some days later by one Ensign Shoolbraid (Pieris 1950, 395).[10]

8. Wāriyapola was already famous as a Sinhalese patriot. When the Kandyan Convention was signed in 1815, it was he, according to a legend questioned by Obeyesekere (2017, 234–235), who had taken down the prematurely hoisted British flag, insisting it could not be flown until after the actual signing. After stealing the tooth relic, he remains with the rebels. In November 1818, he is arrested by the British, tried, and convicted of treason. He is subsequently imprisoned in Jaffna for several years. In popular Sinhalese lore, legends soon develop around him: the gods, it is said, provided him with daily sustenance. It is also said that he usually carried the relic sewn into a fold of his robe on his left shoulder, and so he continually inclined his head in the opposite direction so as not to disrespect it. This changed his posture permanently and made him list to the right. See Pieris 1950, 396.

9. Seventy years later, Lawrie (1896, 203) could declare that the story of the English suppression of the 1817–1818 rebellion "cannot be related without shame." It decimated the Kandyan leadership, and, in addition to the people actually killed, many died of cholera and smallpox and general privations. On the smallpox epidemic in 1819, see Skinner 1891, 18–19.

10. An account of their arrests may be found in Brohier 1933, 38–41. The Pretender, Vilbave, had by then gone back to Uva, and was not caught; instead, he drops out of the picture entirely, returning to live among the Veddas in a remote region of Vellassa province. The British, realizing that he is more or less harmless without the support of the chiefs, make no determined effort to capture him. Eventually, however, twelve years later, in 1830, they do happen to find him and arrest him. He is tried and convicted of high treason but then granted a pardon (Powell [1973] 1984, 271).

The Recovery of the Tooth

By all accounts, the British recovery of the tooth relic that follows their capture of the leaders of the insurrection is a "happy accident" (Brohier 1933,
43). The villagers who helped in capturing Madugalle also tell the British
soldiers that they have seen a suspicious monk in the forest, with several attendants carrying largish bundles. Shoolbraid goes to investigate. When he
catches up with the men, he has their bundles searched. Inside, to their surprise, the soldiers find the tooth relic and all its gem-studded inner caskets.
And the monk turns out to be none other than Wāriyapola. When they hear
the news, Brownrigg and D'Oyly can hardly believe their luck and order the
relic brought back to Kandy. Brownrigg now finally admits that the relic was
stolen . . . now that it is in their hands again! (Pieris 1950, 395–396; see
also CO 54/73, 3B).

The relic's procession back to the temple is not without ceremony and
decorum. On November 11, it reaches the Nittawela Monastery, about four
kilometers from its destination, where it is held until an auspicious *nekata*
can be found for its return to the temple. While it is there, Brownrigg goes to
see it, laying eyes on it for the first time. He is much impressed by the jewels
of the caskets enclosing it. At the same time, or slightly later, as the tooth
is being returned to the Temple, Dr. John Davy (Brownrigg's physician in
Kandy) also gets to see it. "It is," he says, "of a dirty yellow colour, excepting
towards its truncated base, where it is brownish. Judging from its appearance at the distance of two or three feet (for none but the chief priests are
privileged to touch it), it is artificial, and of ivory, discoloured by age" (Davy
1821, 368, slightly altered).[11]

---

11. Davy includes a line drawing of the tooth which, P. E. Pieris (1950, 566n25) argues,
is rather different from that made a few years later by Jonathan Forbes (1840, 1: 292), so that
it is doubtful whether the two saw the same object. This is perhaps true if Davy's drawing was
intended to be life-size; he does not actually give the dimensions of the tooth but Forbes (1840,
1: 293) does, stating it to be "nearly two inches in length, and one inch in diameter." Parentheti-
cally, the drawing of the tooth in Forbes appears to be upside down, as if it were hanging from
the golden wire that encircles it but which is intended as a support from the bottom to raise the
tooth up above its lotus blossom base when it is exhibited. Tennent (1859, 2: 201) reproduces
the same drawing as Forbes, but Da Cunha (1875, 55) properly inverts it. For another drawing
of the tooth with the wire at the bottom, see figure 11.1 below. Pieris (1950, 566n25) seeks to
explain away the supposed discrepancy in size between the two relics by arguing that Forbes
must have seen a "facsimile" of the tooth similar to that shown to Mr. and Mrs. Heber in 1825
(see Heber 1829, 180). It should be noted, however, that none of this helps resolve whether
the tooth returned in 1818, which was seen in that year by Davy and somewhat later by Forbes
(probably when it was exhibited in 1828, and also when it was shown to Baron Karl von Hügel
in 1834—see Turnour 1837, 868), was the same as the one stolen by the rebels.

Like Brownrigg, Davy is more impressed by the gold and gems of the reliquaries than by the relic itself. In what seems very much like a description of its actual re-enshrinement, he states:

> wrapped in pure sheet-gold, it was placed in a case just large enough to receive it, of gold, covered externally with emeralds, diamonds, and rubies, tastefully arranged. This beautiful and very valuable bijou was put into a very small gold karandua, richly ornamented with rubies, diamonds, and emeralds: this was enclosed in a larger one also of gold, and very prettily decorated with rubies: this second, surrounded with tinsel, was placed in a third, which was wrapped in muslin; and this in a fourth, which was similarly wrapped; both these were of gold, beautifully wrought, and richly studded with jewels: lastly the fourth karandua, about a foot and a half high, was deposited in the great karandua. (Davy 1821, 368–369)[12]

Then Davy adds (1821, 369, italics added) what was to become a line much quoted by subsequent colonial authorities and scholars:

> Here, it may be remarked, that *when the relic was taken, the effect of its capture was astonishing and almost beyond the comprehension of the enlightened: "Now [the people said] the English are indeed masters of the country; for they who possess the relic have a right to govern . . . this, for 2000 years, is the first time the relic was ever taken from us."* And the first Adikar [Molligoda who had remained loyal to the British] observed that whatever the English might think of the consequence of having taken Kappitipola, Pilimé Talawé, and Madugallé, in his opinion, and in the opinion of the people in general, the taking of the relic was of infinitely more moment.

This sentiment—that the British regaining control of the tooth brought an immediate cessation of Kandyan hostilities—perhaps originated with Brownrigg. He, however, believed that it was not so much their *capture* of the relic that impressed and influenced the Kandyans as the fact that the tooth had so serendipitously come back into their possession. As he wrote to Earl Bathurst in London on January 8, 1819:

> The recovery [of the tooth] had a manifest effect on all classes and its having fallen again into our hands in this accidental manner was considered by this

12. For another description of the step-by-step re-enshrinement of the tooth, see Cumming 1892, 1: 294–295.

superstitious people as a demonstration of its being the destiny of the British Nation to govern the Kandyans. By these rapidly succeeding events, tranquility in the Kandyan Provinces may be considered as having been reestablished about the beginning of November. (CO 54/73, 3B–4A)

Storically speaking, this is wonderful stuff; historically, however, it is mostly nonsense. The rebellion stopped because of its ruthless suppression by the army and the arrest of its leaders. Moreover, this was hardly the first time the relic was taken from its rightful owners, despite the claim made above that such a thing had never happened over the last two millennia.[13] Moreover, the English repossession of the tooth hardly meant the end of resistance to their rule; as Malalgoda (1970, 436) has pointed out, between 1817 and 1858, there were no fewer than eight millenarian uprisings against the British in Sri Lanka, though most of these were put down with greater ease than was that of 1817–1818. It may be true that, for some Sinhalese, in the short run, the British regaining the tooth may have acted as an extra psychological blow following their arrest of the leaders of the rebellion, and it is true that very quickly thereafter the active uprising subsided, but the usual Sri Lankan reaction to the loss of the tooth relic was not submission, but a desire to recapture it, as the rebellion of 1817–1818 well exemplifies.

In my opinion, this story—that the British taking of the tooth meant capitulation by the people—was a piece of propaganda propounded by them to "consolidate their hold on the Kandyan kingdom" (Seneviratne 1978, 19). Moreover, it was not primarily directed at Kandyans; it was more generally aimed at lowland Sinhalese and at the British public in Ceylon and in England. More specifically, as we shall see, it was used to justify—to missionaries and others—the colonial regime's sponsorship—monetarily and ritually—of the cult of the tooth in Kandy.

The Execution of Keppetipola and Madugalle

Indeed, with the relic back in the temple, if only to show their legitimacy as rulers, the British make it available once again to devotees, though presumably now with extra precautions. Ironically, two of its most prominent first venerators are Keppetipola and Madugalle, the two chief leaders of the

---

13. For instance, in the thirteenth century, it was captured and taken to South India (see Geiger 1929, 2: 205; and chapter 6 above). Also, of course, the Portuguese claim to have taken it in 1560. (Davy [1821, 369] has a brief footnote on that, stating that people disagree.) For a general study of relic theft in Buddhism, see Trainor 1992.

232 / Chapter Nine

uprising who, on November 25, 1818, request to be allowed to go to the temple to worship the tooth one more time before being executed for treason. This they are allowed to do.

The event is most fully narrated, perhaps, by Dr. Henry Marshall, senior medical officer in the Kandyan provinces, who had been a close acquaintance and admirer of Keppetipola in the days prior to his defection to the rebel cause and even afterward (see Marshall 1846, 216–220). Indeed, Marshall (1846, xiv) chose to feature, as a frontispiece to his book, a line-drawing portrait of Keppetipola.

The execution is scheduled for 8:00 a.m. Early that same morning, the prisoners are taken, at their request, to the Temple of the Tooth, where they desire to pay their last respects to the relic and pronounce their *prārthanāva* or final "earnest wish." The fact that the British permit this is interesting, and it is worth speculating a bit about some of the reasons for it. There is, in Sinhalese Buddhism, a tradition of persons about to die reviewing their meritorious lifetime deeds, and wishing (i.e., making a *prārthanāva*) that they might thereby eventually attain nirvana.[14] It is more likely, however, that the British are here respecting their own traditions of permitting condemned prisoners "final words" or "a last meal" or a "final visit with a priest." But their willingness to honor Keppetipola and Madugalle's wish to do this at the Dalada Maligawa may also be connected to several other things: first, it reflects the fact that a number of British officials respected and admired both Keppetipola and Madugalle, especially the former—not enough to seek to have their sentences commuted, but to speak in favor of letting them have their final wishes. We have already seen how Marshall greatly esteemed Keppetipola. The same is true of Mr. Sawers, D'Oyly's deputy in Kandy, who had befriended Keppetipola when he was an official in Badulla (Keppetipola's hometown), and whose presence Keppetipola specifically requested as a gesture of farewell. On the other hand, Keppetipola's asking British friends for their support and succor in his final moments may have simply been due to his fear that had he turned to any Kandyan friends for such companionship, he might have endangered them by making them suspect in the eyes of the British.

Second, the British allowing this visit to the temple may be sending a message to the remaining Kandyan chiefs that their prestige and honor would be respected, as well as their religious traditions (guaranteed by the Kandyan Convention). The execution of chiefs by a ruler in Kandy was, after

14. On *prārthanāva* and its relation to "dying wishes," see Gombrich 1971, 217–225.

all, nothing new, and all too frequent under Śrī Vikrama. Allowing death with dignity, however, was traditionally and culturally admired. Perhaps implicit in the British actions was a desire to draw a contrast between their style of execution, in the case of Keppetipola and Śrī Vijaya's execution of Ehelepola's wife and children.

Finally, and perhaps more importantly for our purposes, in light of all the uncertainty about the genuineness of the tooth relic, taking Keppetipola and Madugalle to the Dalada Maligawa was perhaps also intended to send a message that the tooth in the temple *was* the authentic relic, or at least was considered to be so by these two Kandyan chiefs, since they would not have desired making their final *prārthanāva* in front of a fake.

In any case, upon arriving (under armed escort) at the temple, Keppetipola meets and greets Mr. Sawers. He then kneels in front of the open door to the inner sanctum, where he recalls the chief acts of merit he has performed during his lifetime—gifts to monks and monasteries, and other good deeds. He then declares his "earnest wish" (*prārthanāva*) that he be reborn in the Himālayas and finally attain nirvana (Marshall 1846, 218).[15] Presumably Marshall is here recording the standard verse for finishing such ritual aspirations: "May I pass away from here and be born in the noble Jambudvīpa on a golden peak in the Himalayas as a divine lord with a life span an aeon long, and, hearing the Dharma from the Buddha Maitreya, then attain nirvana."[16] The monk present then replies that indeed, his merits are great, and reassures him that "as sure as a stone thrown up into the air returns to the earth, so certain[ly] you will, in consideration of your religious merits, be present at the next incarnation of Buddha, and receive your reward" (Marshall 1846, 218).

Keppetipola then makes his last offering to the tooth; having nothing else to give, he unwinds the upper cloth from his body and presents it to the temple, telling Mr. Sawers, who is standing by, that he is sharing this merit with him, and joking to him not to worry that the cloth is dirty and ragged: the merit will be large nonetheless, since it is all he has to give (Marshall 1846, 218).

At this point, there is a sudden commotion behind them in the shrine room (*Asiatic Journal and Monthly Register* 1819, 93). Apparently, Madugalle, having finished his own final earnest wish, has suddenly darted into the inner sanctum of the temple, loudly claiming sanctuary under the protection

15. An earlier, shorter, and occasionally different account of these same events may also be found in *Asiatic Journal and Monthly Register* 1819.
16. De Silva 1980, 88 (slightly altered).

of the tooth.[17] The British, however, are not about to observe any such notion of sacred refuge; Madugalle is promptly seized and dragged out from
behind the dagoba by Lieutenant Mackenzie and some of his men. Keppetipola, Marshall adds, remained calm and self-possessed and was "greatly
surprised at the pusillanimity of his fellow-prisoner" (Marshall 1846, 218).

The contrast between the two chiefs continues to be stressed in the account of their actual execution. From the temple, they are taken to the traditional place of execution by Bogambara Lake, about a kilometer away.[18]
On their way, they are accompanied by a great crowd of Kandyans, including
many chiefs (*Asiatic Journal and Monthly Register* 1819, 93). At Bogambara,
Keppetipola calmly ties up his hair and, sitting down on the ground, he
recites some Pali verses from a small book he takes from the folds of his gar-
ment. When he is finished, he asks that the book be given to Mr. Sawers for
transmission to his younger brother in Uva, and he bends his head forward.
As the executioner decapitates him with a sword, he utters firmly the single
word "Arahan" (meaning "[May I be worthy of becoming] enlightened").
His head is then, according to Kandyan custom, placed on his breast (Marshall 1846, 219).

Such bravery impresses, and it is no surprise that in Sri Lanka today, Keppetipola remains very much a heroic figure.[19] But the British as well seem
to be eager to make Keppetipola into a "noble rebel." The first report of his
execution, in the pages of the *Asiatic Journal and Monthly Register* (1819, 93),
already comments: "His whole behavior was manly and collected, and he
met death with a firmness of resolution worthy of a better cause."[20] Marshall, being Scottish, goes even further. Keppetipola, he declares, reminds
him of "Sir William Wallace, the beloved champion of Scotland . . . whose
exertions and sufferings for the independence of his country may be here

17. The Kandyans at this time recognized not the Dalada Maligawa, but the burial place of
the kings, attached to the Asgiriya Monastery, as a place of sanctuary (see Hardy 1850, 230).
However, there are some historical indications that a shrine of the Temple of the Tooth could
also be considered to be a place of refuge. At least the Veḷaikkāras, who took over custody of the
relic in Polonnaruwa in the twelfth century, promised to protect any who entered its sanctum.
See Wickremasinghe 1928, 255.

18. In 1876, after the lake was filled in, the British built the Bogambara Prison near this site.
Bogambara is sometimes an alternate name given to the whole of Kandy Lake, or sometimes just
to its western extremity (private communication, John Holt, September 20, 1920).

19. For an example of a popular patriotic song about him, see https://www.youtube.com
/watch?v=LJk4VgPpjds. According to Brohier (1933, 49), Keppetipola was deified by villagers
under the name Monaravila Alut Deviyo, on whom see Perera 1917, 19.

20. Madugalle, on the other hand, is commonly presented as a coward in the face of death:
he was too agitated to tie up his own hair and had to be forced both to sit and to bend his head
forward and be held by one of the executioners (Marshall 1846, 219).

stated" (1846, 219–220). And, in a lengthy digression, he goes on to recall how, at the end of the thirteenth century, the Scots, "adopting the Kandyan mode of warfare [sic] . . . betook themselves to the woods, mountains, and morasses" and engaged in a general insurrection against the English power. However, their leader, William Wallace, just like Keppetipola, was "at the last betrayed by some of his countrymen and delivered up to the English . . . charged with high treason, condemned to death . . . tortured [and] decapitated" (Marshall 1846, 220). Marshall even describes the way Wallace's head was boiled and dipped in tar (to preserve it) and then displayed on a pike on the gatehouse of London Bridge.[21]

He fails to see, however, that Keppetipola's head suffers a perhaps analogous but more "genteel" (?) nineteenth-century fate, at his own hands: Marshall somehow acquires Keppetipola's skull and sends it to the Phrenological Society's Museum in Edinburgh, where it is studied by those interested in any posited relationship between cranial size and greatness. More specifically, it is used to try to explain how a man of an inferior race could be so brave (Wickremasinghe 1997, 85–86). In time, however, once Keppetipola comes to be honored by Sri Lankans as a national hero—an early freedom fighter who resisted the colonial yoke—it is felt unsuitable for his skull to be on display in Edinburgh. With the approach of independence in 1948, building pressure for the return of certain national symbols mounts, and, just a few days after independence is granted, Keppetipola's skull is repatriated to Ceylon, thanks in part to the intercession of the Duke of Gloucester.[22] Ironically, however, it is again put on display, being initially housed in the Colombo Museum where, according to a contemporary newspaper account, it comes to be viewed as a "national relic," a "symbol of the new and independent nation-state" (Wickramasinghe 1997, 86, 87). It is reportedly now back in Kandy in a pillar at one end of the square in front of the Temple of the Tooth.

The New Proclamation of 1818

Following the quelling of the rebellion, Governor Brownrigg issues in Kandy, on November 24, 1818, a proclamation that not only officially declares an

---

21. It was the first head so to be shown—the start of a gruesome tradition of displaying the heads and sometimes body parts of "traitors" on the bridge that lasted for over three centuries.

22. As we shall see, the Duke of Gloucester was also instrumental, in 1934, in returning the throne and crown of the king of Kandy to Ceylon, which had been taken to England by Governor Brownrigg's son in 1815.

end to the conflict, but also establishes a somewhat new relationship between the colonial authorities and the Kandyans.[23] In this sense, it differs in tone and in substance from the Kandyan Convention of 1815, which was basically seen as a treaty between two parties—the British and the chiefs; this is much more of a unilateral declaration of new terms by victors to a defeated people. Indeed, in article 7, the Kandyans are reminded that "the sovereign majesty of the King of Great Britain and Ireland . . . is the source alone from which all power emanates and to which obedience is due" (Mendis 1956, 237). In articles 8 and 9, a Board of Commissioners is set up for directing all chiefs and headmen in the specifics of their duties (Mendis 1956, 237). In article 11, all full-body prostrations, from or to any person, are abolished, but "all chiefs and other persons coming before, meeting, or passing any British officer, civil or military . . . shall give up the middle of the road, and, if sitting, rise and make a suitable obeisance, which will be always duly acknowledged and returned" (Mendis 1956, 234). In article 12, these acts of obeisance are extended to the portrait of His Britannic Majesty in the Hall of Audience (Mendis 1956, 234). Finally, a caveat is added at the end of the document that states that "the Governor [acting as representative of the British sovereign] reserves full power unilaterally to change any of the provisions of the proclamation" (Mendis 1956, 243).

In line with these reassertions of their new control, the British now see fit to institute other new modes of ritual protocol which, ironically, make them seem more like Kandyan kings. As he explains to Earl Bathurst in London:

In order to impress by exterior appearances on the minds of the people in general that the British authorities were the real organ of the Supreme Government, and that the native chiefs could only act under their orders, it has been thought expedient to appropriate certain marks of respect and attendance which were paid to the former kings of Kandy, to the Governor as His Majesty's representative in the island, and similar honours on a graduated scale to the other principal officers of government as your Lordship will perceive in the proclamation. Accordingly, on my journey down from Kandy to Ruanwelle, I was attended according to the ancient etiquette, by all the chiefs

23. The complete text of the proclamation may be found in Mendis 1956, 231–243, and also in Davy 1821, 505–517, where it figures as Appendix II. See also CO 54/73 for documents pertaining to the drafting of the proclamation—extensive back-and-forth communication between Governor Brownrigg in Colombo and the Board of Commissioners for the affairs of the Kandyan states, that is, John D'Oyly and James Gay.

in Kandy as far as the ferry of Ganorua, and by the Disawas and Honottales of the 4 & 3rd Korles through which my journey lay. (CO 54/73, 8A–8B)

With regard to religion, there is a commitment in the proclamation to continue to support the Buddhist establishment, somewhat in the manner of the former kings, albeit in a changed context. Thus, in article 21, the custom of exempting all temple lands from taxation is continued (this in the face of various other articles that reform the tax system for everyone else by establishing it at a uniform 10 percent of the income from all paddy lands). The same article also retains the custom of requiring the inhabitants of these temple-villages to perform fixed gratuitous services to their temples, in exchange for this freedom from taxation (Mendis 1956, 236). This is in the face of other articles that generally abolish the tradition of *rājakariya* (corvée labor for the king).

In article 17, while the tradition of the provincial chiefs receiving fees from those whom they appoint to subordinate positions (e.g., village headmen) is generally abolished, it is maintained for appointments in the temple-villages. For these, the Diyawadana Nilame (in the case of the villages of the Temple of the Tooth) and the *basnāyaka nilames* (in the case of those of the *devales*) can continue to receive the usual fee from those whom they recommend for approval by the British Resident (Mendis 1956, 235). In other words, though the colonial government retains ultimate control over these appointments (as did the king before 1815), the old system of patronage is maintained.

More generally, in article 16, the proclamation affirms that "the priests as [well as] all the ceremonies and processions of the Budhoo religion, shall receive the respect which in former times was shown them" (Mendis 1956, 242; see also CO 54/73, 82A). Such a commitment, it was felt, was necessary as a safeguard against future rebellions (Boake 1854, 6). At the same time, however, in the same article, there is a nod toward those on the island and back in England who worried or objected to the affirmation that the Buddhist religion would be "inviolable." That word, significantly, does not appear in the Proclamation of 1818. To the contrary, there is now the affirmation that Buddhism will no longer have a special place religiously; instead, the right of all non-Buddhists of various stripes (including Christians) to profess their own religions and (with the permission of the governor) to build new places of worship wherever those might be appropriate is proclaimed. This latter provision was to have an immediate effect. Following the Kandyan Convention, Governor Brownrigg had, in 1815, denied the request of Christian missionary societies to be able to establish themselves and proselytize in Kandyan lands; after 1818, however, that interdiction is lifted, and missionaries are let in (see De Silva 1973b, 72).

All in all, the Proclamation of 1818 does mark a significant change. As Davy puts it, the old system in which "our hands were tied by the articles of the convention and the chiefs were the rulers of the country" is now gone (Davy 1821, 333). Instead, the colonial regime in Kandy moves to a much more "hands-on" mode of governing. With regard to the tooth relic, this means the start of more careful governmental control. From 1815 to 1818, in the spirit of "non-violation," the Buddhist priests and the heads of the *devales* were pretty much left to do what they wanted in the ways they wanted to (within, of course, certain parameters). Simply put, when the tooth came back in 1815, it was brought back by the Kandyans. To be sure, the British (D'Oyly and Brownrigg in particular) pushed for its return, but they still thought of the relic as something that belonged to the Buddhists. For instance, there was no proclamation then that whoever possessed the relic ruled the island. However, when the tooth comes back in 1818, it is reestablished as a captured object by the British, who now not only assert their authority over it more forcefully but find themselves obligated to take the responsibility that authority entails more seriously. Some Kandyans, in fact, state that this is the first time the tooth has actually fallen into foreign hands, and when Davy objects, asking "what about 1815?," their reply is that "they had never surrendered it [then], and that they considered it in their possession till we [i.e., the British] took if from them by force [in 1818]" (Davy 1821, 369n). The British, moreover, take over the management of the temple's funds, all donations to the relic now being funneled through the newly established Board of Commissioners and invested by the Cutchery (Finance Department) (Boake 1854, 21, citing a report from the 1831 Colebrooke Commission).

In the wider Buddhist world, as well, there is a clear realization that the British are now in charge of the tooth relic. For instance, in 1822, the British diplomat John Crawfurd is sent as an envoy to the Siamese court. While there, the Thai foreign minister, in a private conversation, mentions to him that a few years ago, some Siamese monks had been to Kandy, where they had been received by an English gentleman [most likely, D'Oyly] who impressed them by his knowledge of Buddhism and by his courteous demeanor, and who showed them the tooth relic. The minister then adds that since the British are now rulers of Kandy, might Crawfurd not be willing to intercede with the governor of Ceylon and arrange to have the tooth given to His Majesty the king of Siam, who is very desirous to possess it? To his credit, Crawfurd immediately refuses, stating that the relic is also worshiped in

Ceylon and adding, not altogether accurately, that it "was an invariable rule with the British, wherever they were masters, never to violate the religious feelings of the native inhabitants" (Crawfurd 1830, 1: 188).[24]

The 1828 Exposition of the Tooth

The Kandyans, who had generally felt good about the return of the tooth to the temple in 1815, are somewhat more ambivalent about its situation after 1818. For example, on January 8, 1820, at high noon, Sri Lankans and Europeans alike see bright streaks of light streaming upward in a clear blue sky from the pinnacle of the Dalada Maligawa. These are said to be "*budu-res*" (Pali, *Buddharaṃsi*—rays of the Buddha).[25] The notion that Buddha relics occasionally project such rays of light is something that is already found in Indian Buddhist legends, and is said to have been witnessed by various Chinese pilgrims on the subcontinent, who consider it to be a positive sign (see Strong 2004b, 176). In Sri Lanka in 1820, however, they are given ambivalent interpretations. Some say the rays mean that the teachings of the Buddha will last for a full five thousand years (Forbes 1835, 232nf); others, however, claim that they are "ominous, and boding ill in general" (Davy 1821, 71).

It should be said that 1820 was a time of great upheaval for traditional Kandyan and Buddhist culture. Not only had the tooth relic been recaptured, not only had the true subordination of the Kandyan aristocracy become clear, but the British, whether deliberately or not, systematically undertook to undermine the mores of the people and the general social fabric. For example, 1820 also saw for the first time the establishment (under Governor Barnes) of public taverns in virtually all districts and villages in the central province. Some have claimed that the British policy was to use liquor in Sri Lanka the way they used opium in China, and indeed, alcoholism soon became rampant, along with all its consequences (De Silva 1965a, 16; see also Skinner 1891, 219–220). Perhaps it is in light of such developments

24. See also on this Malalgoda 2002. Even before this, in the 1790s, the king of Ava had boasted to the Thais that they could get the relic anytime they wanted; all they had to do was ask the British for it (see Gesick 1976, 138).

25. Forbes 1840, 1: 337, has a general discussion of *budu-rēs* as a beautiful but unexplained meteorological phenomenon. Davy (1821, 71) mentions them specifically in connection with Kandy in 1820. On their association with the pinnacle of the temple on that date, see also http://infolanka.asia/history/colonial-era/history-of-sri-lanka-and-significant-world-events -from-1796-ad-to-1948.

that we should view the perceptions of the people of Kandy at this time that, though the relic was back in its temple, all was not right with the world.

The British were not oblivious to this malaise. Perhaps in order to counter it and ingratiate themselves to the Sinhalese Buddhist population, or perhaps in order to manifest their position of dominion as custodians of the tooth, or perhaps simply to raise money, or for all three reasons, the British decide to sponsor, in 1828, a special exposition of the tooth, in which the relic itself can be gazed upon and worshipped by devotees at close quarters (unlike in the annual Esala Perahera when the tooth, paraded on top of its elephant, is not actually seen but left in an enclosing karandua). Such an event, though fairly common in ancient times according to a fourteenth-century Sinhala text,[26] had not occurred since 1775, some fifty-three years earlier, during the reign of King Kīrti Śrī, so it is truly a special occasion.

The exposition takes place from May 28 to June 3, 1828, as part of the annual Vesak celebrations.[27] The official announcement, with the imprimatur of Governor Barnes, is issued by George Turnour at the Cutchery in Kandy, on April 28: "Notice is hereby given that a dālada pinkama (festival) will be held at Kandy, with *the sanction of government*, on Thursday, 29th proximo, and the sacred relic exhibited at the Maligawa (temple) to all persons who may desire to attend and make offerings" (Selkirk 1844, 386n, italics in the original).

Over the next month or so, news of the coming event spreads throughout the island, while preparations for it are made in Kandy. In the square outside the temple, a pavilion (*mandapa*) is built measuring over 200 feet by 60 feet, and in the middle of it is set up a silver table on which the relic will be placed in the center of a large lotus blossom of pure gold. Around it are hung "veils" or curtains of various kinds of gold and silver cloth. To one side, bedecked with white cloths, seats are made ready for the monks. In addition, two other pavilions (viewing platforms that will keep their users above and distinct from the crowd) are erected—one for Europeans,

26. The *Daḷadāsirita* [History of the tooth relic] specifies that after the tooth is taken (in a carriage pulled by an elephant) around the city, it should be removed from its casket. Then the head monk of the Uttaramula [fraternity of the Abhayagiri sect] should raise it up and show it to the community of monks. Then he hands it over to the king, who should carry it out to an elevated position and exhibit it to the multitude. See Holt 2017, 312; and Hocart 1931, 36. See also De Silva 1980, 218.

27. Two accounts of eyewitnesses, in particular, will be used here, those found in Forbes 1840 and Colebrooke 1836. In addition, Selkirk 1844 has some interesting materials to add. Vesak is a celebration of the Buddha's birth, enlightenment, and parinirvana that occurs on a full moon day, usually in the month of May.

and a larger one for Sinhalese chiefs. All around the pavilions ornamental arches are constructed and flags are displayed, and drummers are sent around the town to urge the citizens to decorate their homes and neighborhoods. Significantly, the chiefs in attendance include leaders not only from the Kandyan provinces but from the coastal areas of the island as well. The same may be said for the assembled crowds of people: they come from all over.[28] Thus, for the first time under the British, we find a ritual union of the whole of the island of Ceylon, and for the first time in many centuries, the tooth is no longer just a Kandyan emblem but has now (re)become a national symbol of unity (Colebrooke 1836, 161).

On the first day of the festival, at an auspicious hour late in the morning, the tooth is taken out of its shrine and, still within its inner caskets, placed under a silver cupola on the back of a magnificently caparisoned tusker. As the elephant bearing the relic emerges from the gate of the temple, a double line of other elephants kneel down to form a sort of avenue through which it proceeds. Cannons are fired, drums are beaten, musical instruments are sounded, and the assembled crowd erupts into loud and sustained cries of "*sadhu sadhu sā*" (Colebrooke 1836, 162). The moment is so striking that Forbes has it sketched and reproduced as the frontispiece of his book (see fig. 9.1).

In any case, the tooth is then taken around the streets of the city in a procession similar to that of the Esala Perahera, but without the presence of the emblems from the *devales*. The various chieftains go first, on the heels of "the flags of the Maligawa; tom-tom beaters; musicians; drummers and trumpeters; chank-blowers; men bearing torches of various description; [and] . . . whip-crackers" (Colebrooke 1836, 163). Following all this goes the relic on its elephant, surrounded by officers of the temple on foot, and flanked by two other elephants bearing the *adikars*.

In due time, the procession returns to the temple, where the relic is removed from the back of its elephant and handed to the first *adikar*, who then takes it to the silver table where it is to be exhibited. Then the hangings immediately surrounding the altar are closed around the relic, and around Governor Barnes, the *adikar*, and the officiating head monk of the temple.

---

28. We do not have a good accounting of where all the pilgrims to the 1828 exhibition came from, but a tragic accident that occurred when a makeshift bridge over the Mahaweli River at the crossing west of Kandy broke up and precipitated many people into the water gives us some inkling. Those who drowned are said to have included five monks from the Seven Korales (northwest of island), three men from Saffragam (south central), Yatinuwara (west of Kandy), and Galle (far to the southwest). Presumably pilgrims from other parts of the island would be crossing the river at different fords. See Selkirk 1844, 387.

Figure 9.1. The 1828 exposition. From Forbes 1840, frontispiece.

When the curtains are opened again, the tooth has been removed completely from all of the caskets that had enclosed it and, elevated on a stand made of a single gold wire, it has been placed in the center of the gold lotus blossom. Directly in front of this altar is a plain table set up for receiving offerings (Forbes 1840, 1: 293–294).[29]

Interestingly, neither Forbes nor Colebrooke mentions a detail that was much later recalled by the grandson of the man who was *adikar* in 1828. According to him, it was Governor Barnes who "carried the Relic in his [own] hand from the shrine room out on to the esplanade," where he handed it over to the care of the *adikar* (*Overland Times of Ceylon* 1897b, 701). This action was akin to what a Kandyan king would have done. Barnes's involvement in the exhibition thus might have been more than what our British accounts of the event (e.g., Colebrooke 1836) here admit.

Be this as it may, over the next seven days, devotees and others get to come up to this table in order to view and venerate the relic. For this, a sort of "pecking order" is established. Precedence is given, on the first day, to "the English ladies and gentlemen"—at least those who are actually interested. Presumably this includes Governor Barnes, John Forbes (who gives a

---

29. See also the description of the 1828 exhibition in Ferguson 1887, 225–229.

precise description of the relic), and others, but it is not known how many Europeans actually approach the relic at this time. It is evident that Barnes, perhaps conscious of the scandal that followed D'Oyly's public offering of a musical clock to the relic in 1815, makes no public gift or pronouncement on this occasion. In this, according to George Turnour, he is directly refusing an invitation to do so made to him by some Kandyan chiefs, "on the ground that he would do nothing which could imply identity in the Buddhist faith on the part of the authorities" (see Malalagoda 1970, 118–119). On the other hand, as we shall see, Barnes (or a member of his family) had been involved in the presentation of a Burmese Buddha image to the tooth the year before.

After the Europeans have approached the tooth, it is the turn of the monks who have been sitting on the pavilion all this time. Colebrooke (1836, 164) says that each approaches the relic "like a poor man finding a precious stone . . . with ardent looks and the most inexpressible joy, crying aloud, *sádú! sádú!* and worshipping it." This lasts until about ten in the evening, at which point the tooth is put in a golden case and so put to bed for the night. It is not known how the monks (and other Kandyans) felt about the Englishmen and -women, who were not only foreigners but laypersons, being given precedence to themselves in viewing the relic. It must have come as a shock, but our Western sources (which seem to assume that the order that was established was the natural one) make no mention of it.

The next day, in the early afternoon, the relic is again taken out of its case, and all of the Kandyan chiefs line up, having shed their finery and being now clad in the ritual white of devout laymen. Each, in turn, approaches to worship and make offerings of money, cloth, and the like (Colebrooke 1836, 164). After this, for a full five days more, people who have come from all over the island worship the tooth and make offerings. These consist of a large variety of items: "gold chains and gold ornaments; gold, silver, and copper coins of all denominations; cloths, priest's vestments, flowers, sugar, areka-nuts, betel-leaves" (Forbes 1840, 1: 294). The offerings collected are turned over to the Board of Commissioners and appropriated by them to be used for the upkeep of the temple (Report of the Cameron Commission in 1831, quoted in Boake 1854, 20–21). Hardy (1841, 18) specifies that the totals collected amounted to 10,000 rix-dollars (or around £750), which the Board of Commissioners lent out at interest, using the returns from the investment for temple maintenance.

Colebrooke (1836, 164) adds some description of security measures taken on the occasion. Immediately around the relic on its dais are seven monks, together with the chief priest (presumably the Diyawadana Nilame) of the temple. Around them, just outside a first row of curtains, stand seven chiefs with silver daggers. Then two more rows of curtains, each of which is patrolled by guards. Outside this inner circle is a company of Malay (i.e., British mercenary) soldiers, more guards, and then regular police officers. It would appear from all this that memories of the 1818 theft of the relic are still fresh, and that not only are measures taken to ensure that the tooth is protected from any ill-intentioned pilgrim, but there is general mutual distrust between at least three groups: the monks, the chiefs, and the British. In any case, all these measures prevent any mishap, and on June 3, a week after the festivities began, at ten o'clock, the relic is once again taken in procession around the city, and then put back in its shrine within the temple.

TEN

The Relic Disestablished:
Missionary Oppositions to the Tooth

The anxiety of the Kandyans for the preservation of their superstitions is in powerful contrast with the indifference manifested by the Europeans to the interest of
Christianity.

—Robert Spence Hardy (1841, 37)

It is a great pity that it would not be considered right for me to have been able to
persuade [the Kandyans] that the Queen of England has a splendid temple called
the *British Museum* in which she would place [the tooth] and take care of it for
them. That is where it ought to have gone.

—Viscount Torrington in a private letter to the Third Earl Grey, August 15, 1847
(see De Silva 1965b, 57)

In 1838, ten years after the exposition of the tooth, the eminent missionary James Selkirk, on his way to Kandy, encountered a procession of two
hundred persons from a village near Colombo who were walking to present their offerings to the Temple of the Tooth. He found the sight of them
distressing: "old men and women between sixty and seventy years of age,
with each a little talipot leaf as a screen from the heat of the sun, so foot-
sore as hardly to be able to move" (Selkirk 1844, 526). He and his fellow
missionaries distribute Christian tracts to the pilgrims and talk to them,
apparently trying to discourage them from paying adorations to the relic.
But to Selkirk's irritation, they soon throw away their tracts and go on their
way, "full of joy at being so near their journey's end . . . preceded by flags
[and] tomtoms . . . and playing upon a wind instrument called Hēwisi . . . at
every village which they pass through." The sight of them prompts Selkirk to
remember the words of Jesus in Matthew 6.2: "When you give alms, sound

no trumpet before you, as the hypocrites do in the synagogues and in the streets, that they may be praised by men" (Selkirk 1844, 527).

A few days later in Kandy, Selkirk himself goes to the Dalada Maligawa, hoping to see the tooth. There is a certain irony in the fact that his intention is to do exactly the same thing as that which he tried to prevent the Sinhalese villagers from doing, albeit with a different attitude. Accompanied by the third *adikar* (a British appointee—the first and second *adikars* had died of alcoholism and not been replaced), he is shown around by the Diyawadana Nilame and admitted into "the very penetralia" of the temple, though he does not get to see the actual relic. He is struck by the opulence of the place, and also by the fact that food offerings to the tooth "become the portion of the priests," italicizing the fact that this means they *"eat things offered to idols"* (Selkirk 1844, 527).

But Selkirk's real aim in visiting the temple is not so much to criticize Sinhalese religious practices as to criticize the British government's support of them. In an adjacent hall, he sees a number of Buddha images and zeroes in on the one that bears an inscription, in Sinhala, that states it was acquired in Burma and presented to the tooth in 1827 by "Princess" (i.e., Miss) Barnes, whom he identifies, probably wrongly, as the daughter of the late recent governor, Sir Edward Barnes.[1] In addition, he identifies two other images, made of silver, that were presented to the temple by a native official in one of the maritime provinces who was a Christian. He is very critical of these apparent cases of Christians making offerings to what he thinks of as an idol (Selkirk 1844, 531).

We have seen above that already in the time of John D'Oyly's barefoot procession into the temple and his offering of a musical clock to the relic there in 1815, there were Christian objections to government officials being involved in the cult of the tooth. Perhaps because of these, Governor Barnes, on the occasion of the 1828 exposition, was hesitant to be seen making any kind of offering to the relic. By the time of Selkirk and other missionaries, however, Christian activism was no longer limited to targeting officials

---

1. The inscription states that in 1827, "Princess Barnes" had presented to the tooth a silver image of the Buddha taken from a Buddhist temple in Ava during the first Burmese war. Herbert White (1919), however, argues that this could not have been Governor Barnes's daughter. For one thing, Barnes did not get married until 1823 (so any child of his would have been no more than three). Moreover, there is no record of Barnes having ever had a daughter. It might have been given by Barnes's wife, Maria Fawkes, but she probably would not have been called a "princess." White speculates that the statue may have been given in commemoration of the birth (or premature death?) of an otherwise unknown daughter of the governor.

actually participating in the cult of the tooth, but was extended to any kind of monetary or symbolic support for Buddhism.

R. Spence Hardy's Pamphlet

At the end of his diary entry on his visit to Kandy, Selkirk makes reference to a pamphlet by one of his Christian colleagues on the island, entitled *The British Government and the Idolatry of Ceylon*. This was written by Robert Spence Hardy in Sri Lanka in 1839 and then republished in London in 1841.[2] Hardy (1803–1868) was a Wesleyan missionary who spent over twenty years in Sri Lanka. He became thoroughly versed in Sinhalese and Pali Buddhist literature and was, for his day, very well informed about the history, literature, and practices of Sri Lankan Buddhism.[3] In his essay, which calls for the British government to divest itself of its connection with Buddhism in general (and specifically with the Buddha's tooth relic), Hardy builds his case, as though he were a debater, by presenting and appealing to evidence and depending on argumentation. He begins with the assumption—which few of his contemporaries would have disputed—that the British Empire has become the greatest nation in the world "in wealth, power, and extent of influence." This he takes as evidence of God's favor, the reason for which, he argues, is so that "we might carry on with better effect the great work of the world's conversion, from darkness to light" (Hardy 1841, 6). He then turns to apply this general principle to Ceylon:

> The national religion of Ceylon is Buddhism, accompanied by the worship of demons, and the propitiation of malignant infernal spirits. . . . It would be foreign to my present purpose to enter into an examination of its dogmas. I rest my argument for the necessity of its destruction upon the simple fact that it is opposed to the truth—denies the existence of God—is ignorant of the only way of salvation, by faith in our Lord Jesus Christ. [As a consequence,] it is utterly impotent as a teacher of morals, or as a messenger of peace to the awakened consciences of its deluded votaries. In the sacred scriptures [i.e., the Bible] all these errors are summed up in one word, Idolatry. The religion of Buddha is idolatrous, and I contend that it is the bounden duty of the

2. I shall refer to the later edition. Elizabeth Harris (2006, 253) references the 1839 edition published by the Wesleyan Press in Colombo, which I have not seen.

3. In particular, see Hardy 1860, which contains extensive translations from Sinhala works, and Hardy 1850, which describes monastic practices and, among other things, has a straightforward account of the tooth relic (249–251).

[colonial] Government of the country, from its possession of the Truth, to discountenance the system by every legitimate means; and that it can afford no open or implied encouragement to its teachers or its worship, without the commission of an offence in the sight of God. (Hardy 1841, 10)

The problem, Hardy contends (1841, 13), is that the British government in Ceylon has failed in this obligation. Instead, in Kandy,[4] it has taken over the responsibilities and prerogatives of the former Kandyan kings; it has made itself into the sponsor and guardian of religion in that kingdom.

In much of the rest of the pamphlet, he goes on to spell out in detail the many ways in which the British government is doing this, and so, he argues, intolerably associating itself with "idolatry." Some of these concern general British policies toward Buddhist institutions such as honoring the system of land grants made by the Kandyan kings in support of the temples, as well as tax exemptions for temple lands, and appointing and paying the elders in charge of the Malwatta and Asgiriya fraternities. Many of his objections, however, focus specifically on the Temple of the Tooth, which, he says, the government supports in many ways: it approves the issuing of stipends to the forty monks who carry out services there in rotation; it also appoints and pays the lay official of the temple (the Diyawadana Nilame) as well as the various lay officials of the *devales*; the tooth relic itself is officially in the custody of the government agent who keeps the keys to the reliquary in his possession, and who appoints and pays an arachy thirty shillings a month to open and close the temple on a daily basis; from dusk to dawn, when the temple is closed, a soldier in uniform, belonging to the Ceylon Rifle Regiment, stands guard in the lower court; the exhibition of the tooth in 1828 was officially superintended by the government agent, and the 10,000 rix-dollars collected from donations on that occasion were kept in an account controlled by him for purposes of embellishing the temple (Hardy 1841, 18).

Moreover, "the [annual] Perahera of Kandy is principally got up at the expense, and by the command, of the British Government" (Hardy 1841, 24). With regard to this, Hardy presents a copy of an invoice sent to the government cutchery for related expenses. This includes "3£/10/6 for the cost of sundry articles for the use of the malagawa and 4 devales, 16/- for carrying the canopy over the karanduwa, and £3/15/- for oil and rags [i.e., to make torches]" (Hardy 1841, 25, slightly altered).

4. Hardy admits that the situation in the coastal regions of the island is somewhat different.

Apart from this, Hardy (1841, 30) complains that the British government also contributes to the expenses of various other festivals throughout the year, both Buddhist and Brahmanical, as well as for ceremonies that he and his contemporaries term "devil dancing." Hardy is, in fact, quite exercised about this latter point. He goes on immediately (1841, 31) to give a description of a "yakun" (i.e., yakka—possessing demon) exorcism, bemoaning the fact that Sinhalese apply to relief from disease, "not to God in prayer, but to the miserable yakadurā, or devil priest," and he decries the vouchers he has seen, signed by the government agent in Kandy, specifying that they are for payments (of £3/13/2½) "for the Devil Dancing called Waliyakoon." These he presents as evidence that "there are annual invocations of evil spirits, both in Kandy and at various outstations, which are paid for, from the Government revenue, by a British agent . . . [and specified] as being celebrated 'FOR HER MAJESTY'S SERVICE!'" (Hardy 1841, 32, caps in the original). Finally, he concludes:

> I feel as if I should be a partaker in these sins were I silent respecting them, and it is from a sense of duty that I have published these particulars. If the position be true that political power has been granted us [so] that the nations brought under our dominion may receive the benefits of divine revelation, it is evident that the neglect of this duty will bring upon us the anger of heaven; our authority will be taken from us, and given to some other people better disposed to carry forward the counsel of God. (Hardy 1841, 33)[5]

For Hardy, then, it was the manifest destiny of the British to convert the people of Ceylon to Protestantism, and should they fail in this, they would be betraying God's trust. In this, he was somewhat akin to the Portuguese, who felt it was their God-given duty to bring the whole of Asia to Catholicism.

Hardy is savvy enough to realize that there may be objections to his view, and he goes on immediately to try to deal with two of them. The first is that the involvement of the government in Kandy's religious practices helps increase respect for the British and stability of their dominion. This he dismisses as being no excuse—that support of idolatry can never be a means of gaining acceptance by the local population. Again, there are echoes here

---

5. All this is summed up in much milder tones in his later more scholarly work: "There [were] from time to time [after 1818] public exhibitions of the pretended tooth, under the sanction of the British authorities, by which the cause of heathenism was greatly strengthened and the minds of sincere Christians were much grieved" (Hardy 1850, 251).

of the position of some Portuguese clerics, who argued that holding the tooth for ransom would merely show the natives how valuable they thought it was.

The second objection Hardy deals with is that the British had a legal obligation to support Buddhism stemming from the Kandyan Convention of 1815, in which they had assured the Kandyans that not only would Buddhism remain "inviolable," but they "would maintain and protect its [rites],[6] ministers, and places of worship"—assurances that were repeated on many occasions thereafter by Brownrigg and D'Oyly. Here, Hardy contents himself with critique and invective. He declares that he finds the notion that Buddhism should be inviolable to be

> so strange, so unwarrantable, that [he] cannot help expressing [his] extreme surprise that such an error should have been committed by Sir Robert Brownrigg, whose respect for revelation cannot be called in question. If it was meant simply to signify that there should be no overt act on the part of the British Government to subvert the religion of the country, it was very improperly worded; if it meant more, it was blasphemy. (Hardy 1841, 37)

Hardy clearly prefers the wording of the proclamation issued after the 1818 insurrection (see above), arguing (1841, 38) that he sees no reason why, based on that language, the British government "should be considered as bound to interfere with the appointment of heathen priests, the celebration of heathen festivals, and the pecuniary support of some of the most gross superstitions that ever entered into the mind of man."[7]

Hardy, to be sure, was not an advocate of the forceful persecution of Buddhists or the outright interdiction of their religion on the island. At one point, in fact, he criticizes the Portuguese for their actions along these lines (Hardy 1841, 10). But he, along with other missionaries and officials of his time, firmly believed that Buddhism was on the decline and that it would soon die out, if only it were left alone and deprived of support by the government (Hardy 1841, 43).[8]

---

6. Hardy adopts the mistaken reading "rights," on which see above.

7. The same argument, that the Proclamation of 1818 made the provisions of the Kandyan Convention of 1815 moot, is also made forcefully by Boake (1854, 6–9). See also Tennent 1849, 306a. Nonetheless, that proclamation did provide for continued involvement in matters such as the appointing of leading monks and *nilames*.

8. The same argument was made by others. For instance, the colonial secretary in Ceylon, Mr. Anstruther, declared in 1845: "Everyone knows that it is only the Christian British Government that upholds the Buddhist religion, and protects it from the spoliation, contempt and

The 1843 Exhibition of the Relic and the Disestablishment of Buddhism

Hardy's pamphlet is influential among his fellow missionaries in Ceylon, and among missionary societies back in England, and these groups begin to pressure the government to give up even token support of Buddhism.[9] In Colombo, James Stewart-Mackenzie, governor from 1837 to 1841, is moved by the pamphlet, but while he and his successor, Sir Colin Campbell (governor from 1841 to 1847), are generally sympathetic to the missionaries' calls for disassociation, they feel constrained by the legal and administrative structures that govern their supervision of the Kandyan Buddhist institutions. Essentially, their response to the missionaries is that although they would like to do what they can to mitigate the situation, real change in the British policy cannot come without a directive from London (see Boake 1854, 26–29; see also De Silva 1965a, 72–79).

Hardy, of course, realizes this and sends his pamphlet to various missionary organizations in England, asking them to use their influence in the Colonial Office to get the established policies reversed. In particular, the secretary of the Church Missionary Society, Dandeson Coates; the evangelical minister, the Reverend James Stephen (who actually held the position of permanent undersecretary in the Colonial Office from 1837 to 1847); and the influential Baptist preacher, James Peggs, all take up Hardy's cause in the home country and begin pressuring the British government to sever its connections with Buddhism in Kandy (Boake 1854, 33–34; De Silva 1965a, 74–75).

The tooth relic, though by no means the sole focus of Hardy's pamphlet, is nonetheless an important one, and in time, it comes to be seen as a prime symbol of the government's association with Buddhism. Its focal role becomes especially evident in 1843, when a group of Siamese monks ask their Kandyan brethren to be allowed to see the tooth relic. The Kandyan bhikkhus pass the request on to the British authorities, who grant permission for the viewing, and on March 27, 1843, the Siamese pilgrims are shown the

---

abandonment of the Buddhists" (see Boake 1854, 14). J. Emerson Tennent (1849, 287b) felt that "Buddhism is too weak to subsist without external support," but that the kind of support received from a Buddhist sovereign could "never be supplied by a Christian government however liberal and tolerant." See also De Silva 1965a, 71; and Barrow 1857, 185.

9. On Hardy's influence, see Harris 2006, 40ff. Boake (1854, 33) describes the situation as follows: "[it was] expected that matters would gradually return to their former state, and this undoubtedly would have been the result had it not been for the publication of Mr. Hardy's Pamphlet."

relic by the Kandyan monks. But then, whether out of curiosity or a sense of duty, Governor and Lady Campbell, as well as C. R. Buller, the acting government agent for the Central Province, decide to also attend this ceremony. In addition, several other civil servants and their wives are present (De Silva 1965a, 80).

When the Reverend James Peggs reads about this in London, he is outraged. He promptly brings this example of what he thinks of as British officials participating in the ritual worship of the tooth to the attention of Lord Stanley, the secretary of state for war and the colonies. At the same time, he sends him a copy of Hardy's pamphlet, and makes a formal demand that he take action against such things and reprimand both Governor Campbell and C. R. Buller (CO 54/209; see also Boake 1854, 34). Lord Stanley responds by sending an official dispatch to Governor Campbell in Colombo, requesting him to report on the facts of the matter and asking for further details about government officials' involvement in "heathen rites and ceremonies" (CO 54/206, dispatch no. 76). In his reply four months later (in January 1844), Campbell denies that he or any other official took part in the ceremony but admits that the keys to the relic chamber are in the possession of the government agent (Mr. Buller), so he, out of necessity, had to be present at the time of the visit of the Siamese monks for unlocking the shrine and assuring its safety.[10] Moreover, he himself (Mr. Campbell) merely sat in the room on that occasion while the various karanduas were being opened and the tooth was exhibited to the Siamese pilgrims (CO 54/210, dispatch no. 14; see also Boake 1845, 35).

In fact, in time, a story develops that Campbell's involvement had been more complex than this. According to a tale current at least by 1863, the Siamese monks' visit had been arranged by one Tikiri Banda Dunuwille.[11] According to a story that may well be apocryphal, Tikiri Banda (as he was called) and Campbell were both prominently present at the time of exhibition of the tooth. The Siamese monks had brought a jar of attar with them, and after viewing and worshipping the tooth, they asked to be able to rub

10. These keys, already mentioned by Hardy, had long been a symbol and reminder of British involvement in the cult of the relic. As George Turnour (1837, 868), who held various administrative posts in the city during the 1820s and 1830s, put it: "The keys of the [Temple's] sanctum are never absent from my library, excepting during the actual performance of the daily religious ceremonies."

11. Tikiri Banda Dunuwille was a Ceylonese lawyer and coffee plantation manager, who was the son of the Kandyan *adikar* Millave who had been involved in the rebellion of 1818. Later in life, Dunuwille was a famed exile in Malaya, where he had been confined for forgery and for his involvement in the rebellion of 1848 (see Pieris 2011, 462–469). See also Davies 1957.

it with a piece of cotton soaked in the rose-scented oil, which they would then put back in the jar and take home to Siam. This was refused to them by the Kandyan elders, and an argument between them and the Siamese ensued. Campbell, who was standing there, asked what the commotion was about, and Tikiri Banda, grabbing the cotton, told him: "Your Honour, this is what they want: They want to take this small piece of cotton, so; and having dipped it in this oil, so; they wish to rub it on the sacred tooth, so; and having done this, to return it to this jar, so; thereby to consecrate the whole of the contents of this jar." Doing these actions as he described them, he then handed the jar back to the Siamese monks. The Kandyan bhikkhus were outraged, but Colin Campbell was said to be highly amused by Tikiri's trickery, telling him that it was "a pity he had not been born in the precincts of St. James [in London]" (see Cameron 1865, 376–380; McNair 1899, 113–117; and *Straits Times* [Singapore] 1863, 6).[12]

Campbell says nothing of this incident, if indeed it happened, in his letter to Lord Stanley. Instead, he further informs him that the real problem with regard to ending the government's association with Buddhism is not stopping participation by officials in religious rites at the Temple of the Tooth, but the need for the *mahānāyakas* and *basnāyaka nilames* to have government-sanctioned appointments to their posts in the monasteries and *devales*, and to supervise their management of the landed properties belonging to them (see De Silva 1965a, 82). In a later letter, he also warns the secretary that the Reverend Peggs has never been to Ceylon and has little knowledge of the situation of Buddhism there (see De Silva 1965a, 82n3).

The ball is now in Lord Stanley's court. He studies the situation; he consults with various officials in London who have some knowledge of the state's commitments to Buddhism and who worry about the need for some orderly administration of the temple lands; but at the same time, he is influenced by the missionary groups whose views are vigorously promoted by James Stephen within the Colonial Office. Stephen, who takes a great interest in the Ceylon "Buddhism question," doggedly seeks to convince Lord Stanley (and his various successors) to effectuate a clean and complete break with that "heathen" religion. With regard to the tooth relic, Stephen even suggests (though admitting it might provoke an insurrection) that "the obvious course is to destroy it." Perhaps inspired by accounts of the Portuguese action almost three hundred years earlier, he proposes that all the Kandyan chiefs and monks be assembled and that in their presence, "the

---

12. For a different version of this story, see Cumming 1892, 320–321.

relic be reduced to impalpable powder, and scattered upon the waters of the lake" (Boake 1854, 53). Alternatively, Stephen suggests that the tooth could be sent off the island (CO 54/210). As is clear from the chapter epigraph from Lord Torrington above, Stephen was not alone in this opinion.

In due time, in July 1844, Lord Stanley makes up his mind. He writes to Governor Campbell, expressing his view that the government has now reached the point where it can withdraw "from all connexion with Idolatry," and orders him, among other things: to cease being involved in the appointment of individuals to positions of authority in the monasteries, the *devales*, and the Temple of the Tooth; to make over the custody of the tooth relic to the priests; to take no part in its exhibition; to remove the sentry from the temple; and to discontinue grants of money for devil dances (CO 54/210, no. 210; see also Evers 1964, 329–330; and De Silva 1965a, 85). This list of orders appears to have been clearly influenced by Hardy's pamphlet. On the question of the management of the landed properties belonging to the temple, he is less clear. This, he recognizes, is a convoluted matter, which will take time to unravel and needs more study, although he urges Campbell to at least start working on divesting the government of its involvement in that as well (De Silva 1965a, 83; see also CO 54/212, dispatch no. 210).

The eminent historian of Sri Lanka, Kingsley De Silva, has said that this dispatch of Stanley's

> was of very great significance in the history of Ceylon. . . . [His] instructions [to Campbell concerning the tooth relic and other matters] in effect severed the tenuous connection of the British Government with Buddhism. . . . The connection between Buddhism and the State which had lasted with only insignificant interruptions from the very beginning of the recorded history of Ceylon was now at an end. (De Silva 1965a, 85)

Governor Campbell's Non-Action

In fact, it takes a few more years, and a few more governmental directives, for this end to be reached. The larger problem is that Stanley and the missionaries can see only the religious side of the tooth, but not its political necessity. In Tambiah's terms, they are blind to the this-worldly cycle of transactions that the tooth, as a charismatic object, has willy-nilly involved them in. Moreover, although Stanley has said *what* he wants, he has failed to specify *how* he wants it done. He leaves the implementation details of his order up to Campbell and his Executive Council in Colombo, but they, cognizant of the transactional complications involved (and also disagreeing among themselves), find it difficult to take action.

Campbell calls a meeting of the Kandyan chiefs and monastic leaders in April 1845 to explain to them the implications of Stanley's decision, and get their feedback. They are not happy with what they are told. Simply put, with regard to the tooth, they want to know who specifically (if not the government) will have possession of it and financial responsibility for it. They feel strongly that the British decision amounts to reneging on their agreement, in the Kandyan Convention and elsewhere, to protect the Buddhist religion in the manner of the Kandyan kings, and fear it is a first step toward a situation of abandonment and chaos (De Silva 1965a, 86).

In the meantime, Campbell's Executive Council meets in Colombo to discuss what they should do, but they cannot come to an agreement. Arthur Buller, attorney general of Ceylon and the Queen's advocate in the Executive Council (from 1841 to 1847), with the mind of a jurist, essentially argues that what they are being asked to do by Stanley is illegal. From his perspective, the Kandyan Convention of 1815 is a binding treaty that makes it clear in article 5 that "the Sovereign of the British empire is bound by an immutable obligation to maintain and protect the Buddhist religion in Ceylon as fully and in the same sense as Her Majesty is bound to maintain the Anglican Church in England and the Scottish Church in Scotland" (Boake 1854, 37).[13] He feels that as long as the government wishes to honor both that agreement and the Proclamation of 1818, it will "be impossible for the State to dissociate itself from Buddhism" (De Silva 1965a, 89). Moreover, he believes that in addition to this legal obligation, Britain has made a moral commitment not to let the Kandyan national religion "shift for itself." He thinks it best, therefore, that the present status quo be maintained, but that if it becomes necessary to give up the tooth relic due to missionary pressure, "it must be done in a quiet and conciliatory manner, after judicious and friendly discussion and without any unnecessary announcement of a determination to break all connections with the religion of the Kandyans" (De Silva 1965a, 89).

13. The relationship of the British monarch to these two churches is somewhat different, however. While he/she is "Defender of the Faith and Supreme Governor of the [Anglican] Church of England," he/she has no such title in Scotland, but only takes an oath "to preserve the settlement of the true Protestant [Presbyterian] religion as established by the laws made in Scotland." See https://www.royal.uk/queens-relationship-churches-england-and-scotland-and-other-faiths.

Overall, then, Buller's view amounts to a rejection of Lord Stanley's directive and an attempt to reargue something that, however, has already been resolved by the Colonial Office in London. For Governor Campbell and the rest of the Executive Council, this is, politically speaking, an impossible stance. They feel bound to carry out their orders, at least in one fashion or another (see Boake 1854, 37).

In opposition to Buller, Philip Anstruther, who served on the Executive Council as colonial secretary from 1833 to 1845, argues for keeping the obligations of the Kandyan Convention, but reinterpreting them. He states that a distinction needs to be made between *pure* Buddhism, which was guaranteed protection by the British, and *popular* religion, which was not, and in which he places the worship of Hindu gods and "devil dancing." Thus for him, article 5 means they need to continue to support the Buddhist monasteries (by making appointments to them, and recognizing their lands), but not the *devales* and veneration of "demons" (CO 54/217, 87–88).[14] It is not clear whether or not Anstruther thinks the tooth relic is part of "pure" or "popular" Buddhism, but in any case, with regard to it, he takes a different tack: he points out that the Kandyan Convention says nothing about the tooth relic per se—that the British only undertook to protect it after the rebellion of 1818, and did that solely due to the politics of the time; since those political reasons are no long relevant, there is nothing to prevent the British from giving the Kandyan monks custody of the tooth (with the added proviso, however, that if they should ever "lose" or misuse the tooth, the British government would confiscate all temple lands!) (De Silva 1965a, 88). His recommendations, then, amount to a partial implementation of Stanley's directive.

There is a problem, however, that Anstruther fails to address: he does not say which Kandyan monks should be responsible for the tooth or how they should be chosen. With regard to this specific issue, the acting government agent for the Kandyan region, C. R. Buller (not to be confused with his namesake Arthur Buller), proposes that all bhikkhus, chiefs, sons of chiefs, and persons who have held office elect a board of five commissioners "to which [all] the powers exercised by the Government in relation to Buddhism [including custody of the tooth and all its treasures] would be transferred" (De Silva 1965a, 86).

14. Arthur Buller promptly points out to him that this distinction was, in fact, not made in the Kandyan Convention (or in the minds and practices of the Kandyans) (see CO 54/217, 88). Moreover, it belies the fact that, in the Sinhala version of the Convention, the British assurances are extended to both the monasteries and the *devales*.

However, Philip Edmund (P. E.) Wodehouse (who had been assistant colonial secretary and clerk of the Executive Council and assistant judge in Kandy, and who, at the time, was serving as government agent for the Western Province) objects that this scheme will give too much power to a small body of influential chiefs principally in Kandy. He also envisions handing authority over to some kind of board, but he wants to do it with more strings attached; for instance, he is interested in having the Crown retain access to some of the revenue from the temple and the monasteries, and to devote it to educational purposes (another thing that Stanley had proposed) (De Silva 1965a, 86–87).

In the end, Governor Campbell cannot really decide what to do. Faced with all these opinions, he merely summarizes them and, in May 1845, sends them back to the Colonial Office in London, without a recommendation of his own, but with a note of caution saying it is important to proceed without alarming "the prejudices of the people." He also asks Stanley "to leave it to his discretion to determine the proper time and method of effecting the range of policy" (De Silva 1965a, 90; see also CO 54/217).

Upon receipt of this dispatch in the Colonial Office, the Reverend James Stephen is furious at Colombo's inaction, and critical of all their views on this matter, none of which, he thinks, is adequate. Arthur Buller's interpretations of the Kandyan Convention he finds "totally unacceptable"; C. R. Buller's proposal, he feels, would establish a "Buddhist Papacy"; and P. E. Wodehouse's scheme, though somewhat better, still does not go far enough in effectuating the divorce he seeks. He communicates his views to Lord Stanley and convinces the latter to write back to Campbell, which he does in August 1845, telling the governor, essentially, to stop dilly-dallying, to strictly adhere to his instructions in his previous dispatch, and to no longer postpone action on this matter (CO 54/218, dispatch no. 388).

Unable to delay any further, Governor Campbell proceeds to draw up an ordinance, based on a new argument—the principle that governmental responsibilities (such as those embodied in the Kandyan Convention) can be delegated. He envisions the appointment of a committee of sixteen persons, six of whom are to be bhikkhus, who will have primary responsibility for the tooth relic and its treasures, and for making sangha appointments. A separate commissioner will deal with the matter of temple lands. The Kandyans are unhappy with this solution, but Campbell tells them the matter is out of his hands and encourages them to petition the Queen if they wish to protest the new policy (which they do). He then sends the draft of his ordinance (along with the monks' petition) to Stanley in February 1846 (De Silva 1965a, 93; see CO 54/223, dispatch no. 37).

The Gladstone Interlude

By then, however, Stanley had been replaced in the Colonial Office by William Ewart Gladstone (1809–1898), who later goes on to serve four terms as prime minister. Gladstone is much less inclined to listen to the missionaries, and delegates the "Buddhism question," not to James Stephen but to his newly appointed assistant undersecretary of state, Frederick Rogers (1811–1889), who had been a classmate of his at Oxford. Rogers makes a full fresh study of the matter. Ignoring evangelical views, he ends up stressing three points: first, the question of dissociation with Buddhism is a difficult and complex one; second, the Kandyans have legitimate reason to feel they are being betrayed by the new policy; and third, the Colonial Office should listen more to the opinions of local civil servants on the ground in Sri Lanka who have a better understanding of the problems involved. Nonetheless, he recommends that Governor Campbell's draft ordinance be rejected. In his opinion, the proposed committee of sixteen persons would strengthen the Buddhist religion too much by giving it "a most dangerous force and unity" and by providing the bhikkhus with a "dangerous organization" (see Boake 1854, Appendix 9A, 51–65). He adds, with regard to the tooth: "The central committee are to have the custody of the relic, which involves the power of exhibiting it, and of thus bringing together as they please large masses of people, being those most under their own influence, under circumstances which render them most susceptible of mischievous influences" (Boake 1854, 62).

The Reverend Stephen, who is not used to having his views contested within the Colonial Office, writes his own memorandum to Gladstone. He vehemently challenges Rogers's conclusion, insisting once again that "no Christian King" can have any obligation to be the guardian "of all the crimes and pollutions practiced in the Kandian country in the name of Religion" (De Silva 1965a, 94). Nonetheless, he agrees that Governor Campbell's proposed ordinance should be turned down. For him, the Buddhists should not be given any kind of structure to govern themselves but should just be cast loose (De Silva 1965a, 95–96).

Faced with these dual recommendations, Gladstone basically follows Rogers's advice. He decides that the proposed ordinance should be rejected, but that the British government still has a moral obligation to provide some organizational structure for Buddhism. Accordingly, in July 1846, he tells Campbell to produce a new ordinance, but one which finds a solution by which the dissociation of the government with Buddhism is "neither harmful nor beneficial" to the Buddhists (De Silva 1965a, 97).

Earl Grey and the Resurgence of Missionary Influence

Soon after Gladstone sends off this new directive, three things happen: Gladstone is replaced at the Colonial Office by Henry Grey (or the third Earl Grey, as he was known); Campbell is replaced as governor in Ceylon by George Byng, aka the 7th Viscount Torrington; and the policy tack undertaken by Gladstone and Rogers is more or less abandoned. Earl Grey is basically in agreement with James Stephen and the missionaries; he too feels that no treaty (by this he means the Kandyan Convention) can bind the British government "to take an active part in maintaining and encouraging the abominable superstition called the Buddhist religion" (De Silva 1965a, 98). In other words, the pendulum, which had gone one way with Gladstone and Rogers, now swings all the way back to the opposite extreme. Earl Grey ignores Rogers and asks Stephen to draft a new set of instructions for Torrington, which he then adopts verbatim as his own dispatch.

This document represents what K. M. De Silva has called "the highwater mark of missionary influence on Colonial Office policy on Buddhism in Ceylon" (De Silva 1965a, 99). In it, Grey asks Torrington to "separate the British Government from all active participation in practices at once idolatrous and immoral"—something he says is "a plain and simple though most urgent duty." He recognizes that doing this may bring dangers to those who live in Ceylon (dangers in the form of rebellion), but that those dangers must be faced (CO 54/234, dispatch no. 2).

Torrington has misgivings about this and expresses them privately to Grey, but he proceeds forthwith to enact his orders. With regard to the tooth relic, he travels to Kandy in August 1847 and successfully sets up a new administrative structure for its governance. As he puts it in a confidential letter to Grey, "I returned from Kandy on the 12th and look back with some satisfaction to my labours in that district, as I believe I have brought to a conclusion (in obedience to your directions) the Buddhist question which has so long been in agitation—and I have arranged to give up the Tooth and Jewels the 1st of October" (De Silva 1965b, 45). What he forces the Kandyans to accept (actually on the second of October) is the consigning of all administrative responsibilities for the Temple of the Tooth and its relic to a Committee of Three, consisting of two monks (in effect, the abbots of the Malwatta and Asgiriya Monasteries), and one lay chief (in effect, the Diyawadana Nilame of the Temple) (CO 54/229, dispatch no. 134). Despite his self-congratulatory tone, Torrington himself is worried about this solution in the long term. As he puts it to Earl Grey: "Your dispatch of April 1847 direct[ed] me to deliver over the relic—but it [was] by no means clear who ought to receive it. I have given it over to the Priests and a lay Chief, but suppose one of these parties die, who succeeds to his rights?" (see De Silva 1965b, 56).

Moreover, the Kandyans, especially the bhikkhus, are not happy. There are worries that handing over the temple will cause civil unrest, because the people believe that the establishment of Buddhism in the country depends on the civil government having custody of the tooth relic. As one bhikkhu put it: "The Queen [Victoria] is the head of our religion, and that [is as] we wish it to be: that is what you promised and what you are bound to do" (De Silva 1965a, 103–104).

The Committee of Three's responsibility is limited to the Dalada Maligawa and the relic and is not involved in the matter of temple lands and appointments. Even so, Torrington has worries about the potential powers of the committee. Again, as he states in a confidential letter to Earl Grey:

> Mr. Peggs was the gentleman who first started this question of the tooth with Lord Stanley. I think it was unfortunate; my deliberate opinion is that our interference, such as it was, with Buddhism, was tending to its gradual decay and suppression whereas now, the tooth will be exhibited, masses of people will be collected together by its supposed sanctity, and the Religion of Budhoo will be thoroughly revived and rejuvenated by the instrumentality of this Tooth which we carefully locked up. (De Silva 1965b, 46)

The Matale Rebellion of 1848 and the Repossession of the Relic

Torrington's solution for the tooth—the governing Committee of Three—was in effect for less than one year when the so-called "insurrection" of 1848 (also known as the Matale Rebellion) breaks out in Ceylon. It is possible to list several reasons for the rebellion: the British dispossession of peasants from their lands, the development of coffee plantations, the importation of labor from South India, increased taxation of the people, and so on (see De Silva 1981, 277–281). Torrington, however, believes the chief cause to have been the changes in the government's policy toward Buddhism over the previous few decades.

The 1848 insurrection has at least one feature in common with that of 1817–1818. Its charismatic leader, Gongalegoda Banda, claiming to be a grandson of Kīrti Śrī Rājasinha (De Silva 1973a, 30n29), has himself anointed as king. The coronation of this "Pretender" is carried out by the chief monk at the Dambulla Monastery, just north of Kandy. Gongalegoda then assembles a peasant army and sets out to fight the colonizers (Wima-laratne n.d.). Though his forces present a much less serious threat than did those of the rebellion of 1817–1818, the British, fearing a repeat of the events of thirty years prior, overreact to the insurrection. Torrington declares martial law and adopts harsh repressive measures. At one point, the government even arrests and executes a Buddhist monk in his robes for treason (De Silva 1965a, 26–27).[15]

Remembering that in 1818, the rebels had actually stolen the tooth relic from the Temple,[16] Torrington orders C. R. Buller, who is still the government agent in the Central Province, to retake custody of the tooth, thus putting an end to the authority of the carefully crafted Committee of Three. At this time, the Fifteenth Regiment enters the Temple of the Tooth by force and retakes custody of the tooth (Sullivan 1854, 70).[17]

The rebellion is quickly put down, but it has lasting effects on the British dealings with Buddhism, which, though still officially a policy of dissociation, becomes more hands-on and less strict than the one envisioned and advocated by the missionaries.[18] Torrington tells Earl Grey that the present Buddhist policy is not working—that temples are now without legally recognized leaders or have their leadership contested by different claimants. And there is widespread feeling among the chiefs that the British are trying to destroy Buddhism. "Unless we hold some moral control over the Chiefs and Priests," he declares, "unless they have some advantage by supporting the Government, we shall always be liable to Treason and Rebellion" (De Silva 1965b, 107). In time, Torrington goes so far as to recommend that "[we] retrace our way altogether, undo all that has been done since 1840 and revert to the old state of things" (De Silva 1965a, 114). Earl Grey and the Colonial Office are not willing to go that route, but they are now more inclined to adapt a middle path, and especially to accept the need for legal guarantees of temple property (De Silva 1965a, 115).

15. See also Sullivan (1854, 54), who seeks to justify Torrington's action.

16. There were reports that Gongalegoda had been seen casing out the Dalada Maligawa just prior to the 1848 rebellion (see Wimalaratne n.d.).

17. They also take back the drums that had been captured from the regiment in the rebellion of 1818—something that excites the troops even more.

18. This may also have been due in part to the Reverend James Stephen's retirement from the Colonial Office in 1847. J. Emerson Tennent (1849) bemoans the fact that they could have cut off ties with the Buddhists as they were planning, except for the events of 1848.

The Tooth's Status "Resolved"

The matter is forcibly delayed, however, when Torrington is replaced as governor of Ceylon by Sir George Anderson. Anderson's approach may perhaps be characterized as "less deliberation, less consultation, and more action." Quickly realizing that the main problem is that Buddhism in Ceylon lacks any central organization of its own—that, if not a king, it needs a state to structure itself—he simply tells his government agents to resume making appointments of monks and *basnayake nilames* in the monasteries and *devales* of the Kandyan provinces (De Silva 1965a, 117). This causes an uproar among the missionaries in Sri Lanka, but Anderson basically ignores them or criticizes them by pointing out that all the government is doing is to treat Buddhism with an attitude of tolerance, adding a sharp barb: "we must ever recollect that offensive and abusive attacks on a religion by an opposing but dominant party is not toleration but persecution" (De Silva 1965a, 118). The missionaries are not to be ignored or put down, however, and a real antagonism develops between them and the governor.

Eventually, a compromise of sorts is reached by the new secretary for war and the colonies, Sir John Pakington, who replaces Earl Grey in February 1852. Pakington instructs Anderson to publish a declaration that the assurances with regard to Buddhism made in 1815 and 1818 are still guaranteed by the government, which will not be influenced in this matter by other parts of the community (i.e., the missionaries) (De Silva 1965a, 126–127). On the other hand, the British custody of the Temple of the Tooth, reestablished by Torrington in 1848, is to be ended, and the relic is to be handed over once again to the same Committee of Three it had had in 1847, with a warning, however, that the government will not hesitate to retake possession of the relic should it be used for anything other than religious purposes. This, on the whole, pleases the missionaries. Conversely, the annual grant of money to the temple, stopped in 1847, is to be restored once more, as a palliative to the Buddhists (De Silva 1965a, 127, 129).

Governor Anderson moves fast in carrying out all these decisions. On May 20, 1853, he hands over control of the tooth to the Buddhist committee, along with its associated jewels that are estimated to have a value of 60,000 pounds. At the same time, he issues "certificates of recognition" (rather than "official appointments") to the new Mahānāyaka of the Asgiriya Monastery, to the new Diyawadana Nilame of the Temple of the Tooth, and to the new Basnāyaka Nilame of the Kataragama Devale in Kandy, who have all been chosen by newly formed electoral colleges. He then reports these actions the following month to the Duke of Newcastle (who has replaced

Pakington in the Colonial Office), presenting them pretty much as a fait ac-
compli. Newcastle basically accepts all of this with only minor objections,
pronouncing it to be "a good compromise between the demands of the Buddhists and the Christians" (De Silva 1965a, 132–134).

Back in Ceylon, however, the Christian missionaries do not think it is
so good. When they realize what Anderson has done, they object that he
has overstepped his authority in carrying out Pakington's directives. They
petition the Queen to voice their complaint, but the Foreign Office is in
no mood to reopen the matter, and the compromise reached by Pakington
and Anderson basically lasts unchanged until the Buddhist Temporalities
Act of 1931.

Discussion

It is clear from the saga recounted in this chapter that the British had, among
themselves, strong disagreements about the matter of custody of the tooth
and its temple. On the one hand, there were the missionaries and those
who were sympathetic to them who became fixated on the belief that *any*
involvement of the government with the tooth was somehow a violation
of the Christian faith and a promotion of an untrue religion, and so was
unacceptable. For them, the tooth was a symbol of heathenism. They were
joined in this by various government officials in London (and in Colombo)
who agreed with them either for religious reasons or out of a budding belief
in the strict separation of Church and State. On the other hand, there were
civil servants in Ceylon who were in full or partial understanding of the
complexities of the situation, and who were left with the task of actually
dealing with the Buddhists—not only with regard to the tooth relic, but
also concerning the matter of ecclesiastical appointments and temple lands.
They tended to be acutely aware of the moral and/or legal commitments
made by the British in the Kandyan Convention and to a lesser extent in the
Proclamation of 1818. They were less concerned with religious matters than
with political, economic, and administrative issues. They recognized that,
given its history, and given factionalism in the sangha, monks could not
really be the possessors of the tooth without the backing of political power.

Essentially, the problem came down to a debate between two parties
that were not able to see both of the social loops that Tambiah specifies
as operating around a charismatic object such as the Dalada. Another way
to put this is that they were unable to see the relic, in the words of Victor
Goloubew (1932, 460), as being at once "Dalada-roi" [Dalada-King] and
"la très sainte Dalada" [the very holy Dalada]. In other words, there was a

division between those British who could only think of the "tooth as Buddha" (which was only slightly better, in their minds, than the "tooth as a
god"), and those who primarily saw the "tooth as king." As we know, however, the tooth was both Buddha and king.

The zigzag course between these two positions was prolonged, and a
resolution between them delayed, by several factors. First there were the
changes in leadership in the governmental hierarchy both in England and
in Ceylon. Over a period of fifteen years, from 1838 to 1853, the "Buddhism
Question" and the matter of what to do with the tooth relic were reviewed
by no less than six secretaries of state for war and the colonies (Russell,
Stanley, Gladstone, Grey, Pakington, and Newcastle) in London, and four
governors in Colombo (Mackenzie, Campbell, Torrington, and Anderson).
Second, the great distance between Colombo and London, and the fact that
it took at least four months to get an answer to any reports, proposals, or
dispatches, meant that it necessitated a great deal of time for ideas to be exchanged, orders to be issued, actions to be taken. Third, the men ultimately
in charge of the Buddhist policy in the British government, succeeding one
another in the Colonial Office, often had radically different views of what
that policy should be.[19] Even more importantly, they held radically different
views about how hands-on they should be in guiding the implementation
of their policies in the colony. This sometimes gave the governor in Colombo considerable leeway in the actions he decided to take.

Interestingly, there was one point on which both missionaries and their
opponents agreed: the (in the end, mistaken) conviction that Buddhism, in
Ceylon, was on its way out and would gradually fade away and cease being
practiced. They disagreed, however, on the means by which this would take
place, the missionaries asserting that it was government "support" for Buddhism that kept it alive; the civil servants thinking that such support and
control was precisely what was keeping Buddhism in check and preventing
a religious resurgence that might come with a newly found "independence."

This is important, for it is sometimes thought that a primary concern of
those British who felt disinclined to turn over to the Kandyans full responsibility for the tooth relic and its temple was their felt need not to betray the
bhikkhus and the chiefs—to honor the commitment the government had
made (in the Kandyan Convention of 1815 and elsewhere) to support and
protect the Buddhist religion, its "rites, ministers, and places of worship." In
fact, they appear to have been just as concerned not to give the Buddhists an

19. This does not appear to be related to their political affiliations: Russell and Grey were
Whigs; Stanley, Gladstone, and Pakington, Conservatives.

institutional structure whereby they could organize themselves and become a potent political force. The memory of the insurrection of 1817–1818, in which the rebels had stolen the tooth and rallied around it, was never far from their minds. In the end, they chose to dissociate themselves from Buddhism, but in doing so, to split up the responsibilities and authorities they had inherited from the Kandyan kings, by creating a number of circumscribed administrative structures where there had been one. In the case of the relic, this was the Committee of Three, whose domain of authority was limited to affairs of the Temple of the Tooth and its lands.

ELEVEN

Showings of the Tooth: The Story of the King of Siam's Visit (1897)

I will always remember the kind people of Kandy, [but I] will never remember the Dalada Maligawa.

—King Chulalongkorn of Siam, April 22, 1897, upon his departure from Kandy (*Overland Ceylon Observer* 1897a, 96)

The . . . colonial government feared that mis-managed devotion towards [the tooth] threatened colonial security.

—Anne Blackburn (2014, 374)

Though the Pakington–Anderson resolution returned the tooth to the custody of the Kandyan Committee of Three, the British were still rulers of Ceylon. In the eyes of some, this meant that they (or, more specifically, their ruling monarch) were still owners of the tooth. As one Buddhist leader put it in 1897, the relic "was Crown property and not the property of the Sangha." His contemporary, a Kandyan chief, echoed the sentiment. In his view, the relic remained the "personal property" of Queen Victoria, even though, he thought, she was not fulfilling her Buddhist responsibilities as owner (*Overland Times of Ceylon* 1897b, 701). Yet, though both of these politically loaded statements were perhaps theoretically true, practically speaking, they had no relevance in the day-to-day activities at the Temple of the Tooth, which were controlled by the Diyawadana Nilame and the other members of the Committee of Three.

Nevertheless, the British colonial government did feel entitled to request (as well as to veto—though to my knowledge this never happened) public exhibitions and special private showings of the relic, especially in the case of British and foreign dignitaries. In this chapter, I will examine the case of the visit of King Chulalongkorn of Siam in 1897. In chapter 12 below, I will look at that of Queen Elizabeth II in 1954. Together, these two stories will give us an idea of the situation of the tooth from a British perspective, in the late nineteenth and mid-twentieth centuries.

Despite the official dissociation of the colonial government from the tooth relic in 1853, the government agent in Kandy retained one of the keys to the shrine room (even though this symbolic assertion of control was something the missionaries had objected to from Hardy's time on). In effect, this meant that he shared responsibility for the tooth at the time of its public exhibitions or private showings with its official custodians. Leonard Woolf,[1] who was the government agent's office assistant in Kandy for a year, in 1907–1908, describes the situation as follows:

> In my day . . . the Tooth could never be taken out or shown without the consent of both the Manager or Guardian of the Temple, the Diyawadana Nilame (a fine old Kandyan chief called Nugawela) and the Government Agent. In fact, both the G.A. and the Diwa Nilame, as he was usually called, had a key to the shrine, and without the two being present the door could not be unlocked. In practice I, as O.A., kept the G.A.'s key, and arranged with Nugawela Ratemahatmaya for unlocking the door if and when the Tooth was to be shown. (Woolf 1961, 142–143, slightly altered)

Woolf (1961, 143) goes on to say that during his year in Kandy, he opened the shrine only three times: once for the Perahera; once, at his request, for the Empress Eugénie;[2] and once, at the Diyawadana Nilame's request, for Reginald Farrer, the Himalayan botanist, who had become a Buddhist."[3]

---

1. Leonard Woolf (1880–1969), who later married the writer Virginia Stephen (Woolf), was in Ceylon from 1904 to 1911. He was stationed in Jaffna, Hambantota, and Kandy. He is best known, perhaps, for his wonderfully evocative novel of Sri Lankan life, *The Village in the Jungle* (1913).

2. Eugénie (1826–1920), aka Eugénia María de Montijo de Guzmán, was the eighty-one-year-old widow of Napoleon III, who, together with then Governor Hugh Clifford, viewed the relic with Woolf in 1908 (see Woolf 1961, 139–142; and Woolf 1989, 136–137).

3. Reginald Farrer (1880–1920) was an English botanist, best known as a plant collector who brought back hundreds of flowers from his travels in Asia (especially Japan and China), and who single-handedly was responsible for popularizing rock gardening in the United Kingdom (see Shulman 2004). In 1907, in Ceylon, he met Hikkaḍuwe Sumangala (1827–1911), the multilingual abbot of Adam's Peak, and was moved by him to become a Buddhist layman. Armed with a letter of introduction from Hikkaḍuwe, he then visited Kandy and viewed the tooth relic together with a Japanese prince (one of Emperor Meiji's sons) who happened to be there at the same time.

The showing of the relic itself, removed from its nested dagobas, was thus a somewhat special occasion. As William Gregory, governor of Ceylon from 1872 to 1877, put it, "[the tooth] is . . . shown to the multitude [enclosed in its karandua, e.g., at the time of the Perahera] once or twice a year, but on other occasions no one, unless of princely station, or a representative of royalty, such as governors or ambassadors, are permitted to behold it" (Gregory 1894, 281).

This is only partially correct. In addition, according to news reports, foreign Buddhist pilgrims were also sometimes given the privilege of seeing the relic by the temple authorities (with the agreement of the British). Thus, for instance, in 1909, the year immediately following Woolf's tenure in Kandy, the tooth was shown to two Siamese Buddhist monks, one wealthy Burmese layman, and two wealthy Chinese, all from Penang, and to Professor Satis Chandra Vidyabhusana of Calcutta.[4] Moreover, in order to grant opportunities to make merit, as well as to raise money, the tooth was very occasionally exhibited to the general public for several days running, outside its shrine room in the Temple of the Tooth.[5]

The Ritual Undressing of the Relic

In private viewings, the full showing of the relic involves the gradual removal of all of its jewels and nested reliquaries, before the bare tooth itself is exhibited atop its golden wire-stand (see fig. 11.1). The whole process is a ritual event that takes about forty minutes (see Trumbull 1950, 3).[6] Foreign viewers in the nineteenth century had mixed reactions to it. The aforementioned Governor Gregory (1894, 281–282), for instance, did not much enjoy the experience:

> We were led upstairs to a very small room on the upper floor, full of yellow-robed priests. The heat was terrible, and the odour of cocoanut oil and many perspiring human beings was detestable. In a portion of the room inside a

4. See *Straits Times* (Singapore) 1909, 11; *Ceylon Independent* (Colombo) 1909a, 9; and *Ceylon Independent* (Colombo) 1909b, 1. I would like to thank Steven Kemper for copies of these newspaper accounts.

5. For an eyewitness account, see Cumming 1892, 1: 291–293.

6. Sometimes, instead of an actual showing of the tooth, important visitors were merely let inside the inner sanctum of the temple to view the outermost dagoba enclosing the relic. (See, for example, Heber 1829, 180; Zaleski 1891, 86–87; and Haeckel 1911, 146.) On other occasions, in order to save time, the relic was taken out of its innermost reliquary ahead of time, and then visitors were let in to view it.

Figure 11.1. The tooth exposed for viewing. From Cumming 1892, 1: 293.

glass case was a profusion of jewels, chiefly rubies, and, so far as I could judge, very bad ones. A huge silver-gilt dagoba contained minor dagobas, it is said of pure gold, and within the last was the relic, which appeared to me like a crocodile's tooth. It was on a stand supported by a narrow gold band, so the whole of it was to be seen. . . . We were heartily glad to get out of the heat and smell, and walked for a cup of tea to the "old palace" which is quite close.[7]

A more sympathetic account of the ceremony may be found in Reginald Farrer's autobiography, and it is worth recalling here since it may give us some idea of the details of the event witnessed by King Chulalongkorn of Siam, just ten years earlier. Step by step, Farrer describes the removal of the reliquaries and the jewels that adorn them. First, the abbot of the Malwatta Monastery unlocks the shrine room, after receiving the key from the Diyawadana Nilame, in the presence of Leonard Woolf representing the government agent. Gradually, Farrer perceives in the dim interior a gold and silver gilt dagoba covered with wreathes and strings of jewels (see fig. 11.2).

7. Nonetheless, Gregory made a presentation to the temple of two ornate lamps. They were topped by brazen canopies in the shape of a dagoba and placed outside the entrance. See White 1919, 176; and Skeen 1903, 20.

Figure 11.2. The jewel-covered outermost reliquary in 2011. Photo courtesy Igor Grunin.

These are removed one by one by two monks: "ropes, chains, pendants, manacles of gold and emerald, flat heavy plaques and ouches and frontlets of crowded ruby, shapes of fantastic bird and holy symbol wrought very long ago in a mosaic of emerald and pearl . . . the priceless treasures of old Kandyan Kings, the priceless votive offerings of days forgotten." Each treasure is handed to the abbot, who "pauses to hold [each one] for our view that we may note the piety of old dead days" (Farrer 1908, 74). Then this outermost dagoba is unlocked by one of the monks and swung open to reveal a smaller karandua of pure gold, and more gems and jewels are removed from the interstices between the reliquaries since they do not fit together tightly: "armlets and crowns of special sanctity or value; and then, reverently raised and handed round for inspection, the famous seated figure of the Lord Buddha, carved from one solid emerald." When the last dagoba ("a spiry pinnacle so close set with rubies as to seem one solid jewel") is lifted off, there is "a minute thing like a tiny thumbstall of rubies. It is the covering of the very relic. . . . The Abbot is in ecstasy. An eager, fumbling movement, so emotional as to fail at first of its purpose, and the Holy Thing is revealed." The relic is then placed through the ring at the end of the gold wire emerging from a golden lotus; this holds it from closer viewing (Farrer 1908, 75–76).[8]

It is clear from these snippets of Farrer's longer and more detailed account that the jewels are as much a part of the show as the relic itself. They are, in fact, objectifications of the story of the tooth, and as such, they serve to define it as a relic. As Patrick Geary (1990, 5), Robert Sharf (1999, 81), and others have pointed out, a "bare bone" carries no fixed meaning; it is the reliquaries (and the stories) that frame it and give it significance.[9] We can better understand now the insistence of the Kandyans in 1815 that before the tooth could be returned to its temple, the jewels also had to be brought back.

The "meaning" of the relic itself, of course, may vary from person to person, as we shall see in the case of King Chulalongkorn. Interestingly, when Farrer gets to see the "bare tooth," his flowery flight of prose brought on by the jewels more or less stops and he describes the object rather precisely, as a scientist might, as "a small morsel of bone, in shape and size and outline like the two top joints of a man's little finger." He rather thinks it to be "the polished tush of a boar." But this makes no difference to him; as a "modern Buddhist," he understands that the tooth is a symbol of the Buddha; as such, introduced by the unveiling of its jewels, it affectively still embodies for him the holiness and venerability of the Blessed One (Farrer 1908, 77–80).

<hr />

8. Farrer does not describe the eventual closing ritual of "re-robing" the relic in its jewels and karanduas, but for an account of that, see Cumming 1892, 1: 294–295.

9. See also Hahn 2010; Rienjang 2017, 146; and Strong forthcoming b.

The Visit of the King of Siam

With this in mind, I want to turn now to the main topic of this chapter: the story of King Chulalongkorn of Siam's viewing of the Kandyan tooth in 1897, and his reactions to it. In the spring of that year, Chulalongkorn (aka Rama V), on his way to Europe to attend the Diamond Jubilee celebrations marking the sixtieth anniversary of Queen Victoria's coronation, stops for three days in Ceylon. One of his primary goals while there is to see the tooth relic, which, with the permission of the British and the go-ahead of the temple's hierarchs, is to be privately exhibited for him.

When his special train arrives in Kandy on April 21, he is met at the station by a group of British dignitaries headed by Joseph Ridgeway, the then governor of Ceylon. Together, they proceed to the Queen's Hotel, where His Majesty is to stay, across the square from the Temple of the Tooth. The visit to the Dalada Maligawa takes place that very same afternoon, but it ends abruptly when Chulalongkorn asks for but is refused permission to actually handle the relic; he storms out of the temple in anger and returns to his hotel.

The incident has been discussed by a number of scholars.[10] It is perhaps best, however, to begin with an account of it that was published the very next day in the *Overland Ceylon Observer*, a local English-language newspaper.[11] It starts by describing the decorations and preparations outside the temple: the strip of cloth of various colors for His Majesty to walk on; the large canopy just outside the entrance under which he stands while the *Jaya-mangala Gāthā*[12] is recited; the crowd of nearly five hundred monks assembled for the occasion; the welcoming address, in Pali, by the Mahānāyaka of the Malwatta Monastery; the king's reply in English; the display of the royal offerings he has brought for the tooth;[13] and the gifts presented to him on behalf of the Siyam Nikāya.[14] Then it turns to the incident:

> The King began his *puja*, but before many minutes passed a small hitch . . . was freely whispered by the large number assembled. The king it appeared was shewn

10. See Kemper 2017 and 2019; Blackburn 2010, 165–186; Peleggi 2002, 38–39. See also Kemper 2015, 97.

11. Much the same account was published in a Sinhala newspaper, the *Sasrasavi Sandarāsa*. See Blackburn 2010, 181n49.

12. A popular *paritta* (protection) text consisting of nine stanzas extolling the victories of the Buddha over various opponents and wishing for prosperity and good fortune.

13. Fifty silk robes for monks, three hundred candles, a large quantity of incense, a silver and a gold tray, and two tree-shaped ornaments, one of which is of silver and the other of gold.

14. A small shrine containing some relics and two ornate palm-leaf manuscripts.

the Tooth Relic when he expressed a wish to touch it. This was refused, [and thereupon] the King decided to leave the temple immediately and in doing so was heard to say he was very disgusted at all that took place. His Majesty and party returned to the Queen's [Hotel] and gave instructions to his attendants to return to the temple authorities the articles presented to him, and also get back what offerings he had brought to the temple. (*Overland Ceylon Observer* 1897a, 96)

The article then goes on to describe the efforts made by the government agent, Allanson Bailey, to remedy the situation: together with a few other prominent persons, he goes to the Queen's to try to explain to the king why his request to touch the tooth was refused, but to no avail. Later that evening, Chulalongkorn refuses to view the *perehera* that had been specially planned for him, even as the tooth on elephant back processes right by the veranda of the Queen's; instead, he stays inside at the dinner table with members of his party and his hosts, listening to music by the Volunteer and Public Band of Kandy (*Overland Ceylon Observer* 1897a, 96).

Chulalongkorn's special train is scheduled to leave the following morning for Colombo. At the station, before entraining, he formally expresses his thanks for the reception given him but adds that while he will "always remember the kind people of Kandy," he will "never remember the Dalada Maligawa." He then gets aboard and steams off. As he leaves, Bailey, the government agent, calls for "Three Cheers" to be shouted. A few persons, more or less in shock, respond, but it is hardly what might be called a spontaneous eruption of enthusiasm (*Overland Ceylon Observer* 1897a, 96).

The visit of King Chulalongkorn to Ceylon was an official one by a foreign sovereign and, accordingly, the British colonial authorities were ultimately responsible for all the arrangements made for it (Peleggi 2002, 38). Indeed, as we have just seen, both the governor of Ceylon and the government agent, as well as the district judge in Kandy, acted as hosts to the king. Interestingly, however, in the aftermath of his visit, they appear not to have been very worked up about the snafu at the temple; perhaps they just wanted to downplay the incident or cover it up, as the tone of the report in the *Overland Ceylon Observer* suggests.

Others, however, were more openly concerned: a certain group of Buddhist leaders in Colombo, including a prominent voice in the Buddhist reform movement, Colonel Henry Steel Olcott,[15] take it upon themselves in

---

15. Colonel Olcott (1832–1907) was an American who served in the Union Army during the Civil War, was subsequently promoted to colonel, and worked first for the navy and then as a lawyer in New York City. After meeting Helena Blavatsky, he became co-founder of the

the next few days to send an investigatory committee to Kandy to determine exactly what happened at the temple. The committee consists of Olcott, D. B. Perera, and Don Carolis Hevavitarana,[16] and they spend April 26–27 in Kandy interviewing various persons. Olcott then writes up their report and presents it to a Buddhist gathering at Ananda College in Colombo a few days later.

He begins his report with an important clarification. Usually, he explains, four people have authority over exhibiting the tooth relic—the British government agent, the two high priests of the Malwatta and Asgiriya Monasteries, and the Diyawadana Nilame. In this particular case, however, because the Diyawadana Nilame had recently passed away, his post was vacant. Therefore, monastic leaders had preliminarily decided that for the visit of King Chulalongkorn, the Diyawadana Nilame would be replaced by a group of three Kandyan chiefs specially appointed as temple trustees for the occasion: W. A. Dullewe Adikar, C. B. Nugawela, and T. B. Panabokke. The latter, in addition, would act as translator (from Sinhala to English and back), since the monks did not understand English, though Chulalongkorn did and spoke it well (*Overland Times of Ceylon* 1897b, 701).

All of these people agree to talk to Olcott's committee, except for Panabokke, who refuses to answer questions in person. Instead, he writes a letter summarizing his assessment of what happened, while claiming at the same time that his role was merely that of being an interpreter. There was no intention, he states, of insulting the king; he merely told him in a very respectful manner that it was not the custom for anyone to handle the tooth. When he had done so, the king became exasperated and left (*Overland Times of Ceylon* 1897b, 701).

What Panabokke does not reveal here, but what comes out in the rest of the inquiry, is that he never communicated the king's request to touch the relic to the monastic leaders present but took it upon himself to immediately answer it in the negative without translating it. Indeed, when the Malwatta elder is interviewed by Olcott's committee, he declares that because he did not understand English, he did not realize what was happening. Had Chulalongkorn's request been made known to him, he would, of course, have granted it! After all, the previous year, the king's own brother, Prince

---

Theosophical Society. He arrived in Ceylon in 1880, where he formally became a Buddhist and quickly established himself as a leading figure in the movement to revive and reform Buddhism. See Prothero 1996.

16. Don Carolis Hevavitarana (1833–1906) was an early leader of the Buddhist Revival, and the father of Anagarika Dharmapala (on whom see Kemper 2015).

Bhanurangsi, had visited the temple and had been allowed to handle the relic. Moreover, when the chief monks of the Asgiriya and Malwatta monasteries had gotten together a month earlier to discuss the king's prospective visit, they had agreed that, given Chulalongkorn's status as a Buddhist sovereign, he should be allowed to handle the relic casket if he wished. All of this is then confirmed by the testimony of the Asgiriya Mahānāyaka (*Overland Times of Ceylon* 1897b, 701).

The Olcott committee also interviews the two English officials who were present in the temple for the occasion. The first, the government agent Bailey, is of no help; he claims to have not been in the shrine room per se at the time of the misunderstanding, and so had not heard the conversation in question. The second, District Judge H. H. Cameron, however, had been there and had heard everything. He says he was surprised by what Panabokke had said and later asked him why he had refused the king's request to handle the relic. Panabokke, already apparently prevaricating, answered that he was only interpreting the wishes of the high priest (*Overland Times of Ceylon* 1897b, 701).

Olcott's committee then talks to the two other Kandyan chiefs, who, along with Panabokke, were acting as fill-in lay trustees for the temple. Dullewe Adikar has little to add about the incident (he too had not been present in the shrine room at the time), but he gives his opinion that there was no reason why the king should not have been able to touch the tooth, since, back in 1828, then Governor Barnes had with his own hands carried the relic from the temple to the esplanade where it was to be publicly displayed. In addition, he had heard rumors that various persons, including European ladies, had touched the relic.[17] The other trustee, however, C. B. Nugawela, reveals that he *was* in the shrine room and had heard the conversation. According to him, when Panabokke told the king, without consulting anyone, that it was against custom for people to touch the relic, His Majesty had asked, "Can nobody touch it?" Panabokke replied that the priests could touch it, to which Chulalongkorn said: "Then, if they can touch it, why can't I? You insult me!" The king then picked up a book lying on the table and said he would like to take it with him so he could have a copy made. Panabokke asked, "How long will you take it for?" To which the king, according to Nugawela, retorted that he was not going to steal it! "He then stood for a moment looking at the [relic] casket and the emerald

---

17. Could this rumor have formed around Constance Gordon Cumming, whose actions in the temple caused quite a stir, and whose book and sketch of the relic had been published five years earlier (see Cumming 1892)?

image of the Buddha, after which he said 'I shall make no offerings.' As he was going out, he added 'my brother and subject was allowed to touch the relic, but I am not; this is an act of disrespect to me'" (*Overland Times of Ceylon* 1897b, 701).

Weighing all that they had learned from these various testimonies, Olcott's committee concludes, in no uncertain terms, that Panabokke was solely to blame for the incident, and they urge the assembled Buddhists who have just heard their report to censure him—which they do (*Overland Times of Ceylon* 1897b, 700–701).

In its report, Olcott's committee is mute on the question of Panabokke's motives for what he did. The simplest explanation would probably be that he, not being a real Diyawadana Nilame, did not have full knowledge about tooth relic etiquettes and traditions, and so mistakenly assumed that only the high priests could touch it. In fact, temple policy on this matter seems not to have been altogether consistent and was, apparently, often settled on an ad hoc basis. A decade later, an Imperial Japanese prince, visiting at the same time as Reginald Farrer, was *not* allowed to touch the relic.[18] Moreover, twenty-five years earlier, Constance Gordon Cumming (1892, 1: 295) was given to understand that "no human hand might touch the sacred ivory" and observed that the monks themselves handled the relic with a cloth so as to avoid direct contact with it. And as far back as 1821, the generally well-informed Davy (1821, 368) declared that "none but the priests may touch [the relic]." Panabokke thus was perhaps understandably confused. Yet rather than inquire of the monastic elders (for whom he was supposed to be translating) or talk to his fellow trustees, he took it upon himself to assert his own opinion to the king.

Chulalongkorn's reaction to the perceived insult is also understandable. Aware that his brother (and others) had previously been allowed to touch the relic, and conscious of his role as a great royal patron of Buddhism, he naturally thought it was his prerogative to do so and must have wondered whether he was being deliberately slighted (see Kemper 2017).

Western explanations of his attitude, however, have tended to revolve around two views. On the one hand, there are some who blame the Siamese king, mockingly portraying him as acting like a spoiled child—an absolute monarch unused to being told "no." For example, Jules Leclercq (1900, 61),

---

18. Farrer (1908, 76–77) is explicit about this: "In an instant, [the tooth is] fitted through the ring of its Monstrance, and the whole is handed towards the Prince for him to view. Curious, he bends over it, as a man inspecting something interesting in a museum; a gesture forbids him to touch it."

a Belgian magistrate who spent some time in Ceylon, recounts the incident, embellishing it as follows:

> [Chulalongkorn], not satisfied with just seeing [the relic], wanted also to manipulate it (*la tâter*). Upon the refusal of the High Priest, the royal visitor put on a peevish public display of anger. He stomped his feet, he ground his teeth, he tore his hair, he cried his eyes out, and very nearly fainted. He who, in Siam, would have chopped off several heads for such a transgression, could do nothing but take back the rich presents he had had unpacked and leave the temple without looking at anyone.

Others, however, see the king's actions as motivated by his rationalism— his interest in "scientifically" testing the genuineness of the relic. Chulalongkorn's relationship to modernization and Westernization was a complex one, but he was by no means an unenthusiastic advocate of both. Moreover he, and his father before him, had done much to try to reform Siamese Buddhist practices by, among other things, divesting them of "superstitious" elements.[19] Where the veneration of relics fits into his views is not altogether clear, but that did not stop some in Ceylon from declaring that the king's "desire to handle the tooth may have been inspired by incredulity rather than by reverence" (*Overland Ceylon Observer* 1897b).

This thought may, in fact, have been influenced by some of Chulalongkorn's own explanations of his actions vis-à-vis the tooth. In recounting the incident to his half sister/wife, Queen Saowapha, whom he had appointed his regent in Siam while he was in Europe, he explained his motivations as follows: he left the temple because of the lack of courtesy and respect on the part of the monks, and also because he was not sure of the relic's authenticity (Peleggi 2002, 38). In a subsequent conversation with his Belgian adviser, Gustave Rolin-Jaequemyns,[20] Chulalongkorn expanded on this, proclaiming that in his view, the tooth in Kandy is "nothing but an alligator's tooth,"[21] and the priests at the temple "exploiters and charlatans."

19. For a short summary of Chulalongkorn's modernizing accomplishments, see Frankfurter [1911] 2013. For an interesting account of the present-day revival of his image as a great modernizer, see Stengs 2009.

20. Rolin-Jaequemyns (1835–1902) was a Belgian authority on international law and a general adviser to the Siamese government. He lived in Bangkok from 1892 until 1901 and was a frequent presence at the royal court. See Tips 1996.

21. In this, Chulalongkorn is interestingly (and perhaps not coincidentally) close to the suggestion of Leclerc (a contemporary and fellow countryman of the Belgians Jaequemyns and Jottrand) that the tooth was that of a crocodile. See Leclerc 1900, 60. See also Gregory (1894,

Wishing to expose those impostors, he pretended to have feelings of devotion and asked to see the relic up close and kiss it. The monks, however, "foreseeing the danger [that he would realize the fake nature of the relic], took an extreme stand and refused the royal request" (Jottrand 1905, 433–434; Eng. tr., Jottrand 1996, 364).[22]

It may, in fact, be the case that the Buddhist elders at the temple had concerns that this might be Chulalongkorn's intention, for they were wary of any attempt to "test" the relic's genuineness by "scientific" means. Indeed, in his testimony to Olcott's committee in Kandy, the Asgiriya Mahānāyaka recalled that when Chulalongkorn's brother, Prince Bhanurangsi, had been allowed to handle the relic, he had subsequently asked permission to weigh it and measure it. This, the abbot declared, had *not* been permitted then, and should not be allowed for anyone. There is, of course, no evidence that Chulalongkorn had any such intention, but the *mahānāyakas* were clearly on the alert for that possibility.[23]

Returning to the question of Panabokke's motivations, it is important also to focus on one of the more general contexts to this whole incident. Around the time of Chulalongkorn's visit, important developments were taking place in Ceylonese Buddhism, especially among monks and laypersons in the low country. This is not the place to examine the questions of the debates between Buddhist and Christian intellectuals on the island (see Young and Somaratna 1996), of the problem of corruption among certain sections of the sangha, or of the rise of so-called "Protestant Buddhism" (see Gombrich and Obeyesekere 1988, 202–240), but it is important to highlight one development that may help inform the story of Chulalongkorn and the tooth. As we have seen, the structure of Theravāda Buddhism is such

---

282), who thought likewise. There were many other foreigners around at the time with similar opinions, including Buddhists: as we have seen, Farrer (1908, 78–79), despite being a new convert to Buddhism, thought upon seeing it that the tooth was a boar's tusk; and Henry Steel Olcott, another Buddhist, declared it was an animal bone (see Gombrich and Obeyesekere 1988, 206; see also Kemper 2015, 82). More generally on Olcott's dismissive view of relics, the Dalada in particular, see Trainor 1997, 15.

22. Similar sentiments were earlier expressed in a Catholic pamphlet that appeared right after the king's visit (see Anonymous 1898, 77–79).

23. It should be pointed out, however, that in 1858, King Mindon of Burma (another great "modernizer") sent two monks to Kandy to examine the tooth relic in order to compare it to a tooth relic that was enshrined in Ava (and that was much longer). A public exhibition (allowed by the British) was arranged in Kandy, and the Burmese monks were able to examine the relic at their leisure prior to it being shown to the assembled crowd of devotees. The story may be found in Jacobs 1860, 129. A rather different version is recounted in Da Cunha 1875, 62–63. It is not clear whether the two monks actually measured or weighed the tooth, but their motive was to "scientifically" evaluate it.

that it needs a monarch—to support it, to reform it if need be, and to watch over it. In the wake of the British government's disengagement from that royal role (Queen Victoria did not really fit the bill), certain prominent Buddhist leaders began to float the idea of asking Chulalongkorn—as the "last remaining monarch of Southern Buddhism"—to take on the sovereign's role in monastic affairs for Ceylon and also for Burma (where the last Buddhist king had recently been deposed, also by the British), in addition to holding it for Siam. Their idea was to establish a single ecclesiastical council that would not only bring the three countries' Buddhisms together under Siamese royal sponsorship, but also promote the unity of the different sects within Ceylon. One of the leaders of this movement was Hikkaḍuwe Sumangala, a prominent leader of the sangha whom we have already encountered above as the converter of Reginald Farrer.[24] Another was Henry Steel Olcott. Also important was the Venerable Jinavaravaṃsa, whose motivations can only be described as somewhat mysterious. Popularly known in Ceylon as the "Prince Priest," his lay name was Prince Prisdang Jumsai, and he was actually a cousin of King Chulalongkorn (Loos 2016, 96). Educated in England (where he garnered top prizes at King's College in London), he then had a brilliant diplomatic career as an ambassador for Siam in Europe (Jumsai 1977). Called back to his home country, however, he soon fell out of favor with the king (for reasons that are still unclear) and went into exile in Ceylon, where he was ordained as a monk by Waskaduwe Subhuti.[25] While still just a novice, he had a meteoric rise as an influential (and, as a foreigner, somewhat suspect) member of the sangha, denouncing monastic corruption and pressing for reform (Loos 2016, 97–103). Despite his falling out with Chulalongkorn, he remained loyal to him, and sought to demonstrate that in a variety of ways. His hopes to unify all of Theravāda Buddhism under his cousin's aegis may have been one of these ways.[26]

These men decided to take advantage of Chulalongkorn's stopover in Ceylon to formally ask him to endorse their scheme. Accordingly, when the king disembarked in Colombo, he was welcomed not only by British officials, but also by crowds of Buddhists bearing banners reading "Welcome to the Protector of our Religion" (Kemper 2017). Colonel Olcott then read out (in English) a petition from "a general committee representing

24. On Hikkaḍuwe's role in the unification scheme, see Blackburn 2010, 168–177.
25. On Waskaduwe Subhuti, see Guruge 1967, ch. 2.
26. Another may have come a year later when, in 1898, he convinced the British government in India to send the relics of the Buddha recently discovered at Piprahwa (near the Nepalese border) to Chulalongkorn, as "the only reigning Buddhist monarch in the world." On this, see Strong forthcoming a.

the Buddhist Priests and laymen of Ceylon," asking the king to back their proposal to unite "the Buddhists of the three sister nations under one international Ecclesiastical Council with Your Majesty's August patronage and protection." Somewhat blindsided by this, Chulalongkorn replied that he would consider it.[27]

The proposal was eventually turned down by Chulalongkorn, in consultation with Siamese monastic leaders in Bangkok,[28] but the British colonial authorities cannot have been enthusiastic about the idea, which would have undermined their sovereignty and greatly complicated their dealings with the Ceylonese Buddhist sangha. They were thus probably secretly delighted when things went awry at the Temple of the Tooth in Kandy.

Kemper (2017), in fact, suggests that Panabokke may actually have been in league with the British colonial authorities, and was deliberately trying to sabotage an event that would have reinforced Chulalongkorn's status as a monarch for all of Theravāda. In this regard, it should be said that although Panabokke came from a distinguished Kandyan family, his "day job" was acting as a police magistrate in Matale and as a member of the local legislative council. In other words, he worked for the British and they may have felt they could trust him. Kemper recounts coming across, in his research, a small article in the *Overland Ceylon Observer* dated May 13, 1897—barely three weeks after the incident in the temple, and about one week after the condemnation of Panabokke by Olcott's committee. The piece was entitled "Mr. Panabokke's Departure from Matale." Reading the headline, Kemper (2017) at first thought that this must be an account of how, because of the mishap in the temple and Panabokke's "bungled translation," he was being dismissed from his post as a commissioner and police magistrate. That was not the case, however. Instead of being punished, Panabokke was being honored by the British colonial authorities, as a person who had given "universal satisfaction" in the performance of his duties, and whose "departure" from his post in Matale was not a reprimand but a reward: he was being sent to England as an official Ceylonese representative at Queen Victoria's Diamond Jubilee. This was enough to suggest to Kemper that Panabokke was being thanked by the British for doing their bidding when he insulted Chulalongkorn by telling him he was not allowed to handle the tooth (Kemper 2017).

27. The full text of the petition is cited in Blackburn 2010, 169–171.
28. They did so in part because they thought that since Burma and Ceylon were under the rule of Britain, such a move by them in Siam was too potentially problematic to be a good idea. See Blackburn 2010, 183–184.

The theory is intriguing and is perhaps supported by another piece of circumstantial evidence. We have seen that, according to their testimony, the Kandyan *mahānāyakas* had decided, several weeks in advance, to let Chulalongkorn touch the relic if he wanted to. A piece in the *Overland Times of Ceylon*, published the day before the Siamese monarch's arrival in Kandy, suggests they may even have gone further than this. After describing the king's activities in Colombo, the article goes on to print the "official programme" for the rest of his trip, that is, his projected time in Kandy. It tells of how, the next day, His Majesty will be welcomed at the station by the governor and others and escorted to the Queen's Hotel, where luncheon will be served. Then, at 4:00 p.m., he will proceed to the Temple of the Tooth, where he will be received by the *mahānāyakas* of the Malwatta and Asgiriya monasteries. Then, "a grand procession of the Dalada will be arranged by the native chiefs to pass before H.M. the King *who will receive the relic with his own hand and carry it to the shrine*, where H.M. will make a Buddha-puja, while the assembled priests will chant the adoration sutta" (*Overland Times of Ceylon* 1897a, 615, italics added).

As we know, this is not what happened the following day; instead, the tooth was waiting for Chulalongkorn inside the temple, and the *perahera* (snubbed by him) was not held until 8:00 p.m. It is not clear who changed the program, but it had to be done with the approval of Allanson Bailey, the British government agent, who was responsible for arranging the details of the king's visit in Kandy. In any case, the change is, of course, a significant one. Had the original program (which Chulalongkorn must have known about) been followed, the event would have been more akin to Governor Barnes's handling the relic at its exhibition in 1828, or to King Śrī Vijaya's holding it aloft to show it to the crowds at the start of Nāyakkar rule in the seventeenth century (see above, chapter 6; and Geiger 1929, 2: 250). In other words, it would have been a public assertion of a sovereign's role vis-à-vis the relic instead of a private viewing of it. To put it simply, symbolically speaking, it would have proclaimed Chulalongkorn, perhaps not as king of Sri Lanka, but as patron and protector of its Buddhism, and this, the British could not countenance.

There is, of course, no proof that Bailey changed the program with any of this in mind, and no British public admission that they schemed to demean such an important monarch as the king of Siam because of these fears. As we have seen, they welcomed Chulalongkorn as a visiting head of state, and tended to downplay the incident at the Temple of the Tooth. And Chulalongkorn, on his way to the Diamond Jubilee, gave no sign that he suspected the British of anything, and probably did not. But from the British perspective, Chulalongkorn's trip to Kandy was yet another late nineteenth-century instance of the great interest foreign Buddhist monarchs were displaying in the relic. As Blackburn (2014, 374) has put it, at this time, "there was a dramatic flow of wealth and high-status visitors from Cambodia and the Burmese court-in-exile to Kandy and her tooth relic."

From Cambodia, in 1884 and 1886, there were visits by high-ranking monks and by the queen mother of King Norodom, who had just been stripped of all power by the French. In 1889, the exiled queen of Burma went to see the tooth and made offerings to it. She was the wife of King Thibaw, who had just been deposed by the British and was now living in enforced exile in Maharashtra. In 1892, the head of the Burmese sangha arrived along with his suite of monks and lay managers (Blackburn 2010, 189–196). All of these visits were facilitated by Hikkaḍuwe Sumangala, who, as we have seen, had an interest in the unification of all Theravādins. That was enough to give the British pause. An even greater reason, perhaps, was (or should have been) that all of these royals, often accompanied by large parties of wealthy laypersons and monks from their home countries, arrived in Kandy hoping that their veneration of the relic and their meritorious offerings to it would rectify the tragic fate—the bad karma—that had beset them and their sovereigns who had just suffered defeat by British (or French) forces! (Blackburn 2010, 188–189).

In retrospect, it is perhaps a little perplexing that the British allowed these pilgrimages to Kandy. Probably their policy was governed by a combination of liberal inclinations and general respect for all monarchies (even deposed ones), but they cannot have liked these developments. As Blackburn (2014, 374) put it, "the . . . colonial government feared that mis-managed devotion towards [the tooth] threatened colonial security." Thibaw and Norodom, of course, were ex-rulers and so did not present that much of a worry, but Chulalongkorn was an actual monarch who was, moreover, being courted by Ceylonese Buddhists. The British had long feared that Ceylonese "rebels" would get hold of the tooth as they had in 1817–1818, and thereby seek to bolster their right to rule. Now, they had to fear that foreign monarchs, such as Chulalongkorn, backed by local Buddhist forces, might use the tooth in a different way to legitimize not their rule over the island but their role as patron and protector of its Buddhism. And so, they took steps to prevent that from happening.

TWELVE

Showings of the Tooth: The Story of Queen Elizabeth's Shoes (1954)

As I see it, if the Cabinet advises her to accept Sir John Kotelawala's advice [to visit the Temple of the Tooth] and she accepts it, Her Majesty will to a certain extent be doing so in order to maintain the structure of the British Commonwealth in the form it is at present.

—Michael Adeane, Private Secretary to Queen Elizabeth II, February 5, 1954 (see PREM 11/737, 44)

One of the ways in which the British sought to counter the interest of foreign rulers in the tooth relic (besides, perhaps, sabotaging the visit of Chulalongkorn) was to send their own royals to visit the tooth. Thus, starting in the nineteenth century, virtually all the members of the British royal family who visit Ceylon also view the relic, as well as a *perahera* (often specially arranged for them).[1] For them, this has become a *de rigueur* event.

For instance, in 1870, Queen Victoria's second son, Prince Alfred, the Duke of Edinburgh, arrives on the island. He spends most of his time hunting elephants and other wild animals and attending lavish parties. In between, he goes to Kandy. There, according to an eyewitness, he views a nighttime procession of elephants around Kandy Lake, complete with a fireworks display "set off from the harem-island in the lake." The next day (April 14), he goes to the Dalada Maligawa to view the relic. He is met by the Diyawadana Nilame and several monks, who conduct him to the shrine-chamber. To save time, the outer jewel-encrusted karanduas have all already been removed and set aside, "exposing the richly jewelled case of solid gold

---

1. A brief listing of all of the British royal visits to Sri Lanka may be found in Boyle 2013.

in which is held the golden lotus-flower within whose open leaves the sacred tooth reclines" (Capper 1871, 74, slightly altered).

In 1875, it is the turn of Queen Victoria's eldest son, the Prince of Wales, Albert Edward (the future Edward VII). Like his younger brother, he spends most of his time shooting elephants and banqueting, but he also goes to

Figure 12.1. The Prince of Wales views the tooth, 1875. From *The Graphic: An Illustrated Weekly Newspaper*, January 8, 1876.

Figure 12.2. Perahera: the relic leaves the temple, 2011. Photo courtesy Igor Grunin.

Kandy. After being treated to a special *perahera* (he is so delighted by some of the baby elephants participating that he asks to have one of them shipped to England), the prince is taken to the temple. He is escorted in by a yellow-robed "chief priest" (presumably the abbot of either the Malwatta or the Asgiriya Monastery) and given a chance to examine the relic closely, though it is not clear that he is allowed to touch it (Wheeler 1876). The moment is caught by an artist for *The Graphic*, an illustrated weekly newspaper (see fig. 12.1)

In 1901, the Prince of Wales's son, George, tours the island with his wife, the Duchess of Cornwall. In Kandy, various processional arches are constructed for them, by the low-country Sinhalese, by the Malays, by the Tamils, by the Moors, and by the Kandyans. They see the tooth relic and view a *perahera*.[2]

In 1921, Edward, Prince of Wales (the later Edward VIII and uncle of Elizabeth), embarks on a grand tour of Asia to visit "all the British possessions between Gibraltar and the Pacific" (Phillips 1922, 1). In Kandy, on March 22, 1922, he holds a durbar, at which he meets eighty Kandyan chiefs. After that, he is taken to the Temple of the Tooth, where he observes the whole unveiling of the relic, dagoba by dagoba, until they get to the innermost reliquary. Then, "the box was reverently removed and placed on a table; the lid was lifted, and the tooth lay revealed by the flickering light of an oil lamp" (Phillips 1922, 151). Following that, the prince is taken to the "Octagon" (the Patthirippuwa—the library attached to the temple), from which he views a full *perahera*. The writer D. H. Lawrence, residing in Kandy at that time, captured the moment in verse in his poem "Elephant," in which he mockingly contrasts the liveliness of the *perahera* with what he perceives to be the lifelessness of the Prince of Wales watching it (Lawrence 1964, 1: 386–392; see also Ellis 1998, 15–19).

The Duke of Gloucester and the Return of the Kandyan Throne

It is clear from these accounts and others that "seeing the tooth" and viewing a *perahera* becomes an almost obligatory event for visiting British royalty. It is not clear what these various British princes and dukes think of the relic when they see it. At some level, they appear to understand that they are in the sanctum of the ancient kings of Kandy, and that, to that extent, they

2. See Skeen 1901, 16, 25, for pictures of the tour; and *The Times* (London) 1901, 5, for an account of the visit.

have replaced them. But they are careful neither to claim their own sovereign's ownership of the tooth (at least not publicly) nor to honor it with any gifts or offerings. In other words, beyond exercising their privilege of seeing the tooth, they steer clear of any act that might suggest they view it or claim it as a palladium of their rule.

Another sign of this gradual relinquishing of British monarchical claims to be royal successors to the throne of Kandy comes in 1934 with the decision to return to Ceylon the actual ancient throne and crown of the Kandyan kings that were taken away in 1818 and kept in Windsor Castle for over a century. Over 1,500 people, representing all ethnic groups from every part of the island, assemble for the ceremony in the audience hall of the old Kandyan kings. As a representative of the royal family, the Duke of Gloucester arrives and takes his place on the ancient chair (not the throne) of King Kīrti Śrī (r. 1747–1782), the monarch who had done so much for the tooth relic and its temple. Leaving his seat, the duke addresses the crowd, telling them that King George has requested him to return the throne and crown to his Ceylonese subjects, and asking the governor (Reginald Stubbs) to accept these items on behalf of all sections and peoples of the island. He then pulls the tassel that releases the curtain hiding the regalia. The crowd erupts in enthusiastic and sustained applause, and then grows quiet. As an eyewitness put it, "The moment's silence that followed, was nothing like anything experienced in Ceylon. From out of the hall [i.e., from the Temple of the Tooth] came the far away beating of drums, drums, drums" (*Straits Times* 1934, 13). It seemed as though the tooth relic itself (or rather, its ritual guardians) was acknowledging that something significant had taken place in terms of suzerainty.[3]

Elizabeth II and the Tooth

All of this paves the way for the topic of this chapter: the visit of Queen Elizabeth II, the first reigning English monarch to go to Ceylon, in 1954.[4] This being after independence, the situation is a bit different from when all the dukes and princes mentioned above visited the tooth. There is no question

3. The throne, which became an object of contention between Kandyan traditionalists and those who saw it as a symbol of pan-Ceylonese nationalism, was subsequently moved to the museum in Colombo where, in the course of a month, it was visited by over three-quarters of a million people. On debates and controversies surrounding the throne after its return to the island, see Wickramasinghe 2006, 106–111.

4. For a newsreel video of Elizabeth's tour of Ceylon, see https://www.youtube.com/watch?v=T61LCygjlpo.

now—on her part—of her being the "owner" of the tooth, or of her being expected to fulfill her royal duties toward the tooth, or of the British government being able to insist on having her invited. Moreover, conscious of her role as Defender of the Faith and the nominal head of the Anglican Church, the Queen herself (as well as a number of politicians) is worried about offending Christians by visiting a Buddhist shrine. The whole story may be reconstructed from documents conveniently kept in a single file labeled the "Suggested Visit by HM The Queen and HRH The Duke of Edinburgh to the Temple of the Tooth at Kandy . . . Ceylon," found in the Records of the Prime Minister's Office [PREM] in the National Archives in Kew, in London.

The tale actually starts in early February 1952. Princess Elizabeth (this is before she becomes queen) is in Kenya, her first stop on a grand tour of the colonies and Commonwealth countries that she has undertaken as a representative of her father, King George VI. Meanwhile, back in England, a rumor develops that when she gets to Ceylon, she is due to visit, barefoot, the Buddhist Temple of the Tooth and present there an offering of a gift of gold. This is seen as scandalous by a Christian fundamentalist pastor and a member of Parliament who are instrumental in spreading the news (see PREM 11/737, 155–157). When the story comes to Prime Minister Winston Churchill's attention, he is appalled and determined to do something about it, as he fears a significant backlash among Christians both in Great Britain and in Ceylon and other Commonwealth countries, should the princess go ahead with this plan.

A couple of days later, however, the question becomes moot, for on February 6, 1952, Elizabeth's father, King George VI, dies, and the rest of her trip is canceled in order for her to return to London. Nevertheless, Churchill realizes that the issue will probably come up again, since once she becomes queen, Elizabeth is likely to resume her tour of Commonwealth countries as their newly crowned monarch (see PREM/11/737, 146–149).

Indeed, five months later, Buckingham Palace announces that the Queen and her husband, Prince Philip, will resume their royal tour sometime in the year following her coronation (which has been set for June 1953). This time, the secretary of state for Commonwealth relations, Lord Salisbury, is determined not to be blindsided by any plans for Her Majesty to visit the tooth relic when she gets to Ceylon. Aware of Churchill's concerns about this matter, he decides to act preemptively: on July 31, 1952, he informs the prime minister's office that, although he himself personally agrees that it would be a "grave error" for the Queen to view the tooth relic, he thinks he should forewarn the prime minister that the governor-general of Ceylon, Lord Soulbury, "remains firmly of the opinion that Her Majesty *should* visit the Temple and make [to it] a [customary] offering of [three] gold [sovereigns]." As this may cause difficulties, Lord Salisbury suggests that Churchill speak about this with Dudley Senanayake, the prime minister of Ceylon, at the upcoming Commonwealth Economic Conference. In the meantime, he has taken the liberty of asking Sir Cecil Syers, the United Kingdom's high commissioner to Ceylon (the equivalent of an ambassador), for his views on this matter (PREM 11/737, 139–141).

Syers, it turns out, has three pages' worth of views to offer. He, like Lord Soulbury, argues in favor of the Queen making a visit to the temple and viewing the tooth. He points out that while there might be some Christian opposition to this, her Buddhist subjects in Ceylon and elsewhere would be greatly hurt if she did not. The visit, however, should be a private one—just her and Prince Philip, the Diyawadana Nilame, the "priests," and possibly the prime minister of Ceylon. He does not think she needs to present any gold sovereigns to the temple, and recommends that instead, they later send a check for, say, 250 rupees, to help with the upkeep of the building. He does think, however, that she will probably have to remove her shoes. But in no case should she go barefoot: "the Temple entrance, being normally crowded with beggars and crossed by a great number of people in bare feet, is not sanitary. . . . If it is imperative that she should remove Her shoes, then . . . she should wear several pairs of stockings and should use a strong disinfectant afterwards." He does think it would be a good idea for the prime minister to discuss the matter with Dudley Senanayake at the Commonwealth meetings. The Ceylonese prime minister is a very devout Buddhist, "but [sic] he is also a very sensible, right-minded man" (PREM 11/737, 142–145).

As it turns out, Churchill is unable to discuss the issue with Senanayake at the Commonwealth summit in November. Instead, on December 29, 1952, he writes him a letter. This letter is prompted by a memo from Churchill's private secretary/assistant, Jock Colville, who seems (perhaps even more than Churchill) to be against the visit. Colville warns Churchill that the Queen soon expects to receive from the governor-general of Ceylon the program for her visit there, and since the governor-general (Lord Soulbury) is firmly *for* the visit to the temple, Colville fully expects the program will once again include it. This will involve the Queen taking off her shoes and "making a present of gold to the idol."[5] It was unfortunate that Churchill was unable to discuss this matter with Prime Minister Senanayake

5. Colville adds that the archbishop of Canterbury, when informed of this, remarked that "however desirable this might be from the point of view of her Majesty's Buddhist subjects, it would cause a great deal of indignation among her Christian subjects."

in person, but now, both Buckingham Palace and the Commonwealth Relations Office (i.e., Lord Salisbury) think that "in order to forestall unpleasantness, the best course would be for you [Churchill] to *write* to the Prime Minister of Ceylon on the subject explaining the delicacy of the position as regards opinion in this country." Accordingly, he (Colville) has taken the liberty of drafting a letter to that effect. He has already run this draft by Alan ("Tommy") Lascelles (Queen Elizabeth's new private secretary), who agrees with it and with this plan (PREM 11/737, 134–135).

The letter, dubbed "Private," is interesting for the considerable number of additions and deletions made to it by Churchill over the course of several drafts (see PREM 11/737, 136–137). In the final version, however, the prime minister gets straight to the point. He tells Senanayake that

> It would be natural that the Government of Ceylon would wish The Queen to visit this great and beautiful shrine. Nevertheless, I am told that a visit to the Temple would involve The Queen removing her shoes and making a gift of gold at the shrine, and I am sure you will be the first to see that such an act by the Queen would not be possible because of misunderstanding among her Christian subjects in other countries.[6] If you thought that The Queen could visit the Temple without removing her shoes or making a direct offering and, at the same time, not give offence to Buddhist opinion, it would be a happy solution. Before the visit is placed on the proposed programme . . . I ask you to give the matter your personal attention and let me know what course you think would be best so as to avoid difficulties for both our Governments. (PREM 11/737, 128–129)

Prime Minister Senanayake is not long in responding, and easily reads between the lines of Churchill's letter. On January 9, 1953, he writes back a "private" reply to the prime minister saying he has considered the matter very carefully, and that all in all, he "think(s) the most satisfactory solution would be to omit this visit [to the Temple] altogether" (PREM 11/737, 127). Jock Colville promptly communicates this message to his counterparts at Buckingham Palace (PREM 11/737, 126) and at the Commonwealth Relations Office (PREM 11/737, 127), and it seems that the matter is settled. Indeed, when the official program for the Queen's visit to Ceylon is drawn up, it does *not* include a visit to the temple to view the tooth (PREM 11/737, 103).

6. In a penultimate draft of the letter, there follows the sentence "I should have to advise against it" (PREM 11/737, 133). These are words that Churchill added in a still earlier draft (see PREM 11/737, 137), but then crossed out in the final version.

Almost a year goes by. In England, in June 1953, Elizabeth's coronation takes place. In November, the Queen and Prince Philip depart on their Commonwealth tour on the royal yacht *Britannia*. Stops are planned in Bermuda, Jamaica, Fiji, Tonga, New Zealand, Australia, and the Cocos Islands before the royal party's arrival, in April 1954, in Ceylon.[7] No viewing of the tooth relic in Kandy is planned. It seems that the conservative forces, worried about the *religious* (but not apparently the political) implications of the Queen showing any respect to the tooth relic, have won the day. The story, however, does not end there.

In Ceylon, in October 1953, Dudley Senanayake is replaced as prime minister by Sir John Kotelawala, and, a couple of months later, the issue of the Queen's tooth-visit resurfaces. Kotelawala, it turns out, was never informed that the plan for the Queen to view the tooth had been canceled. According to him, because his predecessor's correspondence with Churchill had been labeled "Personal," and "Private," it was never included among the official files that were passed on to him in the course of the governmental transition (PREM 11/737, 110).[8] Nor, apparently, did anyone bother to inform the authorities at the Temple of the Tooth that the visit was canceled.

All this becomes clear on January 27, 1954, when Kuda Banda Nugawela, the Diyawadana Nilame of the Dalada Maligawa, assuming the visit is still "on," writes a letter to Prime Minister Kotelawala. He reminds him that "the right to invite Her Majesty the Queen to view the Sacred Tooth Relic is vested in the two Mahānāyakas of Malwatta and Asgirya, [in himself as] Diyawadana Nilame, and in the Basnāyaka Nilames of the four Devales in Kandy." Therefore, with the agreement of all these persons, he is now "officially extending to Her Majesty an invitation to view the tooth relic and [its] jewellery before she goes to the Octagon to give the Temple Chiefs the mandate to start the Perahera" (PREM 11/737, 112).

It is not clear whether or not this invitation is at Nugawela's own initiative, or whether he was asked to make it by Kotelawala. In any case, the very next day, Kotelawala sends a long letter to Churchill. He apologizes for not writing earlier, before the program for the Queen's visit was set, but explains that he had not known that it was. In any case, conditions in the country and surrounding this issue have now changed. He has just received this

7. "Commonwealth Visits since 1952," https://www.royal.uk/sites/default/files/media/commonwealth_visits_since_1952_3.pdf.

8. Kotelawala also claims that the governor-general (Lord Soulbury) did not know that viewing the tooth was "off," though this is harder to believe since the Queen's private secretary says he informed Soulbury three times that the Queen was now opposed to such a visit (PREM 11/737, 103).

invitation from the Diyawadana Nilame (he encloses a copy), and now recommends that Her Majesty agree to view the tooth and the jewelry, adding
a bit of contextual history:

> When the Kandyan kingdom was ceded to the British in 1815 by the Kandyan
> Convention, there was a special clause in the Convention which provided for
> the protection of the Buddhist faith. Her Majesty's ancestors and her uncles
> had all visited the Temple of the Tooth and had viewed the Sacred relic and
> the Jewelry. Reigning kings of various countries have always viewed the Tooth
> Relic when they visited Ceylon and there is now a persistent demand from
> a very large section of the people of the country that Her Majesty should do
> likewise. Indeed, they say that, quite apart from any other consideration, Her
> Majesty should visit the Temple as Queen of Ceylon and Head of the Com-
> monwealth and not give cause for offence to a large number of Her Buddhist
> and Hindu subjects, who constitute over 86% of the population of the coun-
> try. (PREM 11/737, 110)

He then adds his own reassurance that "there will be no religious ceremony connected with her visit to the temple," but, he warns, "Her Majesty
will only have to remove her shoes on entering the relic Chamber."[9] As
prime minister, and as a Buddhist, he feels "most strongly" that the Queen
should accept this invitation, and he asks Churchill to transmit his letter to
her and to support his recommendation. Finally, he appends what amounts
to a warning:

> It would be very unfortunate if the Queen of Ceylon and Head of the Com-
> monwealth were to decline this invitation and wound the religious suscep-
> tibilities of a large section of Her loyal Subjects. If this were to happen, it
> would create religious dissension between the large Buddhist population
> and the comparatively small Christian population in Ceylon. (PREM 11/737,
> 110–111)

What he does not say, and perhaps does not need to say to Churchill,
is that things are happening, politically, in Ceylon, at this time. Leftist opposition parties, which want Ceylon to become a republic and quit the
Commonwealth, are threatening to boycott the Queen's visit, even to stage
demonstrations, much to the consternation of the new secretary of state

---

9. The word "only" is indicative of an important concession: the Queen will not have to
remove her shoes upon entering the building itself, but only in the upstairs relic chamber.

for Commonwealth affairs, Lord Swinton.[10] When Kotelawala had come into office in October 1953, he had a reputation as a person who would maintain law and order. In particular, he assured Lord Soulbury, the British governor-general, that no troubles would occur to mar the Queen's visit, and he personally took charge of police precautions. According to a story, popular at the time, when N. M. Perera, the head of the Trotskyite party, asked Kotelawala whether orders were given for the police to arrest anyone demonstrating against the Queen, he replied jocularly, but in a way that implied he would crack down harder than that: "Oh! No! orders have been given to take demonstrators to hospital first!" (Fernando 1963, 71).

Given this situation, it is understandable that Kotelawala does not wish to risk discontent from Sinhalese nationalists by not having the queen visit the tooth relic, especially since her program calls for her to view a special royal procession (*rāja-perahera*) from the Octagon, which is accessed from the second floor of the Temple of the Tooth. In other words, she will have to pass right by the shrine room of the temple in order to get to her viewing platform. It seems that some of the potential Nationalist demonstrators would really rather not have the Queen come to Ceylon at all—they want Sri Lanka to shed entirely the vestiges of its former status as a British Crown colony—but ironically, if she does come, they want her to at least pay her respects to the tooth relic, and so to the local Buddhist culture.

As soon as Kotelawala's letter reaches Churchill, he informs Edward Ford (the Queen's assistant private secretary) at Buckingham Palace, who immediately telegraphs the royal party (which, at this point, is touring Australia), telling them not to make any final decision yet with regard to Her Majesty's visit to the tooth relic, since the Ceylonese prime minister feels strongly she *should* go (PREM 11/737, 109). Michael Adeane (the Queen's new private secretary, who is with her on the tour) replies from Australia that this is unfortunate, that they do not wish to reintroduce the viewing of the tooth relic into the Ceylon program, that it is contrary to the Queen's "specific hope that no visit should be recommended," and that he hopes "no change is now to be asked for." Nonetheless (given the relationship between Government and Crown in the constitutional monarchy that is Britain), they will consider it if need be (PREM 11/737, 108; see also PREM 11/737, 103).

10. See the series of "secret" and "confidential" telegrams between London and Colombo in PREM 11/737, 120–123. See also PREM 11/737, 96: "If the invitation were declined, Republican tendencies might well be encouraged (i.e., in Ceylon). This would be particularly unfortunate just when we were hoping that the new Prime Minister is steadying the situation in Ceylon."

Churchill is now genuinely uncertain about which course to take, so he decides to consult further with his secretary of state for Commonwealth affairs, Lord Swinton. Swinton turns for advice to Lord Soulbury, the governor-general of Ceylon, who replies that he has personally spoken with Prime Minister Kotelawala and knows he feels very strongly about this. Moreover, he reports, the stakes are now being raised: the temple authorities in Kandy have indicated that they would consider it to be an insult to the Buddhists of Ceylon for the Queen to turn down their invitation to view the tooth, and that if she did so, *"it would be impossible for the [special] perahera to be held"* (PREM 11/737, 99, italics added). In other words: if no tooth, then no elephants, no torch-light parade, no Kandyan dancers, no drummers, no chiefs processing in their glorious costumes. There would, in fact, be nothing for the Queen to do in Kandy, publicly, and no occasion for the people to celebrate her presence (PREM 11/737, 99). In that case, Kotelawala "might [then] find it necessary to advise her Majesty to abandon [entirely] her visit to Ceylon"—something that, Lord Soulbury points out, "might well produce a bitter controversy throughout the island, of which the Opposition party, who wish Ceylon to be a Republic would take full advantage" (PREM 11/737, 60).[11]

Lord Swinton reports all this to Churchill, reassuring him that the Queen's visit to the tooth would in no way be seen as an act of worship or homage, and then, curiously, returning to the question of the Queen's shoes. Swinton holds out the hope that Her Majesty might not be asked to remove her shoes, if "it can be arranged for her shoes to be shod with some other covering." This, he says, has been common for royal personages visiting mosques in other countries, and he thinks it is what was done for the British princes who visited the Temple of the Tooth in the past.[12] Perhaps the priests could provide her with some kind of foot covering. Then, "no one could possibly suggest that [she] was performing an act of worship or homage." But, regardless of whether she has to take off her shoes or not, he thinks the Queen should now accept the invitation—there are too many potential problems were she to refuse (PREM 11/737, 94–95).

Churchill is interested in the idea of "booties"; he immediately asks Swinton to privately cable Lord Soulbury in Colombo to see if some sort of

---

11. These final two points were contained in a paragraph of the draft of a report on the matter to Churchill and his Cabinet. The paragraph, however, was deleted from the final printed version of the report that actually went to the Cabinet (see PREM 11.737, 51).

12. I have found no mention of this in any sources I have looked at. The sketch in figure 12.1, though inconclusive because it does not show Albert's feet, hints that the Prince of Wales is in full uniform, including his footwear.

shoe covering could be arranged for the Queen. In the meantime, he will put the whole issue of the visit before the Cabinet at its next meeting on February 10 (PREM 11/737, 86).

The following day, a "secret" telegram arrives at 10 Downing Street; it is Governor-General Soulbury's response to Swinton's query: "Regret no alternative to removal of shoes possible. No religious significance attached to it here. Have consulted Bishop of Colombo regarding views of Anglican community. He has no objection to removal" (PREM 11/737, 61). What is not said here is that, apparently at some point before this, someone (the governor-general himself?) had urged Prime Minister Kotelawala to take further steps to see if some arrangement could be made to accommodate the Queen's footwear preference. The chronology involved here is not clear, since the prime minister's actions were not revealed until 2009. In that year, the newspaper man and academic H. S. S. Nissanka wrote a short article for the *Daily News* in Colombo, reminiscing about his days as a young journalist in Kandy. In 1954, he explains, the question of whether or not the Queen should remove her shoes before entering the Dalada Maligawa was "a subject of public debate."[13] The Diyawadana Nilame, K. B. Nugawela, was firm in his insistence that she had to remove her footwear. In order to try to change his mind, Prime Minister Kotelawala sent the inspector general of police, Sir Richard Aluwihare, to Kandy to meet with Nugawela. Aluwihare apparently tried to pressure Nugawela into allowing the Queen to wear her shoes or put on some sort of bootie, but he was reportedly stopped short by the Diyawadana Nilame, who slapped him hard on the cheek and said: "Richard, you can arrest me when I am outdoors, but neither you nor even the Queen has the power to give me orders while I am inside the Maligawa." Nissanka ends his account by saying the police inspector general had the grace not to pursue the matter further, and that he (Nissanka) and his two fellow journalists who witnessed the incident had actually "kept it secret for over fifty years!" (Nissanka 2009).

On the same day, February 5, 1954, Churchill writes his regular weekly prime minister's report to the Queen. Fully one-third of the four-page letter concerns the matter of her visit to the tooth relic. Besides showing us where

13. Given this, it is interesting that the American ambassador to Ceylon at the time, Philip Crowe (1956, 16–18), in his lengthy firsthand account of the Queen's visit to Kandy, makes no mention of her viewing the tooth relic, let alone of the debate about her shoes. Perhaps Crowe is just being discreet. However, the issue (the details of which could easily have been leaked from Kotelawala's office, for he was a notorious raconteur) was apparently common knowledge among Sinhalese intellectuals and politicians (despite the British government's insistence on keeping all of its correspondence on the matter "private" or "confidential").

the matter stands at this moment, it gives us a glimpse into his relationship with his monarch:

> Madam . . . I have received from the Prime Minister of Ceylon a long letter suggesting that Your Majesty should, after all, visit the Temple of the Tooth at Kandy. Jock has already sent a copy of this to Michael Adeane. I thought that before offering any advice to Your Majesty on this proposal, it would be well for me to consult the Cabinet, and I will telegraph their view immediately after our next meeting. I understand that it is no longer proposed that Your Majesty should be asked to present gold at the Shrine, or to take part in any form of Buddhist religious ceremony, so that I think a great deal of misunderstanding which might in such circumstances have arisen in these Islands could probably be avoided. Should we decide to advise Your Majesty to go forward with the ceremony and to visit the Temple, this advice of course would be tendered only in so far as it fitted in with Your Majesty's inclinations.[14] Personally, I am rather impressed by the argument that removing one's shoes in a Buddhist Temple is no more than taking off one's hat in a Christian Church. At any rate I think that people here would understand that. (PREM 11/737, 65–66)

What we can see here is Churchill changing his mind and preparing the Queen for changing hers (which, in any case, she has already indicated a willingness to do). Churchill, of course, holds all the power, but there is, again, a polite charade going on between State and Crown.

On February 10, Churchill and Swindon present the whole situation to the Cabinet, and here the question of the Queen's shoes resurfaces. They now both speak in favor of recommending to the Queen that she formally accept the Ceylonese invitation to visit the tooth, pointing out that all parties are agreed that her taking off her shoes at the temple will have no religious significance whatsoever. The whole visit will only last a few minutes, and "steps will be taken to screen Her Majesty and ensure absolute privacy when she takes off her shoes before entering the Shrine. Immediately she leaves it they will be put on again" (PREM 11/737, 51). Churchill adds that it has been determined that the Queen herself is "anxious to meet the wishes

---

14. Actually, Churchill already knows, from a telegram just received from Michael Adeane (see PREM 11/737.72), that though Elizabeth had hoped this issue would not come up, she is willing to accept the invitation to view the tooth, as long as Churchill agrees to explain her actions to the archbishop of Canterbury (which he does on February 10, 1954 [see PREM 11/737, 45–47]).

of her Ceylonese subjects in this matter," and that therefore "there did not appear to be any ground on which the Cabinet should consider tendering advice in a contrary sense" (PREM 11/737, 48).

The minutes of the meeting do not record an actual vote, but simply that the Cabinet "took note with approval of the Prime Minister's statement" (PREM 11/737, 48). Immediately after the meeting, telegrams giving the Cabinet's decision are sent to the Queen (through Michael Adeane), to Prime Minister Kotelawala, to the UK high commissioner in Colombo, and to the governor-general of Ceylon (Lord Soulbury) (PREM 11/737, 35–40). The decision is also communicated in a long explanatory letter from Churchill to Geoffrey Cantuar, the archbishop of Canterbury (PREM 11/737. 45–47).[15] On February 11, Michael Adeane, still in Australia with the Royal Party, replies by cable to 10 Downing Street: "The Queen is accepting Sir John Kotelawala's advice and is grateful for recommendation" (PREM 11/737, 34).

Much of the rest of the correspondence in the PREM 11/737 file is taken up with strategizing (between Downing Street, Buckingham Palace, Commonwealth Affairs, and the high commissioner in Ceylon) as to how best to handle press coverage of the Queen's visit to the Temple before and after it actually takes place (see PREM 11/737, 14–16). Generally, the plan is to minimize the significance of her visit to the tooth (and especially of her removing her shoes), to point out that it has no religious significance, and to emphasize instead the magnificence of her reception by the people and the Kandyan chiefs and of the special *rāja perahera* being put on for her. There are, however, some snafus, the most distressing of which (to the government and to the palace) is the dispatch from Colombo that appears in the *Times of London* on April 10, 1954. The Queen is soon due to arrive in Ceylon. *The Times*'s special correspondent reports on the preparations being made to welcome her, adding that, though there had been some opposition by the Marxist parties to her visit, these have "utterly failed to rally support. It is said indeed that the Queen's visit is being celebrated with greater enthusiasm than Independence Day which is perhaps not surprising among peoples with so long a tradition of kingship [sic]." So far so good, at least, as far as the palace and the government are concerned. Then, however, comes

15. The archbishop replies on February 10, telling Churchill that he is now perfectly satisfied "that there is to be no religious ceremony and no offering of gold. The mere removal of her shoes is, as you say, a matter of complete indifference and nothing more than an act of courtesy to conform to their custom" (PREM 11/737, 33). Churchill includes a copy of his letter in his next weekly report (February 12) to the Queen (PREM 11/737, 27–29).

the slip-up: "Buddhist susceptibilities have been mollified by yesterday's announcement that when the Queen visits Kandy for the picturesque Raja Perahera, with its elephants and dancers, she will visit the Temple of the Sacred Tooth *as an act of worship*, following the example previously observed by other members of the Royal Family" (*The Times* [London] 1954a, italics added).

This naturally outrages Edward Ford (the Queen's assistant private secretary, who has stayed in London). He writes the very same day to the *Times*'s editor to protest the statement. It is, he states (PREM 11/737, 5),

> the direct opposite of the truth, and considerable trouble has been taken both here and in Ceylon to emphasize that the Queen's visit to the Temple of the tooth is an act of courtesy, and that there is no implication of worship in it. Her Majesty will remove her shoes on entering the room where the tooth is kept in the same way that anyone visiting a sacred mosque puts on overshoes.

Ford goes on to suggest conciliatorily that their special correspondent's dispatch was probably "corrupted in transit," but asks that a correction be published forthwith.[16] Indeed, the *Times* is quick to do so. Two days later, on Monday, April 12, under the subhead "An Act of Courtesy," we find the following note:

> It is emphasized by members of the royal household and by the Ceylon Government, that there is no question of Her Majesty performing an act of worship when she visits the Temple of the Tooth at Kandy, as was suggested in your Correspondent's last dispatch. Her acceptance of the invitation from the lay trustee of the temple is an act of courtesy, and it is pointed out that the Queen will make no offering, one of the obligatory acts of worship when the sacred relic is exposed. (*The Times* [London] 1954b)

A week later, in his report on the actual visit of the Queen to Kandy, the *Times*'s special correspondent has apparently learned his lesson. He spends most of the article, entitled "Kandy Greets the Queen with Splendour," describing the magnificence of her welcome there on April 19: The greatest *rāja perahera* since the time of the Kandyan kings! A record 140 elephants!

---

16. Buckingham Palace was not the only party worried about this. Telegrams pointing out that "Her Majesty . . . will not, repeat not, be performing an act of worship" flew also from the Commonwealth Relations Office and the UK high commissioner in Ceylon (PREM 11/737, 2–3).

A million and a half people come to honor her from all over the island! Only in passing does he state that before the procession, the Queen and her husband, the Duke of Edinburgh, visited the temple, accompanied by six priests, the Ceylonese prime minister, and the Diyawadane Nilame:

> They mounted to the inner sanctuary and saw the sacred relic which had been removed from its nest of jeweled caskets. . . . The interesting experience, shared by members of the royal family on previous visits, has no religious significance. Buddhist opinion will be greatly gratified by Her Majesty's visit— much stir had been made by rumours that she would be unable to accept the invitation. (*The Times* [London] 1954c)

There is no mention of her shoes, and no mention of an offering, although he does say that she gave the two *mahānāyakas* presents of long-handled ceremonial fans (*The Times* [London] 1954c).[17]

Conspectus

The general question of whether or not Europeans could be exempted from the practice of removing their footwear when entering Buddhist sacred places was not unique to Ceylon. It had, for instance, been a big issue in Burma, where it became known as "the shoe question," and where, from the start of colonial rule, Europeans had claimed exemption from the rule—up until 1919, when the policy was ended (Turner 2014, 120–133; see also Schober 2011, 73–75). The issue had many ramifications since, as Alicia Turner (2014, 112) has pointed out, it "served as [a] vital symbolic means of inscribing *and* resisting subordination in colonial relations" (italics added).

In Ceylon, the issue remained alive a bit longer, but it appears to have been definitively settled by independence. Thus, no question was raised when the British foreign secretary Ernest Bevin, along with high-level officials from several Commonwealth countries in Colombo for a conference, all removed their shoes as a matter of course when they viewed the tooth in Kandy. Bevin even indicated he was hoping the visit would prove beneficial for his heart ailment (Trumbull 1950, 1). To be sure, Bevin was not the Queen, for whom the matter was doubtlessly more complex.

---

17. American newspapers were less discreet. The *New York Times*, for example, published a short piece entitled "Queen Removes Shoes to See Buddha's Tooth," but made little of this act in the body of the article (*New York Times* 1954). The *Chicago Tribune*, however made no mention of her shoes, focusing instead on the object of the tooth itself (*Chicago Tribune* 1954).

Even so, it may appear a bit surprising and anachronistic that this question of what Elizabeth should do with her shoes at the Temple of the Tooth should have so preoccupied the highest echelons of government, monarchy, Church, and sangha in both England and Ceylon for the better part of two years. The on-again, off-again, on-again saga is significant, however, for a number of reasons.

First, it shows that some of the objections to the state's dealings with the tooth that were raised by Christians missionaries in the early nineteenth century were still alive in the mid-twentieth century. John d'Oyly in 1815 had walked barefoot into the Dalada Maligawa and made an offering there of a golden musical clock on behalf of King George III—acts that some (though not everyone) viewed as scandalous, and which, along with other things, eventually contributed to the British government's disassociating itself from Buddhism. From the start, the possibility that Queen Elizabeth might do something analogous, even in the context of that disassociation, was viewed with alarm by persons such as Prime Minister Churchill, mainly for its perceived religious reverberations among Christians, primarily in England.

For a while, he (with the cooperation of Prime Minister Dudley Sena-nayake) managed to get the Queen's viewing of the tooth relic removed from the Kandy visit. When it was reintroduced at Prime Minister Kotelawa-la's instigation, there were sustained attempts to reassure possible objectors by belittling the religious significance of anything she might do during her visit. The perceived "offering of gold to an idol" became "a symbolic gift of three gold sovereigns to the temple" which, in turn, became "a contribution of 250 rupees by check for building maintenance." Eventually, even that was eliminated and the Queen ended up only giving two ceremonial fans to the chief monks.

They could not do away with her taking off her shoes, however. They did try: "going barefoot" became "taking off her shoes but making sure she was shod in heavy stockings"; and "taking them off at the entrance of the temple" became "taking them off only at the door of the inner sanctum." Alternatively, "taking her shoes off" became "keeping them on but putting covers over them." When that was nixed by the Diyawadana Nilame and the inevitable had to be accepted, there was still a systematic attempt to deny any possible religious significance of the act. It was described as "just like a man taking off his hat in Church,"[18] ignoring, of course, two facts: first, that

18. In Burma, fifty years earlier, it had been argued that Europeans (presumably all males) would take their hats off when visiting pagodas but that Asians would take their shoes off. See Turner 2014, 123.

a *man's* removing his head covering in a place of worship *is* a religious act of respect for Christians dating back at least to Saint Paul, and second, that, in any case, Queen Elizabeth was a *woman* and almost obligatorily wore a hat in Church, a practice also traceable to the First Letter to the Corinthians and fraught with religious and social significance.[19] Alternatively, it was likened to the habit of some European visitors to mosques of wearing booties over their shoes instead of going barefoot, but that too could only serve to highlight the religious importance of the act.

This is not the place to embark on a discussion of the significance of footwear removal in world religions, but in fact, for British Christians of a certain class in the 1950s (as earlier), taking off one's shoes was not only (and probably not primarily) an act of religious humility (despite the episode of the Burning Bush in the Book of Exodus (3:5), where the Lord says to Moses "put off your shoes from your feet, for the place on which you are standing is holy ground)." It was, rather, a way of distinguishing oneself from the lower classes, and, in the colonial or postcolonial context, of distinguishing oneself from the "natives" or "primitives" (see Turner 2014, 129–130).[20] In other words, even if the overt religious significance of the Queen's taking off her shoes was rejected for Christians, there was no denying that it could be perceived as an act of humbling on her part.

Second, it is only when Prime Minister Kotelawala makes Churchill realize that the *political* repercussions of her not visiting the tooth are great for the newly independent Ceylon and Britain's relationship to its people that he begins to change his stance. The same realization occurs to the Queen. As "Defender of the Faith" and "Supreme Governor" of the Church of England, Elizabeth is acutely aware of her need to be a paragon of propriety in religious matters. Thus, it is important to her that taking off her shoes be seen as having no religious significance. But she, or at least Buckingham Palace, also becomes convinced by political arguments. As she changes her mind and becomes reconciled to the viewing of the tooth, if only to satisfy the wishes of "her many millions of Buddhist subjects," or, as her secretary puts it (see chapter epigraph), "to maintain the structure of the British Commonwealth," the Queen also begins to question somewhat the conservative

---

19. In 1 Cor. 11:5–15 (a much disputed and [re]interpreted passage in modern times), it is essentially stated that any man who worships with his head covered dishonors Christ, but any woman who worships with her head uncovered dishonors both Christ and her husband.

20. When I lived in Kandy in 1969, there were two types of boys' soccer teams: those who played with soccer shoes, and those who played barefoot. It was clear which socio-economic status each belonged to.

position of some of her Christian subjects. Indeed, she tells Adeane: "If going into a temple for a non-religious ceremony . . . is going to cause offence to Christians, it is a sad commentary on their trust in [my] Christian faith" (PREM 11/737, 43, slightly altered).

Third, despite Prime Minister Kotelawala's claims, and the invitation from the Diyawadana Nilame himself, not all Buddhists in Ceylon were necessarily happy with the Queen's visit. The president of the Ceylon Buddhist Congress, for instance, tried to revive a campaign to have the Queen altogether excluded from the Octagon as well as from the Temple of the Tooth, while the editor of *Buddhist World* complained of her refusal to acknowledge local religious sentiments, pointing out that since thousands of non-Christians had attended the Queen's coronation (in 1953) and participated in the service, it would only be "a reciprocal act of courtesy [on her part] for the Queen to place her hands together and deposit a tray of flowers at the temple" (*Living Church* 1954).

Finally, the story of Queen Elizabeth's shoes also illustrates the different situation of the tooth in post-independence Ceylon. Simply put, if the tooth was Queen Victoria's "personal property" at the end of the nineteenth century, it was not Queen Elizabeth's in the 1950s. The end of the colonial era in Ceylon had changed all that. There is a significant difference between Elizabeth's visit and those of the royals who preceded her. When Ceylon was still a colony, viewings of the tooth relic were generally arranged at the request or with the permission of British authorities. Thus, the government agent played an important (though behind the scenes) role in the visits of the various English dukes and princes, and of King Chulalongkorn. It is not clear when Britain, represented by the government agent in Kandy, gave up its key to the Dalada shrine, and hence its symbolic say-so, or partial say-so, on access to the tooth relic. Perhaps it was when the GA moved his residence out of the old royal palace to make way for the Kandyan ancient throne returned by King George in 1934; perhaps it was only at independence in 1948. In any case, by Elizabeth's time, the authorities at the Dalada Maligawa (and also in Colombo) are in full control. They are the ones who invite the queen to view the tooth—and they are the ones who change her mind (and Churchill's mind) after the plan for her to do so is given up.

In this sense, the insistence on the queen's not wearing her shoes is symbolic of the newly independent spirit of Ceylon. No mention is made of any such requirement in the visits considered above. Reginald Farrer would certainly have mentioned it if either he or the Japanese Imperial prince had removed their footwear. It is likewise highly doubtful that Albert, the Prince of Wales, in 1875, took his boots off before entering the Dalada shrine—the question probably did not even come up. Nor, I believe, did King Chula-longkorn, who was dressed in Western military uniform during his visit in 1897. Nothing is said about this in the accounts that we have; however, we know that twenty-five years earlier in 1872, a younger but already Western-izing King Chulalongkorn did *not* remove his footwear during a visit to an-other famous reliquary temple, in Yangon (Rangoon). On that occasion, he and all the members of his entourage marched into the sacred precincts of the Shwe Dagon pagoda *with their boots on*. Moreover, they failed to observe Buddhist ritual observances in the presentation of their offerings. All of this upset the Burmese monks, who, however, concluded that "their Siamese [royal] co-religionists in adopting European manners and customs had be-come imbued . . . also with a European religious element, to the prejudice, perhaps, of their own peculiar Buddhist tenets" (Sahai 2002, 401; see also Mukherjee 2018, 28).[21]

All of these cases, of course, concern shod, booted *men*, and it is possible that the wearing or non-wearing of footwear by women, such as Queen Eliz-abeth, was treated differently—among both Western guests and Buddhist hosts. It is interesting, for instance, that in all of the planning for Elizabeth's visit, no mention is ever made of what Prince Philip might have or not have to do with his shoes. But whether or not the difference is gender based, it is also clearly a reflection of the different power situations in precolonial and postcolonial times.

The story of the British royalty's dealings with the tooth relic did not end, however, with Queen Elizabeth's visit in 1954. As late as November 2013, her son, Prince Charles, made an official trip to Kandy. He did not view the relic outside its nested reliquaries, but he did visit the inner sanctum of the temple. In doing so, he not only took off his shoes and went in his stocking feet, he also made a formal offering of a tray of flowers, with little apparent controversy. News reports were more focused on his dancing the hokey-pokey with a group of Sri Lankan schoolgirls! Times change and attitudes evolve.[22]

---

21. Chulalongkorn's father, King Mongkut, had earlier decided to allow European shoes and socks at royal courts and Buddhist sites (Turner 2014, 112).

22. For photos and an account of Charles's visit, see https://www.templenews.org/2013/11/19/prince-charles-visits-temple-of-the-tooth-relic/. See also https://www.youtube.com/watch?v=GOgM-IF8HX0.

Summary and Conclusion

Part 1 of this book, examining stories about the Portuguese tooth, was basically topical in its approach; I dealt with different presentations of the capture of the tooth (where and how it was taken), of its identification (whose it was), of its trial, and of its destruction. Part 2, on the other hand, was more episodic, more biographical; in temporal succession, I dealt with various events in the life story of the Kandyan tooth as it was viewed by the British.

Despite these different approaches, it is possible to identify a number of leitmotifs that bridge both part 1 and part 2. By way of a conclusion, then, I would like to review and briefly expand upon some of these unitive themes under the following headings: (1) multiplicity of views of the tooth; (2) the tooth as an object and the discoveries of Buddhism; (3) jewels and bones; (4) the tooth and the two dimensions of the fetishism of objects; and (5) the tooth as a cosmopolitan object.

Multiplicity of Views of the Tooth

By and large, whether dealing with the Portuguese or the Kandyan tooth, Westerners have had mixed feelings about it. There is no uniform view of the tooth either in our storytellers or in those about whom their stories were told—no single attitude that we can point to as *the* Western stance toward the relic(s). More generally, the many tales about the tooth may be seen as reflections of the many Western attitudes toward Buddhism and/or Asian religions in general in the sixteenth to twentieth centuries. These views varied greatly from individual to individual and from group to group and, though some evolution may be detectable, a variety of mindsets generally coexisted and competed with one another. In no particular order, I will only briefly recall here a number of the different attitudinal moves we encountered in this regard:

(a) Animalization, as a way of dismissing, demeaning, and "de-deifying" the tooth. From the Portuguese, as we have seen, we got the view that the tooth was that of a monkey, but also that replicas of the relic were carved out of staghorn, or out of the tooth of a buffalo; or, in the case of the Kandyan tooth, that it was the tooth of a crocodile or a boar. Animalization is often combined with jocularity and debasing, in which jokes are told about the credulity of believers, or about the larger-than-human size of the tooth itself and the implications of that about the monstrosity of its original owner. At the same time, all this went hand-in-glove with a theory of the evolution of religion that saw animal worship as one of its most primitive phases.

(b) Demonization. This was made most clear in the story of the trial of the relic in Goa in which the Portuguese concluded the tooth was Satan's own. It also appeared, however (though less graphically), in Hocart's identification of the Kandyan relic as being the tooth of a yakṣa (demon), or in Hardy's preoccupation with government support of "devil dancing," which, he claimed, was associated with the tooth. Demonization in this sense, as we have seen, places a belief or practice at the low end of a spectrum of heathenism.

(c) Idolization. Somewhat akin to demonization, but more to the middle of this spectrum, was the view of the tooth as an idol, an object of misguided worship. This was apparent in the Portuguese destruction of the tooth in Goa in the context of its policy of iconoclasm. It was also reflected in the outrage and dismay of the British missionaries who viewed the tooth as a prime example of idolatry—the antithesis of what Britain should support. And it could still be found to some extent in the worries of Winston Churchill and Queen Elizabeth about the reactions of ideological descendants of those committed Christians toward even token signs of honoring the tooth.

(d) Then there is commodification—esteeming the tooth with an eye on its possible monetary value, whether gained or lost. This could be seen in the stories of Dom Constantino's fidalgos in Goa, who wished to hold the tooth for ransom by the highest bidder or take it on a grand money-making tour of their own; or in the tabulation by the British Prize Committee in Kandy of the value of the jewels they were having to concede to the temple. Commodification applied to the tooth relic was a way of secularizing its veneration.

(e) A fifth theme may be found in the practical utilitarianism of persons such as John D'Oyly and Governors Brownrigg and Barnes, who sought to use the tooth to bolster their colonial regime and claimed that its support was necessary to please and appease the Kandyan chiefs and monks, and to avert an insurrection. This was mixed with a realization of the political importance of the tooth as an emblem of sovereignty, something that was also recognized by the Portuguese in their dealings with Vijayanagar and Pegu.

(f) Finally, we should not forget instances of tolerance and genuine respect for the tooth, exemplified in some (not all) of D'Oyly's actions but also in Reginald Farrer's attitudes, and in the views of persons such as Roberto De Nobili and Bartolomé de las Casas, who would probably have shown interest in the tooth had they known about it, and tolerated and accommodated its worship.

The Tooth as an Object and the Discoveries of Buddhism

We have seen that the tooth is first and foremost an object—a movable, stealable thing. The first Portuguese who laid hands on it, whether in Jaffna or on Adam's Peak, probably had no idea of what it was. Its importance, however, was hinted at by the presence around it of other objects (jewels, a reliquary), and its identity was then affirmed by stories, told both by local people and by Westerners. In the case of the Portuguese, this involved a gradual transition from viewing the tooth as being that of a monkey, to claiming it to be Hanumān's, to seeing it as the Buddha's—an evolution that I portrayed as related to the changing geopolitical situation in South Asia, and to the concomitant growth in the ability of the Portuguese to make distinctions between various types of "heathens." Similarly, there was a growth in British awareness; they did not go into Kandy in 1803 thinking they would conquer a *Buddhist* kingdom. Rather, as we have seen, they seemed more or less oblivious, if not to the actual existence of the tooth, at least to its importance as a Buddhist object. It was only after 1815 that its identity and significance began to dawn on them, for much the same reasons that it had dawned on the Portuguese.

In his study of Sri Lankan relics, Kevin Trainor (1997) called for a "rematerialization" of the Sri Lankan Theravāda tradition. One could also make a call for a rematerialization of the Western Buddhological tradition, for a reconsideration of the fillips that brought Westerners into awareness of Buddhism as a religion. In both the Portuguese and the British cases, as we have seen, it was not texts or doctrines that first occasioned the Western discovery and definition of Buddhism, but objects such as the tooth and stories about them. To be sure, the British, coming later, had an advantage over the Portuguese; for one thing, they knew (or some of them knew) the

Portuguese story from Do Couto and others. But they also knew, from the Kandyans, the Sri Lankan pre-story of the tooth as the Buddha's. In either case, however, this Buddhism that they discovered was one defined not by the Four Noble Truths, but by its connection to kingship and sovereignty, and by its inspiration among the people of fervent devotion to the Buddha.

Jewels and Bones

Another way of viewing the dual importance in the tooth of kingship and Buddhahood is by looking at the material expression this was given in the opposition and complementarity of objects that, for shorthand purposes, I have called "jewels and bones." British descriptions of the Dalada Maligawa often stress the magnificence of the jewels decorating the nested reliquaries containing the tooth (see fig. 11.2) and, despite the occasional complaints of claustrophobic visitors about oppressive heat and redolent odors (and the hint that some of the rubies might have been of inferior quality), the sanctum of the temple itself is commonly portrayed as a place of brilliant gold and gemstones. These jewels, as I have suggested, are more than ornamentation or votive offerings; they are obligatory elements in the overall experience of the relic. The monks' insistence in 1815 that the Dalada's treasures had to be found and brought back prior to the return of the tooth itself was not just a clever way to make sure the temple's wealth did not get treated by the British Army as so much war booty; it was also a reflection of the crucial role played by all that gold and all those gems in the ritual life of the tooth. And it should be noted that both Prime Minister Kotelawala and the Diyawadana Nilame invited Queen Elizabeth not just to see the tooth, but to view the "tooth and jewels."

In the discussion in chapter 11 of Reginald Farrer's visit to the temple, I made the Buddhological claim that the jewels themselves could be viewed as a type of relic—symbolizing the purity and permanence of the Buddha in conjunction with the bare bone of the tooth that embodied his corporeality and impermanence. More relevantly here, it is also possible to see the jewels as reinforcing the royal (and divine) dimensions of the relic—its identity as what Goloubew (1932, 460–461) has called the "Dalada-king"—while the tooth per se may be seen as symbolic of its more ascetic monastic aspect— what, in this context, might be seen as its identity as the "Dalada-monk." The jewels and the bone together thus serve to show that in his tooth relic, the Buddha is both king and monk.

In this context, we have seen that the British generally seem to have been more comfortable with the jewels than with the bone—with the "royal" rather than the "religious" symbolism; with the *laukika* (this-worldly) rather than the *lokottara* (supramundane) dimension. The jewels had an inherent universal value the British were familiar with (if only from their own monarch's crown jewels) and that they readily associated with sovereignty. The yellowish piece "of discolored ivory" (Davy 1821, 268) that was the bone, however, could be esteemed only by a projection to the unfamiliar— whether that be the Buddha, or "heathen absurdities," or the rejected relics of Roman Catholicism. In this light, part of Queen Elizabeth's problem may have been the fact that she was being brought face to face with the bare tooth, removed from all its reliquaries. Had the tooth remained hidden— had she only viewed the sparkling jewel-encrusted gilded silver of the outer karandua—who knows?—she might well have gone ahead and offered a tray of flowers, as did her son, Prince Charles, fifty years later.

The Portuguese had similar attitudes, but they need to be described a bit differently: rather than saying they were *more comfortable* with the jewels, I am inclined to think they were more *un*comfortable with the bone. The "jewels," which were far fewer in number than in the case of the Kandyan tooth, they were willing to keep. The bone, however, they resolved to destroy. This, I have argued, was not only because they feared it was the Devil's, but because they had, from their own Catholic tradition, a more vivid understanding of the power of relics than did the British.

Friedrich Max Müller, in an oft-quoted passage, once asked why the Portuguese navigators recognized at once some of the objects they saw among the populations they visited as *feitiços* (fetishes). It was, he says, "because they themselves were fetish-worshippers . . . and probably carried with them some beads or crosses or images that had been blessed by their priests before they started their voyage" (Müller 1880, 61). The same thing might be said of relics: the Portuguese had no trouble seeing the tooth they captured in Jaffna (or elsewhere) as a relic—even as a *"mui grande reliquio,"* as Do Couto (1783, 17: 317) called it. It was, however, a heathen object, a sort of anti-relic. To be sure, their destruction of it was an act of religious intolerance, but it was one that took the un-tolerated seriously.

The Tooth and the Two Dimensions of the Fetishism of Objects

Another (but related) way of looking at the jewel-bone polarity is by focusing on the two dimensions or "social loops" of the fetishism of objects defined by Tambiah and referred to several times in the course of this book. As mentioned, Tambiah (1984, 335–337) posited that charismatic objects such as the tooth relic could ideologically and devotionally connect

Buddhist practitioners to the Buddha, a connection that could advance them on the "otherworldly" path of making merit and attaining enlightenment. At the same time, the same relic could be used for this-worldly purposes, "in the corridors of politics [and] the stratagems of commerce" (Tambiah 1984, 336). These two dimensions were also perceived by Westerners dealing with the tooth, but with a difference: while for Buddhists, as Tambiah makes clear, the two aspects of the tooth were like the two sides of a single coin (or amulet), for Westerners, there was a tendency to bifurcate the two dimensions and to prefer to retain one in preference over the other. As we have seen, by and large, believing Christians such as the Portuguese and the British in our stories could not accept *for themselves* the tooth as a religious object. Simply put, their otherworldly myopia did not allow them to engage the relic-as-Buddha. Thus, the Portuguese destroyed the bone and the British divorced themselves from it. They were, however, willing to engage in this-worldly (especially political) transactions with the tooth and use to their own benefit its "Dalada-king" dimension. The Portuguese, having gotten rid of the tooth-object, had to do this through stories that reified the relic as a symbol of sovereignty and so let them score geopolitical points against Vijayanagar, Pegu, and Kandy. The British, however, having not destroyed the tooth, could engage it materially by protecting, sponsoring, and benefiting from its cult in Kandy.

To be sure, over the years, the degree of their engagement declined in the face of opposition from Christian missionaries for whom the religious identity of the tooth as "Buddha" trumped that of "King," as well as in the light of the objections of Christian politicians who insisted on the separation of "Religion" from "State." As we have seen throughout the chapters of part 2, the tooth is a marker that can be used to trace the evolving shifts in British colonial attitudes toward Sri Lanka and Buddhism, from ignorance to usurpation to condemnation to dissociation. And even thereafter, remnants of the British engagement with the tooth could still be seen lingering in the cases of the visits of King Chulalongkorn in 1897 and of Queen Elizabeth in 1954. Colonialism may stop, but the tooth relic lives on—not only in the minds of Sri Lankans, but in the imagination of Westerners.

The Tooth as a Cosmopolitan Object

Finally, I want to return to the question of the multicultural cosmopolitan character of the tooth. The relic in Sri Lanka has often been viewed as a symbol of Sinhalese Buddhist sovereignty, an emblem uniting the island against foreign rulers; indeed, this may be what it was at certain points in

Sri Lankan history and what it perhaps is today. As we have seen, however, it can also be viewed as a cosmopolitan object, something that bridges divides between countries, cultures, even continents. Put simply, the tooth is both a Sri Lankan and a foreign object. In its first capacity, it could and did serve the purposes of Sinhalese nationalist rulers; in its latter capacity, it was an ideal bolster for non-Sinhalese sovereigns. As pointed out in chapter 6, the tooth was a perfect palladium for the Nāyakkars because its cult (like they themselves) exhibited both Buddhist and Hindu elements, overlapping those two religio-cultural traditions (in as much as they may be deemed to have been distinct from one another).

This same multiculturality is reflected, I think, in the multiple identities given (sometimes simultaneously) to the tooth by the Portuguese. It had either belonged to a Hindu god (Hanumān) or to the Buddha, both of whom, however, shared something in common: in the stories the Portuguese told about them, they were portrayed as foreign figures who came to Sri Lanka from India, and who then went away again, but chose either to leave their tooth on the island or to send it back there from their deathbeds so they could be venerated there. Whether Hanumān's or the Buddha's, the tooth relic was thus a symbol of the indigenization of a foreign culture.

It is in this sense that I have argued that the tooth was also a good palladium for the British, who, like it, came from abroad and stayed. Just as the Nāyakkar cult of the tooth had both Hindu and Buddhist elements, it may be possible, in the early nineteenth century, to speak of the cult of the tooth as also having some British aspects.[1] The inclusion of British military bands in the *peraheras* that returned the tooth in 1815 and in 1818, for instance, was hardly traditional. Nor was D'Oyly's offering of a musical clock on that occasion. Nor was the pecking order of viewers at the 1828 exhibition of the tooth that saw English ladies and gentlemen go first, prior to the assembled monks. In these examples, we can see how the cosmopolitan tooth, in its multiculturalism, can open itself to amalgamating new elements. There were limits, however, to how far this amalgamation was allowed to go. Unlike the footprint on Adam's Peak which, Do Couto suggested, was that of Saint Thomas, unlike the reclining image of the Buddha in Mulgirigala, which was thought to be that of Adam on his deathbed, the tooth was never given a Christian identity, despite Peter Courtenay's ([1913] 2005, 147) suggestion that Muslims thought of it as the tooth of Adam.

---

1. It never got to have Portuguese elements except, perhaps, in the ritual of its destruction.

Final Story

But the saga of the tooth was famous enough that its mythos got domesticized by Western storytellers. To illustrate this further with a concrete example, I want to end with one more tale. In August 1942, in the midst of the second world war, a certain English admiral named Studholme Brownrigg wrote a short letter to the Colonial Office in London.[2] He had recently inherited an ivory object that had been in his family for generations and which they always referred to as "Buddha's Tooth." To the best of his knowledge, it had been acquired by his great-grandfather in 1815, in a temple in Kandy, Ceylon, under what circumstances he was not sure. His great-grandfather was a nephew of Robert Brownrigg, the governor of Ceylon at the time.[3] In any case, the admiral recalled reading that in 1934, the Duke of Gloucester had repatriated the Kandyan throne to Ceylon, and he was now thinking he would like to do the same with his family's heirloom by returning it to the temple from whence it came, and where, he felt, it belonged. Was there any way the Colonial Office could help him with this? (CO 54/979/2, 1).

At first, the Colonial Office treated this as an unusual but more or less routine request, but when Andrew Caldecott, the wartime governor of Ceylon, was apprised of the letter and read therein the words "Buddha's tooth," "Kandy," "1815," and "Brownrigg," he went into panic mode. It is easy to imagine the questions that must have bubbled up in his mind: Had Governor Robert Brownrigg in 1815 somehow acquired the Dalada? Had he asked his nephew to take it back to England, the same way he had had his son accompany back the Kandyan throne? Had it been kept in the family all this time? If so, was the relic in Kandy a fake? He immediately classified the whole inquiry as "confidential," and declared that what the admiral was proposing was a very delicate matter and would risk raising the specter of a long-ago "sacrilegious theft from a Buddhist temple." He should do nothing until they could investigate all this further (CO 54/979/2, 6).

In due time, it became clear that the admiral's ivory object was not the tooth. For one thing, it was much too large, being described as a "deformed or twisted elephant's tusk"—something that the admiral's cousin had

2. Studholme Brownrigg (1882–1943) was an officer in the Royal Navy, who fought in both World War I (where he distinguished himself at the Battle of Jutland) and World War II.

3. The admiral's great-grandfather, John Studholme Brownrigg (1786–1853), went out to India at age fifteen and had various posts in the military there and elsewhere in Asia, including, apparently, visits to Ceylon. He was promoted to captain in 1815 but five years later resigned from the army and returned to England, where he served as a member of Parliament and built a career as a merchant.

thought might look good as a display item in the entrance of Admiralty House in Chatham (CO 54/979/2, 5). Even so, Governor Caldecott's fears were well founded, for questions still remained; large elephant tusks are common votive decorations in the Dalada Maligawa, as well as other temples in Sri Lanka, and this one had obviously been stolen. Thus, Caldecott recommended that the admiral be told that, though he was free to do what he wanted with the tusk, if he sent it back to Ceylon, he should in no case mention any of his correspondence with anyone in the government. As far as they were concerned, he was on his own—it was a private matter (CO 54/979/3, 3).

In the end, it is not clear (at least to me) what happened to Admiral Brownrigg's tusk. By the time the Colonial Office wrote to him to inform him of all this, in January 1943, he had perished at sea; the transport convoy that he had come out of retirement to command encountered a violent storm in the North Atlantic. His ship broke apart and all on board were drowned. However, the story of his family's "Buddha's tooth" and of his well-intentioned desire to repatriate it as a relic serves as a reminder not only of how the fame of a "foreign" relic can persist in the Western imaginaire, but also of how stories can make such an object potent and meaningful, even when it is not "genuine."

REFERENCES

ARCHIVAL MATERIALS
(AT NATIONAL ARCHIVES, KEW, RICHMOND, ENGLAND)

[CO = Colonial Office; PREM = Records of the Prime Minister's Office]

CO 54/53. Ceylon, Original Correspondence. Despatches. 1814, September–December.

CO 54/55. Ceylon, Original Correspondence. Despatches. 1815, January–April.

CO 54/56. Ceylon, Original Correspondence. Despatches. 1815, June–September.

CO 54/58. Ceylon, Original Correspondence. Offices and Individuals. 1815.

CO 54/71. Ceylon, Original Correspondence. Despatches. 1818, July–November.

CO 54/72. Ceylon, Original Correspondence. Offices and Individuals. 1818.

CO 54/73. Ceylon, Original Correspondence. Despatches. 1819, January–March.

CO 54/206. Ceylon, Original Correspondence. Despatches. 1843, November–December.

CO 54/209. Ceylon, Original Correspondence. Individuals. 1843.

CO 54/210. Ceylon, Original Correspondence. Despatches. 1844, January–March.

CO 54/212. Ceylon, Original Correspondence. Despatches. 1844, July–September.

CO 54/217. Ceylon, Original Correspondence. Despatches. 1845, April–June.

CO 54/218. Ceylon, Original Correspondence. Despatches. 1845, July–September.

CO 54/223. Ceylon, Original Correspondence. Despatches. 1846, January–February.

CO 54/234. Ceylon, Original Correspondence. Despatches. 1847, March–April.

CO 54/229. Ceylon, Original Correspondence. Offices (except Treasury). 1846.

CO 54/979/2. Admiral Sir S. Brownrigg: offer to return alleged "Buddhas Tooth" to Ceylon. August 1, 1942–November 30, 1942.

CO 54/979/3. Admiral Sir S. Brownrigg: offer to return alleged "Buddhas Tooth" to Ceylon. October 1, 1942–January 31, 1943.

CO 416/19. Commissioners of Eastern Inquiry, Ceylon. Kandyan Provinces, No. G.1–G.8. 1829–1830.

CO 416/20. Commissioners of Eastern Inquiry, Ceylon. Kandyan Provinces, 1829–1830.

PREM 11/737. "Suggested Visit by HM The Queen and HRH The Duke of Edinburgh to the Temple of the Tooth at Kandy in the Event of a Royal Visit to Ceylon."

UNSIGNED NEWSPAPER ARTICLES

Asiatic Journal and Monthly Miscellany. 1818. "Asiatic Intelligence—Ceylon." 5 (June): 609–617.

Asiatic Journal and Monthly Register for British India and Its Dependencies. 1816a. "Asiatic Intelligence—Ceylon." 1 (January–June): 90–92.

———. 1816b. "An Account of the Late Conquest of Kandy." 1 (January–June): 117–120, 226–231.

———. 1816c. "Asiatic Intelligence—Ceylon." 2 (July–December): 102–103.

———. 1819. "Execution of Kappitipola and Madugalle." 8 (July–December): 92–94.

Catholic Messenger and the Western World (Davenport, IA). 1932. "Novena of Grace Recalls Extraordinary Death and Miracles of Saint Francis Xavier." 50, no. 13 (March 3): 6.

Ceylon Independent (Colombo). 1909a. "Buddha's Tooth." August 25, p. 9.

———. 1909b. "Return of Viscount Kitchener from Kandy." September 16, vol. 22, no. 67, p. 1.

Chicago Tribune. 1954. "Seven Cases Open and Queen Gazes on Tooth of Buddha." April 20.

Living Church. 1954. "Ceylon." 128 (January 17).

London Quarterly Review. 1840. "Chinese Affairs." 66: 294–319.

New York Times. 1954. "Queen Removes Shoes to See Buddha's Tooth." April 20, p. 4.

Overland Ceylon Observer. 1897a. "The King of Siam at Kandy." April 22, p. 96.

———. 1897b. "The Māligāwa Incident." April 29, p. 523.

Overland Times of Ceylon. 1897a. "Official Programme." April 20, pp. 614–615.

———. 1897b. "The Siamese King and the Ceylon Buddhists." May, pp. 700–702.

Straits Times (Singapore). 1863. "Malacca." December 19, p. 6.

———. 1909. "A Golden Shrine." June 29, p. 11.

———. 1934. "Royal Pageantry in Ceylon. Duke Returns Kandyan Throne & Crown." October 5, p. 13.

Sunday Observer (Colombo). 2016. "Where the Sacred Tooth Relic Was Hidden." August 1.

The Times (London). 1901. "The Duke of Cornwall's Tour." April 15, p. 5.

———. 1954a. "The Queen of Ceylon." April 10, p. 6.

———. 1954b. "Ceylon Greets the Queen." April 12, p. 8.

———. 1954c. "Kandy Greets the Queen with Splendour." April 20, p. 8.

BOOKS AND ARTICLES

Abeyasinghe, Tikiri. 1980–1981. "History as Polemics and Propaganda: An Examination of Fernao de Queiros, *History of Ceylon.*" *Journal of the Royal Asiatic Society, Sri Lanka Branch* 25: 28–68.

Aksland, Markus. 2001. *The Sacred Footprint: A Cultural History of Adam's Peak.* Bangkok: Orchid Press.

Alexander, Alexander. 1830. *The Life of Alexander Alexander.* Edited by John Howell. 2 vols. Edinburgh: William Blackwood.

Almond, Philip C. 1987. "The Buddha of Christendom: A Review of the Legend of Barlaam and Josaphat." *Religious Studies* 23: 391–406.

———. 1988. *The British Discovery of Buddhism.* Cambridge: Cambridge University Press.

Amiel, Charles, and Anne Lima. 1997. *L'inquisition de Goa. La relation de Charles Dellon 1687.* Paris: Editions Chandeigne.

An Yang-Gyu. 2003. *The Buddha's Last Days: Buddhaghosa's Commentary on the Mahāparinibbāna Sutta.* Oxford: Pali Text Society.

Anderson, Thomas Ajax. 1809. *Poems Written Chiefly in India.* London: Philanthropic Society.

Anonymous. 1898. *Buddha's Tooth, Worshipped by the Buddhists of Ceylon in the Pagoda called Dalada-Maligawa at Kandy.* Mangalore: Codialhail Press.

———. 2018. "Arahat Maha Kassapa Thera Tooth Relic Temple, Galapatha." *SriLankaView*. https://www.srilankaview.com/places_interest/galapatha.htm.

———. n.d. "Victims of Francis Xavier Oppose the Public Display of his Corpse, Demand Return to France." *Indiafacts. Truth be Told*. http://indiafacts.org/victims-of-fran cis-xavier-oppose-the-public-display-of-his-corpse-demand-return-to-france/#.VHSB cGdh7TO.

App, Urs. 2010. *The Birth of Orientalism*. Philadelphia: University of Pennsylvania Press.

———. 2012. *The Cult of Emptiness: The Western Discovery of Buddhist Thought and the Invention of Oriental Philosophy*. Rorschach: University Media.

Appadurai, Arjun. 1986. *The Social Life of Things: Commodities in Cultural Perspective*. Cambridge: Cambridge University Press.

Arasaratnam, Sinnappah. 1978. *François Valentijn's Description of Ceylon*. London: Hakluyt Society.

Atkinson, Geoffroy. 1920. *The Extraordinary Voyage in French Literature*. New York: B. Franklin.

Auction House of Mr. Thomas King. 1820. "Regalia of the King of Kandy. A Catalogue of Splendid and Valuable Collection of Jewellery Forming the Regalia of the King of Kandy." London: W. Smith.

Ayyar, P. V. Jagadisa. 1920. *South Indian Shrines*. Madras: Madras Times.

Balbi, Gasparo. 1590. *Viaggio dell'Indie Orientali*. Venice: Camillo Borgominieri.

———. 2003. ["English translation of Burma-relevant part of his *Viaggio*"]. *SOAS Bulletin of Burma Research* 1, no. 2: 26–34.

Baldaeus, Philippus. 1672. *Naauwkeurige Beschrijvinge van Malabar en Choromandel der Zelver aangrenzenden Ryken en het machtige Eyland Ceylon*. Amsterdam: Johannes Janssonius van Waasberge and Johannes van Someren.

———. [1703] 2000. *A Description of ye East India Coasts of Malabar and Coromandel with their Adjacent Kingdoms & Provinces & of the Empire of Ceylon*. Translated by Anonymous. New Delhi: Asian Educational Services.

Bandaranayake, Senake. 1986. *The Rock and Wall Paintings of Sri Lanka*. Colombo: Lake House.

Barbosa, Duarte. 1866. *A Description of the Coasts of East Africa and Malabar in the Beginning of the Sixteenth Century*. Translated by Henry E. J. Stanley. London: Hakluyt Society.

Barrow, George. 1857. *Ceylon: Past and Present*. London: John Murray.

Bechert, Heinz. 1963. "Mother Right and Succession to the Throne in Malabar and Ceylon." *Ceylon Journal of Historical and Social Studies* 6, no. 1: 25–39.

Bell, Aubrey F. G. 1924. *Diogo Do Couto*. Oxford: Oxford University Press.

Bell, H. C. P. 1888–1889. "Treaty of Peace Between the Dutch and Sinhalese, Dated 14th February 1766." *The Orientalist* 3: 115–118.

Bennett, J. W. 1843. *Ceylon and its Capabilities; an Account of its Natural Resources, Indigenous Productions, and Commercial Facilities; to which are added Details of its Statistics, Pilotage and Sailing Directions*. London: W. H. Allen and Co.

Berkwitz, Stephen C. 2007. *The History of the Buddha's Relic Shrine: A Translation of the Sinhala Thūpavaṃsa*. Oxford: Oxford University Press.

———. 2013. *Buddhist Poetry and Colonialism: Alagiyavanna and the Portuguese in Sri Lanka*. Oxford: Oxford University Press.

———. 2016. "Reimagining Buddhist Kingship in a Sinhala *Praśasti*." *Journal of the American Oriental Society* 136, no. 2: 325–341.

Bernand, Carmen, and Serge Gruzinski. 1988. *De l'idolatrie: une archéologie des sciences religieuses*. Paris: Editions du Seuil.

Biedermann, Zoltán. 2016. "The Temporal Politics of Spiritual Conquest: History, Geography and Franciscan Orientalism in the Conquista Espiritual do Oriente of Friar Paulo da Trindade." *Cultural & History Digital Journal* 5, no. 2. http://cultureandhistory.revistas.csic.es/index.php/cultureandhistory/article/view/101/345.

———. 2018. *(Dis)connected Empires: Imperial Portugal, Sri Lankan Diplomacy, and the Making of a Habsburg Conquest in Asia.* Oxford: Oxford University Press.

Biedermann, Zoltán, and Alan Strathern, eds. 2017. *Sri Lanka at the Crossroads of History.* London: UCL Press.

Blackburn, Anne M. 2001. *Buddhist Learning and Textual Practice in Eighteenth-Century Lankan Monastic Culture.* Princeton, NJ: Princeton University Press.

———. 2010. *Locations of Buddhism: Colonialism and Modernity in Sri Lanka.* Chicago: University of Chicago Press.

———. 2014. "The Sphere of the *Sāsana* in the Context of Colonialism." In *Networks of Material, Intellectual and Cultural Exchange.* Singapore: Institute of Southeast Asian Studies. 1: 371–382.

———. 2015. "Buddhist Connections in the Indian Ocean: Changes in Monastic Mobility, 1000–1500." *Journal of the Economic and Social History of the Orient* 58: 237–266.

Boake, Barcroft. 1854. *A Brief Account of the Origin and Nature of the Connexion between the British Government and the Idolatrous Systems of Religion Prevalent in the Island of Ceylon and of the Extent to which that Connexion still Exists.* Colombo: Ceylon Times.

Bosman, Willem. 1705. *A New and Accurate Description of the Coast of Guinea Divided into the Gold, the Slave, and the Ivory Coasts.* Translated from the Dutch by Anonymous. London: Rose and Crown.

Boxer, Charles Ralph. 1948. *Three Historians of Portuguese Asia (Barros, Couto, and Bocarro).* Macau: Imprensa Nacional.

———. 1955. "Captain João Ribeiro and his History of Ceylon, 1622–1693." *Journal of the Royal Asiatic Society of Great Britain and Ireland* 1955: 1–12.

Boyle, Richard. 2013. "British Royal Encounters with Sri Lanka." *Explore Sri Lanka,* November. http://webcache.googleusercontent.com/search?q=cache:zu92GZJ8fOsJ:exploresrilanka.lk/2013/11/british-royal-encounters-with-sri-lanka/+&cd=4&hl=en&ct=clnk&gl=us.

Bracciolini, Poggio. 1857. "The Travels of Nicolò Conti in the East in the Early Part of the Fifteenth Century." Translated by J. Winter Jones. In *In the Fifteenth Century. Being a Collection of Narratives of Voyages to India.* Edited by R. H. Major. London: Hakluyt Society. Part 2.

Breazeale, Kennon. 2004. "Early Fifteenth Century Travels in the East." *SOAS Bulletin of Burma Research* 2, no. 2: 100–117.

Brockey, Liam Matthew. 2005. "Jesuit Pastoral Theater on an Urban Stage: Lisbon, 1588–1593." *Journal of Early Modern History* 9: 1–50.

———. 2015. "The Cruelest Honor: The Relics of Francis Xavier in Early-Modern Asia." *Catholic Historical Review* 101: 41–64.

Brohier, R. L. 1933. *The Golden Age of Military Adventure in Ceylon: An Account of the Uva Rebellion, 1817–1818.* Colombo: Plâté, Ltd.

Brucker, Joseph. 1913. "Malabar Rites." *Catholic Encyclopedia.* https://en.wikisource.org/wiki/Catholic_Encyclopedia_(1913)/Malabar_Rites.

Burridge, Tom. 2010. "Monkey Security for Delhi Games." https://www.bbc.com/news/av/world-south-asia-11448350/monkey-security-for-delhi-games [BBC News report, October 1].

Burrun, B. 2015. "Histoire: Le Prince de Kandy exilé jusqu'à sa mort à Maurice." *LeMauricien.com.* http://www.lemauricien.com/article/histoire-prince-kandy-exile-jusqu-sa-mort-maurice.

Buultjens, A. E. 1899. "[J. G. Van Angelbeek's(?) Journal of] Governor Van Eck's Expedition against the King of Kandy, 1765." *Journal of the Royal Asiatic Society (Ceylon Branch)* 16: 36–78.

Bynum, Caroline Walker. 1995. *The Resurrection of the Body in Western Christianity 200–1336.* New York: Columbia University Press.

Calladine, George. 1922. *The Diary of Colour-Serjeant George Calladine, 19th Foot, 1793–1837.* Edited by M. J. Ferrar. London: Eden Fisher & Co.

Calvin, John. 1970. *Three French Treatises.* Edited by Francis M. Higman. London: Athlone Press.

Cameron, John. 1865. *Our Tropical Possessions in Malayan India: Being a Descriptive Account of Singapore, Penang, Province Wellesley, and Malacca; their Peoples, Products, Commerce, and Government.* London: Smith, Elder and Co.

Camões, Luís de. 1997. *The Lusíads.* Translated by Landeg White. Oxford: Oxford University Press.

Candidus (pseud.). 1816. "Letter to the Editor of the Asiatic Journal." *Asiatic Journal and Monthly Register for British India and Its Dependencies* 1 (January–June): 225–226.

Capper, John. 1871. *The Duke of Edinburgh in Ceylon: A Book of Elephant and Elk Sport.* London: Provost & Co.

Carita, Helder. 2007. "Portuguese-Influenced Religious Architecture in Ceylon: Creation, Types and Continuity." In *Re-Exploring the Links: History and Constructed Histories between Portugal and Sri Lanka.* Edited by Jorge Flores. Wiesbaden: Harrassowitz Verlag. Pp. 260–278.

Carletti, Francesco. 1964. *My Voyage around the World: The Chronicles of a 16th Century Florentine Merchant.* Translated by Herbert Weinstock. New York: Pantheon Books.

Cervantes, Fernando. 1994. *The Devil in the New World: The Impact of Diabolism in New Spain.* New Haven, CT: Yale University Press.

Cervantes, Miguel de. 1885. *The Ingenious Gentleman Don Quixote of La Mancha.* Translated by John Ormsby. London: Smith, Elder & Co.

Chavannes, Edouard. 1894. *Mémoire composé à l'époque de la grande dynastie T'ang sur les religieux éminents qui allèrent chercher la loi dans les pays d'occident, par I-Tsing.* Paris: Ernest Leroux.

Clericus Damnionensis (pseud.). 1815. ["Letter to the Editor"]. *Ceylon Government Gazette.* May 3.

Colebrooke, W. M. G. 1836. "Account of a Ceremonial Exhibition of the Relic termed 'the Tooth of Buddha,' at Kandy, in Ceylon, in May 1828. Translated and abridged from the original Singhalese, drawn up by a Native Eye-Witness." *Journal of the Royal Asiatic Society* 3: 161–164.

Coleridge, Henry James. 1881. *The Life and Letters of St. Francis Xavier.* 2 vols. London: Burns and Oates.

Collis, Maurice. 1943. *The Land of the Great Image.* New York: New Directions Books.

Cordiner, James. 1807. *A Description of Ceylon Containing an Account of the Country, Inhabitants, and Natural Productions; with Narratives of a Tour round the Island in 1800, the Campaign in Candy in 1803, and a Journey to Ramisseram in 1804.* 2 vols. London: Longman, Hurst, Rees, and Orme.

Courtenay, P. 1900. *Le Christianisme à Ceylan.* 2 vols. Lille: Desclée, De Brouwer, & Co.

———. [1913] 2005. *History of Ceylon.* Abridged translation by M. G. Francis. New Delhi: Asian Educational Services.

Crawfurd, John. 1830. *Journal of an Embassy from the Governor-General of India to the Courts of Siam and Cochin China; Exhibiting a View of the Actual State of Those Kingdoms.* 2 vols. London: Henry Colburn and Richard Bentley.

Cronin, Vincent. 1959. *A Pearl to India: A Life of Roberto de Nobili*. New York: E. P. Dutton.

Crowe, Philip K. 1956. *Diversions of a Diplomat in Ceylon*. Princeton: D. Van Nostrand Co.

Cūḷavaṃsa. 1980. Edited by Wilhelm Geiger. London: Pali Text Society.

Cumming, Constance Frederica Gordon. 1892. *Two Happy Years in Ceylon*. 2 vols. New York: Charles Scribner's Sons.

D'Oyly, John. 1917. Diary of Mr. John D'Oyly. Edited by H. W. Codrington. *Journal of the Ceylon Branch of the Royal Asiatic Society* 25, no. 69.

———. 1929. *A Sketch of the Constitution of the Kandyan Kingdom (and other Relevant Papers)*. Colombo: H. Ross Cottle, Government Printer.

Da Cunha, J. Gerson. 1875. *Memoir on the History of the Tooth-Relic of Ceylon*. London: W. Thacker & Co.

Dāṭhāvaṃsa. 1884. Edited by T. W. Rhys Davids. *Journal of the Pali Text Society*: 109–150.

Davids, T. W. Rhys. 1874. "[Review of] *The Dāṭhāvaṃsa; or History of the Tooth-Relic of Gotama Buddha*. By M. Coomâra Swâmy." *The Academy* 6 (September 26): 339–341.

Davies, Donald. 1957. "Tricky Tickery—the Tale of a Knave." *Straits Times* (Singapore) (December 1): 14.

Davies, Robert. 1870. "A Memoir of Sir Thomas Herbert, of Tinterne, in the County of Monmouth, and of the City of York, Baronet." *Yorkshire Archaeological and Topographical Journal* 1: 182–214.

Davy, John. 1821. *An Account of the Interior of Ceylon, and of its Inhabitants. With Travels in that Island*. London: Longman, Hurst, Rees, Orme, and Brown.

De Barros, João. [1563] 1777. *Da Asia de João De Barros. Dos feitos, que os Portuguezes fizeram no descubrimento, e conquista dos mares, et terras do Oriente. Decada Terceira, Parte Primeira*. Lisbon: Regia Officina Typographica.

De Brosses, Charles. 1760. *Du culte des dieux fétiches, ou parallèle de l'ancienne religion de l'Egypte avec la religion actuelle de Nigritie*. Paris: n.p.

De Bussche, L. 1817. *Letters on Ceylon; Particularly Relative to the Kingdom of Kandy*. London: J. J. Stockdale.

De Kloguen, Denis Louis Cottineau. 1831. *An Historical Sketch of Goa, the Metropolis of the Portuguese Settlements in India*. Madras: Gazette Press.

De la Boullaye-le-Gouz, François. 1653. *Les Voyages et Observations du Sieur De La Boullaye-le-Govz, gentil-homme angevin*. Paris: Gervais Clousier.

De Silva, C. R. 1977. "The Rise and Fall of the Kingdom of Sitawaka (1521–1593)." *Ceylon Journal of Historical and Social Studies* 7: 1–43.

———. 2009. *Portuguese Encounters with Sri Lanka and the Maldives: Translated Texts from the Age of the Discoveries*. Farnham: Ashgate.

De Silva, K. M. 1965a. *Social Policy and Missionary Organizations in Ceylon 1840–1855*. London: Longmans, Green and Co.

———. 1965b. *Letters on Ceylon 1846–50. The Administration of Viscount Torrington and the "Rebellion" of 1848*. Kandy: K. V. G. De Silva and Sons.

———. 1973a. "The Kandyan Kingdom and the British—The Last Phase, 1796–1818." In *University of Ceylon History of Ceylon, Volume Three*. Edited by K. M. De Silva. Peradeniya: University of Ceylon. Pp. 12–33.

———. 1973b. "Religion and the State in the Early Nineteenth Century." In *University of Ceylon History of Ceylon, Volume Three*. Edited by K. M. De Silva. Peradeniya: University of Ceylon. Pp. 66–76.

———. 1981. *A History of Sri Lanka*. Berkeley: University of California Press.

De Silva, Keshini. 2017. "The Tale of a Grinding Stone." http://exploresrilanka.lk/2017/09/the-tale-of-a-sacred-grinding-stone/.

De Silva, Lynn. 1980. *Buddhism: Beliefs and Practices in Sri Lanka.* Battaramula: SIOLL School of Technology.

De Silva, R. K., and W. G. M. Beumer. 1988. *Illustrations and Views of Dutch Ceylon 1602–1796: A Comprehensive work of Pictorial Reference with Selected Eye-Witness Accounts.* London: Serendib Publications.

De Silva, W. Arthur. 1915–1916. "The Popular Poetry of the Sinhalese." *Journal of the Ceylon Branch of the Royal Asiatic Society* 24: 27–66.

De Sousa, Francisco. 1710. *Oriente Conquistado a Jesu Christo pelos padres da Companhia de Jesu da Provincia de Goa.* Lisbon: Valentim da Costa Deslandes.

De Souza, Teotonio R. 1979. *Medieval Goa: A Socio-Economic History.* New Delhi: Concept Publishing Co.

Deeg, Max. 2005. *Das Gaoseng-Faxian-Zhuan als religionsgeschichtliche Quelle.* Wiesbaden: Harrassowitz Verlag.

Dellon, Gabriel. 1688. *Relation de l'inquisition de Goa.* Paris: Daniel Horthemels.

Dewaraja, Lorna Srimathie. 1972. *A Study of the Political, Administrative and Social Structure of the Kandyan Kingdom of Ceylon, 1707–1760.* Colombo: Lake House Publishers.

———. 2018. *The Kandy Äsala Maha Perahära.* Colombo: Vijitha Yapa Publications.

Dhaninivat (Prince). 1965. "Religious Intercourse between Ceylon and Siam." *Paranavitana Felicitation Volume on Art and Architecture and Oriental Studies.* Edited by N. A. Jayawickrama. Colombo: M. D. Gunasena. Pp. 135–141.

Dharmadasa, K. N. O. 1976. "The Sinhala-Buddhist Identity and the Nayakkar Dynasty in the Politics of the Kandyan Kingdom, 1739–1815." *Ceylon Journal of Historical and Social Studies* 6, no. 1: 1–23.

Di Varthema, Ludovico. [1510] 1863. *The Travels of Ludovico di Varthema in Egypt, Syria, Arabia Deserta and Arabia Felix, in Persia, India, and Ethiopia A.D. 1503 to 1508.* Translated by John Winter Jones. Edited by George Percy Badger. London: Hakluyt Society.

Diffie, Bailey W., and George D. Winius. 1977. *Europe and the World in the Age of Expansion: Foundations of the Portuguese Empire, 1415–1580.* Minneapolis: University of Minnesota Press.

Dīgha Nikāya. 1911. Edited by J. Estlin Carpenter. London: Pali Text Society.

Disney, A. R. 2009. *A History of Portugal and the Portuguese Empire.* Cambridge: Cambridge University Press. 2 vols.

Do Couto, Diogo. 1780. *Da Asia. Dos feitos, que os Portuguezes fizeram na conquista, e descubrimento das terras e mares do Oriente. Decada Quinta, Parte Segunda.* Lisbon: Regia Officina Typographica.

———. 1783. *Da Asia. Dos feitos, que os Portuguezes fizeram na conquista, e descubrimento das terras e mares do Oriente. Decada Setima, Parte Segunda.* Lisbon: Regia Officina Typographica.

———. 1786. *Da Asia. Dos feitos, que os Portuguezes fizeram na conquista, e descubrimento das terras e mares do Oriente. Decada Oitava.* Lisbon: Regia Officina Typographica.

———. [1612] 1937. *O Soldado Prático.* Lisbon: Libraria Sá Da Costa.

———. 2016. *Dialog of a Veteran Soldier Discussing the Frauds and Realities of Portuguese India.* Translated by Timothy J. Coates. Dartmouth, MA: Tagus Press.

Dolapihilla, Punchibandara. 1959. *In the Days of Sri Wickramarajasingha, Last King of Kandy.* Maharagama: Saman Press.

Doniger [O'Flaherty], Wendy. 1988. *Other Peoples' Myths: The Cave of Echoes.* New York: Macmillan Publishing Co.

Dooley, Eugene A. 1931. *Church Law on Sacred Relics.* Washington, DC: Catholic University of America.

Dreyer, Edward L. 2007. *Zheng He: China and the Oceans in the Early Ming Dynasty, 1405–1433*. New York: Pearson Longman.

Du Jarric, Pierre. 1610. *Histoire des choses plus mémorables advenues tant ez Indes Orientales, que autre païs de la descouverte des Portugais, en l'establissement et progrez de la foy Chrestienne et Catholique: et principalement de ce que les Religieux de la Compagnie de Iesus y ont faict, et enduré pour la mesme fin. Depuis qu'ils y sont entrez jusqu'à l'an 1600*. Bordeaux: Simon Millanges.

Duangmee, Phoowadon. 2012. "Rites of Passage." *The Nation* (Bangkok) (August).

Dubois, Jean-Antoine. [1807] 1906. *Hindu Manners, Customs and Ceremonies*. Translated by Henry K. Beauchamp. Oxford: Clarendon Press.

Duncan, James. 1990. *The City as Text: The Politics of Landscape Interpretation in the Kandyan Kingdom*. Cambridge: Cambridge University Press.

Eaton, Richard. 2006. *A Social History of the Deccan, 1300–1761: Eight Indian Lives*. Cambridge: Cambridge University Press.

Eire, Carlos M. 1986. *War against the Idols: The Reformation of Worship from Erasmus to Calvin*. Cambridge: Cambridge University Press.

Eliade, Mircea. 1969. *The Quest: History and Meaning in Religion*. Chicago: University of Chicago Press.

Elliot, Walter. 1886. *The International Numismata Orientalia. Coins of Southern India*. London: Trübner & Co.

Ellis, David. 1998. *D. H. Lawrence: Dying Game, 1922–1930*. Cambridge: Cambridge University Press.

Evers, Hans-Dieter. 1964. "Buddhism and British Colonial Policy in Ceylon, 1815–1875." *Asian Studies* 2, no. 3: 323–333.

Falcao, Nelson. 2003. *Kristapurāṇa: A Christian-Hindu Encounter. A Study of Inculturation in the Kristapurāṇa of Thomas Stephens, S.J. (1549–1619)*. Gujarat: Gurati Sahitya Prakash.

Faria e Souza, Manuel. 1666–1675. *Asia Portuguesa*. Lisbon: Officina de Henrique Valente de Oliveira, Impressor del Rey. 3 vols.

———. 1695. *The Portugues' Asia: or, the History of the Discovery and Conquest of India by the Portuguese*. 3 vols. Translated by John Stevens. London: C. Brome.

Farrer, Reginald. 1908. *In Old Ceylon*. London: Edwin Arnold.

Faure, Bernard. 2018. *Les mille et une vies du Bouddha*. Paris: Editions du Seuil.

Fellowes, Robert (aka Philalethes). 1817. *The History of Ceylon from the Earliest Period to the Year MDCCCXV; with Characteristic Details of the Religion, Laws & Manners of the People and a Collection of their Moral Maxims and Ancient Proverbs*. London: Joseph Mawman.

Ferguson, Donald. 1897. "Pedro Teixeira." *Journal of the Royal Asiatic Society of Great Britain and Ireland*: 933–939.

———. [1908] 1993. *The History of Ceylon from the Earliest Times to 1600 A.D. as Related by Joao de Barros and Diogo do Couto*. New Delhi: Navrang. Originally published in the *Journal of the Ceylon Branch of the Royal Asiatic Society* 20, no. 60: 1–445.

———. 1911. "Mulgiri-Gala." *Journal of the Ceylon Branch of the Royal Asiatic Society of Great Britain and Ireland* 22, no. 64: 197–244.

Ferguson, John. 1887. *Ceylon in the Jubilee Year. With an Account of the Progress Made since 1803, and of the Present Condition of its Agricultural and Commercial Enterprises; the Resources Awaiting Development by Capitalists; and the Unequalled Attractions Offered to Visitors*. 3rd ed. London: John Haddon and Co.

Fernando, J. L. 1963. *Three Prime Ministers of Ceylon—An Inside Story*. Colombo: M. D. Gunasena.

Flores, Jorge, and Maria Augusta Lima Cruz. 2007. "A 'Tale of Two Cities,' a 'Veteran Soldier,' or the Struggle for Endangered Nobilities: The Two *Jornadas de Huva* (1633, 1635) Revisited." In *Re-Exploring the Links: History and Constructed Histories between Portugal and Sri Lanka*. Edited by Jorge Flores. Wiesbaden: Harrassowitz Verlag. Pp. 95–124.

Forbes, Jonathan. 1835. "The Dangistra Daladâ, or Right Canine Tooth of Gautama Buddha." *Ceylon Almanac and Compendium of Useful Information* 3: 231–235.

———. 1840. *Eleven Years in Ceylon Comprising Sketches of the Field Sports and Natural History of that Colony and an Account of its History and Antiquities*. 2 vols. London: R. Bentley.

Fortescue, J. W. 1921. *A History of the British Army*. London: Macmillan and Co. Vol. 5.

Frankfurter, Oscar. [1911] 2013. *The Late King Chulalongkorn*. New Delhi: Isha Books.

Fritz, John. 1985. "Was Vijayanagara a Cosmic City?" In *Vijayanagara—City and Empire: New Currents in Research*. Edited by Anna Libera Dallapiccola and Stéphanie Zingel-Avé Lallemant. Stuttgart: Steiner Verlag. Pp. 257–273.

———. 1986. "Vijayanagara: Authority and Meaning of a South Indian Capital." *American Anthropologist* 88: 44–55.

Fuente del Pilar, José Javier. 2005. "Pedro Teixeira y su viaje por Mesopotamia." *Arbor* 180, no. 711–712: 627–643.

Gaspard, E. 1918. "Ceylon According to Du Jarric." *Ceylon Antiquary and Literary Register* 4, no. 1 (July): 5–20.

Gatellier, Marie. 1991. *Peintures murales du Sri Lanka, école Kandyenne XVIII–XIXe siècles*. Paris: Ecole Française d'Extrême-Orient.

Geary, Patrick. 1986. "Sacred Commodities: The Circulation of Medieval Relics." In *The Social Life of Things: Commodities in Cultural Perspective*. Edited by Arjun Appadurai. Cambridge: Cambridge University Press. Pp. 169–191.

———. 1990. *Furta Sacra: The Theft of Relics in the Central Middle Ages*. Princeton, NJ: Princeton University Press.

Geiger, Wilhelm. 1912. *The Mahāvaṃsa or the Great Chronicle of Ceylon*. London: Pali Text Society.

———. 1929. *Cūḷavaṃsa, Being the more Recent Part of the Mahāvaṃsa*. 2 vols. Translated from the German by C. Mabel Rickmers. London: Pali Text Society.

———. 1960. *Culture of Ceylon in Medieval Times*. Edited by Heinz Bechert. Wiesbaden: Otto Harrassowitz.

Gesick, Lorraine Marie. 1976. "Kingship and Political Integration in Traditional Siam, 1767–1824." PhD diss., Cornell University.

Gibb, H. A. R., trans. and ed. 1929. *Ibn Battuta, Travels in Asia and Africa, 1325–1354*. London: Routledge and Kegan Paul.

Gimlette, John. 2016. *Elephant Complex: Travels in Sri Lanka*. New York: Alfred A. Knopf.

Goloubew, Victor. 1932. "Notes et mélanges: Le temple de la dent à Kandy." *Bulletin de l'Ecole Française d'Extrême-Orient* 32: 441–474.

Gombrich, Richard F. 1971. *Precept and Practice: Traditional Buddhism in the Rural Highlands of Ceylon*. Oxford: Clarendon Press.

Gombrich, Richard F., and Gananath Obeyesekere. 1988. *Buddhism Transformed: Religious Change in Sri Lanka*. Princeton, NJ: Princeton University Press.

Gooneratne, Brendon, and Yasmine Gooneratne. 1999. *This Inscrutable Englishman: Sir John d'Oyly, Baronet, 1774–1824*. London: Cassell.

Gray, Albert 1887. *The Voyage of François Pyrard of Laval to the East Indies, the Maldives, the Moluccas and Brazil*. 2 vols. London: Hakluyt Society.

Gregory, William. 1894. *Sir William Gregory, K.C.M.G., Formerly Member of Parliament and Sometime Governor of Ceylon. An Autobiography.* Edited by Lady [Elizabeth] Gregory. London: John Murray.

Guṇasékara, B. 1900. *The Rājavaliya or a Historical Narrative of Sinhalese Kings.* Colombo: George J. A. Skeen.

Gunawardana, R. A. L. H. 1979. *Robe and Plough: Monasticism and Economic Interest in Early Medieval Sri Lanka.* Tucson: University of Arizona Press.

———. 1994. "Colonialism, Ethnicity and the Construction of the Past; the Changing 'Ethnic Identity' of the Last Four Kings of the Kandyan Kingdom." In *Pivot Politics: Changing Cultural Identities in Early State Formation Processes.* Edited by Martin van Vakel, Renée Hagesteijn, and Pieter van de Velde. Amsterdam: Het Spinhuis. Pp. 197–221.

Gupta, Pamila. 2004. "The Relic State: St. Francis Xavier and the Politics of Ritual in Portuguese India." PhD diss., Columbia University.

———. 2010. "Discourses of Incorruptibility: Of Blood, Smell and Skin in Portuguese India." *Ler História* 58: 81–97.

———. 2014. *The Relic State: St. Francis Xavier and the Politics of Ritual in Portuguese India.* Manchester: Manchester University Press.

Guruge, Ananda. 1967. *From the Living Fountains of Buddhism.* Colombo: Department of Cultural Affairs.

Haeckel, Ernst. 1883. *A Visit to Ceylon.* Translated by Clara Bell. 2nd American ed. Boston: S. E. Cassino and Co.

Hahn, Cynthia. 2010. "What Do Reliquaries Do for Relics?" *Numen* 57: 284–316.

Hamilton, J. H. F. 1888. "The Antiquities of Meḍamahanuwara." *Journal of the Ceylon Branch of the Royal Asiatic Society* 10, no. 36: 310–325.

Hardy, R. Spence. 1841. *The British Government and the Idolatry of Ceylon.* London: Crofts and Blenkarn.

———. 1850. *Eastern Monachism: An Account of the Origin, Laws, Discipline, Sacred Writings, Mysterious Rites, Religious Ceremonies, and Present Circumstances of the Order of Mendicants Founded by Gautama Buddha.* London: Williams and Norgate.

———. 1860. *A Manual of Buddhism, in its Modern Development.* London: Williams and Norgate.

Harris, Elizabeth J. 2006. *Theravāda Buddhism and the British Encounter: Religious, Missionary and Colonial Experience in Nineteenth-Century Sri Lanka.* London: Routledge.

Harvard, William Martin. 1823. *A Narrative of the Establishment and Progress of the Mission to Ceylon and India.* London: n.p.

Harvey, Godfrey Eric. [1925] 1967. *History of Burma from the Earliest Times to 10 March 1824, the Beginning of the English Conquest.* New York: Octagon Books.

Head, Thomas. 1993. "Bodies of Truth: The Genesis and Abandonment of the Ritual Proof of Relics by Fire." Paper delivered at the Davis Seminar, Princeton University.

Heber, Reginald. 1829. *Narrative of a Journey through the Upper Provinces of India, from Calcutta to Bombay, 1824–1825 (with Notes Upon Ceylon).* London: John Murray.

Henn, Alexander. 2014. *Hindu-Catholic Encounters in Goa: Religion, Colonialism, and Modernity.* Bloomington: Indiana University Press.

Herath, Dharmaratna. 1994. *The Tooth Relic and the Crown.* Colombo: n.p.

Herbert, Thomas. [1634] 1638. *Some Yeares Travels into Divers Parts of Asia and Afrique.* Revised edition. London: Iacob Blome and Richard Bishop.

Hewavissenti, Amal. 2010. "The Last Days of Ehelepola Adikaram: A Grudge That Rewrote History." *Sunday Observer* (Sri Lanka), September 19.

Heydt, Johann Wolffgang. 1744. *Allerneuester geographisch- und topographischer Schau-Platz von Africa und Ost-Indien; oder ausführliche und wahrhafte Vorstellung und Beschreibung von den wichtigsten der Holländisch-Ost-Indischen Compagnie in Africa und Asia zugehörigen Ländere, Küsten und Insulen, in accuraten See- und Land-Karten.* Willhermsdorff: Johann Carl Tetschner.

———. 1952. *Heydt's Ceylon, Being the Relevant Sections of the Allerneuester Geographisch- und Topographischer Schau-Platz von Africa und Ost-Indien.* Translated by R. Raven-Hart. Colombo: Ceylon Government Press.

Himbutana, Gopitha Peiris. 2006. "Ven. Thotagamuwe Sri Rahula Thera: Scholar Monk Par Excellence." *Budusarana* (Lake House). https://amazinglanka.com/wp/thotagamuwe -sri-rahula.

Hocart, A. M. 1931. *The Temple of the Tooth in Kandy.* Memoirs of the Archaeological Society of Ceylon, vol. 4. London: Luzac and Co.

Holt, John C. 1991. *Buddha in the Crown: Avalokiteśvara in the Buddhist Traditions of Sri Lanka.* New York: Oxford University Press.

———. 1996. *The Religious World of Kīrti Śrī: Buddhism, Art and Politics in Late Medieval Sri Lanka.* New York: Oxford University Press.

———. 2004. *The Buddhist Viṣṇu: Religious Transformation, Politics, and Culture.* New York: Columbia University Press.

———. 2007. "Buddhist Rebuttals: The Changing of the Gods and Royal (Re)legitimization in Sixteenth- and Seventeenth-Century Sri Lanka." In *Re-Exploring the Links: History and Constructed Histories between Portugal and Sri Lanka.* Edited by Jorge Flores. Wiesbaden: Harrassowitz Verlag. Pp. 145–170.

———. 2017. *Theravada Traditions: Buddhist Ritual Cultures in Contemporary Southeast Asia and Sri Lanka.* Honolulu: University of Hawai'i Press.

Htin Aung, Maung. 1967. *A History of Burma.* New York: Columbia University Press.

———. 1997. "A King of Burma and the Sacred Tooth Relic." *Sunday Times Plus* (Colombo). April 6.

Huonder, Anthony. 1913. "Pierre de Jarric." *Catholic Encyclopedia,* vol. 8. https://en .wikisource.org/wiki/Catholic_Encyclopedia_(1913)/Pierre_du_Jarric.

Hurd, William. 1780. *A New Universal History of the Religious Rites, Ceremonies, and Customs of the Whole World: or a Complete and Impartial View of all the Religions in the Various Nations of the Universe, both Antient and Modern, from the Creation down to the Present Time.* London: Alexander Hogg.

Ichimura Shohei. 2015. *The Canonical Book of the Buddha's Lengthy Discourses, Volume I.* Berkeley: Bukkyo Dendo Kyokai.

Ilangasinha, H. B. M. 1992. *Buddhism in Medieval Sri Lanka.* Delhi: Sri Satguru Publications.

Irissou, Louis. 1946. "François Martin, apothicaire et explorateur." *Revue d'Histoire de la Pharmacie* 116: 105–112.

Jacobs, Alfred. 1860. "Le Bouddhisme: Son législateur et son influence sur le monde moderne." *Revue des deux mondes,* March: 108–132.

Janson, Horst W. 1952. *Apes and Ape Lore in the Middle Ages and the Renaissance.* London: Warburg Institute.

Jayawickrama, N. A. 1962. *The Inception of Discipline and the Vinaya Nidāna.* London: Luzac.

Johnston, Arthur. 1810. *Narrative of the Operations of a Detachment in an Expedition to Candy in the Island of Ceylon, in the year 1804.* London: C. and R. Baldwin.

Joosse, Leendert Jan. 2015. "Philippus Baldaeus." In *Christian-Muslim Relations 1500–1900.* Edited by David Thomas. Consulted online on April 12, 2019. http://dx.doi .org/10.1163/2451-9537_cmrii_COM_26816.

Jottrand, Emile, M. et Mme. 1905. *Au Siam: Journal de voyage*. Paris: Librairie Plon.

Jottrand, Emile, Mr. and Mrs. 1996. *In Siam: The Diary of a Legal Adviser of King Chulalongkorn's Government*. Translated by Walter E. J. Tips. Bangkok: White Lotus.

Jumsai, M. L. Manich. 1977. *Prince Prisdang's Files on his Diplomatic Activities in Europe, 1880–1886*. Bangkok: Chalermnit.

Kamps, Ivo. 2001. "Colonizing the Colonizer: A Dutchman in *Asia Portuguesa*." In *Travel Knowledge: European "Discoveries" in the Early Modern Period*. Edited by Ivo Kamps. New York: Palgrave. Pp. 160–184.

Kapferer, Bruce. 1983. *A Celebration of Demons: Exorcism and the Aesthetics of Healing in Sri Lanka*. Bloomington: Indiana University Press.

Karashima, Noboru, ed. 2014. *A Concise History of South India: Issues and Interpretations*. Oxford: Oxford University Press.

Kayserling, Meyer. 1907. "Texeira, Pedro." In *The Jewish Encyclopedia*. Edited by Isidore Singer. New York: Funk & Wagnalls Co. Vol. 12: 76.

Kemper, Steven. 1991. *The Presence of the Past: Chronicles, Politics, and Culture in Sinhala Life*. Ithaca, NY: Cornell University Press.

———. 2015. *Rescued from the Nation: Anagarika Dharmapala and the Buddhist World*. Chicago: University of Chicago Press.

———. 2017. "Chulalongkorn, the Lankan Proposal, the Tooth Relic, the Prince Priest, and the 'Grievous Insult.'" Lecture given at Kings College, London, Buddhist Research Studies Seminar. May 5. Available at https://vimeo.com/217919958.

———. 2019. "The King and the Sacred Tooth Relic." Unpublished lecture. Bates College, Lewiston, Maine. May 21.

Kircher, Athanasius. [1667] 1987. *China Illustrata*. Translated by Charles D. Van Tuyl. Bloomington: Indiana University Press.

Knighton, William. 1845. *The History of Ceylon from the Earliest Period to the Present Time*. London: Longman, Brown, Green and Longmans.

Knox, Robert. [1681] 1966. *An Historical Relation of Ceylon*. Dehiwala: Tisara Press.

Kriekenbeek, J. G. 1918. "Greeving's Diary." Edited by Violet M. Methley. *Journal of the Royal Asiatic Society (Ceylon Branch)* 26: 166–180.

L'Estra, François. 1677. *Relation ou journal d'un voyage fait aux Indes Orientales*. Paris: Estienne Michallet.

Lévi-Strauss, Claude. 1963. "The Structural Study of Myth." In *Structural Anthropology*. Translated by Claire Jacobson and Brooke Grundfest Schoepf. New York: Basic Books. Pp. 202–228.

Lahiri, Latika. 1986. *Chinese Monks in India: Biography of Eminent Monks Who Went to the Western World in Search of the Law during the Great T'ang Dynasty, by I-ching*. Delhi: Motilal Banarsidass.

Landström, Björn. 1967. *Columbus: The Story of Don Cristóbal Colón, Admiral of the Ocean*. New York: Macmillan.

Law, Bimala Churn. 1925. *The Dāṭhāvaṃsa (A History of the Tooth-Relic of the Buddha)*. Lahore: Punjab Sanskrit Book Depot.

Lawrence, D. H. 1964. *The Complete Poems of D. H. Lawrence*. Edited by Vivian de Sola Pinto and Warren Roberts. 2 vols. New York: Viking Press.

Lawrie, Archibald Campbell. 1896. *A Gazetteer of the Central Province of Ceylon (Excluding Walapane)*. Vol. 1. Colombo: George Skeen.

Le Blanc, Vincent. 1648. *Les voyages fameux du Sieur Vincent LeBlanc, Marseillois*. Paris: Gervais Clovster.

———. 1660. *The World Surveyed: Or, the Famous Voyages and Travailes of Vincent le Blanc, or White, of Marseilles*. Translated by F. B. Gent. London: John Starkey.

Leclercq, Jules. 1900. *Un séjour dans l'île de Ceylan*. Paris: Plon-Nourrit et Cie.

Legge, James. [1886] 1965. *A Record of Buddhistic Kingdoms*. New York: Paragon Books.

Lesbre, Emmanuelle. 2002. "Une vie illustrée du Buddha (*Shishi yuanliu*, 1425), modèle pour les peintures murales d'un monastère du XVe s. (Jueyuan si, Sichuan oriental)." *Arts Asiatiques* 57: 69–101.

Levathes, Louise. 1994. *When China Ruled the Seas: The Treasure Fleet of the Dragon Throne, 1405–1433*. Oxford: Oxford University Press.

Lévi, Sylvain. 1900. "Les missions de Wang Hiuen-ts'e dans l'Inde (suite et fin)." *Journal asiatique*: 401–468.

Li Rongxi. 1996. *The Great Tang Dynasty Record of the Western Regions*. Berkeley: Numata Center for Buddhist Translation and Research.

Liu Xinru. 1996. *Silk and Religion*. New Delhi: Oxford University Press.

Longhurst, A. H. 1917. *Hampi Ruins Described and Illustrated*. Madras: Government Press.

Loos, Tamara. 2016. *Bones around my Neck: The Life and Exile of a Prince Provocateur*. Ithaca, NY: Cornell University Press.

Lopez, Donald S. Jr. 2013. *From Stone to Flesh: A Short History of the Buddha*. Chicago: University of Chicago Press.

———. 2016. *Strange Tales of an Oriental Idol: An Anthology of Early European Portrayals of the Buddha*. Chicago: University of Chicago Press.

Lubac, Henri de. 1952. *La rencontre du Bouddhisme et de l'Occident*. Paris: Aubier.

Lutgendorf, Philip. 2007. *Hanuman's Tale: The Messages of a Divine Monkey*. New York: Oxford: Oxford University Press.

MacCormack, Sabine. 2006. "Gods, Demons, and Idols in the Andes." *Journal of the History of Ideas* 67, no. 3: 623–647.

Magone, Rui. 2012. "The Fô and the Xekiâ: Tomás Pereira's Critical Description of Chinese Buddhism." In *In the Light and Shadow of an Emperor: Tomás Pereira, S.J. (1645–1708), the Kangxi Emperor and the Jesuit Mission in China*. Edited by Artur K. Wardega and António Vasconcelos de Saldanha. Newcastle upon Tyne: Cambridge Scholars Publishing. Pp. 252–274.

Mahāvaṃsa. 1908. Edited by Wilhelm Geiger. London: Pali Text Society.

Malalgoda, Kitsiri. 1970. "Millennialism in Relation to Buddhism." *Comparative Studies in Society and History* 12, no. 4: 424–441.

———. 1976. *Buddhism in Sinhalese Society 1750–1900*. Berkeley: University of California Press.

———. 2002. "Ceylon, Siam and the Tooth Relic." Paper presented at the 13th Conference of the International Association of Buddhist Studies. Bangkok.

Malville, John McKim. 1994. "The Compleat Devotee and the Cosmic City: Hanuman at Hampi." In *Art, the Integral Vision: A Volume of Essays in Felicitation of Kapila Vatsyayan*. Edited by B. N. Saraswati, S. C. Malik, and Madhu Khanna. New Delhi: D. K. Printworld. Pp. 147–164.

Marshall, Henry. 1846. *Ceylon: A General Description of the Island and its Inhabitants; with an Historical Sketch of the Conquest of the Colony by the English*. London: William H. Allen and Co.

Martin De Vitré, François. 1604. *Description du premier voyage faict aux Indes Orientales par les François en l'An 1603, contenant les moeurs, loix, façon de vivre, religions & habits des Indiens*. Paris: Laurens Sonnius.

Masuzawa, Tomoko. 2005. *The Invention of World Religions, or How European Universalism Was Preserved in the Language of Pluralism*. Chicago: University of Chicago Press.

Mathew, K. S. 1986. "Trade in the Indian Ocean and the Portuguese System of Cartazes." In Newitt 1986, 69–84.

McNair, J. F. A. 1899. *Prisoners their own Warders: A Record of the Convict Prison at Singapore in the Straits Settlements*. London: Archibald Constable and Co.

Méndez-Oliver, Ana L. 2016. "Chaotic, Effeminate and Promiscuous 'Bodies' in John Huyghen van Linschoten's *Itinerario*." *Anais de História de Além-Mar* 17: 337–358.

Mendis, G. C. 1956. *The Colebrooke-Cameron Papers. Documents on British Colonial Policy in Ceylon 1796–1833*. Vol. 2. Oxford: Oxford University Press.

Methley, Violet M. 1918. "The Ceylon Expedition of 1803." *Transactions of the Royal Historical Society* 1: 92–128.

Mickle, William Julius. n.d. "The Life of Camoëns." http://www.sacred-texts.com/neu/lus/lus02.htm.

Millāva, Disāva of Vellassa. 1817. "Account of the Ceremony of Peraherra, Presented to His Exc. The Governor of Ceylon, August 19, 1817." *Ceylon Government Gazette*, September 13, 1817. Reprinted in *Asiatic Journal and Monthly Register for British India and its Dependencies* 6 (June 1818): 19–23.

Mills, J. V. G. 1970. *Ma Huan, Ying-Yai Sheng-Lan: "The Overall Survey of the Ocean's Shores."* Cambridge: Cambridge University Press.

Moderator (pseud.). 1816. "Letter to the Editor of the *Asiatic Journal*." *Asiatic Journal and Monthly Register for British India and Its Dependencies* 1 (January–June): 219–221.

Mukherjee, Sraman. 2018. "Relics in Transition: Material Mediations in Changing Worlds." *Ars Orientalis* 48: 20–42.

Müller, Friedrich Max. 1880. *Lectures on the Origin and Growth of Religion*. London: Longmans, Green and Co.

Mythologus (pseud.). 1816a. "Letter to the Editor of the *Asiatic Journal*." *Asiatic Journal and Monthly Register for British India and Its Dependencies* 1 (January–June): 19–21.

———. 1816b. "Letter to the Editor of the *Asiatic Journal*." *Asiatic Journal and Monthly Register for British India and Its Dependencies* 1 (January–June): 114–116.

Newitt, Malyn, ed. 1986. *The First Portuguese Colonial Empire*. Exeter Studies in History No. 11. Exeter: Department of History and Archaeology, University of Exeter.

Nilakanta Sastri, K. A. 1959. "Inroads by Pandya and Vijayanagara Empires." *University of Ceylon History of Ceylon*. Edited by H. C. Ray and K. M. De Silva. Peradeniya: University of Ceylon Press. Vol. 1, part 2: 684–690.

———. [1955] 2002. *A History of South India from Prehistoric Times to the Fall of Vijayanagar*. New Delhi: Oxford University Press.

Nilsson, Jan-Erik. n.d.a. "The Portuguese Carrack *São Tiago (Santiago)*, taken by the Dutch 14 March 1602." http://gotheborg.com/glossary/santiago.shtml.

———. n.d.b. "Kraak Porcelain." http://www.gotheborg.com/glossary/kraak.shtml#T.

Nissanka, H. S. S. 2009. "Kandy in 1940s and 50s . . ." *Daily News* (Colombo). March 31.

Obeyesekere, Gananath. 1984. *The Cult of the Goddess Pattini*. Chicago: University of Chicago Press.

———. 2002. "Colonial Histories and Vädda Primitivism: An Unorthodox Reading of Kandy Period Texts." G. C. Mendis Memorial Lecture. http://artsrilanka.org/essays/body.html. See also http://vedda.org/obeyesekere5.htm.

———. 2017. *The Doomed King: A Requiem for Śri Vikrama Rājasinha*. Colombo: Sailfish.

Ohnuki-Tierney, Emiko. 1987. *The Monkey as Mirror: Symbolic Transformations in Japanese History and Ritual*. Princeton, NJ: Princeton University Press.

An Old English Politician (pseud.). 1816. "Letter to the Editor of the *Asiatic Journal." Asiatic Journal and Monthly Register for British India and Its Dependencies* 1 (January–June): 210–214.

Oldenberg, Hermann. [1879] 1982. *The Dīpavaṃsa: An Ancient Buddhist Historical Record.* New Delhi: Asian Educational Services.

Paranavitana, Karunasena Dias, and Rajpal Kumar de Silva. 2002. *Maps and Plans of Dutch Ceylon.* Colombo: Central Cultural Fund, Sri Lanka-Netherlands Association.

Parr, Charles McKew. 1964. *Jan van Linschoten: the Dutch Marco Polo.* New York: Thomas Y. Crowell Co.

Parry, Jonathan P. 1994. *Death in Banaras.* Cambridge: Cambridge University Press.

Pathmanathan, S. 2007. "The Portuguese in Northeast Sri Lanka (1543–1658): An Assessment of Impressions Recorded in Tamil Chronicles and Poems." In *Re-Exploring the Links: History and Constructed Histories between Portugal and Sri Lanka.* Edited by Jorge Flores. Wiesbaden: Harrassowitz Verlag. Pp. 29–47.

Pe Maung Tin and G. B. Luce. [1923] 1960. *The Glass Palace Chronicle of the Kings of Burma.* Rangoon: Rangoon University Press.

Pearson, Joseph. 1929. "The Throne of the Kings of Kandy." *Journal of the Ceylon Branch of the Royal Asiatic Society* 31, no. 82: 380–383.

Peleggi, Maurizio. 2002. *Lord of Things: The Fashioning of the Siamese Monarchy's Modern Image.* Honolulu: University of Hawai'i Press.

Pelliot, Paul. 1933. "Les grands voyages maritimes chinois au début du XVe siècle." *T'oung pao* 30: 237–452.

Percival, Robert. 1803. *An Account of the Island of Ceylon, Containing its History, Geography, Natural History, with the Manners and Customs of its Various Inhabitants; to which is Added The Journal of an Embassy to the Court of Candy.* London: C. and R. Baldwin.

Perera, A. D. T. E. 1984. "Daḷadā Perahāra." *Encyclopaedia of Buddhism, Volume IV.* Edited by Jotiya Dhirasekera. Colombo: Government of Sri Lanka Press. Pp. 294–299.

Perera, Arthur A. 1917. *Sinhalese Folklore Notes.* Bombay: British India Press.

Perera, Edward W. 1904. "Alakéswara: His Life and Times." *Journal of the Ceylon Branch of the Royal Asiatic Society* 18, no. 55: 281–312.

———. 1910. "The Age of Srī Parākrama Bāhu VI (1412–1467)." *Journal of the Royal Asiatic Society, Ceylon Branch* 22: 6–45.

Perniola, V. (S.J.). 1989. *The Catholic Church in Sri Lanka. The Portuguese Period. Original Documents translated into English.* 3 vols. *Ceylon Historical Journal,* Monograph Series, vols. 12, 15, and 16. Dehiwala: Tisara Prakasakayo.

Phayre, Arthur P. [1883] 1967. *History of Burma including Burma Proper, Pegu, Taungu, Tennaserim, and Arakan.* 2nd ed. New York: Augustus M. Kelley.

Phillips, Percival. 1922. *The Prince of Wales' Eastern Book: A Pictorial Record of the Voyages of H.M.S. "Renown" 1921–1922.* London: Hodder and Stoughton.

Picart, Bernard, Jean-Frédéric Bernard, and Antoine Augustin Bruzen de la Martinière. 1723–1743. *Cérémonies et coutumes religieuses de tous les peuples du monde représentées par des figures dessinées de la main de Bernard Picart, avec une explication historique, & quelques dissertations curieuses.* 9 vols. Amsterdam: J. F. Bernard.

Pieris, Aloysius. 1985. "The Cult of the Sacred Tooth Relic—Its Origin and Meaning." *Dialogue* (Colombo), n.s. 10: 63–72.

Pieris, Anoma. 2011. "The 'Other' Side of Labor Reform: Accounts of Incarceration and Resistance in the Straits Settlements Penal System, 1825–1873." *Journal of Social History* 45: 453–479.

Pieris, Paulus Edward. 1913. *Ceylon: The Portuguese Era, being a History of the Island for Period 1505–1658.* 2 vols. Colombo: Colombo Apothecaries Co.

332 / References

———. 1920. *Ceylon and the Portuguese 1505–1658.* Tellippalai: American Ceylon Mission.

Ribeiro, João. [1685] 1701. *Histoire de l'isle de Ceylan écrite par le Capitaine J. Ribeyro, & présentée au Roi de Portugal en 1685.* Translated by Abbé Le Grand. Amsterdam: J. L. De Lorme.

———. [1685] 1899. *Ribeiro's History of Ceilão, with notes from de Barros, de Couto and Antonio Bocarro.* Translated by P. E. Pieris. Galle: Albion Press.

———. [1685] 1989. *Fatalidade historica da ilha de Ceilão.* Lisbon: Alfa Publications.

Rienjang, Wannaporn ["Kay"]. 2017. "Relic Cult Practice in Eastern Afghanistan with Comparison to Dharmarajika Pakistan." PhD diss., University of Cambridge.

Roberts, Michael. 2003. *Sinhala Consciousness in the Kandyan Period 1590s to 1815.* Colombo: Vijitha Yapa Publications.

Robson, James. 2009. *Power of Place: The Religious Landscape of the Southern Sacred Peak (Nanyue 南嶽) in Medieval China.* Cambridge, MA: Harvard University Press.

Rocher, Ludo. 1984. *Ezourvedam: A French Veda of the Eighteenth Century.* Amsterdam: John Benjamins Publishing Co.

Rockhill, W. W. 1915. "Notes on the Relations and Trade of China with the Eastern Archipelago and the Coast of the Indian Ocean During the Fourteenth Century, Part II." *T'oung pao* 16, no. 3: 374–392.

Rodrigues da Silva Tavim, José. 2016. "'O culto ao diabo' na Inquisição de Goa, Segundo o *Reportorio* de João Delgado Figueira (1623)." *Anais de História de Além-Mar* 17: 271–302.

Rogers, John D. 2004. "Early British Rule and Social Classification in Lanka." *Modern Asian Studies* 38: 625–647.

Ruppert, Brian D. 2000. *Jewel in the Ashes: Buddha Relics and Power in Early Medieval Japan.* Cambridge, MA: Harvard University Press.

Sahai, Sachchidanand. 2002. *India in 1872 as Seen by the Siamese.* Delhi: B. R. Publishing.

Said, Edward. 1978. *Orientalism.* London: Routledge and Kegan Paul.

Saldin, Tony. 2003. "Banishment of the first Ceylonese Family to Australia." *Sunday Island.* January 12. http://www.worldgenweb.org/lkawgw/odeane.html.

Saraiva, António José. 2001. *The Marrano Factory: The Portuguese Inquisition and Its New Christians 1536–1765.* Translated by H. P. Salomon and I. S. D. Sassoon. Leiden: E. J. Brill.

Schober, Juliane. 2011. *Modern Buddhist Conjunctures in Myanmar: Cultural Narratives, Colonial Legacies, and Civil Society.* Honolulu: University of Hawai'i Press.

Schopen, Gregory. 1997. *Bones, Stones, and Buddhist Monks.* Honolulu: University of Hawai'i Press.

Schurhammer, Georg. 1929. "Unpublished Manuscripts of Fr. Fernão de Queiroz, S.J." *Bulletin of the School of Oriental Studies* 5: 209–227.

Schwartz, Stuart B. 2008. *All Can Be Saved: Religious Tolerance and Salvation in the Iberian Atlantic World.* New Haven, CT: Yale University Press.

Scott, David. 1994. *Formations of Ritual: Colonial and Anthropological Discourses on the Sinhala Yaktovil.* Minneapolis: University of Minnesota Press.

Selkirk, James. 1844. *Recollections of Ceylon after a Residence of nearly Thirteen Years with an Account of the Church Missionary Society's Operations in the Island: and Extracts from a Journal.* London: J. Hatchard and Son.

Seneviratne, H. L. 1976. "The Alien King: Nayakkars on the Throne of Kandy." *Ceylon Journal of Historical and Social Studies,* n.s. 6, no. 1: 55–61.

———. 1978. *Rituals of the Kandyan State.* Cambridge: Cambridge University Press.

Sewell, Robert. 1900. *A Forgotten Empire (Vijayanagar): A Contribution to the History of India.* London: Swan Sonnenschein.

Sharan, Ishwar. 1991. *The Myth of Saint Thomas and the Mylapore Shiva Temple*. New Delhi: Voice of India.

Sharf, Robert H. 1999. "On the Allure of Buddhist Relics." *Representations* 66: 75–99.

Shirodkar, P. P. 1998. *Researches in Indo-Portuguese History*. 2 vols. Jaipur: Publication Scheme.

Shorto, H. L. 1963. "The 32 *Myos* in the Medieval Mon Kingdom." *Bulletin of the School of Oriental and African Studies* 26: 572–591.

———. 1970. "The Gavampati Tradition in Burma." In *R. C. Majumdar Felicitation Volume*. Edited by Himansu Bhusan Sarkar. Calcutta: Firma K. L. Mukhopadhyay. Pp. 15–30.

Shulman, Nicola. 2004. *A Rage for Rock Gardening: The Story of Reginald Farrer, Gardener, Writer and Plant Collector*. Boston: D. R. Godine.

Sikand, Yoginder. 2003. *Sacred Spaces: Exploring Traditions of Shared Faith in India*. New Delhi: Penguin Books.

Silva, Kapila D. 2011. "Mapping Meaning in the City Image: A Case Study of Kandy, Sri Lanka." *Journal of Architectural and Planning Research* 28: 229–251.

———. 2017. "The Symbolic Authenticity of Kandy, Sri Lanka." In *Cultural Landscapes of South Asia: Studies in Heritage Conservation and Management*. Edited by Kapila D. Silva and Amita Sinha. London: Routledge. Pp. 144–158.

Siriweera, W. I. 1993/1995. "The City of Jayawardena Kotte: History, Form and Function." *Sri Lanka Journal of the Humanities* 19: 1–22.

Sirr, Henry Charles. 1850. *Ceylon and the Cingalese; their History, Government, and Religion; the Antiquities, Institutions, Produce, Revenue, and Capabilities of the Island; with Anecdotes Illustrating the Manners and Customs of the People*. London: William Shoberl. Vol. 1.

Sivasundaram, Sujit. 2013. *Islanded: Britain, Sri Lanka, and the Bounds of an Indian Ocean Colony*. Chicago: University of Chicago Press.

Skeen, George J. A. 1901. *The Royal Visit to Ceylon, April 1901*.

———. 1903. *A Guide to Kandy with Maps*. Colombo: A. M. and J. Ferguson.

Skeen, William. [1870] 1997. *Adam's Peak: Legendary Traditional and Historic Notices of the Samanala and Srî-Páda with a Descriptive Account of the Pilgrims' Route from Colombo to the Sacred Foot-Print*. New Delhi: Asian Educational Services.

Skilling, Peter. 2018. "Relics: The Heart of Buddhist Veneration." In *Relics and Relic Worship in Early Buddhism*. Edited by Janice Stargardt. London: British Museum Press. Pp. 1–11.

Skinner, Thomas. 1891. *Fifty Years in Ceylon: An Autobiography*. Edited by Annie Skinner. London: W. H. Allen and Co.

Snoek, G. J. C. 1995. *Medieval Piety from Relics to the Eucharist*. Leiden: E. J. Brill.

Somasunderam, Ramesh. 2008. "British Infiltration of Ceylon (Sri Lanka) in the Nineteenth Century: A Study of the D'Oyly Papers between 1805 and 1818." PhD diss., University of Western Australia.

———. 2015. *British Infiltration of Ceylon (Sri Lanka) in the Nineteenth Century: A Study of the D'Oyly Papers between 1805 and 1818*. Pannipitiya: Stamford Lake Publishers.

Stadtner, Donald M. 2011. *Sacred Sites of Burma: Myth and Folklore in an Evolving Spiritual Realm*. Bangkok: River Books.

———. Forthcoming. *Sacred Sites of Sri Lanka*. Bangkok: River Books.

Stein, Burton, 1980. *Peasant State and Society in Medieval South India*. Oxford: Oxford University Press.

Stengs, Irene. 2009. *Worshipping the Great Moderniser: King Chulalongkorn, Patron Saint of the Thai Middle Class*. Singapore: NUS Press.

Strathern, Alan. 2005. "Fernão de Queiros: History and Theology." *Anais de história de além-mar* 6: 47–88.

———. 2007. *Kingship and Conversion in Sixteenth-Century Sri Lanka. Portuguese Imperialism in a Buddhist Land.* Cambridge: Cambridge University Press.

Strathern, Alan, and Zoltán Biedermann. 2017. "Introduction: Querying the Cosmopolitan in Sri Lankan and Indian Ocean History." In *Sri Lanka at the Crossroads of History.* Edited by Zoltán Biedermann and Alan Strathern. London: UCL Press. Pp. 1–19.

Strong, John S. 2001. *The Buddha: A Beginner's Guide.* Oxford: Oneworld Publications.

———. 2004a. "Buddhist Relics in Comparative Perspective: Beyond the Parallels." In *Embodying the Dharma: Buddhist Relic Veneration in Asia.* Edited by David Germano and Kevin Trainor. Albany: State University of New York Press. Pp. 27–50.

———. 2004b. *Relics of the Buddha.* Princeton, NJ: Princeton University Press.

———. 2010. "'The Devil Was in That Little Bone': The Portuguese Capture and Destruction of the Buddha's Tooth-Relic, Goa, 1561." In *Relics and Remains.* Edited by Alexandra Walsham. Past and Present Supplement 5. Oxford: Oxford University Press. Pp. 184–198.

———. 2015. *Buddhisms: An Introduction.* Oxford: Oneworld Publications.

———. 2016. "The Buddha, Fact and Fiction: A Kaleidoscopic History of Western Views of the Buddha." In *History as a Challenge to Buddhism and Christianity.* Edited by Elizabeth J. Harris and John O'Grady. Sankt Ottilien: EOS Books. Pp. 139–165.

———. 2017. "The Lifestory of the Buddha." In *Narrating Religion.* Edited by Sarah Iles Johnston. Farmington Hills, MI: Macmillan Reference USA. Pp. 209–226.

———. Forthcoming a. "Interpretations and (Mis)understandings: Three Case Studies of Illustrations of the Buddha's Biography." In *Narrative Visions and Visual Narratives in Indian Buddhism.* Edited by Naomi Appleton. Sheffield: Equinox.

———. Forthcoming b. "Beads and Bones: The Case of the Piprahwa Gems." *Jewels, Jewelry, and Other Shiny Things in the Buddhist Imaginary.* Edited by Vanessa Sasson. Honolulu: University of Hawai'i Press.

Strong, John S., and Sarah M. Strong. 1995. "A Tooth Relic of the Buddha in Japan: An Essay on the Sennyū-ji Tradition and a Translation of Zeami's Nō Play 'Shari.'" *Japanese Religions* 20: 1–33.

Subrahmanyam, Sanjay. 2012. *Courtly Encounters: Translating Courtliness and Violence in Early Modern Eurasia.* Cambridge, MA: Harvard University Press.

———. 2017. *Europe's India: Words, People, Empires, 1500–1800.* Cambridge, MA: Harvard University Press.

Sullivan, Edward. 1854. *The Bungalow and the Tent; or, a Visit to Ceylon.* London: Richard Bentley.

Sumangalavilāsinī: Buddhaghosa's Commentary on the Dīgha Nikāya. 1971. 2nd ed. Edited by William Stede. London: Pali Text Society.

Tambiah, Stanley J. 1976. *World Conqueror and World Renouncer: A Study of Buddhism and Polity in Thailand against a Historical Background.* Cambridge: Cambridge University Press.

———. 1984. *The Buddhist Saints of the Forest and the Cult of Amulets.* Cambridge: Cambridge University Press.

Taw Sein Ko. 1892. *The Kalyāṇī Inscriptions Erected by King Dhammacetī at Pegu in 1476 A.D.* Rangoon: Superintendent of Government Printing.

Taylor, Meadows. 1879. *A Student's Manual of the History of India.* 4th ed. London: Longmans, Green, and Co.

Tennent, James Emerson. 1849. "Memorandum on Buddhism and the Means of Severing the Connexion between the British Government and the Buddhist Rites and Temples in Ceylon." Unpublished manuscript in CO 544/296, pp. 283–331.

———. 1859. *Ceylon: An Account of the Island.* London: Longman, Green, Longman and Roberts. 2 vols.

Texeira, Pedro. 1610. *Relaciones de Pedro Teixeira d'el origen, descendencia, y succession de los reyes de Persia, y de Harmuz, y de un viage hecho por el mismo autor dende la India Oriental hasta Italia por tierra.* Antwerp: Hieronymus Verdussen.

———. 1715. *The History of Persia: Containing the Lives and Memorable Action of its Kings from the first Erecting of that Monarchy to this Time.* Translated by John Stevens. London: Jonas Brown.

———. 1902. *The Travels of Pedro Teixeira: Narrative of my Journey from India to Italy.* Translated by William F. Sinclair, with further notes by Donald Ferguson. London: Hakluyt Society.

Thomas, P. 1919. "Buddha's Tooth." *Catholic Missions* (New York) (February): 32–34.

Tips, Walter E. J. 1996. *Gustave Rolin-Jaequemyns and the Making of Modern Siam: The Diaries and Letters of King Chulalongkorn's General Adviser.* Bangkok: White Lotus.

Tolfrey, William. 1815. *A Narrative of the Events which have Recently Occurred in the Island of Ceylon Written by a Gentleman on the Spot.* London: T. Egerton.

Trainor, Kevin M. 1992. "When Is a Theft Not a Theft? Relic Theft and the Cult of the Buddha's Relics in Sri Lanka." *Numen* 39: 1–26.

———. 1997. *Relic, Ritual, and Representation in Buddhism: Rematerializing the Sri Lankan Theravāda Tradition.* Cambridge: Cambridge University Press.

Trindade, Paulo da. [1630–1636] 1962–1967. *Conquista espiritual do Oriente.* Edited by Fernando Félix Lopes. 3 vols. Lisbon: Centro de Estudos Históricos Ultramarinos.

Trumbull, Robert. 1950. "Tooth of Buddha Shown to Bevin in Rarely Performed Ceylon Rite." *New York Times.* January 16. Pp. 1, 3.

Tun Aung Chain. 2004. *Selected Writings of Tun Aung Chain.* Yangon: Myanmar Historical Commission.

Turner, Alicia. 2014. *Saving Buddhism: The Impermanence of Religion in Colonial Burma.* Honolulu: University of Hawai'i Press.

Turner, L. J. B. 1918. "The Town of Kandy about the year 1815 A.D." *Ceylon Antiquary and Literary Register* 4: 76–83.

Turnour, George. 1837. "Account of the Tooth Relic of Ceylon, Supposed to be Alluded to in the Opening Passage of the Feroz lāt Inscription." *Journal of the Asiatic Society of Bengal* 6, no. 2: 856–868.

Valentijn, François. 1726. *Oud en Nieuw Oost-Indien.* Vol. 5. Dordrecht: Joannes van Braam.

Vālmīki. 2005. *Rāmāyaṇa Book Four: Kiṣkindhā.* Translated by Rosalind Lefeber. Clay Sanskrit Library.

———. 2006. *Rāmāyaṇa Book Five: Sundara.* Translated by Robert P. Goldman and Sally J. Sutherland Goldman. New York: New York University Press.

Van der Aa, Jean Baptiste. 1899. *Ile de Ceylan, croquis, moeurs et coutumes: Lettres d'un missionnaire.* Louvain: F. Giele.

Van Linschoten, Iohn [Jan] Hvighen [Huyghen]. 1598. *His Discours of Voyages into ye Easte & West Indies.* London: Iohn Wolfe.

Van Linschoten, Jan Huyghen. [1598] 1885. *The Voyage of John Huyghen Van Linschoten to the East Indies, from the Old English Translation of 1598.* Edited by Arthur Coke Burnell and P. A. Tiele. 2 vols. London: Hakluyt Society.

Verghese, Anila. 1995. *Religious Traditions at Vijayanagara as Revealed through Its Monuments.* New Delhi: Manohar.

Villiers, John. 1986. "The Estado da India in Southeast Asia." In Newitt 1986, 37–68.

Vimalananda, Tennakoon, and F. R. Jayasuriya. 1966. *The Child Hero of Ceylon*. Colombo: M. D. Gunasena.

Viterbo, Sousa. 1906. *O Thesouro do Rei de Ceylão*. Historia e Memorias da Academia Real das Sciencias de Lisboa, n.s. 2nd classe, Sciencias Moraes e Politicas, e Bellas Lettras. Vol 10, part 2, Fasc. 2. Lisbon: Typographia da Academia.

Waduge, Shenali D. 2014. "Sri Lanka Must Demand the Return of the Remains of Ven. Thotagamuwe Sri Rahula from Goa, if the DNA Tests Prove Positive." *Lankaweb* November 27. http://www.lankaweb.com/news/items/2014/11/27/sri-lanka-must -demand-the-return-of-the-remains-of-ven-thotagamuwe-sri-rahula-from-goa-if-the -dna-tests-prove-positive/.

Wagenaar, Lodewijk. 2016. *Cinnamon and Elephants: Sri Lanka and the Netherlands from 1600*. Amsterdam: Rijks Museum.

Waldschmidt, Ernst. 1950–1951. *Das Mahāparinirvāṇa-sūtra*. 3 parts. Abhandlungen der deutschen Akademie der Wissenschaften zu Berlin, Philosophisch-historische Klasse, 1949, no. 1, and 1950, nos. 2–3. Berlin: Akademie Verlag.

Walshe, Maurice, tr. 1987. *Thus Have I Heard: The Long Discourses of the Buddha*. London: Wisdom.

Walters, Jonathan S. 1991/1992. "Vibhīṣaṇa and Vijayanagar: An Essay on Religion and Geo-politics in Medieval Sri Lanka." *Sri Lanka Journal of the Humanities* 17/18: 129–142.

———. 1996. *The History of Kelaniya*. Colombo: Social Scientists' Association.

Weinman, Aubrey N. 1963. "Prins's Embassy to the Kandyan Court 1770." *Journal of the Dutch Burgher Union of Ceylon*. 53, nos. 1 and 2: 1–11, and nos. 3 and 4: 36–46.

Wheatley, Paul. 1971. *The Pivot of the Four Quarters: A Preliminary Enquiry into the Origins and Character of the Ancient Chinese City*. Chicago: University of Chicago Press.

Wheeler, George. 1876. *India in 1875–76. The Visit of the Prince of Wales. Chronicle of his Royal Highness's Journeyings in India, Ceylon, Spain, and Portugal*. London: Chapman and Hall.

White, Herbert. 1919. "The Barnes Buddha." *Ceylon Antiquary and Literary Register* (January 4): 175–176.

Whiteway, R. S. 1899. *The Rise of Portuguese Power in India 1497–1550*. Westminster: Archibald Constable.

Wicki, Ioseph. 1954. *Documenta Indica III (1553–1557)*. Rome: Monumenta Historica Societatis Iesu.

Wickramasinghe, Nira. 1997. "The Return of Keppetipola's Cranium: Authenticity in a New Nation." *Economic and Political Weekly* 32, no. 30: PE85–PE92.

———. 2006. *Sri Lanka in the Modern Age: A History of Contested Identities*. Honolulu: University of Hawai'i Press.

Wickremasinghe, Don Martino De Zilva. 1928. *Epigraphia Zeylanica II*. London: Humphrey Milford.

Wickremeratne, U. C. 1973. "Lord North and the Kandyan Kingdom, 1798–1805." *Journal of the Royal Asiatic Society of Great Britain and Ireland* 105: 31–42.

Wickremesekera, Channa. 2004. *Kandy at War: Indigenous Military Resistance to European Expansion in Sri Lanka 1594–1818*. New Delhi: Manohar Publishers.

Wieger, Léon. [1913] 2002. *Les vies chinoises du Buddha*. St. Michel en l'Herm: Editions Dharma.

Wijayaratna, Môhan. 1987. *Le culte des dieux chez les bouddhistes singhalais*. Paris: Cerf.

Wijesinghe, Mahil. 2016. "Mulgirigala Rock Cave Temple: The Dutch Link." *Sunday Observer* [Colombo]. December 4.

Wimalaratne, K. D. G. n.d. "Gongale Goda Banda (1809–1849): The Leader of the 1848 Rebellion." http://www.lankalibrary.com/geo/gongalegoda.htm.

Winius, George Davison. 1985. *The Black Legend of Portuguese India: Diogo do Couto, His Contemporaries and the* Soldado Prático. New Delhi: Concept Publishing Company.

Wojciehowski, Hannah Chapelle. 2011. *Group Identity in the Renaissance World*. Cambridge: Cambridge University Press.

Woolf, Leonard. [1913] 1981. *The Village in the Jungle*. Oxford: Oxford University Press.

———. 1961. *Growing: An Autobiography of the Years 1904 to 1911*. New York: Harcourt Brace Jovanovich.

———. 1989. *Letters of Leonard Woolf*. Edited by Frederic Spotts. New York: Harcourt, Brace, Jovanovich.

Wyatt, David K. 2001. "Relics, Oaths and Politics in Thirteenth-Century Siam." *Journal of Southeast Asian Studies* 32: 3–66.

Xavier, Angela Barreto, and Ines G. Županov. 2015. *Catholic Orientalism: Portuguese Empire, Indian Knowledge (16th–18th Centuries)*. New Delhi: Oxford University Press.

Young, R. F., and G. P. V. Somaratna. 1996. *Vain Debates: The Buddhist-Christian Controversies of Nineteenth-Century Ceylon*. Vienna: Sammlung De Nobili.

Yule, Henry, and A. C. Burnell. 1903. *Hobson-Jobson: A Glossary of Colloquial Anglo-Indian Words and Phrases, and of Kindred Terms, Etymological, Historical, Geographical and Discursive*. New ed. by William Crooke. London: John Murray.

Zaleski, Mgr. 1891. *Ceylan et les Indes*. Paris: Albert Savine.

Županov, Ines G. 1999. *Disputed Mission: Jesuit Experiments and Brahmanical Knowledge in Seventeenth-Century India*. New Delhi: Oxford University Press.

———. 2010. "Jesuit Orientalism; Correspondence between Tomás Pereira and Fernão de Queiros." In *Tomás Pereira, S.J. (1648–1708) Life, Work and World*. Edited by Luís Filipe Barreto. Lisbon: Centro Científico e Cultural de Macau, I.P. Pp. 43–74.

———. n.d. "Managing Sacred Relics in Jesuit Asia (Sixteenth and Seventeenth Centuries." https://igs.duke.edu/sites/default/files/atoms/files/Managing%20Sacred%20Relics%20in%20Jesuit%20Asia%20%28Sixteenth%20and%20Seventeenth%20Centuries%29_Zupanov.pdf.

Zwalf, Wladimir. 1985. *Buddhism, Art and Faith*. New York: Macmillan.

INDEX

Page numbers in italics refer to figures.

Adam, 61–62; and Eve, 62, 71; footprint of, 22n6, 61n42; identified with Pangu, 60; identified with the Buddha as first man, 42, 63; tomb of, 58n33, 62, 313; tooth relic of, 71, 313. *See also* Adam's Peak
Adams Berg. *See* Mulgirigala
Adam's Bridge, 24, 79, 82, 85. *See also* Palk Straits
Adam's Peak, 9, *20*, 55, 91, 161n14; the Buddha's visit to, 90, 91, 95; as burial place of Adam, 58n58; as burial place of the Buddha, 58, 60; confusion of with Mulgirigala, 36, 40, 60–63; cosmopolitan nature, 71; footprint on, 22n6, 45, 57, 59, 60, 61n42, 63, 70, 71, 88–91, 146, 149; as site of paradise, 61. *See also* capture of tooth by the Portuguese: near Adam's Peak; Mulgirigala; Portuguese tooth: found near Adam's Peak; Śrī Pada
Adeane, Michael, 285, 295, 298, 299, 304
African troops used by the British, 160, 176, 225n4
Aggreen, Daniel, 41, 169
Alagakkonara, 50
Albert Edward, Prince of Wales, 286, 296n12, 304
Alfred, Duke of Edinburgh, 285
Almond, Philip, 2, 3, 96n52
Aluwihare, Richard, 297
amulets, 6, 312
Anawrahta, King, 49, 103
Anderson, George, 262–63, 264, 267
Anotatta, Lake, 179
Anstruther, Philip, 250n8, 256

anunāyakas, 194, 227
Anurādhapura, *20*, 45, 48, 89n38, 212n11, 228
ape's tooth, 73n1. *See also* monkey's tooth
Apollonia, Saint, 139
App, Urs, 3, 95
Appadurai, Arjun, 3, 94
Aracan, 40
Āryacakravarti. *See* Jaffna: Āryacakravarti rulers in
Asgiriya Vihāra, 154, *157*, 172n27, 180, 194, 211, 234n17, 259, 288; *mahānāyaka* of, 194, 195, 248, 253, 262, 276, 279, 282, 293, 301; rivalry with Malwatta Vihāra, 214
Aśoka, 48n9, 97
Atkinson, Geoffroy, 33
Augustinians, 32, 136
auto-da-fé, 12, 129, 133–38
Ava, 103, 239n24, 246n1, 279n23
Avalokiteśvara, 61, 164n18

Badulla, 224, 232
Bago. *See* Pegu
Bāhiranidāna, 91n40
Bailey, Allanson, 274, 282
Baldaeus, Philippus, 23, 35–36, 39, 42, 45, 56, 59–62, 74, 79
barefoot, 302, 303n20; D'Oyly going, 246, 302; possibility of Elizabeth II going, 290–91, 303. *See also* shoe removal
Barlaam and Josaphat, story of, 88
Barnes, Edward, 239–43, 246, 309; handling of the tooth relic, 276, 282

Barnsley, George X., 175n37
Barreto, Melchior Nunes, 95n50, 140
basnāyaka nilame. See *devales: basnāyaka nilames* of
Basto, Pedro de, 38n40
Bathurst, 3rd Earl of: correspondence with R. Brownrigg, 181n13, 184, 185, 206, 226, 230, 236; and Kandyan Convention, 177, 190, 191, 193; and Kandyan jewels, 207
Batticaloa, *20*, 166, 168, 207, 224n3
Bayinnaung, King, 101, 102n63, 103, 104, 113n8, 147
Bell, Aubrey, 66n51
Bellarmino, Roberto, 141
Bengal, 27, 40, 77, 93, 171, 176
Bennett, John Whitchurch, 195, 203
Bergeron, Pierre, 28n17, 33–34
Beruwala, 59–60
Bevin, Ernest, 301
Bhanurangsi, Prince, 276, 279
Bhuvanekabāhu VI, 52, 67n53
Biedermann, Zoltán, 32, 61n42, 156n3
Bisnagar. See Vijayanagara
Blackburn, Anne, 267, 283
Boake, Barcroft, 191, 250n7, 251n9
Bogambara Lake, 234
Botelho, Filipe, 100
Botelho, Francisco Marques, 111, 133
bowl relic, 48, 49n10, 58, 90, 103n66
Boxer, Charles Ralph, 88
Bragança, Constantino da (viceroy), 11, 92, 118, 121, 132, 134n15, 308; and capture of tooth, 29, 38, 63, 69, 149; and CCCCC medallion, 128, 138, 146; and debate over the tooth, 25, 109; defenders of his actions, 33, 39, 128, 146; and destruction of tooth, 24, 31, 33, 79n12, 105, 125–26; and invasion of Jaffna, 25, 38, 65, 66, 110, 146
British Commonwealth, 16, 78n10, 285, 290–95, 300n16, 301
Brownrigg, John Studholme, 314n2
Brownrigg, Lady, 220–21
Brownrigg, Robert, 14, 15, 181n13, 219, 308, 314; and 1815 invasion of Kandy, 182, 184–87; and Kandyan Convention, 187–91, 193, 237, 250; and Kandyan monks, 193–96, 223; and Kandyan regalia, 206–7, 314; and rebellion of 1817–1818, 224, 225nn4–5, 226, 235,

236n23; and statue of Tārā, 207; and Temple of the Tooth treasures, 197, 200, 201; and tooth relic, 206, 213, 220, 221, 226–30, 238
Brownrigg, Studholme, 314–15
Bucer, Martin, 141
Buckingham Palace, 16, 290, 292, 295, 299, 300n16, 303
Budão. See Buddha
Buddha: cremation and relics of, 45–46, 97; evolving European views of life story of, 2–3, 4n4, 57, 87–91, 94–96, 98, 157; and the gods in Kandy, 164, 192, 193, 203, 205; images of, 60, 62, 212, 215, 243, 246, 272, 277; as said to have come from Delhi, 57, 95, 98; as straddling various lands, 89n38; as symbolized by jewels and bones, 4–5, 310; in trial of the tooth, no mention made of, 120, 138; visit of to Pegu, 30, 89–92, 98; visits of to Sri Lanka, 91; visit of to the Andaman Islands, 59. See also Fô (Buddha); Śākyamuni; Shaka; Xaca
Buddhasāmi. See Muttusāmi, King
Buddhism: belief in its decline in Sri Lanka, 250, 251n8, 260, 264; British colonial government's attitudes toward, 14, 15, 189–94, 218, 219, 223, 237, 262–64, 312; British dissociation with, 251–57, 258–60, 268, 302; distinguished from Hinduism, 87, 191–92; distinguished from popular religion, 191–92, 247, 256; missionary attitudes toward, 191, 247–50, 251–54, 259–60, 262; Nāyakkars and, 13, 159; Portuguese realization of its distinctiveness, 86, 88, 92, 94–95, 106, 120, 307; Portuguese realization of its pan-Asian nature, 86, 94–99, 106; Portuguese view of it as rival to Christianity, 99–100, 147; Western discoveries of, 2–3, 39, 106, 309–10
Buddhist World, 304
Budu, 63, 98. See also Buddha
budu-res (rays of the Buddha), 239
Buller, Arthur, 255–57
Buller, C. R., 252, 256, 261
Bynum, Caroline, 120

Cain and Abel, story of, 62–63
Caldecott, Andrew, 314–15
Calicut, 27, 100

Calvin, John, 141
Cameron, H. H., 276
Camões, Luís de, 36, 128, 132
Campbell, Colin, 251, 258, 259, 264;
    and the 1843 exhibition of the tooth,
    251–54; indecision of with regard to
    Buddhism, 254–57
Cankili I, 64–68
Cantuar, Geoffrey (archbishop of Canter-
    bury), 291n5, 298n14, 299
capture of the tooth by the Portuguese, 44;
    near Adam's Peak, 19, 22, 36, 40, 42,
    45, 56, 62, 71; in Jaffna, 3, 9, 12, 19,
    23–27, 30–34, 36, 38, 45, 56, 57, 63,
    69, 70, 119, 138, 146, 311
Carletti, Francesco, 29n22
Casey, Edward, 70
Catarina, Queen of Kandy, 104
Catarina, Queen Regent of Portugal, 65,
    131, 132
CCCCC medallion, 127, 138, 146
Cervantes, Fernando, 118
Charles, Prince of Wales, 305, 311
Chulalongkorn, King, 15, 267–83, 312
Churchill, Winston, 290–99, 302, 303,
    304, 308
Clifford, Hugh, 268n2
Coates, Dandeson, 251
Cochin, 27, 52n18, 121
Colebrooke, W. M. G., 242, 243
Colebrooke-Cameron Commission, 160
Colombo, 20; attack of by Sinhalese forces,
    54n27, 176; bishop of, 297; Chulalong-
    korn's arrival in, 280–82; Ehelepola in,
    180, 225; and 1803 attack on Kandy,
    166, 170, 174; established by the Portu-
    guese, 52; as seat of British government,
    190, 195–96, 235n23, 251–55, 264, 296,
    299; Śrī Vikrama taken to, 178, 187
Columbus, Christopher, 58
Colville, Jock, 291–92
Committee of Three, 259–62, 265, 267
Compostella, Santiago de, 22, 27
Constantino, Dom. See Bragança, Constan-
    tino da (viceroy)
Coomaraswamy, Muthu, 12
Cordiner, James, 63n47, 170
Coromandel, 35, 40, 164
cosmopolitanism, 71, 146, 153, 160, 161–
    65. See also tooth as object: as cosmo-
    politan object

Counter Reformation, 131n9, 141
Courtenay, Peter, 71, 313
Coutinho, Francisco, 128
Crawfurd, John, 238–39
Crowe, Philip, 297n13
crypto-Hindus, 132, 134n17
crypto-Jews, 26, 133, 134nn16–17
Cūḷavaṃsa, 54n26, 55n29, 162, 165
Cumming, Constance Gordon, 276n17,
    277

Da Asia, 57; manuscript history, 29–30
Da Cunha, J. Gerson, 111n6, 229n11
dagoba of the tooth relic, 226–28, 234,
    269n6, 270–72, 288; taken away by Van
    Eck, 167. See also karandua; reliquaries
Dalada, 164, 165, 171, 200, 206, 208, 214,
    223, 279n21, 282, 314; as Dalada-King,
    263, 310, 312; as Dalada-monk, 263,
    310. See also Kandyan tooth
Daḷadā-ge, 38
Dalada Maligawa, 51, 154, 171, 178, 180,
    194, 196, 198–99, 209–10, 234n17,
    260, 315. See also Temple of the Tooth
    in Kandy
Daḷadāsirita, 240n26
Daḷadāvittiya, 172n27
Dambadeniya, 49, 212n11
Dantapura, 47–48
Dāṭhādhātughara, 48
Dāṭhāvaṃsa, 12, 47, 48, 105n73, 142
Davids, T. W. Rhys, 12
Davie, Adam, 174, 175
Davy, John, 15, 76n5, 154, 155, 157,
    165n20, 228–30, 238, 239n25, 277
De Barros, João, 29, 32, 89; account of
    Adam's Peak, 57, 59, 70, 90, 146; on life
    of the Buddha, 57, 98
debate on what to do with the tooth. See
    trial of the tooth in Goa
De Bussche, L., 185
De Conti, Nicolò, 81
Defender of the Faith, 16, 255n13, 290,
    303
De Kloguen, Denis L. Cottineau, 128
De la Boullaye-Le-Gouz, François, 125,
    148n1
Delgamuwa, 20, 23n7, 28, 51, 54–55, 70,
    153, 163n17
Delhi, Kingdom of, 57n31, 78n10; the Bud-
    dha said to be from, 57, 95, 98

Dellon, Charles Gabriel, 134–37
De Mello, Diogo, 166
de Mello, Martin Alfonso, 92n43, 93
demons, 24, 38, 80n16, 83, 87, 91, 148, 179. *See also* demon-worship; devil-dancing
demon-worship: British views of, 191, 192n29, 247, 249, 256; Portuguese anxiety about, 33, 118, 119, 145
De Nobili, Roberto, 121–22, 132, 309
de Orta, Garcia, 137n23
De Silva, K. M., 254, 259
De Sousa, Francisco, 38–39, 45, 73–76, 86, 94n46, 97–99
de Souza, Martin Affonço, 64, 65
destruction of the tooth by the Portuguese in Goa, 3, 11, 15, 19, 24, 29, 33, 38, 44, 94, 100, 104, 125–49, 308; British on, 12, 253; Do Couto on, 127–28; Dom Constantino praised for, 33, 39, 146; Du Jarric on, 125–26; and Hindu funerals, 129–30; and iconoclasm, 130–33; and the Inquisition, 111, 133–38; possible historicity of, 145; reasons for, 6, 7, 10, 25, 31, 39, 85, 86, 94, 99, 107, 117, 311; Sri Lankan views on, 68, 101, 104–5, 153; Texeira on, 126–27, 130
devales, 154, 164n18, 172, 180, 194–97, 203–5, 209, 211n10, 219, 220, 241, 256; *basnāyaka nilames* of, 194, 204, 237, 238, 248, 253, 254, 262, 293; confiscation of by Dharmapala, 52; and *peraheras*, 172, 220, 241; properties of, 195–97, 237, 253; and return of the gods in 1815, 193, 194, 203–5, 219; and Sinhala Kandyan Convention, 192–93, 256n14. *See also* Kataragama (god); Nātha; Pattini; Saman; Viṣṇu
Devarāja II, 84
Devil, 33, 38, 97, 115, 119; tooth as a relic of, 3, 11, 93, 112, 118–20, 133, 311. *See also* demons; Satan
devil-dancing, 249, 254, 256, 308
Dewaraja, Lorna, 158, 177n1
Dhammazedi, King, 50, 91
Dharmapala. *See* João Dharmapala, King
Dharmapala, Anagarika, 275n16
Dhātuvaṃsa, 46
Dīpavaṃsa, 91n40
Divāguhā, 91
Di Varthema, Ludovico, 81

Diyawadana Nilame, 54, 195, 207, 214, 237, 243, 246, 248, 262, 275, 285; and the Committee of Three, 259, 267; co-ordination of with British government agent, 268, 270; and Elizabeth II, 291, 293, 294, 297, 302, 304, 310; and return of the tooth relic in 1815, 207, 209, 212. *See also* Kapuwatte (Diyawadana Nilame); Nugawela, Kuda Banda (Diyawadana Nilame); Nugawela, Kuda Bandara (Diyawadana Nilame)
Do Couto, Diogo, 29–30, 43, 133; account of tooth relic, 30–32, 111–13, 127–28; and footprint on Adam's Peak, belief of as belonging to Saint Thomas, 88n37, 313; and identification of the tooth as the Buddha's, 75, 147, 149; influence on other scholars, 8, 19, 23, 32, 33, 36, 38, 39, 57, 62, 94n46, 310; interest in Buddhism, 88; on invasion of Jaffna, 64–66, 86; on King Bayinnaung and Pegu, 101–4, 147; on the life story of the Buddha, 88–89, 91; on relics, 138
Dolapihilla, Punchibandara, 171, 172n27, 172n29
Dominic, Saint, 135
Dominicans, 32, 66, 110, 123
Doṇa, 46. *See also* Droṇa
Dondra, 60–61
Doniger, Wendy, 19
Don Quijote, 32n27
D'Oyly, John, 13, 183–87, 219, 223, 238, 250, 308, 309; and capture of Śrī Vikrama, 182, 186, 187; and Gajaman Nona, 183; and Kandyan Convention, 187–89, 190n27, 192, 193; and Kandyan monks, 194–96, 207, 211; and offering of musical clock, 217–19, 243, 246, 302, 313; and Prize Committee, 198–200, 211, 212; and recovery of temple's treasures, 196–97; and recovery of the tooth in 1818, 229; and re-enshrinement of the tooth, 214–19; and return of the gods to the *devales*, 203–5, 219; and return of the tooth to the temple in 1815, 14, 201, 206–14; and theft of tooth in 1818, 226, 227
Droṇa, 97. *See also* Doṇa
Du Jarric, Pierre, 25–27, 36, 63, 69, 74, 79, 81, 93, 110–11, 126–27
Dullewe Adikar, W. A., 275–76

Dunuwille, Tikiri Banda. *See* Tikiri Banda

Dutch: and the British, 159, 169, 174, 182; and Kandy, 161, 167–69, 172n28; and the Portuguese, 22, 29, 37, 75, 99, 153; in Sri Lanka, 153, 154, 182

Dutch East India Company, 35, 39, 41, 56

Dutch-German narrative lineage, 8, 9, 45

Edward, Prince of Wales, 288

Ehelepola, 180n7, 194, 195, 200, 211–13, 223, 226; execution of family of, 181, 181–82n13, 233; exile of to Mauritius, 180n10, 225n7; help to British, 182, 183n15, 186; hopes to be made king, 184, 186, 188, 189, 195, 204, 216; rebellion against Śrī Vikrama, 180, 181; and signing the Kandyan Convention, 193n32

Eliade, Mircea, 5

Elizabeth II, Queen, 16, 268, 289–305, 308, 310–12

Esala Perahera, 69n57, 159, 163, 164n18, 165, 170, 240, 248, 269, *287*

Eugénie, Empress, 268

Ezourvedam, 122

Falcão, Aleixo Dias, 111, 133

Faria e Souza, Manuel, 36–37, 45, 73, 74, 75n2, 77, 79, 109, 125; account of the trial of the tooth, 112–17; on tooth as the Devil's, 118–20; on whiteness, 78

Farrer, Reginald, 268, 270, 272, 277, 279n21, 280, 304, 309, 310

Faxian, 48

fetishism of objects, 6, 77, 107, 138, 307, 311

fidalgos (noblemen), 11, 66, 110, 111, 140, 308

Fô (Buddha), 94n47, 95–97

Fonseca, João Vicente da, 21

Forbes, Jonathan, 76, 229n11, 239n25, 241, 242

Ford, Edward, 295, 300

Fortescue, J. W., 177

Franciscans, 22, 32, 53, 110, 118

Franco-Portuguese narrative lineage, 8, 9, 45, 56, 63

Gajaman Nona, 183

Galapatha Rājamahāvihāra, 59

Galle, 3, 19, *20*, 28, 42, 63

Gampola, 49, 50, 84

Gandhāra, 5, 46

Gaspar, Dom (archbishop), 22, 31, 40, 109n1, 110, 111, 121, 127

Gavāmpati, 91–92

Geary, Patrick, 4, 139, 272

gentiles, 26, 75, 87, 90, 112–15, 128, 131–32. *See also* heathenism

George III, 173, 189

George IV, 191; as prince regent, 177, 189, 191, 195, 206

George V, 289, 304; as duke of Cornwall, 288

George VI, 290

Getambe, *209*, 210

Gladstone, William Ewart, 258–59, 264

Gloucester, Duke of, 206n3, 235, 288–89, 314

Goa, 1, 21, 23–29, 32, 34, 37–38, 52n18, 57, 64, 65, 100, 103, 121–22, 126–30; and Hanumān, 79, 85; iconoclasm in, 131–33; tooth relic in, 6, 11, 15, 22, 23, 31, 35, 39, 42, 45, 68–69, 92–93; Xavier's body-relic in, 99, 138–43. *See also* destruction of the tooth by the Portuguese in Goa; Inquisition in Goa; trial of the tooth in Goa

Golden Calf, 125, 130, 131n8

Goloubew, Victor, 13, 149, 153, 164, 263, 310

Gongalegoda Banda, 260, 261n16

Greeving (assistant surgeon), 175n37

Gregory, William, 269, 270n7

Grey, 3rd Earl (Henry Grey), 245, 259–61, 262, 264

Gupta, Pamila, 99, 142

hair relic, 58, 91

Hampi, 81–82

Hanguranketa, 166, 172, *209*, 226, 228

Hanumān, 21, 24, 25, 34, 35, 78, 79–80; and Jaffna, 36, 69, 70, 80n15, 93; as patron deity of Vijayanagara, 16, 80, 81–86, 148

Hanumān's tooth, 3, 10, 24, 39, 45, 56, 59, 73, 76, 106, 118, 119, 147, 309

Hardy, R. Spence, 247; and devil-dancing, 249, 308; objection to government support of Buddhism, 243, 248–50; pamphlet on idolatry in Sri Lanka, 15, 247–50, 251, 252, 254; and the tooth relic, 251, 252, 268

Harvard, William Martin, 192
heathenism, 308, 309, 311; British views of, 249n5, 252, 253, 263; Portuguese views of, 7, 32, 38, 71, 75, 86, 87, 106, 120. *See also* gentiles; idolatry
Helmont, Govert, 62
Henn, Alexander, 131n9, 132
Herbert, Thomas, 79n12, 87
Hevavitarana, Don Carolis, 275
Heydt, Johann Wolffgang, 8, 41–42, 45, 56, 60; in Kandy, 169; and Mulgirigala, 63
Hikkaḍuwe Sumangala, 268n3, 280, 283
Hindagala, 209, 210, 212–14
Hinduism, 9, 24n10, 118, 146; British views of, 191, 218, 256; funerary practices of, 12, 129, 130; at Kandyan court, 158, 160, 162, 180; oppression by the Portuguese, 130–34; temples of, 52, 54, 67, 70, 139. *See also* Hinduism and Buddhism, syncretistic relations
Hinduism and Buddhism, syncretistic relations, 13, 70, 71, 87, 94, 95, 106, 149, 191, 192n29; in Jaffna, 66, 67; in Kandy, 154, 162, 164, 184n18, 313; in Kotte, 51, 56, 162
Hiripitiye, Keerawelle, 54
Hocart, A. M., 77, 164, 308
Holt, John, 164n18
Huduhumpola, 212–14
Humphreys (British soldier), 175n37

iconoclasm, Portuguese, 12, 130–32, 308
idolatry: Biblical examples of, 11, 114–17, 120, 130–31; British worries about, 15, 16, 216–18, 246–49, 254, 291, 302, 308; Las Casas on, 123; Portuguese opposition to, 1, 7, 25, 26, 31, 32, 85, 95n49, 110, 111, 113, 123, 131, 138. *See also* idols, Portuguese views of
idols, Portuguese views of, 34, 36, 40, 87, 90, 92, 95, 109n1, 112–17, 119, 129, 138. *See also* idolatry
Ignatius of Loyola, Saint, 140
Indra, 46, 49, 63n46, 156, 163, 178, 205
Ingirisi Hatana, 172n27
Inquisition in Goa, 6, 12, 95n49, 111, 112, 123, 129, 145, 146; and destruction of the tooth, 133–37
Islam. *See* Muslims

Jaffna, 20, 35, 36, 50, 52, 70, 74, 93; Āryacakravarti rulers in, 49–51, 66–67, 80, 84, 85; Hanumān and, 79, 80n15, 85; Kotte rule over, 52, 67; Portuguese war with, 30, 34, 63–66, 117, 118, 126; theories of how the tooth got to, 31, 66–69, 104, 147; Vijayanagara and, 84, 85. *See also* capture of the tooth by the Portuguese: in Jaffna; Nallur
Jansen, Arent, 41
Japan, 39, 95, 97–100, 148, 268
Jesuits, 12, 24, 25, 27, 37, 38, 39, 110, 121, 122; and pan-Asian nature of Buddhism, 96, 99, 148; in Sri Lanka, 100, 105n73. *See also* Xavier, Francis, relic of
jewels, 4, 5, 125, 197, 198, 307, 309; and bones, 310–11; requirement of for ritual in Temple of the Tooth, 14, 200, 203; and the tooth relic, 239–40, 259, 262, 269–70, 272; as war booty, 7, 207, 308
Jinavaravaṃsa, 280
João III, 64, 65, 131
João VI, 37
João da Austria. *See* Vimaladharmasuriya, King
João Dharmapala, King, 31, 52, 53n22, 67n53, 100, 101, 102n65, 119
Johnston, Arthur, 176
Jornada de Uva (F. Botelho), 100
Jottrand, Emile, 278n21
Jumsai, Prisdang. *See* Jinavaravaṃsa

Kaffirs, 160, 225n4. *See also* African troops used by the British
Kalinga, 46–47, 142, 156n4
Kandy, 20, 209; cosmology of, 154–56, 178–80; description of, 154, 165; evacuations of by the Kandyans, 165, 167, 171, 178n2, 185, 197, 204; invasion by the British, 5, 13, 170–76, 182–86, 206; invasion by the Dutch, 167, 200; invasion by the Portuguese, 166; king's audience hall in, 168, 172, 187, 194, 210, 211, 221, 236, 289; king's palace in, 38, 55, 154, 156, 157, 166–79, 185, 187, 210, 211; monastic leaders in, 194, 195, 248, 253, 255, 262, 275, 277, 279; New Year's celebrations in, 210–11, 219. See also *devales*; Nāyakkar kings; Temple of the Tooth in Kandy

Kandyan Convention, 13, 160, 168, 177, 187–89, 190n27, 193, 223, 232, 264, 294; British reactions to, 177, 191, 237; confusion between "rites" and "rights," 189n26, 219, 250n6, 264; D'Oyly and, 168, 195, 203, 205, 219; interpretations of, 255–57, 259, 263; "inviolable," use of the word, 14, 178, 189, 191, 193, 237, 250; Sinhala version of, 192, 193, 203, 205

Kandyan tooth, 2, 4, 6, 12–13, 15, 78, 148, 153, 164; Chulalongkorn and, 273–83; description of, 229, 311; Elizabeth II and, 289–301; exposition in 1828, 239–44, 248; exposition in 1843, 251–54; Nāyakkar kings and, 13, 51n17, 67, 161–64, 313; recovery by the British in 1818, 5, 14, 206, 223, 229–31, 238; return to Kandy in 1815, 205–19; ritual of its veneration, 162, 220; ritual undressing of, 269–72; size of, 76, 229n11, 272, 308; theft of in 1818, 5, 14, 226–27, 244, 314; thought to be a boar's tusk, 78, 164, 272, 279n21, 308; thought to be a buffalo's tooth, 40, 41, 105, 106, 148, 308; thought to be a crocodile's tooth, 270, 278, 308; thought to be a yakṣa's fang, 78, 164, 308. See also reliquaries; showings of the tooth relic; Temple of the Tooth in Kandy

Kandy Lake, 154, 156, 157, 173, 208, 234n18, 285; digging of, 179, 180n8

Kāṇherī, 22, 88

Kapuwatte (Diyawadana Nilame), 195, 199, 200; and the 1815 return of the tooth, 207–10, 212, 214, 215

karandua, 230, 240, 248, 252, 269, 272, 285, 311. See also reliquaries

Kārtikeya. See Kataragama (god)

Kataragama (god), 30n25, 51n16, 71, 163, 164n18, 192, 204; devale in Kandy, 154, 157, 262

Kataragama (town), 71n61, 224, 226

Kelaniya, 47, 48, 84, 85, 193

Kemper, Steven, 15, 104n71, 269n4, 281

Keppetipola, 227, 231; execution of, 231, 234–35; fate of his skull, 235; and rebellion of 1817–1818, 225, 226, 228; and tooth relic, 232–33

Khema, 47

Kircher, Athanasius, 148

Kīrti Śrī Rājasiṃha, King, 159, 160, 163, 165, 199, 240, 260, 289

Kiṣkindhā, 81

Knox, Robert, 166, 182n13

Kobbekaduwa, the Venerable, 194, 208, 210–15

Konappu Bandara. See Vimaladharma-suriya, King

Kotelawala, John, 285, 293, 295–97, 299, 303, 304, 310

Kotte, 20, 51; and Jaffna, 34, 52, 67, 71, 68–69; and kings of Pegu, 31, 32, 37, 81, 91n41, 101–4, 119, 147; Portuguese dominance of, 23, 52; religious syncretism in, 51; tooth taken to Delgamuwa from, 53, 54, 147; and Zheng He, 50. See also João Dharmapala, King; Temple of the Tooth in Kotte; Vidiye Bandara

Kublai Khan, 58

Kumarihami, 181, 181–82n13

Kundasale, 208, 209

Kurunegala, 49

Kuṣṭharājagala, 61

Labujagāma vihāra, 55

langurs, 76; at the Delhi games, 78n10; and Hanumān, 78. See also monkeys

Las Casas, Bartolomé de, 123, 309

Lascelles, Alan, 292

laukika (this-worldly), 7, 311

Lawrence, D. H., 288

Lawrie, Archibald, 195n36, 228

Le Blanc, Vincent, 33–36, 45, 63, 69, 74, 78, 79, 81, 109, 125

Leclercq, Jules, 277

L'Estra, François, 61n40

Lisbon, 21, 29, 36, 37, 41, 65, 96, 132; Inquisition in, 133n14, 135–36

lokottara (supramundane), 7, 311

Lopez, Donald, 3

Lusignan, George, 227

Lutgendorf, Philip, 73n1, 77, 78

Luther, Martin, 141

Lyttleton, W. H., 214, 216

MacCormack, Sabine, 123

MacDowall, Hay, 171, 173, 174, 177, 205

MacKay, Alexander, 197

Madugalle: execution of, 231, 234n20; and rebellion of 1817–1818, 225, 228–29; and tooth relic, 230–34

Madurai, 121, 122n22, 157, 158
Magone, Rui, 96n55
Mahākassapa, tooth relic of, 59–60
Mahānavami Festival, 82
mahānāyaka. See Asgiriya Vihāra:
  mahānāyaka of; Malwatta Vihāra:
  mahānāyaka of
Mahāparinibbāna sutta, 45, 213
Mahāvaṃsa, 49n10, 61, 91
Mahaweli River, 156, 165, 171, 174–75,
  195, 204, 241n28
Ma Huan, 59–60
Malabar Coast, 35, 40, 122n22
Malabar Rites Controversy, 122n22
Malabars, 160, 170, 180, 181, 186, 188,
  195, 204, 224
Malacca, 26, 52n18, 94, 140
Malalgoda, Kitsiri, 224n2, 231
Malay mercenaries in Kandy, 160, 171, 173,
  174, 176, 244
Malwatta Vihāra, 154, *157*, 172–73, 180,
  194, 208, 211, 213, 259, 270, 275–76,
  288; *mahānāyaka* of, 194, 195, 248, 273,
  279, 282, 293, 301; rivalry with Asgiriya
  Vihāra, 214. *See also* Kobbekaduwa, the
  Venerable
Mannar, *20*, 34, 64–65, 66n52, 126
Marco Polo: on the life of the Buddha, 90;
  and tooth relic on Adam's Peak, 58, 59,
  70, 71, 146
Marshall, Henry, 223, 232–35
Matale, 184n19, 209, 281; rebellion in, 260
Mayadunne, King, 54, 67
McGilvray, Dennis, 80n15
Mecca, 26, 89n38
Medamahanuwara, 166, *209*
Mediwaka, 208, *209*
Melchior, Father, 118
Mendis, Solias, *47*, 48
Mendosa, André Furtado de, 28–29n18
Millāva, 220–21
Mindon, King, 279n23
Ming Yuan, 48
missionaries: and British policies toward
  Buddhism, 189, 191, 219, 237, 238, 251,
  261, 264; and the Portuguese in Asia, 3,
  24, 35, 39, 64, 96, 97, 118, 121, 139; in
  Sri Lanka, 6, 32, 53, 71, 192, 247, 262;
  and the tooth, 2, 7, 15, 245–65, 302,
  308, 312. *See also* Hardy, R. Spence; mis-
  sionary societies in London

missionary societies in London, 193, 246,
  251, 253, 258, 259. *See also* Coates,
  Dandeson; missionaries; Peggs, James;
  Selkirk, James; Stephen, James
Molligoda, 180, 181, 188, 195, 200, 204,
  205, 207, 209, 215; cooperation with
  the British, 185, 212, 225, 230; suspicion of Ehelepola, 213
monkeys: colonial views of peoples as,
  77; Portuguese views of, 76–77; in the
  Rāmāyaṇa, 80–82, 85. *See also* langurs;
  monkey's tooth
monkey's tooth, 3, 9, 10, 21–30, 33, 34, 38,
  42, 45, 56, 62–63, 74, 75–77, 79n12,
  80, 92, 100–101, 126, 147, 308–9;
  identification attributed to uneducated
  Portuguese, 38, 75–76; identification
  contested, 10, 32, 39, 40, 75, 76, 79n11,
  105, 149; identification said to be due to
  linguistic confusion, 76–77, 80. *See also*
  ape's tooth; monkeys
Moors. *See* Muslims
Mulgirigala, 9n10, *20*, 40–42, 60–63, 70,
  71, 91n40, 313; as burial place of Adam,
  61; as burial place of the Buddha, 60
Müller, Friedrich Max, 311
Murugan, 80. *See also* Kataragama (god)
Muslims, 52, 59, 86, 100, 134; and Adam's
  Peak, 9, 57, 58n33, 70, 71, 313; in
  Kandy, 160, 161, 288
Muttusāmi, King, 13, 159, 170–76, 189
Mylapore, 65

nāgas, 46, 62, 97
Nallur, 9, 30n25, 52, 67–69, 71, 80. *See also*
  Jaffna
Nānumura Mangallaya, 210
Napoleon, 37, 171n26, 176, 184
Nātha, 51, 83n26, 154, 163, 164n18, 192,
  204; *devale* in Kandy, *157*, 194, 205,
  211, 220
Nāyakkar kings, 148, 157–61, 180, 224;
  British attitudes toward, 159, 160, 164,
  184, 188, 189, 218; caste and, 157–59;
  corvée labor and, 154, 178–80, 227, 237;
  disaffection of Kandyan people with,
  178–82; religious beliefs of, 158, 159;
  South Asian origins of, 13, 149, 158–60,
  180. *See also* Kīrti Śrī Rājasiṃha, King;
  Rājasiṃha II; Śrī Vijaya Rājasinha, King; Śrī
  Vikrama, King

nekata (auspicious moment), 5, 171, 204, 208, 210–14, 216, 229
Newcastle, Duke of, 262–63, 264
Nissanka, H. S. S., 297
Nittawela Monastery, 229
Norodom, King, 283
Noronha, Afonso de (viceroy), 23, 140
North, Frederick, 171
Nugawela, C. B., 275, 276
Nugawela, Kuda Banda (Diyawadana Nilame), 293, 297
Nugawela, Kuda Bandara (Diyawadana Nilame), 268
Nunez, Duarte, 131

Obeyesekere, Gananath, xi, 4, 89, 158n9, 170n4, 172n29, 175n36, 176, 179, 180n9, 181, 182n13, 183n17, 190n27, 192n30, 196n37, 225, 228n8
Ocean of Milk, 180. *See also* Kandy Lake
Octagon, 293, 295, 304. *See also* Patthirippuwa
Olcott, Henry Steel, 274n15, 279n21, 280; as chair of committee investigating the Chulalongkorn incident, 274–77, 279, 281
otherworldly myopia, 11, 118, 121, 312

pagode, 35, 38, 53, 56, 87, 166, 169; Portuguese meaning of, 22
Pakington, John, 262–63, 264, 267
Palk Straits, 24, 64, 82, 85. *See also* Adam's Bridge
palladium. *See* tooth as object: as palladium
Panabokke, T. B., 275–77, 279, 281
Pāṇḍi (legendary king), 179
Paṇḍu (Indian king) 47, 142
Parākramabāhu III, 49
Parākramabāhu VI, 50, 51, 162
Pārakumbā sirita, 51
Patthirippuwa, 154, 156, 196, 211, 288. *See also* Octagon
Pattini, 51n16, 154, 163, 164n18, 192, 204; *devale* in Kandy, 157, 211n10
Peggs, James, 251–53, 260
Pegu, 10, 33, 78, 92, 100, 106, 115, 146, 147, 309, 312; acquisition of tooth from Kotte, 101–3, 119; the Buddha's travel to and death in, 30, 89–91, 98; interest in tooth, 22, 25, 31–38, 40, 50, 53n21, 81,

93, 97, 110, 113, 139; refusal of tooth from Kandy, 104–5, 119. *See also* Bayinnaung, King
Peradeniya, 180, 212, 224n3
perahera, 55, 223, 268, 285, 313; in 1815, 14, 216; in 1817, 219–21; in 1828, 240; for British princes, 282, 288, 293; for Elizabeth II, 295–96, 299–300; snub by Chulalongkorn, 282. *See also* Esala Perahera
Percival, Robert, 170
Pereira, Thomas, 96–97
Perera, D. B., 275
Perera, N. M., 295
Perumal, 24, 25. *See also* Viṣṇu
Philip, Duke of Edinburgh, 290, 291, 293, 305
Pieris, P. E., 37, 68–70, 193, 229n11
Pilimatalawa (the elder), 170
Pilimatalawa (the younger), 225, 228, 230
Pimenta, Nicolaus, 23–27, 45, 74, 79, 85, 92, 109, 125
Piṭigoda, 207–9
Polonnaruwa, 48, 49, 234n17
Portuguese tooth, 2, 3, 8; demonization of, 11, 117–20, 308; fake replicas of, 100–105, 119, 213; found in Jaffna, 9, 12, 19, 23–27, 30, 32–34, 36, 38, 45, 56, 57, 63–70, 119, 138, 146, 311; found in Southern Sri Lanka, 60–63; found near Adam's Peak, 3, 9, 19, 23, 28, 39, 45, 56–58, 138, 146; imprints of, 34, 36, 103, 113n8; and Japan, 97, 98; and the relic of Saint Francis Xavier, 12, 99, 138–43, 145; said to have been extracted by the Buddha from his own mouth, 57, 90–92, 97; sources identifying it as the Buddha's tooth, 30, 32, 33, 38–40, 73, 74, 75–76, 86; sources not identifying it as the Buddha's tooth, 23, 36, 42, 73, 74; stories of, 19–42, 44, 145–49. *See also* capture of the tooth by the Portuguese; destruction of the tooth by the Portuguese in Goa; Hanumān's tooth; monkey's tooth; ransoms offered for the Portuguese tooth; trial of the tooth in Goa; white monkey's tooth
prārthanāva (final earnest wish), 232–33
Prize Committee, 197–201, 207, 211–12, 308
Proclamation of 1815, 160n11, 184, 190

Proclamation of 1818, 235–38, 250, 255, 263

Protestant Buddhism, 279

Pusulpitiya Monastery, 209, 212

Pybus, John, 169

Pyrard de Laval, François, 27–29, 74, 92, 125

Queiros, Fernão de, 37–38, 45, 74, 109; account of invasion of Jaffna, 64–66; affirmation of captured tooth as the Buddha's, 75, 86; on the Buddha's life story, 89n38, 96–97; on Buddhism in competition with Christianity, 99; claim that Vidiye brought the tooth to Jaffna, 68–69; on the distinctiveness of Buddhism, 94, 95; on the pan-Asian nature of Buddhism, 95–97, 99; on the Temple of the Tooth in Kandy, 38, 105; *Temporal and Spiritual Conquest of Ceylon* not published for two and a half centuries, 37–38, 41, 68n54, 96, 98n57

Rachel, theft of idols from her father, 115, 117

Raigama, 52, 84

Rājasiṃha II, 158n8, 179

Rājasinha, King of Sītāwaka, 54, 55, 104, 163n17

Rājāvaliya, 50n11, 91n40

Rāma, 10, 24, 79–83, 85, 148

Rāmacandra Temple, 82

Rāmāyaṇa, 10, 24, 80nn14–16, 81–83, 85n32, 147, 148

Rambelli, Fabio, 7n7, 132

Rambukpota, 227

ransoms offered for the Portuguese tooth, 1, 7, 23–26, 38, 44, 97, 101, 308; amounts offered, 92–93; debate over, 109–12, 116, 250; Do Couto's account of, 93–94; evolving identity of offerors, 92; rejection of, 128, 138, 145

Ratnapura, 9n60, 40, 54, 55, 60, 164n17

Rāvaṇa, 24, 83, 148

Rebellion of 1817–1818, 223–25, 228, 235, 256, 261, 265; and tooth relic, 2, 5, 14, 227, 231

Rebellion of 1848, 252n11, 260–61

Reinders, Eric, 132

relics: attempted thefts of, 140n28; as capturable objects, 48, 139; Catholic views of, 12, 99, 110, 138, 139, 140n27, 141, 311; Chulalongkorn's view of, 278; as extended bodies, 5; indestructability of, 141–42; as objectifications of charisma, 6–7; Olcott's view of, 279n21; original distribution of the Buddha's, 46, 92, 97, 213; and the Portuguese empire, 142–43; and rainmaking, 98; and rays of light, 239; as special objects, 4, 139. *See also* bowl relic; hair relic; Kandyan tooth; Portuguese tooth; tooth as object; tooth in pre-Portuguese times

reliquaries, 4, 101, 201, 305, 309; nesting reliquaries of the tooth relic, 14n13, 105, 163, 167, 200n41, 226, 227, 248, 269, 270, 271, 272, 288, 305, 310, 311. *See also* dagoba of the tooth relic; karandua

return of the gods in 1815, 203–5, 206, 216, 219

Ribeiro, João, 90, 94; belief that the Buddha was Saint Thomas, 89n37

Ridgeway, Joseph, 273

Rienjang, Wannaporn, 5

Robson, James, 9, 70, 71

Rogers, Frederick, 258–59

Rogers, John, 159

Rolin-Jaequemyns, Gustave, 278

Rumley, Edward, 175

Said, Edward, 2

Śaivism, 13, 30n25, 66, 67, 71, 80, 158, 164n18

Śakra. *See* Indra

Śākyamuni, 59, 96, 122. *See also* Xaca

Salisbury, Marquess of, 290–92

Saman, 55; *devale*, 51, 184n19

Saowapha, Queen, 278

Sapumal, 51, 52, 67, 71

Satan, 97, 118, 119; tooth of, 117–20, 126, 308. *See also* Devil; Portuguese tooth: demonization of

Sawers, Simon, 232–34

Sebastião I, 65

Selkirk, James, 240n27, 245–47

Senanayake, Dudley, 291–93

Seneviratne, H. L., 159

Shah, Mujahid, 83

Shaka, 95, 98. *See also* Śākyamuni; Xaca

Sharf, Robert, 272

shoe removal, 216, 301, 303, 305; and D'Oyly, 216; and Elizabeth II, 16, 285, 291–304. *See also* barefoot

Shoolbraid, Thomas, 228–29
showings of the tooth relic, 267–69; by
    Barnes, 239–44, 248; to Chulalongkorn,
    273, 275–79; to Elizabeth II, 289–301;
    to Farrer, 268, 270–72; by Śrī Vijaya,
    163, 282; to various foreign monks,
    165, 251–54; to various foreign royals,
    283, 285–86, 288, 305
Shwe Dagon, 305
Siam, 15, 40, 78, 95, 97, 165; monks from,
    159, 164, 165, 220n17, 238, 251–53,
    269. See also Chulalongkorn, King
Siamese monks: and Esala Perahera, 159,
    164; and higher ordination in Kandy,
    159, 165; visit to tooth relic in Kandy,
    220n17, 238, 251, 252, 257, 269
Simons, Cornelis, 62
Sinhalese: cultural golden age, 67; national-
    ism, 295, 313; and the Nāyakkars, 158–
    60, 164, 165, 182n13, 184, 189, 218;
    and the Rāmāyaṇa, 80n14; traditions
    about the Buddha's visits to the island,
    91, 95; traditions about the tooth relic,
    13, 45–56, 68, 105, 126, 171, 312
Sirimeghavaṇṇa, 92n43, 161
Sirr, Henry Charles, 223
Sītā, 24, 79–81, 83, 85n32
Sītāwaka, 52, 54, 55, 67, 104
Śiva, 22n6, 24n10, 51, 80, 122
Sivasundaram, Sujit, 160
Skanda. See Kataragama (god)
Skeen, George, 105n73
Soulbury, Baron of, 290–91, 293n8, 295–
    97, 299
Śrī Pada, 9, 19, 22n6, 40, 42, 50n14, 60,
    63, 70, 89n38. See also Adam's Peak
Śrī Vijaya Rājasinha, King, 158, 162–63,
    282
Śrī Vikrama, King, 157, 160n12, 164, 171,
    172n29, 173, 175n36, 178–84, 187,
    188, 221, 233; capture of, 13, 170, 182,
    186, 196, 206; and construction projects
    in Kandy, 156, 178–79; exile of, 178,
    187, 224; Kandyan disaffection with,
    178–82; maligned as cruel tyrant, 164;
    propensity for violence, 181–82
Stanley, Lord, 252, 258, 260, 264; advocacy
    of dissociation with Buddhism, 253,
    254; and Campbell, 255–57
Stephen, James, 251, 253, 254, 257–59,
    261n18

Stephens, Thomas, 122, 132
Stewart-Mackenzie, James, 251, 264
storical approach, 4, 9, 12, 13, 46, 70, 145–
    49, 214, 231
Strathern, Alan, 32n27, 51, 71, 94n47,
    95n49, 99n60, 156n3
Stubbs, Reginald, 289
Subrahmanyam, Sanjay, 1, 3, 7, 8, 120
Sugriva, 81
Swinton, Viscount, 295–97
Syers, Cecil, 291
syncretism, religious and cultural, 13, 51,
    56, 67, 71, 87, 162, 164n18. See also
    Hinduism and Buddhism, syncretistic
    relations

Tambiah, Stanley, 6, 10, 11, 106, 107, 120,
    156n3, 219, 254, 263, 311, 312
Tamils, 35, 36, 51, 71, 80n15, 122, 171; in
    Jaffna, 66, 68; in Kandy, 67, 157, 161,
    164; language of, 36, 54, 121, 122, 159;
    prejudices against in Kandy, 159, 160,
    180, 182n13, 184
Teldeniya, 186, 187, 209
Temple of the Tooth in Kandy, 2, 41, 105,
    154, 155, 156, 157, 161; administra-
    tion of, 195, 259, 262, 265, 267, 269,
    304; British management of, 237, 238,
    243, 248, 250, 252n10, 253–54, 257;
    British occupation of, 176, 196n37,
    261, 262; British subsidies of, 248–49;
    and Committee of Three, 259–61, 262,
    265, 267; construction history, 28,
    48, 55, 104, 162, 179; early foreigners
    in Kandy oblivious to, 168–69, 170;
    Keppetipola's visit to, 232–33; landed
    properties of, 195–96, 209n8, 237,
    256–57, 260–63; pilgrims to, 245;
    ransacked or burned by foreigners,
    166, 167, 173; rituals in, 205, 210, 241;
    shrine room in, 162, 163, 231, 246, 271;
    theft of the tooth from, 5, 14, 226–28;
    treasures of, 7, 14, 171, 185, 194, 197–
    201, 202, 211–12, 262, 272, 294; visit
    of British royalty to, 285–88, 305; visit
    of Chulalongkorn to, 273–83; visit of
    Elizabeth II to, 284–305. See also Dalada
    Maligawa; Diyawadana Nilame
Temple of the Tooth in Kotte, 23, 50, 51,
    53, 103, 162
Temudo, Jorge, 65, 109, 118

Tennent, J. Emerson, 57, 229, 251n8, 261n18
Texeira, Pedro, 26–27, 74, 75n2, 79, 85, 92, 126; on ways to destroy the tooth, 127, 130
theft of the tooth relic: attempted by Ming Yuan, 48; in Kandy in 1818, 226–27, 244, 314; stories of in India, 45–46
Theravāda, 85n32, 91n41, 99n60, 164n18, 279–81, 283, 309
Thibaw, King, 283
Thoen, Jan Egbertus, 175n37, 181
Thomas, Saint, 22n6, 88–89n37, 313. See also Mylapore
throne of Kandyan kings, 187; returned to Sri Lanka, 235n22, 288–89, 304, 314; taken to England, 206
Thūpavaṃsa, 46
Tikiri Banda, 252–53
Times of London, 299–300
Tolfrey, William, 181n13, 188n22, 190, 197
tooth as object, 1, 2nn2–3, 3, 4, 10–12, 45, 105, 118, 173, 307, 309–10, 312, 315; as cosmopolitan object, 13, 153, 161, 165, 312–13; as fetish, 77, 138; as a "foreign" object, 55, 148, 149, 163, 313; as indestructible, 47, 54, 55, 105n73, 142; as a movable object, 45, 48, 309; multiplicity of views of, 307–9; as object of value, 11, 12, 31, 94, 106, 139, 308; as palladium, 10, 13, 48, 66, 104, 161, 162, 168, 203, 226, 289, 313; touchability of, 15, 229, 274–77, 282, 288
tooth in pre-Portuguese times: attempted destructions of, 45, 47, 55; attempted theft of by Chinese pilgrim, 48; capture of by various foreign kings and generals, 47, 49, 50, 58, 67; at the cremation of the Buddha, 46, 156n4; and Faxian, 48; Marco Polo on, 58, 59, 70, 71, 146; Sinhalese traditions on its movements, 45–56
tooth relic. See Kandyan tooth; Portuguese tooth; tooth as object; tooth in pre-Portuguese times
Torrington, 7th Viscount of (George Byng), 245, 254, 264; and 1848 rebellion, 260–62; establishes Committee of Three, 259–60, 262
Toscano, Antonio, 102, 103n67

Toṭagāmuwa Sri Rahula, 84, 85, 143
Trainor, Kevin, 309
transactions, cycle of, 6, 10, 106, 116, 120, 219, 254, 255, 312
trial of the tooth in Goa, 11, 15, 109–20, 308; arguments against destroying the tooth, 112–13, 116; arguments for destroying the tooth, 114–16, 117; Biblical citations at, 114–16, 117, 131; early accounts, 109–12; Faria e Souza on, 112–17
Trincomalee, 20, 166, 174, 207
Trindade, Paulo da, 32–33, 45, 53, 73–75, 78, 94, 103; on the Buddha's life story, 89–90
Turner, Alicia, 301
Turnour, George, 61, 240, 243, 252n10

Uva, 100, 212, 224–26, 228n10, 234

Vajira, Kumburugamuwe, 70
Valentijn, François, 23, 39–41, 45, 56, 60, 62, 73, 74, 79, 81
Valladolid Debate, 122
Van der Aa, Jean Baptiste, 105n73
van Domburg, Diederik, 41
Van Eck, Lubbert Jan, 167–69
Van Linschoten, Jan Huyghen, 8, 21–23, 43, 93, 109; and capture of the tooth on Adam's Peak, 56, 62, 70–71; and classification of religions, 86–87; influence on other Dutch scholars, 35–36, 39–42, 146; on making of a fake tooth, 125, 126, 148; on Vijayanagara, 100–101
van Spilbergen, Joris, 168
Veddas, 164, 224, 228n10
Vellassa, 220, 224, 225n3, 228n10
Vibhīṣaṇa, 83–85, 147
Victoria, Queen, 15, 260, 267, 273, 280, 281, 285, 286, 304; and Church of England, 255; and Church of Scotland, 255
Vidiye Bandara, 54, 67; taking of tooth to Jaffna, 68, 69, 147
Vidyabhusana, Satis Chandra, 269
Vijaya, King, 194, 205
Vijayanagara, 10, 35, 40, 65n49, 81, 84–86, 92, 93, 106, 146–48, 157; end of suzerainty, 85–86; and Hanumān, 25, 81–83, 148. See also Hampi
Vilbave, 224, 226, 228n10

Vimaladharmasuriya, King, 28, 31, 32n27, 55, 104, 119, 147
Vīrakrama Śrī Kīrti, King, 226
Viṣṇu, 24n10, 51, 60, 97, 122, 163, 164n18, 192, 204; *devale* in Kandy, 154, 157, 205, 211n10, 220
von Hügel, Karl, 229n11

Wagenaar, Lodewijk, 167
Wallace, William, 234–35
Walters, Jonathan, 83–84
Wāriyapola, 227–29
Waskaduwe Subhuti, 280
Watapuluwa, 175n34, 175n36
Weligama, 61–62
Wheatley, Paul, 156
white monkey's tooth, 10, 25, 33, 34–37, 45, 71–75, 78–79
Wijayaratna, Môhan, 80n15, 85n32

Wilson, Silvester, 224, 225n3
Wodehouse, P. E., 257
Wojciehowski, Hannah, 21n2, 76, 111, 119, 134n16, 136
Woolf, Leonard, 12, 76, 268–70

Xaca, 39, 94n47, 97, 148. *See also* Śākyamuni; Shaka
Xavier, Angela Barreto, 122n22, 131n8
Xavier, Francis, relic of, 6, 12, 64, 65, 99, 131, 134n16, 145

yakṣa (demon), 78, 164, 249, 308
Yapahuwa, 49
Yongle, Emperor, 50
Yule, Henry, 58, 88n36

Zheng He, 50, 59, 81
Županov, Ines, 122n22, 131n8, 139, 142